Cultural Memory and Early Civilization
Writing, Remembrance, and Political Imagination

Now available to an English-speaking audience, this book presents a groundbreaking theoretical analysis of memory, identity, and culture. It investigates how cultures remember, arguing that human memory exists and is communicated in two ways, namely interhuman interaction and in external systems of notation such as writing, which can span generations. Dr. Assmann defines two theoretical concepts of cultural memory, differentiating between the long-term memory of societies, which can span up to 3,000 years, and communicative memory, which is typically restricted to 80–100 years. He applies this theoretical framework to case studies of four specific cultures – including state, international law, religion, and science – illustrating their functional contexts and specific achievements. Ultimately, his research demonstrates that memory is not simply a means of retaining information, but rather a force that can shape cultural identity and allow cultures to respond creatively to both daily challenges and catastrophic changes.

Jan Assmann is Professor Emeritus of Egyptology at the University of Heidelberg and an Honorary Professor at the University of Constance. He has published forty-five monographs including, most recently, *The Price of Monotheism* (2009), *Of God and Gods: Egypt, Israel and the Rise of Monotheism* (2008), *Religion and Cultural Memory* (2006), and *Death and Salvation in Ancient Egypt.*

Cultural Memory and Early Civilization

Writing, Remembrance, and Political Imagination

JAN ASSMANN

University of Constance, Germany

CAMBRIDGE
UNIVERSITY PRESS

CAMBRIDGE UNIVERSITY PRESS
Cambridge, New York, Melbourne, Madrid, Cape Town,
Singapore, São Paulo, Delhi, Tokyo, Mexico City

Cambridge University Press
32 Avenue of the Americas, New York, NY 10013-2473, USA

www.cambridge.org
Information on this title: www.cambridge.org/9780521188029
© Verlag C.H. Beck oHG, München 2007 and 2009, 2011

First published in Germany for Verlag as *Das kulturelle Gedächtnis: Schrift, Erinnerung und politische Identität in frühen Hochkulturen*

First English edition 2011

Printed in the United States of America

A catalog record for this publication is available from the British Library

Library of Congress Cataloging in Publication data

Assmann, Jan.
Cultural memory and early civilization : writing, remembrance, and political
imagination / Jan Assmann.
  p.   cm.
Includes bibliographical references and index.
ISBN 978-0-521-76381-3 (hbk.) – ISBN 978-0-521-18802-9 (pbk.)
1. Civilization, Ancient.   2. Memory – Social aspects – History.   3. Collective
memory – History.   4. Group identity – History.   5. Interpersonal communication –
History.   6. Written communication – History.   7. Politics and culture – History.
8. Egypt – Civilization.   9. Israel – Civilization.   10. Greece – Civilization.   I. Title.
CB311.A75 2011
930 – dc22   2011001971

ISBN 978-0-521-76381-3 Hardback
ISBN 978-0-521-18802-9 Paperback

Contents

Foreword (1992)

For several years now, the subject of memory has been an increasingly important focal point for both Eastern and Western minds. I do not regard this as a matter of chance. On the contrary, it seems to me that we are passing through a transitional period in which at least three factors have combined to bring this theme to the forefront. First there are new electronic media for external storage (a kind of artificial memory), and these have brought about a cultural revolution as significant as the invention of the printing press and, in much earlier times, of writing. Second and connected to this, our entire cultural tradition is now permeated with what George Steiner has called a "post-culture," in which something now coming to an end – which Niklas Luhmann termed "Old Europe" – nevertheless lives on as the subject of memory and of commentary. Thirdly, and perhaps most importantly of all, something else is also coming to an end that affects our very lives as individuals. A generation of contemporary witnesses to some of the most terrible crimes and catastrophes in the whole of human history is now dying out. Generally, a period of forty years is regarded as the threshold beyond which the collective memory begins to fade: the recollections of the living become fewer and fewer, and the various forms of cultural memory become problematical. Even if sometimes the debate over history, memory, and mnemotechnics may appear abstract and academic, it seems to me to nevertheless lie at the very heart of current discourse. Everything points to the fact that the concept of memory constitutes the basis for a new paradigm of cultural studies that will shed light on all the interconnected fields of art and literature, politics and sociology, and religion and law. In other words, everything is in flux, and this book itself is in its own way part of that fluidity. It does not claim to offer conclusions, but it sets out to provide directions and connections.

My research, carried out with Aleida Assmann at the Wissenschaftskolleg in Berlin in 1984 and 1985, acted as the starting point for this book. To this institution I therefore offer my special thanks. Without the opportunity to attend the lectures, courses, and discussions on a wide variety of subjects, I would never have dared to venture so far beyond the frontiers of my own special subject, Egyptology. In particular, I would like to thank Christian Meier, Peter Machinist, and Michel Strickman, who were all members of a close-knit circle dedicated to discussing the whole question of comparative cultural studies.

The topic of "cultural memory" arose from a study group engaged on the "Archäologie der literarischen Kommunikation," documented in *Schrift und Gedächtnis* [Writing and Memory] (1983), *Kanon und Zensur* [Canon and Censorship] (1987) and *Weisheit* [Wisdom] (1991), and further developed at various conferences and lectures.[1] This book is the direct result of preparations for and evaluations of the conferences, in particular of the second conference held in January 1985 at the Wissenschaftskolleg in Berlin. A first version, written as an introduction – also in Berlin – with Aleida Assmann was aborted after 150 pages because it simply was not possible to cover the subject in any depth within the narrow framework of an introduction. After a few more years of intermittent collaboration, it seemed sensible to continue our research independently because despite the common ground of memory our studies were taking us in different directions. Aleida Assmann has published her own findings under the title *Erinnerungsräume. Funktionen und Wandlungen des kulturellen Gedächtnisses*[2] [*Arts of Memory....*]. Her work focuses on the forms and functions of cultural memory from antiquity through to the (post)modern age,

---

[1] The series continued with "Text und Kommentar" [Text and Commentary] (1995), "Schleier und Schwelle" [On Secrecy, 3 vols.] (1997–1999), "Einsamkeit" [Solitude] (2000), "Aufmerksamkeiten" [Attention] (2001), "Hieroglyphen" [Hieroglyphs] (2003), "Verwandlungen" [Transformations] (2005), and "Vollkommenheit" [Perfection] (2010).

[2] Munich 1999, 4th ed. 2009. Engl., Cultural Memory and Western Civilization (Cambridge University Press, 2011).

and to a certain degree it can be considered a continuation of my present book, which concentrates mainly on the early written cultures of the Middle East and the Mediterranean.

A sabbatical in 1987 and 1988 enabled me to work on the case studies discussed in Part II of the book. The first, more theoretical part developed in Part I grew from my preparations, together with Tonio Hölscher, for the lecture series on "Kultur und Gedächtnis" (1986 and 1988), "Kultur und Konflikt" (1988 and 1990), and "Revolution und Mythos" (1990), in collaboration with Dietrich Harth, and the conferences on "Kultur als Lebenswelt und Monument" (1987 and 1991), and "Mnemosyne" (1989 and 1991), in collaboration with Aleida Assmann and Dietrich Harth. I am indebted to all of these colleagues for their endlessly inspiring supply of ideas. A further, most welcome opportunity to discuss the central themes was provided by lectures at the SFB Freiburg on "Mündlichkeit und Schriftlichkeit" [The Oral and the Written], at the Stuttgart Zentrum für Kulturtheorie, at the Freiburg Graduiertenkolleg on "Vergangenheitsbezug antiker Gegenwarten" [Past Reference in Classical Presents], and at the Essen Kulturwissenschaftliches Institut – most of these delivered jointly by myself and Aleida Assmann. Finally, my thanks go to E. P. Wieckenberg, without whose indefatigable encouragement my tentative probings would never have grown into a book.

Foreword (2010)

Twenty-five years ago when Aleida Assmann and I discovered "Cultural Memory" as a topic for a common book project, we embarked on what was then a small river of discourse. Today, the river has grown into a sea. Cultural memory has become a central concern, not only for archaeology and comparative literature, the two disciplines in the context of which we started, but also within all branches of cultural studies as well as history, arts, and even politics. However, the very fact that we began our research at such an early stage when the foundations of this field had still to be set down may have saved our books from becoming soon outdated by being just part of a passing fashion. There is very little that I found necessary to change for the English edition except for updating the bibliography. The field has since evolved in many directions, but the theoretical foundations proved stable as did the ancient world with which the case studies are concerned.

For an Egyptologist, cultural memory is a likely concept to study, especially for two reasons. First, Egypt was reputed, in antiquity, to be the civilization with the longest memory whose monuments and annals stretched back into time immemorial. The past stood visibly and constantly before Egypt as a model to follow, and the Egyptians made great efforts not to let the monuments of their past fall into ruin and oblivion. Is this a special case? Or, is it a typical form of a culture or society to deal with its past? Second, do we think of Ancient Egypt as part of our own past or rather as a foreign, exotic world? Is it a matter of memory or of (re)discovery? And what is the difference? What is the nature of this mysterious shadow-line that separates remembered from discovered past, for example, the Homeric epics or the biblical psalms from the Pyramid Texts?

Completely different were the questions about the past that started to occupy the public debates in Germany during the years from 1985 to 1990, when we started to work on our common project. They concerned the recent past and its importance for the political (re)invention both of Germany after the union with the former German Democratic Republic (GDR) and of Europe aspiring to ever closer forms of political union. The "past" and "identity" were the two focal points around which we tried to build our concept of cultural memory. My task was to deal with the ancient world whereas Aleida's was to pursue the topic up to modernity and postmodernism. However, due to external reasons, the work that was planned as a common enterprise was published separately at seven years distance. It is only now, in its English version and at its new home with Cambridge University Press, that our original concept is realized and the two parts reunite, not between two covers but as a pair belonging together and complementing each other.

We are very grateful that this has become possible, first of all to Werner Kelber (Rice University) who insisted on English editions of the works and did not give up until he found a publisher; then, to Beatrice Rehl who charged herself so efficiently with getting this project into the program of Cambridge University Press, and to Emily Spangler, Brigitte Coulton, and Ginger Boyce who with great care saw the manuscript through its various stages of production. David Henry Wilson did an admirable job in translating my at times rather heavy German text into his fluent and elegant English prose. Linda Shortt attended with indefatigable care to finding and verifying existing English translations for the many quotes and checking the exact terminological correspondents. The Constance Cluster of Excellence "Cultural Foundations of Integration" and the Athenaeum Stiftung Dietrich Goetze supported the publication with their generous funding.

Constance, August 2010, Jan Assmann

Introduction

In the Pentateuch, we are told four times that children must be taught the meaning of rituals and laws:

And when thy son asketh thee in time to come, saying, What mean the testimonies, and the statutes, and the judgments, which the Lord our God hath commanded you? Then thou shalt say unto thy son, We were Pharaoh's bondmen in Egypt; and the Lord brought us out of Egypt with a mighty hand.... (Deut. 6:10)

And it shall come to pass, when your children shall say unto you, What mean ye by this service? That ye shall say, "It is the sacrifice of the Lord's Passover, who passed over the houses of the children of Israel in Egypt, when he smote the Egyptians.... (Exod. 12:26)

And it shall be when thy son asketh thee in time to come, saying, What is this? That thou shalt say unto him, By strength of hand the Lord brought us out from Egypt, from the house of bondage.... (Exod. 13:14)

And thou shalt shew thy son in that day, saying, This is done because of that which the Lord did unto me when I came forth out of Egypt.... (Exod. 13:8)

That which unfolds before us here is a little drama of personal pronouns and remembered history. The son talks of "you" and "us" (the Lord our God), and the father answers with "we" or with "I/me." These verses are made into the "Midrash of the Four Children" as part of the Haggadah, the liturgy that accompanies the Jewish ceremonial meal of Seder, which is nothing less than a lesson to teach children about the exodus from Egypt. Four questions (including the one that is not asked in Exod. 13:8) are distributed among four children: the clever, the bad, the simple, and the one who does not yet know how to ask questions. The cleverness of the clever child is exemplified by the manner in which he distinguishes between concepts (testimonies, statutes, judgments) and expands the second person "you" into the first person "our." The father tells him the story using "we" to incorporate the questioner. The badness of the bad child is evinced by his exclusive "ye":

How does the bad child ask his question? "What mean ye by this service?" "Ye" does not include himself! And so, just as he excludes himself from the group, you must also shut him out by answering: "This is done because of that which the Lord did unto me when I came forth out of Egypt." (Pesach Haggadah)

This little drama touches on three of the themes of this book: identity ("we," "you," and "I"), memory (the story of the exodus from Egypt that provides the basis and the substance of "we"), and reproduction and continuity (the relationship between father and son). During the feast of Seder the child learns to say "we" because he is drawn into a story and a memory that form and fill the concept of the first-person plural.[1] This is, in fact, a problem and a process that underlies every culture, but it rarely comes so sharply into focus as it does here.

This book deals with the connection between these three themes of memory (or reference to the past), identity (or political imagination), and cultural continuity (or the formation of tradition). Every culture formulates something that might be called a connective structure. It has a binding effect that works on two levels – social and temporal. It binds people together by providing a "symbolic universe" (Berger and Luckmann) – a common area of experience, expectation, and action whose connecting force provides them with trust and with orientation. Early texts refer to this aspect of culture as justice. However, it also links yesterday with today by giving form and presence to influential experiences and memories, incorporating images and tales from another time into the background of the onward moving present, and bringing with it hope and continuity. This connective structure is the aspect

---

[1] On the catechism as a form of historical memory and identity formation, see A. de Pury and T. Römer, 1989, "Memoire et catechisme dans l'Ancien Testament," *Histoire et conscience historique* (CCEPOA 5, 1989), 81–92.

of culture that underlies myths and histories. Both the normative and the narrative elements of these – mixing instruction with storytelling – create a basis of belonging, of identity, so that the individual can then talk of "we." What binds him to this plural is the connective structure of common knowledge and characteristics – first through adherence to the same laws and values, and second through the memory of a shared past.

The basic principle behind all connective structures is repetition. This guarantees that the lines of action will not branch out into infinite variations but instead will establish themselves in recognizable patterns immediately identifiable as elements of a shared culture. The ceremonial feast of Seder once again provides a clear illustration of this: this Hebrew word actually means "order" and refers to the strictly prescribed course that the feast must follow. Even the terms "prescribe" and "follow" go to the heart of the whole concept – namely, time. On the one hand, the internal, temporal, organization of the ceremony is fixed, and on the other, each celebration is linked to its predecessor. Because all such festivals follow the same "order," they entail repetition just like the patterns on wallpaper in the form of unending rapport. I call this principle "ritual coherence." Seder night, however, not only repeats the ceremony of the previous year by following the same ritual but also re-presents or "presentifies"[2] an event from a far more remote past: the Exodus. Repetition and presentification are two very different forms of a single reference. The term "Seder" refers only to the repetition, whereas the presentification or realization of the experience is expressed by the term *Haggadah* – the book that is read on this occasion. This is an often richly illustrated collection of blessings, songs, anecdotes, and homilies that all relate to the escape from Egypt. They may be seen as interpretations of the biblical tradition and are meant above all to explain these events to children. The *Haggadah* is also a prescription, with the emphasis on "script," because it is an interpretation of a text. Memory of the past is brought to present life through the explanation of a tradition.

All rituals combine these two elements of repetition and re-presentation or presentification. The more rigidly they stick to an established order, the more predominant the aspect of repetition is.

---

[2] On the concept of *presentification* see Chapt. 2 , n. 5.

The more freedom they give to individual expression, the more the aspect of re-presentation comes to the fore. These provide the two poles between which the dynamic process develops that gives writing its all-important function in the connective structure of cultures. It is through the written element of traditions that the dominance of repetition gradually gives way to that of re-presentation – ritual gives way to textual coherence. A new connective structure emerges out of this, which consists not of imitation and preservation but of interpretation and memory. Instead of liturgy we now have hermeneutics.

Different studies are examined in this book in an attempt to extrapolate a typological analysis of textual coherence from this concept of culture. My focus is on comparisons between and variations in the changes and characteristics that mark the connective structure, and I examine the process that leads to its establishment, consolidation, loosening, and even dissolution. The term "canon" is used to identify a principle that elevates a culture's connective structure to a level at which it becomes impervious to time and change. Canon is what I might call the *mémoire volontaire* of a society, in contrast to both the more fluid "stream of tradition" of early civilizations and the self-regulating *memoria* of postcanonic culture, the contents of which have lost their binding force. Societies conceive images of themselves, and they maintain their identity through the generations by fashioning a culture out of memory. They do it – and this is a crucial point for this book – in completely different ways. I investigate *how* societies remember, and how they visualize themselves in the course of their remembering.

Although current discussions of posthistory and postmodernism would provide us with sufficient material for study, this book deals only with the Ancient World. That is partly because it is my own specialized field, and partly because, in her book *Erinnerungsräume: Formen und Wandlungen des kulturellen Gedächtnisses* [Arts of Memory], Aleida Assmann focuses on the cultural memory of the modern age. However, despite this limitation, this book also transcends the borders of my specialty, Egyptology, in a manner that some may find unacceptable and that certainly requires a word of explanation. The arguments and concepts developed in Part I of the book are illustrated in Part II by case studies drawn from Mesopotamia, the Hittites, Israel, and Greece, as well as Ancient Egypt. In my defense, I would like to emphasize that

I am not concerned here with presenting research material as such – which would naturally be restricted to my own special field – but my object is to reconstruct cultural connections or, to be more precise, to establish the links among (collective) memory, written culture, and ethnogenesis as a contribution to a general theory of culture.

Such contributions have been and are being made by scholars from a wide variety of fields. They include Johann Gottfried Herder and Karl Marx, Jacob Burckhardt, Friedrich Nietzsche, Aby Warburg, Max Weber and Ernst Cassirer, Johan Huizinga and T. S. Eliot, Arnold Gehlen and A. L. Kroeber, Clifford Geertz, Jack Goody and Mary Douglas, Sigmund Freud and René Girard, and the list goes on and on. Poets and novelists, sociologists, economists, historians, philosophers, ethnologists – only archaeologists have for the most part remained strangely silent on this topic. However, there can be no doubt that a study of early civilizations can shed a great deal of light on the nature, function, origin, communication, and transformation of culture, and that is precisely my starting point.

It is normal to present definitions at the start of such a study. The reader has every right to know what is meant by the term "cultural memory," why it is both valid and meaningful, what phenomena it may help to illuminate more efficiently than other terms, and how it transcends the more established concept of tradition. Cultural memory refers to one of the exterior dimensions of the human memory, which initially we tend to think of as purely internal – located within the brain of the individual, and a subject of encephalology, neurology, and psychology but not of historical cultural studies, the contents of this memory. However, the contents of this memory, the ways in which they are organized, and the length of time they last are for the most part not a matter of internal storage or control but of the external conditions imposed by society and cultural contexts. Maurice Halbwachs was the first to focus directly on this phenomenon, and his arguments form the subject of my first chapter. I would like to distinguish between four areas of this external dimension, and cultural memory is just one of them:

1. "Mimetic memory." This refers to action. We learn different forms of behavior through imitation. The use of written instructions relating to machinery, cooking, construction, and

so on, is a relatively modern and never comprehensive development. Action can never be completely codified. Other areas such as everyday manners, customs, and ethics still depend on mimetic traditions. It is this mimetic aspect that René Girard has made the central platform of his numerous books, which develop a cultural theory that draws much of its impact from this one-sidedness.

2. "The memory of things." From time immemorial human beings have surrounded themselves with "things," from private everyday objects such as beds, chairs, crockery, clothes, and tools to houses, streets, villages, towns, cars, and ships.[3] They all represent our concepts of practicality, comfort, beauty, and, to a certain extent, our own identity. Objects reflect ourselves – they remind us of who we are, of our past, of our forebears, and so on. The world of things in which we live has a time index that refers not only to our present but also, and simultaneously, to different phases and levels of our past.

3. "Communicative memory." Language and the ability to communicate are again developed not from within oneself but through interchange with others, with circular or feedback interplay between interior and exterior. The individual physiology and psychology of consciousness and memory are inexplicable, and as a result they demand a systemic explanation that will incorporate interaction with other individuals. A person's consciousness and memory can only be formulated by way of his or her participation in such interactions. However, we need not go into further detail here, as this aspect is covered in our discussion of Maurice Halbwachs's theory of memory.

4. "Cultural memory." This is the handing down of meaning. This is an area in which the other three aspects merge almost seamlessly. When mimetic routines take on the status of rituals, for example, when they assume a meaning and significance that go beyond their practical function, the borders of mimetic action memory are transcended. Rituals are part of cultural memory because they are the form through which cultural meaning is both handed down and brought to present life.

---

[3] This corresponds to what Maurice Halbwachs calls *entourage matériel.*

The same applies to things once they point to a meaning that goes beyond their practical purpose: symbols; icons; representations such as monuments, tombs, temples, idols; and so forth, all transcend the borders of object-memory because they make the implicit index of time and identity explicit. This aspect is the central point of Aby Warburg's "social memory." The degree to which the same can be said of our third area, language and communication and the role played by writing, is the real subject matter of this book.

At this point, I would like to look back at the history of this line of inquiry. At the end of the 1970s, a circle of specialists in cultural studies came together – experts on the Old Testament, Egyptology, Assyriology, Classical Philology, Literature, and Linguistics – to research the "archaeology" of the text or, to be precise, of the literary text. At that time, these questions were approached on a very abstract, theoretical level. The objective of this new study group was to move away from theory and into two different dimensions: temporal depth and cultural distance. Several books resulted from this project under the collective heading *Archäologie der literarischen Kommunikation* [Archaeology of Literary Communication]. At the group's first conference on the topic of "The Oral and the Written," the term "cultural memory" was proposed within the context of the literary text. Konrad Ehlich defined this as a *wiederaufgenommene Mitteilung* [message returned to later] within the framework of a *zerdehnte Situation* [extended situation]. The original setting of the text is the institution of the messenger.[4]

Out of this concept of the extended situation emerged what Aleida Assmann and I – continuing the research of Jurij Lotman and other culture theorists – have called cultural memory in our own work.[5] Exactly what this means can best be described in technical terminology. The extension of the communicative situation requires possibilities of intermediate, external storage. The system of communication

4 Konrad Ehlich, "Text und sprachliches Handeln. Die Entstehung von Texten aus dem Bedürfnis nach Überlieferung", in A. Assmann/J. Assmann/ Chr. Hardmeier (eds.), *Schrift und Gedächtnis. Archäologie der literarischen Kommunikation I.* München 1983 24–43.
5 Aleida Assmann and Jan Assmann, "Schrift, Tradition und Kultur", in W. Raible (ed.), *Zwischen Festtag und Alltag*, Tübingen 1988, 25–50; J. Assmann, "Kollektives Gedächtnis und kulturelle Identität," in J. Assmann and T. Hölscher (1988a), 9–19.

therefore has to develop an external area where communications and information – of cultural importance – can be processed through forms of coding, storage, and retrieval.[6] This requires institutional frameworks, specialization, and, under normal circumstances, systems of notation such as knotted cords, *churingas*, calculi, and, finally, writing. Writing emerged everywhere from such systems of notation, which were developed within the functional context of extended communication and the required mode of intermediate storage. There are three typical fields or functional contexts for symbolic representation: economics (e.g., near-eastern counters), political power (Egypt), and identity-giving myths (e.g., Australian *churingas* and songlines).

The invention of writing opened up the possibility of an all-encompassing, revolutionary transformation of this external area of communication, and in most cases, this transformation actually occurred. At the stage of pure orality or orality plus notation systems prior to writing, the intermediate and external modes of communication storage remained closely linked to the actual system of communication. Cultural memory coincides almost completely with whatever meaning is circulating within the group. It is only through writing that this external area of communication is able to take on an independent and increasingly complex existence of its own. Only now can a memory be formed to extend the message or meaning beyond the limitations of its original time and its original mode of communication, just as the individual memory can extend beyond the range of present consciousness. Cultural memory feeds tradition and communication, but that is not its only function. Without it there can be no infringements, conflicts, innovations, restorations, or revolutions. These are all eruptions from a world beyond the current meaning, through the recalling of the forgotten, the revival of tradition, or the resurfacing of what has been suppressed. They represent the typical dynamism of written cultures that led Claude Lévi-Strauss to categorize them as "hot societies."

---

[6] Under the key term *extériorisation*, André Leroi-Gourhan, *Le geste et la parole*, Paris 1965 describes the technological evolution of external data storage from primitive tools, through writing, card indexes, and punch cards, to the computer, and he calls this a *mémoire extériorisée* (1965, 64). The bearer is not the individual or, as with animals, the species, but the *collectivité ethnique*. Merlin Donald (1991, 308–15) speaks of "External Storage Systems" (ESS) using "exograms."

As with all the more complex instruments, writing – in an even more distinct manner – gives rise to a dialectic of expansion and loss. The automobile, as an externalization of natural movement, allows for a hitherto undreamed-of expansion in the range of human travel, but if overused, it also reduces our natural, unaided mobility. The same applies to writing: as an externalized memory, it facilitates a hitherto undreamed-of expansion in our capacity to store and retrieve information and other forms of communication, while simultaneously leading to a shrinkage of our natural memory bank. This problem, which was already noted by Plato, still preoccupies psychologists.[7] It is not just the individual who is affected by these possibilities of external storage; even more important, the whole of society and the communications that help to formulate that society are affected. This externalization of meaning in turn opens up another very different dialectic. The positive new forms of retention and realization across the millennia are counterbalanced by the negative forms of loss through forgetting and through suppression by way of manipulation, censorship, destruction, circumscription, and substitution.

We need a term to describe these processes and to relate them to historical changes in the technology of storage systems, in the sociology of the groups concerned, in the media, and in the structures of storage, tradition, and the circulation of cultural meaning – in short, to encompass all such functional concepts as tradition forming, past reference, and political identity or imagination. That term is cultural memory. It is "cultural" because it can only be realized institutionally and artificially, and it is "memory" because in relation to social communication it functions in exactly the same way as individual memory does in relation to consciousness. Cancik and Mohr suggest (1990) that instead of the "metaphor" of collective memory we should use the time-honored concept of tradition, leading to a foreshortening of cultural phenomenology and its dynamics, similar to reducing the concept of individual memory to that of consciousness. However, we should not allow ourselves to be led astray by a battle over terminology. No matter what name one gives to this externalization of social tradition and communication, it is a phenomenon in its own right:

---

7 F. H. Piekara, K. G. Ciesinger, K. P. Muthig, "Notizenanfertigen und Behalten," *Zeitschrift für Pädagogische Psychologie* 1987, 1, H.4, 267–280.

a cultural sphere that combines tradition, awareness of history, myth in action, and self-definition, and that – a crucial point – is subject to the vast range of historically conditioned changes, including those brought about by the evolution of media technology.

In borderline cases, this comprehensive area of memory, which extends far beyond whatever meaning has been communicated or handed down, takes on such a solid consistency that it can even contradict the social and political reality of the present. I refer to such cases with the labels "contra-present memory" (G. Theissen) and "anachronous structures" (M. Erdheim). These are enhanced, artificial forms of cultural memory that use cultural mnemotechnics to produce and maintain "nonsimultaneity."

This study of cultural memory therefore focuses on such processes of transformation and enhancement, examining the decisive changes within the connective structure of a given society. In particular, I consider and analyze two approaches that highlight these changes although, in my opinion, they do not go far enough in explaining them. The first, which goes back to the 18th century, was the central point of A. Weber's all-embracing theory of culture and was subsumed by K. Jaspers under the simple heading of the Axial Age, whereas its sociological consequences were explained by S. N. Eisenstadt. It traces the changes back to innovations connected solely with the history of ideas: visions of a transcendental basis for living and for understanding life as set out by individuals like Confucius, Laotse, Buddha and Zoroaster, Moses and other prophets, Homer and the tragedians, Socrates, Pythagoras, Parmenides, Jesus and Muhammad – ideas that were then taken up by new generations of the intellectual elite and put into operation to radically transform the reality in which they were living.

The second approach, of much more recent vintage, is today represented mainly by the Hellenist Eric A. Havelock and the anthropologist Jack Goody, together with an expanding group of evolutionary (Niklas Luhmann) and media (Marshall McLuhan) theorists. They see these and other transformations mainly as the effects of technological developments such as the invention of writing and of the printing press.

It is greatly to the credit of both approaches that they draw attention to the changes and uncover many important connections. However, they suffer from the fact that neither pays sufficient heed to the connections focused on by the other. The media-based account runs the risk of reducing all these processes to a single technological cause, whereas the ideas-based interpretation remains astonishingly blind to the fundamental importance of writing, with its ever increasing influence on cultural traditions and social institutions.

With this study of cultural memory, I hope to overcome such problems by placing the written culture in the wider context of what on the one hand Aleida Assmann calls the "construction of cultural time" and on the other of collective identity formation or political imagination. Against this background, that which could be described as changes in the cultural memory is illustrated by four examples that are neither systematic nor completely representative but are meant to offer a starting point for what could be an unlimited series of further studies. By selecting Egypt, Israel, Greece, and (briefly) cuneiform cultures I have, however, tried to focus on as wide a variety as possible of typical processes that transform cultural memory.

PART I

THE THEORETICAL BASIS

1

Memory Culture

Preliminary Remarks

THE ART AND THE CULTURE OF MEMORY

The concept of *ars memoriae* or *memorativa* is firmly rooted in western tradition. The Greek poet Simonides, who lived during the 6th century BCE, is regarded as its founder. The Romans classified this form of art as one of five categories of rhetoric, and that was how it was handed down to the Middle Ages and the Renaissance. The underlying principle was as follows: "Those who would like to employ this part of their abilities should choose localities, then form mental images of the things they wanted to store in their memory, and place these in the localities. In this way, the order of the localities would preserve the order of the things, while the images would present the things themselves" (Cicero, *De Oratore* II 86, 351–354).[1] The author (1st century BCE) of the *Rhetorica ad Herennium*, the most important classical text on the art of memory, distinguished between "natural" and "artificial" memory. *Ars memoriae* is the basis of artificial memory. It helps the individual to absorb and retain an extraordinary amount of knowledge, for example, for rhetorical use. This tradition remained effective until well into the 17th century, and has been documented by the English historian Frances Yates in a now classic book that has paved

---

[1] Cicero, *On the Ideal Orator*, trans. with introduction by James M. May and Jakob Wisse (Oxford: Oxford University Press, 2002), 219.

the way for countless new studies.[2] However, this *art of memory* has very little in common with what is subsumed here under the concept of memory culture (*Erinnerungskultur*). The art of memory relates to the individual and presents techniques to help form personal memory. By contrast, "memory culture" is concerned with a social obligation and is firmly linked to the group. The question here is: "What must we not forget?" This question is generally a more or less explicit and a relatively central element of any group. Where it is central and integral to the group's identity and image of itself, one can speak of "memory communities" (Pierre Nora[3]). In other words, memory culture is linked to the "memory that forms a community" (K. Schmidt, see n. 63). Unlike the art of memory that was a classical invention – albeit not exclusive to the West – memory culture is universal. It is virtually impossible to think of any social group where it is not to be found, in no matter how weak a form. That is why its history cannot be written in the way Frances Yates was able to deal with the art of memory. It is only possible to highlight some generic features that can be illustrated by recourse to some examples chosen arbitrarily. However, just as the Greeks occupy a special place in the field of classical *ars memoriae*, there is one nation that stands out in the history of memory culture – despite its universality – namely, the Israelites. They gave it a new form, and this was as influential for western history – among others – as the classical art of memory. Israel formed and preserved itself in accordance with the imperative "keep and remember."[4] Thus the Israelites became a people in a new and emphatic sense: they became the prototype of nationhood. Max Weber, who contrary to the spirit of his own time saw clearly the "perceived" or, as we would say today, the imagined nature of nationhood, wrote: "And behind all ethnic diversities there is somehow naturally the notion of the 'chosen

---

[2] Frances Amelia Yates, *The Art of Memory* (Chicago: University of Chicago Press, 1966. Herwig Blum, *Die antike Mnemotechnik* (Hildesheim: Olms, 1969); Dale F. Eickelmann, "The Art of Memory: Islamic Education and its Social Reproduction," *Comparative Studies in Society and History* 20 (1978), 485–516; Aleida Assmann and Dietrich Harth (eds.), *Mnemosyne* (Frankfurt: S. Fischer, 1991), especially Part II, "Art of Memory – Memory of Art"; Anselm Haverkamp and Renate Lachmann (eds.), *Gedächtnis als Raum. Studien zur Mnemotechnik* (Frankfurt: Suhrkamp, 1991).

[3] *Les lieux de memoire*, 3 vols., (Paris: Gallimard 1984–1987).

[4] "Shamor ve zakhor be-dibur echad" (Remember and preserve, in a single commandment) are the words of the Sabbath song *Lekha Dodi*.

people,'"[5] and this insight shows just how the principle of ethnic differences enabled Israel to develop a form that could serve as a model for the ideal. Any people that sees itself as a unit unlike other peoples, imagines itself somehow to be chosen. Weber was writing at a time when nationalism was at its peak, and it is only now that we can see just how universally valid this idea is. The principle of memory follows on from that of "being chosen"– being chosen means nothing less than a complex network of rigidly fixed obligations not allowing under any circumstances memory to fade away. Thus, Israel developed an enhanced form of memory culture that corresponds exactly to the artificial type described in *Rhetorica ad Herennium*.

REFERRING TO THE PAST

What space is to the art of memory, time is to memory culture. Perhaps, though, I should take that one step further: what the art of memory is to learning, memory culture is to plans and hopes – that is, to the formation of an identity, including the social construction of meaning and time. Memory culture depends mainly, though not exclusively, on various links with the past. It is fundamental to the thesis that the past only comes into being insofar as we refer to it. Initially, this may seem odd. Nothing appears more natural than the formation of the past – it comes into being through the passing of time. Thus by tomorrow, today will be history in the form of yesterday. But societies can react to this natural process in completely different ways. As Cicero maintained of the "barbarians," people may "live into the day" and happily let today sink into the oblivion of the past; alternatively, they may strain every sinew to make today last indefinitely, for instance – like Cicero's Romans – their "plans should aim at what endures" (*De Oratore* II 40, 169),[6] or similar to the Egyptian Pharaohs who "set the morrow before their eyes" and "place into their hearts the demands of eternity." Anyone who during today fixes his eyes on tomorrow must preserve yesterday from oblivion by grasping it through memory. This is how the past is reconstructed, and this is the sense in which we can say that the past comes into being when we refer to it. The two

---

[5] Max Weber, *Economy and Society* (see Chapter 3, note 31), 391.
[6] Cicero, *On the Ideal Orator*, 167 (see chapt. 1, n. 1).

concepts of "memory culture" and "reference to the past" mark the boundaries of our study, and they distinguish it from those elements of memory that can be subsumed under *ars memoriae.*

In order to refer to the past, it goes without saying that the past must be brought into our consciousness. This presupposes two things:

1) It cannot have disappeared completely, and so there must be some kind of documentation;
2) this documentation must denote some kind of characteristic difference from today.

The first condition speaks for itself. The second can be best explained through the phenomenon of language change. Change is inevitable. There are no natural, living languages that remain permanently fixed. Language shifts are usually slow and unobtrusive, and the speaker is normally unaware of them. Awareness comes only when older stages of the language remain preserved under particular conditions (e.g., special forms as used in religious worship, or in texts that are passed down word for word from one generation to another, as with scriptures), and when the difference between these older versions and the current language has become so marked that the former seem like a language of their own and not a variation of the familiar idiom. This dissociation can sometimes even be noticed in oral traditions, but generally it only comes to light in written cultures, for instance when sacred or classical texts have to be learned at school.[7]

There are, however, many other factors, and many nonlinguistic levels that may make us conscious of the differences between old and new. Every substantial break in continuity or tradition can produce the past whenever the break is meant to create a new beginning. A Renaissance or a Reformation will always be shaped by a recourse to the past. Cultures rediscover this past while developing, producing, and constructing a future. This can be illustrated with the example of the earliest Renaissance recorded in human history: the neo-Sumerian revival of Sumerian traditions during the Ur III period, (end

---

[7] I have described how this happens in Egypt, in Jan Assmann, "Die Entdeckung der Vergangenheit. Innovation und Restauration in der ägyptischen Literaturgeschichte," in H. U. Gumbrecht and U. Link-Heer (eds.), *Epochenschwellen und Epochenstrukturen im Diskurs der Literatur- und Sprachhistorie* (Frankfurt: Suhrkamp, 1985), 484–499.

of 3rd millennium) after the interlude of the Sargonide Dynasty. For Egyptologists, a more obvious example is the slightly later Middle Kingdom (beginning of 2nd millennium), which is also significant because it too saw itself as a Renaissance. The name that the founder of the 12th Dynasty, Amenemhet I, gave himself as a kind of governmental manifesto was *whm mswt* (Repeater of Births), which is simply another way of saying "renaissance."[8] The kings of the 12th Dynasty revived forms from the 5th and 6th Dynasties;[9] they established cults for their royal predecessors,[10] classified the literary traditions of the past,[11] took the person of Snofru – a king from the early 4th Dynasty – as their model,[12] and thus created the "Old Kingdom" in the sense of a past, whose memory they used to establish a sense of continuity, legitimacy, authority, and self-confidence. In their inscriptions, the same kings displayed that very pathos of eternalization – "setting the morrow before their eyes" – mentioned earlier.

The rupture between yesterday and today, in which the choice to obliterate or preserve must be considered, is experienced in its most basic and, in a sense, primal form in death. Life only assumes the form of the past on which a memory culture can be built through its end, through its irremediable discontinuity. One might even call it the primal scene of memory culture. There is a difference between the autobiographical memory of the individual looking back from a certain vantage point over his own life, and the posthumous commemoration of him by posterity, and it is this distinction that brings out the specifically cultural element of collective memory. We say that the dead will live on in the memory of others, as if this were some kind of natural prolongation of their life. In reality, though, this is an act

---

[8] Detlef Franke, *Das Heiligtum des Heqaib auf Elephantine. Geschichte eines Provinzheiligtums im Mittleren Reich* (Heidelberg: Orientverlag, 1994), gives a detailed and compelling justification for this interpretation of Amenenhet I's Horus name.

[9] The "archaism" of the 12th Dynasty has been revealed particularly by Dieter Arnold's excavations at the royal cemetery in Lischt.

[10] Donald B. Redford, *Pharaonic King-Lists, Annals and Day Books* (Mississauga: Benben, 1986), 151 ff.

[11] Jan Assmann, *Ma'at: Gerechtigkeit und Unsterblichkeit im alten Ägypten* (Munich: C. H. Beck, 1990), chapter 2.

[12] Erhart Graefe, "Die gute Reputation des Königs 'Snofru'," in *Studies in Egyptology*, Fs.Lichtheim (Jerusalem: Magnes 1990), 257–263.

of resuscitation performed by the desire of the group not to allow the dead to disappear but, with the aid of memory, to keep them as members of their community and to take them with them into their progressive present.

The most vivid representation of this form of memory culture is the upper class Roman custom of parading their ancestors by way of portraits and masks (Latin *persona*: the dead man as a "person") in family processions.[13] The Egyptian custom whereby this memory culture that posterity normally implemented for the deceased, deliberately bridging the gap between life and death, was in fact initiated by the person during his own lifetime appears particularly strange in this context. The Egyptian official would arrange his own tomb and have his own biography inscribed on it, not in the sense of a memoir, but as an anticipatory obituary.[14] As the earliest and most widespread form of memory culture, the memory of the dead clearly illustrates that phenomena exist that are simply not covered by the conventional concept of "tradition." This masks the break that leads to the birth of the past, focusing our attention on continuity. Of course, some of those elements described by the terms "memory culture" or "cultural memory" may also be called tradition, but this leaves out the aspect of reception, the bridging of the gap, and also the negative factors of oblivion and suppression. This is why we need a concept that embraces both aspects. Dead people and memories of dead people cannot be handed down. Remembrance is a matter of emotional ties, cultural shaping, and a conscious reference to the past that overcomes the rupture between life and death. These are the elements that characterize cultural memory and take it far beyond the reaches of tradition.

---

[13] A strikingly similar custom developed in Egypt after the Old Kingdom; see Hermann Kees, *Totenglauben und Jenseitsvorstellungen der alten Ägypter: Grundlagen und Entwicklung bis zum Ende des Mittleren Reiches* (Leipzig: Hinrichs, 1926), 253 ff. The major processions also included wooden statues of important ancestors.

[14] See Jan Assmann, "Schrift, Tod und Identität. Das Grab als Vorschule der Literatur im alten Ägypten," in A. and J. Assmann (eds.), *Schrift und Gedächtnis. Archäologie der literarischen Kommunikation I* (Munich: Fink, 1983), 64–93; "Sepulkrale Selbstthematisierung im Alten Ägypten," in A. Hahn and V. Kapp (eds.), *Selbstthematisierung und Selbstzeugnis: Bekenntnis und Geständnis* (Frankfurt: Suhrkamp, 1987), 208–232.

THE SOCIAL CONSTRUCTION OF THE PAST:
MAURICE HALBWACHS

In the 1920s, the French sociologist Maurice Halbwachs developed his concept of the *mémoire collective*, which was then mainly outlined in three works: *Les cadres sociaux de la mémoire* (1925),[15] *La topographie légendaire des évangiles en terre sainte. Étude de mémoire collective* (1941),[16] and *La mémoire collective* (published posthumously in 1950, based mostly on work done during the 1930s).[17] Halbwachs studied at the lycée Henri IV under Bergson, in whose philosophy the premise of memory played a central role (H. Bergson 1896). He was also a student of Durkheim's, whose concept of collective consciousness gave him a solid basis in his quest to overcome Bergson's subjectivism and interpret memory as a social phenomenon. Halbwachs went on to teach sociology at Strassburg and subsequently at the Sorbonne. In 1944, just as he was offered a chair at the Collège de France, the Germans deported him; he was murdered on March 16, 1945, in the concentration camp at Buchenwald.[18]

Individual and Collective Memory

The central thesis that Halbwachs adheres to throughout his work is the social conditioning of memory. He is not in the least interested in the physical, that is, the neurological and encephalological basis of memory,[19] but establishes instead the social frame of reference without which no individual memory can either form or preserve itself. "No memory is possible outside frameworks used by people

[15] A new edition by Gérard Namer appeared in 1994 (Paris: Albin Michel). For a detailed appreciation of Halbwachs's theory of memory, see Gérard Namer, *Mémoire et société* (Paris: Klincksieck, 1987).

[16] Reprint 1971. A critical reedition by Marie Jaisson and Eric Brian will appear in the collection "Sociologie d'aujourd'hui," PUF, Paris.

[17] See the critical re-edition by G. Namer and M. Jaisson (Paris: Albin Michel, 1997).

[18] See Annette Becker's biography of M. Halbwachs: *Maurice Halbwachs: un intellectuel en guerres mondiales 1914–1945* (Paris: Agnes Vienot editions, 2003); for Halbwachs' tragic death see ibid., 413–450.

[19] Therefore he also rejects Bergson's mind/body dualism, see Henri Bergson, *Matière et mémoire* (Paris: Alcan, 1896).

living in society to determine and retrieve their recollections."[20] This means that a person who has grown up in complete isolation – though Halbwachs never puts the argument in such a direct way – would have no memory, because memory can only be fashioned during the process of socialization. Despite the fact that it is always the individual who "has" memory, it is created collectively. This is why the term collective memory should not be read as a metaphor, because while the group itself does not "have" a memory, it determines the memory of its members. Even the most personal recollections only come about through communication and social interaction. We recall not only what we have learned and heard from others but also how others respond to what we consider to be significant. All such experiences depend on intercourse, within the context of an existing social frame of reference and value. There is no memory without perception that is already conditioned by social frames of attention and interpretation.[21]

The concept of social frameworks (*cadres sociaux*) introduced by Halbwachs runs along surprisingly similar lines to E. Goffman's theory of "frame analysis" that delves into the social prestructure or organization of everyday experiences.[22] What Halbwachs undertakes is a frame analysis of memory – analogous to Goffman's analysis of experience – and he uses the same terminology. He even goes so far as to make the collective group the subject of memory, and he coins expressions like "group memory" and "memory of the nation," which take on the status of metaphors.[23] We do not need to follow him that far. The subject of memory is and always was the individual who nevertheless depends on the "frame" to organize this memory. The advantage of this theory lies in the fact that it simultaneously explains both remembering and forgetting. If persons – and societies – are only able to remember what can be reconstructed as a past within the referential framework

---

[20] Maurice Halbwachs, *On Collective Memory*, ed. and trans. Lewis A. Coser (Chicago: University of Chicago Press, 1992), 43.

[21] Ibid., 169.

[22] Erving Goffman, *Frame Analysis An Essay on the Organization of Experience* (New York: Harper 1974).

[23] Frederic C. Bartlett, *Remembering: A Study in Experimental Social Psychology* (Cambridge: Cambridge University Press, 1932) strongly objected to such expressions (though his approach was similar).

of their own present, then they will forget things that no longer have such a referential framework.[24]

To put it differently: a person's memory forms itself through his or her participation in communicative processes. It is a function of their involvement in a variety of social groups – ranging from family through religion to nation. Memory lives and survives through communication, and if this is broken off, or if the referential frames of the communicated reality disappear or change, then the consequence is forgetting.[25] We only remember what we communicate and what we can locate in the frame of the collective memory.[26] From the individual's point of view, memory is a conglomeration that emerges from participation in different group memories. From the perspective of the group, memory is a matter of knowledge that is distributed among and internalized by each member. All memories go to make up an independent system, whose elements both determine and support one another, whether in the individual or in the group. This is why it is so important for Halbwachs to distinguish between the individual and the collective, even though the former always has to be part of the latter. Memory is individual in the sense that it is a unique link between the collective memory (of the various group experiences) and the experiences specific to the person concerned. Strictly speaking, it is the emotions rather than the memories that are individual because emotions are closely connected with our bodies, whereas memories necessarily have their origin in the thoughts of the different groups to which we belong.

Figures of Memory

Just as thinking may be abstract, remembering is concrete. Ideas must take on a form that is imaginable before they can find their way into

---

[24] In Chapter 5 forgetting will be viewed through changes in the framework.

[25] "Forgetting is explained by the disappearance of these frameworks or a part of them, either because our attention was not in a position to fix itself on them, or because it is focused elsewhere.... However, forgetting... or the deformation of certain recollections, is also explained by the fact that these frameworks change from one period to another." Thus not only remembering but also forgetting is a social phenomenon.

[26] Halbwachs, *On Collective Memory* chapt. 4: "The Localization of Memories," 52–53.

memory, and so we have an indissoluble merging of idea and image. "But if a truth is to be settled in the memory of a group it needs to be presented in the concrete form of an event, of a personality, or of a locality" (*On Collective Memory*, 200).[27] On the other hand, if an event is to live on in the memory of a group, it must be enriched with the meaningfulness of a significant truth. "As soon as each person and each historical fact has permeated this memory, it is transposed into a teaching, a notion, or a system of ideas" (*On Collective Memory*, 188). That which are "memory figures" emerge out of this interplay between concepts and experiences.[28] These are characterized by three special features: a concrete relationship to time and place, a concrete relationship to a group, and an independent capacity for reconstruction.

Reference to Time and Place. Memory figures need to be given substance through a particular setting and to be realized in a particular time. In other words, they are always related concretely to time and place, even if this is not necessarily in an historical or a geographical sense. Collective memory's reliance on this concrete orientation creates points of crystallization. The substance of memories is connected to time both through the adherence to primal or outstanding events and through the periodic rhythms to which these memories refer. For instance, the calendar of festivals mirrors a collectively "experienced time" that may be secular or ecclesiastical, agricultural or military, depending on the nature of the group. *Inhabited space* provides a similar anchorage: what the house is to the family, village and land are to the farmer; what cities are to town-dwellers, the countryside is to rural communities. These are all spatial frames for memories, and even – or especially – during absence, they are what is remembered as home. Another spatial element is the world of objects that surround or belong to the individual – his *entourage matériel* that both supports and contributes to his

[27] Halbwachs, "The Legendary Topography of the Gospels in the Holy Land," in *On Collective Memory*, 193–235, here 200.

[28] In this context, Halbwachs himself speaks of "memory images," see especially *Les cadres sociaux de la mémoire* (Paris: F. Alcan, 1925), 1 ff.; the term "memory figures" also denotes culturally formed, socially binding "memory images," but it seems preferable to use "figure" in this case as it refers not only to iconic but also to narrative forms.

identity. This world of objects – tools, furniture, rooms, their particular layout, all of which "offer us an image of permanence and stability" (1985b, 130)[29] – also has a social dimension: its value and its status symbolism are both social factors.[30] The tendency toward localization applies to every form of community. Any group that wants to consolidate itself will make an effort to find and establish a base for itself, not only to provide a setting for its interactions but also to symbolize its identity and to provide points of reference for its memories. Memory needs places and tends toward spatialization.[31] Halbwachs illustrates this point with the example of the "The Legendary Topography of the Gospels in the Holy Land" – a work that we will examine more closely in another context. Group and place take on a symbolic sense of community that the group also adheres to, when it is separated from its own space, by symbolically reproducing the holy sites.

Reference to the Group. Collective memory is dependent on its bearers and it cannot be passed on arbitrarily. Whoever shares it thereby demonstrates his membership in the group, and so it is not only bound to time and place but also to a specific identity. In other words, it is related exclusively to the standpoint of one real and living community. The temporal and spatial elements together with the different forms of communication within the particular group operate within an existential context that is also filled with ideas, emotions, and values. All of these factors combine to create a history of home and life that is full of meaning and significance for the image and aims of the group. Memory figures are also "models, examples, and elements of

[29] Quoted from Auguste Comte; see also Arnold Gehlen's term "Aussenhalt" (external belongings) in *Urmensch und Spätkultur* (Berlin: de Gruyter, 1956), 25 f. and elsewhere.

[30] Cf. Arpag Appadurai, *The Social Life of Things. Commodities in Cultural Perspective*, (Cambridge: Cambridge University Press, 1986).

[31] See Cicero: "tanta vis admonitionis inest in locis, ut non cine causa ex iis memoriae ducta sit disciplina" (*de finibus bonorum et malorum* 5, 1–2): "So great a power of memory lies in places that it is not without cause that mnemotechnics are derived from them" (quoted by Hubert Cancik and Hubert Mohr, "Erinnerung/Gedächtnis," in *Handbuch religionswissenschaftlicher Grundbegriffe* 2 [Stuttgart: Kohlhammer, 1990], 299–323, quote 312). This approach is further developed by Pierre Nora in his monumental work *Les lieux de mémoire*, 3 vols. (Paris: Gallimard, 1984, 1986, 1992).

teaching. They express the general attitude of the group; they not only reproduce its history but also define its nature and its qualities and weaknesses" (Halbwachs, *On Collective Memory*, 59). Halbwachs uses the hierarchy of the medieval feudal system to illustrate the relationship between collective memory and the image a group has of itself and its social function. The various coats-of-arms and titles symbolized people's claims to rights and privileges. The rank of a family was to a large extent "clearly defined by what it and others know of its past" (*On Collective Memory*, 128). They had to "appeal to the memory of society in order to obtain an allegiance that was later legitimized by stressing the usefulness of the services rendered and the competence of the magistrate or functionary" (*On Collective Memory*, 121–122).

The social group that forms a memory community preserves its past mainly through two factors: its peculiarity and its durability. Through the image that it creates for itself, it emphasizes externally the difference that it plays down internally. It also forms a consciousness of its identity over time in order that remembered facts are always selected and proportioned according to parallels, similarities, and continuities. The moment a group becomes aware of a radical change, it ceases to be a group and makes way for another constellation. But because every group strives for durability, it tends to block out change as far as possible and to perceive history as an unchanging continuance.

Reconstructivism. There is another element of collective memory that is closely linked to the group: its reconstructive character. Memory cannot preserve the past as such, "only those recollections subsist that in every period society, working within its present-day frameworks, can reconstruct" (*On Collective Memory*, 189). In the words of the philosopher H. Blumenberg, there are "no pure facts of memory."

There is no more impressive proof of the breadth and originality of Halbwachs's thinking than the fact that, although he was a philosopher and a sociologist, he chose to illustrate his thesis with such recondite material as the history of the holy sites of Christianity in Palestine. Christian topography is pure fiction. The holy sites do not commemorate facts attested to by contemporary witnesses, but they represent ideas of faith whose roots were sunk there long after the events (Halbwachs, *Topographie légendaire*, 157). The authentic collective memory, drawn from live experience, of the community of the disciples – nowadays we might call it the Jesus Movement – as a *communauté affective* is a typical selection based on emotional involvement, and is restricted to the sayings, parables, and sermons of Jesus. The biographical elaboration of these memories did not come until later after expectations of the Apocalypse had faded. At this point it became important to embed the remembered sayings in biographical episodes that would furnish them with the order of time and place. There were no places incorporated in those memories, and therefore after Jesus's death they were augmented with particular settings by people well acquainted with the geography of Galilee. When Paul came on the scene, however, the focus of memory shifted from Galilee to Jerusalem. Here there are absolutely no "authentic memories," because the trial and execution of Christ took place without the disciples. At this point Jerusalem became central as theological attention shifted to focus on the passion and resurrection of Jesus: these decisive elements had to be reconstructed; thus everything that happened in Galilee was pushed into the background as a prelude to the main event.

The new idea, made binding by the Council of Nicaea, was that Jesus as the Son of God died to redeem the sins of mankind. This took on the status of memory and became a memory figure as the story of the Passion. The Jesus memory was reconstructed by way of the cross and the resurrection, and Jerusalem became the commemorative setting. This new doctrine and the new Jesus memory that incorporated it then took on concrete form through a *système de localisation* that gave it spatial links through churches, chapels, holy sites, memorial plaques, Calvary, and so on. Later systems of localization proceeded to extend or build over these in a kind of palimpsest that gave expression to the various changes in the Christian doctrine.

Memory, then, works through reconstruction. The past itself cannot be preserved by it, and thus it is continually subject to processes of reorganization according to the changes taking place in the frame of reference of each successive present. Even that which is new can only appear in the form of the reconstructed past, in the sense that traditions can only be exchanged with traditions, the past with the past (*On Collective Memory*, 185). Society does not adopt new ideas and replace the past with them; instead it assumes the past of groups other than those that have hitherto been dominant. "In this sense, there is no social idea that would not at the same time be a recollection of the society" (*On Collective Memory*, 188). Thus collective memory operates simultaneously in two directions: backward and forward. It not only reconstructs the past but it also organizes the experience of the present and the future. It would therefore be absurd to draw a contrast between the "principle of memory" and the "principle of hope," because each conditions the other and each is unthinkable without the other.[32]

Memory versus History

Halbwachs believes that a group incorporates its past in a form that excludes any kind of change. This is reminiscent of the characteristics of the societies C. Lévi-Strauss calls "cold."[33] In fact the exclusion of change from Halbwachs's collective memory plays such a crucial role that he is able to call "history" its exact opposite, because it works in a reverse way from collective memory. The latter only focuses on similarity and continuity, whereas the former perceives nothing but difference and discontinuity. Whereas collective memory looks at the group from inside – and is at pains to present it with an image of its past in which it can recognize itself at every stage and so exclude any major changes – history leaves out any periods without change as empty interludes in the story in order that the only worthwhile historical facts are those that reveal an event or a process resulting in something new. Group memory, then, lays emphasis on its distinction from all other group memories – its uniqueness – and history eliminates all such differences and reorganizes its facts within a

[32] D. Ritschl, *Memory and Hope. An Inquiry Concerning the Presence of Christ* (New York: Macmillan, 1967).

[33] See Claude Lévi-Strauss, *La pensée sauvage* (Paris: Plon, 1962), 360; Engl. *The Savage Mind* (Chicago: University of Chicago Press, 1966), 203f.; *Structural Anthropology, vol. 2*, trans. Monique Layton (Chicago: University of Chicago Press, 1976), 26–32. In light of this distinction, to which I return in another context, the question arises as to whether there are not also groups – "hot societies" – that become conscious of their own change and are capable of accepting their new self-image.

homogeneous historical context in which nothing is unique, every-thing is comparable to everything else, each individual episode is linked to other episodes, and they are all of equal significance.[34] There are many different collective memories, but there is only one history, and this shuts out all connections with individual groups, iden-tities, and reference points, reconstructing the past in a tableau with-out identity, in which – to quote Ranke – everything is "immediate to God" because it is "independent of any group judgement" that would naturally be in accordance with its own particular leanings. The (ideal) historian is free from all such influences and obligations, and therefore "tends towards objectivity and impartiality."[35]

For Halbwachs, then, history is not memory, because there is no such thing as a universal memory – only a collective, group-specific, fixed-identity memory: "Every collective memory has a group as its carrier which is bound by time and space. The totality of past events can only be brought together in a single tableau on condition that these can be separated from the memory of the groups that have kept their recollections of them, that the bonds with which they were attached to the psychological life of the social milieu where they took

---

34 Halbwachs, *On Collective Memory*, 75, (see chapt. 1, n. 20) : "Despite the variety of places and times, history reduces events to terms that appear to be compa-rable, which allows it to link one to the other, like variations on one or several themes."

35 Halbwachs, *Das kollektive Gedächtnis* (Frankfurt: Fischer 1985), 72. Cf. Lucian's claim that a historian should be "apolis" (i.e., not partial to any political group in writing history) (*Luciani Samosatensis opera*, ed. W. Dindorf, vol. 2 [Leipzig: Teubner, 1929] 148 § 41). It is clear that here Halbwachs represents a positivistic concept of his-tory from which more recent historians have long since distanced themselves. All historiography is bound to its time and to the interests of its writers or their patrons. This is why the distinction between "memory" and "history" (in the sense of "histo-riography") – as Halbwachs draws it – no longer stands up to scrutiny, and instead historiography is classified as a particular kind of social memory, as suggested by Peter Burke, "Geschichte als soziales Gedächtnis" (History as Social Memory), in A. Assmann and D. Harth, *Mnemosyne*, 289 ff. (see chapt. 1, n. 2). However, this results in the loss of an important category: that of the neutrality of history writing. Regard-less of the influences of time and special interests, ever since Herodotus there has been a preoccupation with the past that stems purely from "theoretical curiosity," the need to know, and this is clearly very different from those forms of history that we call "memory culture" that are always related to the identity of the remembering group. In the sense of the distinction drawn later in this chapter, scholarly historiography is one form of "cold" memory.

place are cut, and that only their chronological and spatial schema is maintained" (*Das kollektive Gedächtnis*, 73).

On the one hand are the many histories in which the different groups record their memories and their image, and on the other hand is one single history in which historians record the facts they have drawn from the many histories. These facts in themselves, however, are mere abstractions that mean nothing to anyone; they are remembered by no one, and are stripped of all references to identity and memory. The time in which history places its data is particularly abstract. Historical time is a *durée artificielle* that is neither experienced nor remembered by any group as a "duration." And so for Halbwachs it stands outside reality. It is a functionless artifact, isolated from the bonds and obligations imposed by life, that is, social life in a specific time and place.

According to Halbwachs, the relationship between memory and history is one of sequence. The moment at which the past is no longer remembered, that is, lived, is the moment at which history begins. History generally begins at the point where tradition ceases and the social memory dissolves. In other words, the historian takes over from where collective memory leaves off. "For history the real past is that which is no longer incorporated into the thoughts of existing groups. It seems that history must wait until the old groups disappear, along with their thoughts and memories, so that it can busy itself with fixing the image and the sequence of facts which it alone is capable of preserving"[36] (*Das kollektive Gedächtnis*, 100).

Halbwachs distinguishes collective memory not only from history but also from all organized and objective forms of memory subsumed under the concept of tradition. For him tradition is not a form but rather a distortion of memory. This is the point at which I find myself unable to go along with him. The borderlines between memory and

---

[36] This need to wait has been succinctly described by the historian Ernst Nolte as the past's "not-wanting-to pass away." The nerve end that Nolte has struck relates to the continual confusion in the so-called Historians' Quarrel between the spheres of memory and history. The passing from memory to history, however, is not always just a matter of time. Some events never cease to be "figures of memory" for a specific group such as, 680 AD (the battle of Kerbela) for the Shi'ites or 1389 (the battle on the Kosovo) for the Serbs.

tradition can be so flexible that it seems pointless to try and introduce rigid conceptual distinctions. For this reason, I prefer the term (collective) memory as a general heading, and then to distinguish between "communicative" and "cultural" memory. This distinction will be explained in the second section of this chapter, in which I also return to Halbwachs's concept of tradition.

Summary

There is a certain irony in the fact that the theorist of social memory is now largely forgotten.[37] Even if the name Halbwachs has become more familiar in recent times, this does not by any means apply to his work. The fact that I have devoted this much space to his ideas does not mean that I am unaware of the many weaknesses that, with hindsight, are now all too clear. For instance, his terminology lacks the sharpness that would make his ideas truly communicable.[38] It is also astonishing for us today that he never systematically or coherently considered the vital role played by writing in the compilation of collective memories. He seems instead to be under the spell of Bergsonian terms such as "life" and "reality." What fascinated him, and many of his contemporaries, was a sociology that was supposed to explore the secret of a living connection with a *temps vécu* (in contrast to a *temps conçu* and a *durée artificielle*).

Of course all this points toward Nietzsche, and therefore it is all the more surprising that the name is scarcely ever mentioned (apart from in a totally different context, *On Collective Memory*, 120). Unlike Nietzsche, Halbwachs was not a culture critic. He did not automatically

[37] Since this statement was written (in 1990), this situation has changed completely. There are several biographies of and books on Halbwachs who is by now generally recognized as one of the founding fathers of modern memory studies.

[38] This applies particularly to his treatment of religion in *On Collective Memory*, chapter 6, (see chapt. 1, n. 20), which proposes that *all* religion is a kind of institutionalized memory and "aims at preserving unchanged through the course of time the remembrance of an ancient period without any admixture of subsequent remembrances" (ibid., 93) This is precisely the point at which on the one hand the distinction between "culture" and "religion" becomes questionable, while on the other it becomes essential to distinguish between the many different types of religion. We are therefore not giving any further consideration to the religious theories propounded in *On Collective Memory*.

condemn anything that projected beyond the format of organic coherences as a functionless, even dangerous artifact. His interest remained analytical, and in relation to the basic structures of collective memory his approach was mainly that of a social psychologist. His pioneering work on collective memory centered on the juxtaposition of memory and group, and he used various examples to illustrate how group memory and group identity were inextricably bound up together. (He rarely used the term "identity," and that of the "we" identity, developed by Georges Gurvitch, a close colleague in Paris during the 1930s and 1940s, never occurs in his work. The idea itself, though, is omnipresent.)

As a social psychologist, Halbwachs did not look beyond the group, and he never considered expanding his theory of memory into the realm of a theory of culture. The perspective of cultural evolution also did not enter his field of vision. Nevertheless, the basic structures that he developed are fundamental to the analysis of culture, and many of his findings remain valid when applied to the mechanisms of its evolution. Of course the transition from live, communicated memory to institutionalized commemoration requires much more detailed study, and above all there needs to be an explicit analysis of the (r)evolutionary achievements of writing.

It may well be that Halbwachs himself would have regarded this transition to the highly complex system of culture, with its multiplicity of groups and memories, as an unacceptable shift into the realm of metaphor. However, it is also possible that he intended to expand his socio-psychological findings into the field of culture studies and theory in his later work. We should not forget that his writing remained fragmentary, and it was his daughter Jeanne Alexandre who edited his magnum opus from the papers he left behind.[39] His book on the topography of the legends of the Holy Land, which is a move toward just such an expansion, must be seen as the latest but not the last book that he would have written had he lived longer.

Halbwachs is often sharply criticized for his use of the concept of memory for socio-psychological phenomena. This is condemned as an unwarranted metaphorical transfer from the individual to the

---

[39] See G. Namer's critique of J. Alexandre's rather biased edition in his re-edition of 1997 (see chapt. 1, n. 15).

collective level. It is said to obscure "the particular way in which the past is present in human culture and communication."[40] But for Halbwachs, collective memory was anything but a metaphor because he wanted to show that even individual memories were a social phenomenon. The fact that only individuals can have a memory because of their neurological equipment makes no difference to the dependence of their memories on the social frame. One should not confuse the concept of the collective with theories of a collective unconscious, along the lines of Jungian archetypes, because this is the complete opposite of Halbwachs's theory. For Jung the collective memory was 1) biologically hereditary, and 2) a *mémoire involontaire* that, for instance, expressed itself in dreams. Halbwachs was concerned only with what was communicable, not with what was heritable, and with the *mémoire volontaire*.[41] In my view, it is not the "socio-constructivist" expansion but, on the contrary, the individual and psychological contraction of the memory concept that obscures the ways in which the past is given communicative and cultural presence. Groups "inhabit" their past just as individuals do, and from it they fashion their self-image. Trophies, certificates, and medals adorn the cabinets of clubhouses as well as the shelves of individual sportsmen, and there is not much point in calling one tradition and the other memory.

The concept of the past that I adopt from Halbwachs is one that can be called socio-constructivist. What Peter L. Berger and Thomas Luckmann have shown to be true of reality as a whole was applied by Halbwachs, forty years earlier, to the past: it is a social construction whose nature arises out of the needs and frames of reference of each particular present. The past is not a natural growth but a cultural creation.

[40] Cancik and Mohr, "Erinnerung/Gedächtnis," 311 (see chapt. 1, n. 31).

[41] The distinction between *mémoire volontaire* and *mémoire involontaire* is due to Marcel Proust, see *Remembrance of Things Past: Swann's Way: Within a Budding Grove*, trans. Terence Kilmartin and C. K. Scott-Moncrieff, Vol. 1 (New York: Knopf, 1982), 45–50, esp. 46 f. For Proust as for Halbwachs, the pictures of voluntary memory "preserve nothing of the past itself" that, in this form of memory, is "in reality all dead." Proust, therefore, discarded voluntary memory and turned to the all too rare moments of "involuntary memory" as the only true ways of accessing the past. Halbwachs, on the other hand, concentrated on voluntary memory because of its very inauthenticity and social constructedness.

FORMS OF COLLECTIVE MEMORY

Communicative and Cultural Memory

"The Floating Gap": Two Modi Memorandi. In his book *Oral Tradition as History*[42] (1985), the ethnologist Jan Vansina describes a phenomenon of unwritten historical memory that is as strange as it is typical:

Accounts of origin, group accounts, and personal accounts are all different manifestations of the same process in different stages. When the whole body of such accounts is taken together there appears a three tiered whole. For recent times there is plenty of information that tapers off as one moves back through time. For earlier periods one finds either a hiatus or just one or a few names, given with some hesitation. There is a gap in the accounts, which I will call the floating gap. For still earlier periods one finds again a wealth of information and one deals here with traditions of origin. The gap is not often very evidence [sic.] to people in the communities involved, but it is usually unmistakable to the researchers. Sometimes, especially in genealogies, the recent past and origins are run together as a succession of a single generation.

[...] Historical consciousness works on only two registers: time of origin and recent times. Because the limit one reaches in time reckoning moves with the passage of generations, I have called the gap a floating gap. For the Tio (Congo), c. 1880, the limit lay c. 1800, while in 1960 it had moved to c. 1880.[43]

Vansina's "floating gap" is familiar to all historians who deal with oral traditions.[44] This is the phenomenon of the "dark ages," known especially from Ancient Greece. Greek mythology throws a bright if not strictly historical light on the heroic age of Mycenaean culture, which archaeologists classify as "Late Helladic." Greek historiography of the classical age goes back over exactly those eighty to one hundred years

---

[42] First published in 1961 under the title *De la tradition orale*; the first English translation appeared in London 1965.

[43] Jan Vansina, *Oral Tradition as History* (Madison: University of Wisconsin Press, 1985), 23 f.

[44] Jürgen von Ungern-Sternberg and Hansjörg Reinau (eds.), *Vergangenheit in mündlicher Überlieferung*, Colloquium Rauricum (Stuttgart: Teubner, 1988); see esp. Meinhard Schuster, "Zur Konstruktion von Geschichte in Kulturen ohne Schrift," in ibid., 57–71.

that Vansina calls "recent past" and that could typically be captured by a contemporary memory through experience and hearsay. Herodotus begins his history with Kroisos as "the man of whom I know for sure that he commenced hostilities against the Greeks," thereby marking out precisely the area of memory confirmed by contemporary witnesses. The floating gap designated by archaeologists as a dark age that archaeological finds have pinpointed as the centuries from 1100 to 800 BCE, comes between these. The term "dark age," however, is viewed from the researcher's perspective, whereas with the concept of memory our focus is more on the inner perspective of the particular societies – a distinction that plays only a minor role for Vansina.

In the latter context, it is clear that one cannot speak of a gap, whether floating or fixed. In the cultural memory of a group, both levels of the past merge seamlessly into one another. This is most evident in the earliest and most typical form of cultural mnemotechnics, the genealogy, which Vansina also refers to. The classical historian Fritz Schachermeyr, in his last work *Die griechische Rückerinnerung* (1984), studied the genealogies of the Greek aristocracy and came upon the same structures[45] that Vansina noted among African and other tribal societies. Keith Thomas made the same observation about England in the early modern age. "Numerous genealogies leaped quickly from mythical ancestor to modern times; as one antiquarian put it, they were like head and feet without a body, two ends without a middle."[46] The genealogy is a form that bridges the gap between the present and the time of origin, legitimizing a current order or aspiration by providing an unbroken link with the very beginning. This does not mean, however, that there is no difference between the two times that are linked together. Both records of the past – the two ends without a middle – correspond to two memory frames that differ from each

---

45 Generally these genealogies comprise 10–15 generations. They begin with the well-known names – not necessarily historical but certainly mythological (immanent in the system) – of legendary Greek heroes, and end with historically known characters two to four generations before the particular name-bearer. In between, there are imaginary names to provide the links in the chain, the length of which is prescribed by whatever is required by the circumstances.

46 Keith Thomas, *The perception of the past in early modern England* (London: University of London, 1983), 9.

other in certain fundamental areas. I call these the "communicative" and the "cultural" memory.[47]

The communicative memory comprises memories related to the recent past. These are what the individual shares with his contemporaries. A typical instance would be generational memory that accrues within the group, originating and disappearing with time or, to be more precise, with its carriers. Once those who embodied it have died, it gives way to a new memory. This, too, is formed, vouched for, and communicated solely by way of personal experience and covers the three to four biblical generations that must stand accountable for a debt. The Romans referred to this as *saeculum*, by which they meant the end point when the last surviving member of a generation (and carrier of its particular memories) has died. In his account of the year 22, Tacitus notes the death of the last contemporary witness to have experienced the Republic.[48] Half of the generational limit of eighty years – that is, forty years – seems to represent a critical threshold. I return to this in Chapter 5, in connection with Deuteronomy. After forty years those who have witnessed an important event as an adult will leave their future-oriented professional career, and will enter the age group in which memory grows as does the desire to fix it and pass it on. Over the past ten (now twenty-five) years, the generation that experienced the traumatic horrors of Hitler's persecution and annihilation of the Jews has been confronted with this situation. That which continues to be living memory today, may be only transmitted via media tomorrow. This transition was also evident during the 1980s when there was a spate of written testimonies by survivors and an intensified accumulation of archive material. The forty years mentioned in Deuteronomy was just as applicable then. In fact it was exactly forty years after the end of the World War II on May 8, 1985, that Richard von Weizsäcker's commemorative speech

---

[47] For more on this distinction, see Aleida and Jan Assmann, "Schrift, Tradition, Kultur," in W. Raible (ed.), *Zwischen Festtag und Alltag* (Tübingen: Narr, 1988); Jan Assmann, "Stein und Zeit. Das monumentale Gedächtnis des alten Ägypten," in J. Assmann and T. Hölscher (eds.), *Kultur und Gedächtnis* (Frankfurt: Suhrkamp, 1988), 87–114.

[48] Tacitus, *Annales* III, 75; see H. Cancik-Lindemaier and H. Cancik, "Zensur und Gedächtnis. Zu Tac. Ann. IV 32–38," in A. and J. Assmann (eds.), *Kanon und Zensur* (Munich: Fink, 1987), 175.

to Parliament set in motion a memory process that a year later was to lead to the well-known crisis of the "Historikerstreit" (Historians' Quarrel).

The directness of experience is the subject of "oral history," a branch of historical research that relies not on the usual written accounts but exclusively on memories extracted orally from people. The historical picture that emerges from these recollections and anecdotes is a "history of the everyday" or "a history from below." All such studies confirm that even in literate societies, living memory does not extend beyond eighty years (L. Niethammer 1985). The floating gap comes next; this is followed by textbooks and monuments, for example, the official version rather than myths of origin.

Here are two modes of remembering – two uses of the past – that need to be carefully distinguished even though they are largely connected in real historical culture. Collective memory functions in two ways: through the mode of "foundational memory" that relates to origins, and that of "biographical memory" that concerns personal experiences and their framework – that is, the recent past. The foundational mode always functions – even in illiterate societies – through fixed objectifications both linguistic and nonlinguistic, such as rituals, dances, myths, patterns, dress, jewelry, tattoos, paintings, landscapes, and so on, all of which are kinds of sign systems and, because of their mnemotechnical function – supporting memory and identity – capable of being subsumed under the general heading of *memoria*. The biographical mode, on the other hand, always depends on social interaction, even in literate societies. Foundational memory is more a matter of construction than of natural growth (and its anchorage in fixed forms means that its implementation is somewhat artificial), whereas biographical memory works the opposite way. Cultural memory, unlike communicative, is a matter of institutionalized mnemotechnics.

Cultural memory, then, focuses on fixed points in the past, but again it is unable to preserve the past as it was. This tends to be condensed into symbolic figures to which memory attaches itself – for example, tales of the patriarchs, the Exodus, wandering in the desert, conquest of the Promised Land, exile – and that are celebrated in festivals and are used to explain current situations. Myths are also figures of memory, and here any distinction between myth and history is eliminated. What counts for cultural memory is not factual but remembered history. One might even say that cultural memory transforms factual into remembered history, thus turning it into myth. Myth is foundational history that is narrated in order to illuminate the present from the standpoint of its origins. The Exodus, for instance, regardless of any historical accuracy, is the myth behind the foundation of Israel; thus it is celebrated at Pesach and thus it is part of the cultural memory of the Israelites. Through memory, history becomes myth. This does not make it unreal – on the contrary, this is what makes it real, in the sense that it becomes a lasting, normative, and formative power.

Such examples show that cultural memory is imbued with an element of the sacred. The figures are endowed with religious significance, and commemoration often takes the form of a festival. This, along with various other functions, serves to keep the foundational past alive in the present, and this connection to the past provides a basis for the identity of the remembering group. By recalling its history and reenacting its special events, the group constantly reaffirms its own image; but this is not an everyday identity. The collective identity needs ceremony – something to take it out of the daily routine. To a degree, it is larger than life. The ceremony as a means of communication is itself a forming influence, as it shapes memory by means of texts, dances, images, rituals, and so on. One might therefore compare the polarity between communicative and cultural memory to that between everyday life and the festival, and perhaps even speak of everyday memory and festival memory,[49] though I would not wish to go to quite such lengths. I return later to the link between cultural memory and the sacred.

The polarity between communicative and cultural memory also has a sociological character through what I call its "participatory structure." This is as different for the two forms of collective memory as their time structures are different. The group's participation in communicative memory varies considerably: some people know more than others, and the memories of the old reach further back than those of the young. But even though some individuals are better informed than others, there are no specialists, no experts in this informal tradition, and the relevant knowledge is acquired at the same time as

---

[49] Cf. Wolfgang Raible (ed.), *Zwischen Festtag und Alltag* (Tübingen: Narr, 1988).

language and other forms of everyday knowledge. Everybody has equal competence.

By contrast, participation in cultural memory is always highly differentiated. This even applies to illiterate and egalitarian societies. The original task of the poet was to preserve the group memory, and even today in oral societies this remains the task of the griot. One of them, the Senegalese Lamine Konte, has described the role of the griot as follows[50]: "At the time when virtually throughout Africa there were no records, the task of remembering and narrating history had to be handed to a special social group. It was believed that a successful communication of history needed a musical background, and so the oral tradition was entrusted to the griot or extempore singer, who was given the status of musician. And so they became the preservers of the common memory of African peoples. Griots are also poets, actors, dancers and mime artists, and they use all these arts in their performances" (*Unesco-Courier 8*, 1985, 7).

Cultural memory always has its special carriers. They include shamans, bards, griots, priests, teachers, artists, scribes, scholars, mandarins, and others. The extraordinary (as opposed to everyday) nature of these cultural memories is reflected by the fact that these specialist carriers are separated from everyday life and duties. In illiterate societies, the form of their specialization will depend on what is required of the memories. The most demanding requirement is a word-for-word rendition. In this instance, human memory is used as data storage, or as a precursor of the written record. This is typically the case in matters of ritual that must always follow a strict "prescription" even when there is no script to fix the formula. The best known example of such memorized, codified rituals is the Rigveda. The magnitude of this task and the essential nature of this knowledge are reflected by the elevated social status of the memory specialists. In the Indian caste system, the Brahmins rank above the Kshatriya, who constitute the ruling class. In Rwanda, the texts that form the basis of the eighteen royal rituals are learned verbatim by specialists who are ranked

---

[50] On the function of the griot in Africa, see also Claudia Klaffke, "Mit jedem Greis stirbt eine Bibliothek" (With every old man there dies a library), in A. and J. Assmann (eds.), *Schrift und Gedächtnis* (Munich: Fink, 1983), 222–230; Patrick Mbunwe-Samba, "Oral Tradition and the African Past," in R. Layton (ed.), *Who needs the past?: indigenous values and archaeology* (London: Unwin Hyman, 1989), 105–118.

as the highest dignitaries in the land. Mistakes, however, may be punishable by death. Three of these dignitaries know the complete texts of all eighteen rituals by heart, and they share the divinity of the ruler himself (P. Borgeaud 1988, 13).

Participation in cultural memory is not diffuse in still another sense. In contrast to communicative memory, it does not spread itself around spontaneously but has to be thoroughly prepared and vetted. Its distribution is controlled, and whereas on the one hand it makes participation obligatory, on the other it withholds the right to participate. It is subject to restrictions that are more or less rigid. In some cases, people must prove their competence (or their membership) by means of formal tests (as in classical China), or by mastering relevant forms of communication (e.g., from Greek in the Greco-Roman world, French in 18th-century Europe, to Wagner operas to be played on the grand piano at home). Meanwhile, others are excluded from such knowledge. In Jewish and Ancient Greek culture these "others" included women; in the golden age of the educated middle classes, it was the lower strata of society that were left out.[51]

In its temporal dimension, the polarity of collective memory corresponds to that between the festival and everyday life; in its social dimension, it is that between a knowledgeable elite, the specialists in the field, and the ordinary members of the group. How, then, are we to visualize this polarity of memory? Are they two independent systems that – analogous to colloquial and written language – coexist although they remain distinct from one another, or are they, as Wolfgang Raible has suggested, the extremes on a scale that is flexible in its transitions?[52] It may well be that each case has to be decided on its merits. There are certainly cultures in which cultural memory is sharply distinct from communicative memory, so that one can speak of a "biculture." Ancient Egypt would fall under this category.[53] But other societies, including our own, fit in better with the model of the

---

[51] Cf. Aleida Assmann, *Arbeit am nationalen Gedächtnis. Eine kurze Geschichte der deutschen Bildungsidee* (Frankfurt: Campus-Verlag, 1993).

[52] Wolfgang Raible (ed.), *Zwischen Festtag und Alltag* (*Scriptoralia* 6, Tübingen 1988), introduction.

[53] J. Assmann, "Gebrauch und Gedächtnis. Die zwei Kulturen des pharaonischen Ägypten", in: A. Assmann, D. Harth, (eds.), *Kultur als Lebenswelt und Monument* (Frankfurt 1991, 135–152).

sliding scale. Even the example of colloquial and literary language can by no means be pinned down to a cut-and-dried diglossia, and in many cases it is more aptly described as two extremes of a sliding scale. However, there is also a degree of internal differentiation between the two types of memory through association with the festive and sacred, and this distinction cannot be defined by the scale image. With this qualification in mind, I will now formalize the scale model with regard to the ideal type of an oral society and set out the poles as follows:

	Communicative Memory	Cultural Memory
Content	Historical experiences in the framework of individual biographies	Mythical history of origins, events in an absolute past
Forms	Informal, without much form, natural growth, arising from interaction, everyday	Organized, extremely formal, ceremonial communication, festival
Media	Living, organic memories, experiences, hearsay	Fixed objectifications, traditional symbolic classification and staging through words, pictures, dance, and so forth
Time structure	80–100 years, with a progressive present spanning three–four generations	Absolute past of a mythical, primeval age
Carriers	Nonspecific, contemporary witnesses within a memory community	Specialized tradition bearers

Ritual and Festival as Primary Forms of Organizing Cultural Memory

Without the possibility of written storage, human memory is the only means of preserving the knowledge that consolidates the identity of a group. There are three functions that must be performed in order to fulfill the necessary tasks of creating unity and guiding action: storage, retrieval, and communication – or poetic form, ritual performance, and collective participation. It is generally accepted that the poetic form has the mnemotechnical aim of capturing the unifying knowledge in a manner that will preserve it.[54] Also familiar is the fact that this knowledge is customarily performed through multimedia staging in which the linguistic text is inseparable from voice, body, mime, gesture, dance, rhythm, and ritual action.[55] It is the mode of participation that I will focus on here. How does the group gain access to the cultural memory, which at this level is already the province of the specialists (minstrels, bards, shamans, griots, and so on)? The answer lies in assembly and personal presence. In illiterate societies there is no other way to participate in the cultural memory. Consequently occasions must be established to bring about such gatherings, namely festivals. Through regular repetition, festivals and rituals ensure the communication and continuance of the knowledge that gives the group its identity. Ritual repetition also consolidates the coherence of the group in time and space. The festival as a primary form of memory organization divides up the time structure of illiterate societies into the everyday and the ceremonial. In the ceremonial or "dream time" of the major gatherings, the setting expands into the cosmic realm, embracing the time of the creation, of all origins, and also of the great upheavals that took place when the world was young. Rituals and myths capture the sense of reality, and it is through their scrupulous observation, preservation, and transmission – together with the identity of the group – that the world continues to function.

Cultural memory extends the everyday world with a further dimension of negations and potentials, and, through this, it compensates for the deficiencies of normal life. It endows life with a kind of dual time that is maintained throughout all stages of cultural evolution and that is most prevalent in illiterate societies through the distinction between the everyday and the festive. In Antiquity, the festivals and the Muses were regarded as having healing powers. In his *Laws* Plato describes how children's education is wasted in later life because of the grind of daily affairs: "So, taking pity on this suffering that is natural to the human race, the gods have ordained the change of holidays as times of rest from labor. They have given as fellow celebrants the Muses,

---

54 See also Eric Alfred Havelock, *Preface to Plato* (Cambridge, MA: Belknap Press of Harvard University, 1963), who speaks of "preserved communication."
55 See, for example, Paul Zumthor, *Introduction à la poésie orale* (Paris: Seuil, 1983).

with their leader Apollo, and Dionysus – in order that these divinities might set humans aright again."[56]

The festival refocuses on the background of our existence that has been pushed aside by everyday life, and the gods themselves revive the order that has either been taken for granted or forgotten. Originally, there was only one order, which was festive and sacred and which had a guiding influence on everyday life. The original function of the festival was purely to structure time, not to separate the routine from the sacred. This structure or rhythm created a general time framework that gave the everyday its proper place. The best example of this original nondistinction between the sacred and the profane is the Australian concept of the spirits of the ancestors, whose journeys and actions on Earth provide the model for all regulated human activities, from rituals to lacing up one's shoes. The festival only becomes the setting for another order, time, and memory at a more developed cultural level when everyday matters have separated themselves into a different order.[57]

As seen before, the distinction between communicative and cultural memory is linked to the difference between the everyday and the festive, the profane and the sacred, the ephemeral and the lasting, the particular and the general. It can perhaps best be grasped in terms of the fluid as opposed to the fixed,[58] but care must be taken not to equate this contrast with the difference between the oral and the written. Oral tradition is structured in exactly the same way as written, with exactly the same distinction between communicative and cultural, everyday and festive. In illiterate societies, however, the oral method is naturally more difficult because it must first learn to separate those elements that belong to cultural memory from those that are everyday. This is made much clearer in written cultures, because

---

[56] Plato, *The Laws of Plato*, trans. with notes and an interpretative essay by Thomas L. Pangle (New York: Basic Books, 1979), *leg.* 653 d, 33. See Rüdiger Bubner, "Ästhetisierung der Lebenswelt," in W. Haug and R. Warning (eds.), *Das Fest* (Munich: Fink, 1989), 651–662.

[57] For more details, see Jan Assmann, "Der zweidimensionale Mensch. Das Fest als Medium des kulturellen Gedächtnisses," in J. Assmann and T. Sundermeier (eds.), *Das Fest und das Heilige. Religiöse Kontrapunkte des Alltags, Studien zum Verstehen fremder Religionen 1* (Gütersloh: Mohn, 1991), 13–30.

[58] See Aleida Assmann, "Kultur als Lebenswelt und Monument," in Assmann and Harth (eds.), *Mnemosyne* (see chapt. 1, n. 2).

undeniably cultural memory has an affinity to writing,[59] whose fixed texts are far less fluid than the ceremonial activities that give a group its identity.

Memory Landscapes: The "Mnemotope" of Palestine

The primal element in all mnemotechnics is placement.[60] This is the basis of Frances Yates's study of *The Art of Memory* (1966) in the West, as well as mnemotechnics in Antiquity[61] and in Islam.[62] Significantly, place also plays the main role in collective and cultural mnemotechnics – the culture of memory. The term "places of memory" is quite common in French, and Pierre Nora used it as the title for his project (*Les lieux de mémoire*). The art of memory works with imaginary settings, and memory culture with signs based on Nature. Even, or indeed especially, entire landscapes may serve as a medium for cultural memory. These are not so much accentuated *by* signs ("monuments") as raised to the status *of* signs, that is, they are *semioticized*. The most impressive examples of this are the "totemic landscapes" or "song lines" of the Australian Aboriginals. At their major festivals they consolidate their group identity by making pilgrimages to particular places that are associated with memories of their ancestors (T. G. H. Strehlow, 1970). The ancient cities of the Orient were structured by festive streets, and during major festivals the principal gods would move along them in procession (J. Assmann, 1991b). Rome in particular created a sacred landscape during Antiquity (H. Cancik 1985–1986), consisting of topographical texts of cultural memory, that is, "mnemotopes" or places of memory. Maurice Halbwachs's description of the *topographie légendaire* as a form of expression for the collective memory [...] should be read against this background (see above). What Halbwachs set out to show through the commemorative landscape

---

59 Writing, however, need not necessarily fix things permanently. It can also create a fluid effect by removing the close connection between collective memory and particular features of ceremonial communication, thereby depriving the interchange between the two *modi memorandi* of their ceremonial function.

60 See also Note 26, as well as the "fields and distant palaces of memory," mentioned by Augustine, *Confessions* 10, 8, 12 ff.

61 H. Blum, *Die antike Mnemotechnik*, 1969.

62 D. F. Eickelmann, "The Art of Memory: Islamic Education and its Social Reproduction," Comparative Studies in Society and History 20 (1978), 485–516.

of Palestine was that not only every epoch but also every group and every faith creates, in its own way, locations and monuments for its own particular memories. This study can be seen as the unfolding of a metaphor, and it is striking to see how spatial metaphors dominate his description of memory functions: frame, space, places, localize – these are key terms that occur over and over again. Thus it seems pertinent to investigate the concrete location of memories in a landscape such as Palestine that is so rich in memories and meanings: the Holy Land as a mnemotope.

Transitions

Memories of the Dead, Commemoration. I have already touched briefly on the subject of the dead, appropriately at the beginning of this study. "Appropriately" because death is both the origin and the center of what I mean by memory culture. This relates above all else to the past, and once we are conscious of the distinction between yesterday and today death has to be the primal experience of that distinction, whereas memories of the dead are the primal form of cultural memory. In the context of the differentiation between the communicative and the cultural, however, this subject must be addressed in order to examine it from another angle. It is clear that the memory of the dead occupies an intermediate position between the two forms of social memory. It is communicative in so far as it represents a universally human form, and it is cultural to the degree in which it produces its particular carriers, rituals, and institutions.

Memory of the dead can be divided into "retrospective" and "prospective." The first is the more universal, original, and natural form.[63] It is the one through which a group goes on living with its dead, keeping them present, and thereby building up an image of

---

[63] See Karl Schmid (ed.), *Gedächtnis, das Gemeinschaft stiftet* (Munich: Schnell and Steiner, 1985), in particular the essay by Otto G. Oexle, "Die Gegenwart der Toten," in H. Braet and W. Verbeke (eds.), *Death in the Middle Ages, Mediaevalia Lovanensia, Series I, Studia 9* (Leuven: Leuven University Press, 1983), 74–107. Also Otto G. Oexle, "Memoria und Memorialüberlieferung im frühen Mittelalter," in *Frühmittelalterliche Studien* 19 (1976), 70–95; Karl Schmid and Joachim Wollasch (eds.), *Memoria. Der geschichtliche Zeugniswert des liturgischen Gedenkens im Mittelalter*, Münstersche Mittelalter-Schriften 48 (Munich: Fink, 1984).

its own unity and wholeness, of which the dead naturally form a part (O. G. Oexle 1983, 48 ff.). The farther back into history that the group goes, the more dominant the retrospective link to its ancestors is (K. E. Müller 1987). The prospective element consists in "achievement" and "fame" – the manner in which the dead have rendered themselves unforgettable. Of course, that which makes an individual special will vary from culture to culture. In Egypt, achievement was measured by the fulfillment of social norms; in Greece it was a matter of success in competition and thus of surpassing social norms. Deeds become memorable not by merely exploiting human potential, but by exceeding it: Pindar immortalized the winner of the pan-Hellenic Games in odes; the founders of colonies lived on through hero worship. The retrospective dimension, on the other hand, is based on *pietas in the Roman sense* (as "respect toward the dead") through which the living contribute to the unforgotten status of the dead.

Ancient Egypt represents a special case as it connects prospective and retrospective elements. This link was not established solely by the fact that as soon as an individual achieved high office, he was in a position to organize a monument to himself and thus to prospectively ensure his own remembrance.[64] Underlying this process was also a particular concept of reciprocity: one can only expect from posterity the same amount of respect that one shows for one's own forebears. Thus the social network of interdependence takes on an eternalized form. Ancient Egypt is an extreme example that is not even limited to its vast necropoleis with their mighty tombs; these monuments are only the outer sign of unforgettable achievements in the form of a life led according to the code of ethics: according to an Egyptian proverb, "The (true) monument of a man is his virtue." The virtues of reciprocity, for instance, gratitude, a sense of family and citizenship, solidarity, loyalty and respect, were central to this code of ethics. They determined the shape of life before death, and by including the virtues of the dead they were prolonged into the afterlife.[65] The imperatives

---

[64] "Furthermore, I have completed this tomb and created its inscription in person, while I was still alive," a high priest from the 11th to 12th Dynasty wrote on his tomb in Assiut (quoted by Franke, *Das Heiligtum des Heqaib*, 23, [see chapt. 1, n. 6]).

[65] The Egyptian expression for this principle, however, is not "thinking of one another" but "acting for one another." Thus texts define the basic formula of Egyptian ethics

of Egyptian ethics entailed thinking of others in order not to break the social network, and they were supplemented by the appeal to "Remember!" – which Egyptian monuments address ten thousand times to the commemorative memory. But these monuments need not necessarily be material. A name can live on merely through the sound of a voice: "A man lives when his name is spoken," runs another Egyptian proverb.

The principle of the two-dimensional *memoria* (prospective achievement and retrospective respect) is to be found with varying degrees of intensity in all societies. The hope of living on in the group memory and the idea that the dead can accompany the living through the progressive present are among the basic, universal structures of human life (M. Fortes 1978 a). Memory of the dead is in fact a paradigmatic way of "establishing the community" (K. Schmidt 1985), because the link with them consolidates identity. This bond with particular names always entails some sort of socio-political integration, and monuments, in the words of the historian R. Koselleck, are "identity providers for the survivors" (R. Koselleck 1979). Whether the monument is a war memorial with thousands of names, or the anonymous Tomb of the Unknown Warrior, the motif of group identification is unmistakable. "Void as these tombs are," writes B. Anderson, "of identifiable mortal remains or immortal souls, they are nonetheless saturated with ghostly national imaginings" (1983, 17). The cult of relics is another socially binding and stabilizing instance of mortuary commemoration, and we should keep in mind the fact that the cathedrals in our medieval cities were built as central, civic symbols to house the relics of a saint – preferably a well-known one, or best of all an apostle – and sometimes the authorities had to battle hard to acquire them (B. Kötting 1965). The memorial hall for Mao Tse Tung presents a

---

as Ma'at (= truth-order-justice-fairness). "The reward for the doer lies in the fact that actions are performed for him: that means 'Ma'at' in the heart of the divinity." But this "acting for one another" actually means the same as the "thinking of one another" found in commemorative memory, as is made clear by the following lament:

To whom shall I talk today?
One no longer remembers yesterday.
One no longer acts for him who has acted today.

(See J. Assmann, *Ma'at*, 60–69 [see chapt. 1, n. 11]).

similar case: his successor legitimized his rule by worshiping at the tomb of his predecessor. Mao Tse Tung's mummy is protected by all kinds of complicated technical measures against robbery or violation in the event of a possible political revolution, and this too exemplifies the identity function of the cult of relics. Anyone who can take possession of an important relic acquires a major instrument of legitimation.

Memory and Tradition. Communicative memories by their very nature can only last for a limited time. No one has demonstrated this more clearly than Maurice Halbwachs, whose theory of memory has the priceless advantage of also being a theory of forgetting. The problem of the endangered communicative memory and the culturally fixed memory will be dealt with through a special case study using the example of Deuteronomy (Chapter 5). For the moment, however, I return to Halbwachs and his theoretical principles.

Halbwachs distinguishes between memory and tradition in a manner similar to our own distinction between biographical and foundational, or communicative and cultural memory. What interests him is the transition from *mémoire vécue* (lived memory) into two different forms of written record that he calls *histoire* and *tradition*. The former consists in the critical overview and impartial archiving of events stored in the memory, and the latter in the ever-present process of capturing and keeping by all means possible the live impressions made by a remorselessly receding past. In this case, instead of constantly having to reconstruct events anew, there are fixed traditions. These become separated from communicative, everyday references and take on a canonical, commemorative substance.

The example that Halbwachs uses to illustrate the phases of tradition, from lived or communicated memory to that which is carefully preserved, is the early history of Christianity. During the first phase, the period of "formation," past and present are one in the consciousness of the group: "In this period Christianity was in effect still very close to its origins; it wasn't easy to distinguish what was remembrance from what was consciousness of the present. Past and present were confused because the evangelical drama did not yet seem to be at its end" (*On Collective Memory*, 94).

"During this phase of live, emotional involvement, in its natural state of collective memory, early Christianity provides a typical example of a communicative group that does not live through its memories but through its goals, though it is also conscious of its historical unity. In this period Christianity is far from representing the past in preference to the present, and it lacks the clear-cut course that will eventually be marked out by the early church. Few situations are 'considered incompatible with Christianity'" (*On Collective Memory*, 97); as it is still caught up in the present, it integrates contemporary trends rather than running counter to these. Its position can be summed up by the fact that all its concepts and memories are "still immersed in the social milieu" (112). There is, then, still a unity between society and memory, and there is no distinction between clergy and laity: "But up to this moment religious memory lives and functions within the entire group of believers. It is conflated in the law with the collective memory of the entire society" (98).

Everything changes in the second phase, which according to Halbwachs begins in the 3rd to 4th century. It is only now that "religious society retreats and establishes its tradition, that it determines its doctrine and imposes on the laity the authority of a hierarchy of clerics who are no longer simply functionaries and administrators of the Christian community but who constitute instead a closed group separated from the world and entirely turned towards the past, which they are solely occupied with commemorating" (*On Collective Memory*, 98).

With the inevitable changes in the social milieu, the embedded memories begin to fade. At the same time the texts begin to lose their initially clear meaning, and become in need of interpretation. From now on, instead of communicative memory we have the organization of memory. The clergy takes on the task of interpreting the texts that no longer speak directly to the particular age, but have become to a degree alienated from the present. Dogma has to work out and fix the framework of possible interpretations that must adapt memories to fit in with the prevailing doctrine. Just as the historian can only step forward when the collective memory of the participants has disappeared, so too the exegete only has a role when direct understanding of the text is no longer possible. "As the meaning of forms and formulas became partially forgotten, they had to be interpreted," writes

Halbwachs (*On Collective Memory*, 117), in this way, he moves along much the same lines as the Protestant theologian Franz Overbeck, who puts this in somewhat sharper focus: "Posterity has given up understanding them, and has reserved the right to interpret them."[66]

OPTIONS OPEN TO CULTURAL MEMORY: "HOT" AND "COLD" MEMORY

The Myth of a "Sense of History"

Some forty years ago, the time had come to put an end to the common misconception that illiterate peoples had no consciousness of history, and hence no history. In his now famous inaugural lecture in Münster on *The Historical Consciousness of Illiterate Peoples* (1968), Rüdiger Schott helped to clear the way for a far more differentiated view. Today, the concept of oral history has completely eradicated the idea that history depends on writing. "Historical consciousness" has become an anthropological universal, though this was already proposed in 1931 by the cultural anthropologist E. Rothacker, who regarded historical consciousness or "a sense of history" as a basic instinct "to preserve, remember and narrate events and forms of the past."[67] Schott defines this "sense of history" as "an elementary quality of humans which is directly connected to their cultural faculty." He pins down the function of this "basic instinct," showing that "oral communications of history are even more bound to the groups whose destinies they describe than written records." Not only are they bound to these groups, but they themselves exert a binding power of their own. They create a bond because they record the events on which the group "bases the consciousness of its unity and its peculiarity (*Eigenart*)." What Schott identifies as a "sense of history," the American sociologist E. Shils – to whom we are indebted for a pioneering work on the sociology of

---

[66] Franz Overbeck, *Christentum und Kultur* (Basel: Schwabe, 1919), 24. Just as Nietzsche distinguishes between history and memory, Halbwachs's distinction between writing and memory links up with the distinction drawn by Nietzsche's friend Franz Overbeck between "Urgeschichte" and "Geschichte," "Urliteratur" and "Literatur."

[67] Erich Rothacker, "Das historische Bewusstsein," in *Zeitschrift für Deutschkunde* 45 (1931). Quoted by Rüdiger Schott, "Das Geschichtsbewußtsein schriftloser Völker," *Archiv für Begriffsgeschichte* 12 (1968), 166–205, here 170.

tradition – calls a "sense of the past"[68]: knowledge of the past, respect, attachment, imitation, rejection of the past could not exist without this intellectual organ.

An acceptance of a sense of history or the past is so unquestionable that today it is virtually taken for granted. In fact now we are more interested in the question of why this basic human instinct is so much more developed in some societies or cultures than in others.[69] However, there are some societies in which this sense or instinct – if such it is – seems not only to be less developed but is even consciously rejected, and for that reason I have my doubts as to whether there really is such a thing as an historical sense; the term "cultural memory" seems more cautiously suitable. My starting point for this – incidentally very much in line with Nietzsche – is the fact that man's basic, natural disposition would seem to favor forgetting rather than remembering, and so the question that really needs to be raised is why he would be interested at all in investigating, recording, and resuscitating the past. Instead of referring to a particular sense or instinct, I think it would be more meaningful to ask in each individual case what has made people do something with their past. It seems to me particularly striking that until a relatively late era there was no specifically historical interest in the past, but a more general and focused interest in legitimation, justification, reconciliation, change, and so forth, as well as in those functional frameworks we have discussed under the headings of memory, tradition, and identity. In this sense, we may ask for tranquilizers or stimulants of historical memory – for factors that may stop things or start them. Ancient Egyptian culture is a particularly good example of this. Here we have a society that was confronted by its past in an overwhelmingly grandiose manner, supplemented by annals and lists of kings, and yet it did practically nothing with any of them.

"Cold" and "Hot" Options

The beginnings of this approach are to be found in Claude Lévi-Strauss and his famous distinction between "cold" and "hot" societies,

---

[68] E. Shils, *Tradition*, Chicago 1981, 51–52.

[69] "There is, however, an extraordinary difference from one people to another in the degree to which this 'historical sense' unfolds, and the manner in which it has developed." Ibid.

to which R. Schott also refers. According to Lévi-Strauss, cold societies are those that strive "by the institutions they give themselves, to annul the possible effects of historical factors on their equilibrium and continuity" (1966, 233–234).[70] Hot societies, on the other hand, are characterized by "an avid need for change," and they have internalized their history (*leur devenir historique*) in order to make it the driving force behind their development. "Cold," however, should not be taken as simply a term – or even a metaphor – for what others call a lack of history or of historical consciousness. What Lévi-Strauss is referring to is not a lack of anything, but a positive achievement that is attributed to a particular kind of "wisdom" and of "institution." Cold is not the zero setting of culture – it is a status that has to be created. And so the question is not just to what degree and in what forms societies create an historical consciousness, but also how and with what institutions and social mechanisms a society manages to freeze change. Cold societies do not live by forgetting what hot societies remember – they simply live with a different kind of memory, and in order to do that, they must block out history. For this they need the techniques of cold memory.

For Lévi-Strauss the distinction is a convenient term for the "clumsy distinction between 'peoples without history' and others" (1962, 233). It means the same to him as the distinction between primitive and civilized, illiterate and literate, acephalous and state societies. The two terms are therefore just the extremes in the process of civilization that inevitably leads from cold to hot, and herein lies the full sum of his insight. In my view, he does very little else with it. I want, however, to develop it a great deal further, and my interpretation rests on two observations:

1. There are societies that are civilized and literate, and yet are still cold in the sense that they put up desperate resistance to the penetration of history. I only mention two classic examples: Ancient Egypt and medieval Judaism. In both cases, one can see very clearly that resistance to history serves another memory. In the case of Egypt, I have described this as "the monumental memory,"[71] and for medieval Judaism Y. H. Yerushalmi (1982)

---

[70] Lévi-Strauss, *La pensée sauvage*, 309; Engl. *The Savage Mind*, 233–234 (see chapt. 1, n. 33).

[71] J. Assmann, "Stein und Zeit," 107–110 (see chapt. 1, n. 47).

simply used the imperative "Zakhor!" (Remember) as the title of his impressive study. Rather than merely rename primitive and civilized cultures as cold and hot in the context of the evolutionary scheme of things, it seems to me more productive to view the two terms as cultural options, or political memory strategies that exist at all times, independently of writing, calendar, technology and forms of power. Under the cold option, writing and ruling bodies may also become means of freezing history.

2. Societies or cultures need not be completely cold or hot: they may contain elements of both, to be distinguished – using the terms coined by the ethnopsychologist M. Erdheim – as cooling and heating systems. The former are, on the one hand, those institutions with the aid of which cold cultures freeze historical change (Erdheim uses the example of initiation rites[72]), and on the other, separate institutions within societies that are otherwise hot, for example, the military[73] or the church.

In the light of the distinction between cold and hot in relation to history, our question concerning the stopping and starting of historical consciousness becomes a little clearer. The tranquilizing element serves the cold option, whereby change is frozen. The meaning that is remembered here lies in recurrence and regularity, as opposed to the unique and the extraordinary; and, in continuity, as opposed to change and upheaval. The stimulant serves the hot option, in which meaning, importance, memorableness are in service of the reversal, of change, growth and development, but also conversely of deterioration, corruption and decline.

The Alliance between Power and Memory

One strong incentive for memory is power. In acephalous societies "historical knowledge . . . seldom extends beyond a few generations before it swiftly fades into a nebulous, 'mythical' past in which all events are conceived on the same time level" (Schott 1968, 172). This

---

72 Mario Erdheim, "Adoleszenz und Kulturentwicklung," in M. Erdheim, *Die gesellschaftliche Produktion von Unbewußtheit* (Frankfurt: Suhrkamp, 1984), 271–368, 272 ff.
73 Mario Erdheim, "'Heisse' Gesellschaften – 'kaltes' Militär," *Kursbuch* 67 (1982), 59–70.

is the "floating gap" that J. Vansina (1985) speaks of: the gap between the living memory of contemporaries, a span of some eighty years – which research into oral history has confirmed as being a universe of collective memory and the sanctified traditions concerning origins. Here if anywhere is the natural state of collective historical consciousness. By contrast, "a more sharply divided time perspective (opens up) only among those peoples which have a chiefdom or other central political institutions." Classic examples are Polynesian dynasties, with chiefdom genealogies covering up to twenty-two generations, or the Tallensi in Africa, whose equally extensive genealogies locate each individual's roles and rights within the overall political system (M. Fortes 1945). Further examples of this alliance between power and memory are the Sumerian and Egyptian lists of kings. It is unquestionable that power requires origin, and this is called the "retrospective" side of the phenomenon.

The alliance between power and memory also has a "prospective" side. Rulers usurp not only the past but also the future because they want to be remembered, and to commemorate their own deeds by monuments, ensuring that their glory will be narrated, sung, immortalized or, at the very least, recorded in archives. Power "legitimizes itself retrospectively and immortalizes itself prospectively." Practically everything that has come down to us from the historical sources of the Ancient Orient belongs to this official, politico-ideological function. In an Egyptian text from the Middle Kingdom (ca. 1900 BCE), which forecasts a time of bliss after a time of chaos, one of the signs of restored order is that the "son of a man (= of noble birth) will be able to make a name for himself for ever and ever."[74] The literature of the Middle Kingdom sought to spread the conviction that social order was only possible through the Pharaonic state (G. Posener 1956; J. Assmann 1990). The most important element of this order was the immortality of the individual that depended on the memory of the group. Without the state, the framing conditions of social memory would fall apart, thus blocking the path to immortality.

---

[74] Hns Goedicke, ed., *The prophecy of Neferti* (Baltimore: Johns Hopkins University Press, 1977), 52 f.: "Rejoice, you people of his time, the son of a man will make his name for ever and ever."

The Alliance between Power and Forgetting

There is a third way of understanding the alliance between power and memory. For this we must return to Lévi-Strauss's theory that power in the sense of politically organized inequality produces heat. Hot cultures, according to his imagery, function like "steam engines," in which the falling energy levels caused by class differences provide the driving force for change (Erdheim 1988, 298). Erdheim links the relationship between statehood and the hot option to a preference for linear history: "Hot cultures lean towards the state, and states towards the centralization of power. The linearization of history is the temporal, and the centralization of power the spatial aspect of one and the same process, namely the constitution of power" (Erdheim 1988, 327).

It is clear that Erdheim has placed the entire process on its head. It is not that hot cultures lean toward the state, but that state-organized cultures lean toward cultural heat. This, however, does not stem from the rulers. It is natural that those who are ruled, oppressed, and under-privileged should strive for change. The linearization of history is a syndrome of the underclasses, as is evident from its most extreme form, apocalypticism, that throughout the Old (and possibly the New) World represents the ideology of revolutionary resistance movements (see Hellholm 1983). Oppression is a stimulant for linear historical thinking, for the formation of frameworks within which change, reversal, and revolution appear meaningful (Lanternari 1960). This, then, is far more of an alliance between power and forgetting. In fact, there have been and there still are forms of power that use every available means of communication and technology in order to put up desperate resistance to the penetration of history, as in Levi-Strauss's *sociétés froides*. Tacitus describes such forms of prescribed oblivion in Imperial Rome (H. Cancik-Lindemaier/H. Cancik 1987). In modern times, G. Orwell presents just such a strategy in his novel *1984*: "History has stopped. Nothing exists except an endless present in which the Party is always right."[75]

---

[75] Georg Orwell, *Nineteen Eighty-Four*, with introduction by Bernard Crick (Oxford: Clarendon Press, 1984), 290.

A. Assmann has shown that many details of these methods correspond to the "structural amnesia" of oral traditions and they can be seen as the exact equivalent of the way cold cultures function, albeit here under modern conditions: "Events and the intrusions of chance cannot be eliminated, but what *can* be prevented is their consolidation into history."[76] Under oppression, memory can become a form of resistance – this aspect of cultural memory is addressed more closely in the discussion in A. and J. Assmann (1988, Section 7, 78 ff.).

Documentation – Controlling or Giving Meaning to History?

Nothing seems more reasonable than to presume that together with the Sumerians, the Egyptians, with the longest memories and traditions reaching back uninterrupted over thousands of years, would have developed a very special consciousness of history. Here if anywhere one would expect profound interest in the past, with a rich store of anecdotes about the great kings of former times, all of whom stand there before us in their monuments, and perhaps also with epic poems about the mighty deeds of the founders, along with tales of war, conquest, feats of engineering, and so on. And yet the sources offer none of this. You will find some traces of narrated past in Herodotus who recorded the oral history of the Late Period, but official sources approach the past from a very different angle. If we may anticipate, the point here is that the lists of kings and the annals prove to be a tranquilizer and not an incentive when it comes to the writing of history. One could call these "cold memory."

The topos of Egypt as the nation with the longest memory goes back to Herodotus. He calculated the length as covering 341 generations, or 11,340 years. That is how far back into the past Egypt's documented history is believed to stretch. He writes, "The sun, however, had within this period of time, on four occasions, moved from his wonted course, twice rising where he now sets, and twice setting where he now rises. Egypt, however, was in no degree affected by these changes; the

---

[76] A. and J. Assmann, "Schrift, Tradition und Kultur," 35 f. (see chapt. 1, n. 17).

productions of the land, and of the river, remained the same; nor was there anything unusual either in the diseases or the deaths."[77]

I will not dwell on the abstruse astronomy – obviously Herodotus confused some issues – but his conclusions are much more interesting.[78] What can the Egyptians learn from their well-documented hindsight over thousands of years? Simply that nothing has changed. This is the purpose served by the lists of kings, annals, and other documents,[79] which demonstrate not the importance but the triviality of history. The lists of kings open up the past, but they do not invite us to look any further. By recording the facts, they stifle the imagination, because they show that nothing happened that is worth telling us about.

For the Egyptians – still according to Herodotus – the triviality of history results from the fact that it is manmade. "Thus the whole number of years is eleven thousand, three hundred and forty; in which entire space, they said no god had ever appeared in human form [...] However, in times anterior to them it was otherwise; then Egypt had gods for its rulers, who dwelt upon the earth with men, one being always supreme above the rest. The last of these was Horus, the son of Osiris, called by the late Greeks Apollo. He deposed Typhon, and ruled over Egypt as its last god-king."[80]

History only begins to be of interest when it concerns the gods. But that is precisely when for us it ceases to be history and turns into mythology. The time of the gods is the time of the great events, changes, and upheavals that gave rise to the world as we have known it for the last 12,000 years. That is the time that one can tell stories about, and those stories are what we now call myths. They tell

---

77 Herodotus II 142 see G. Rawlinson, *History of Herodotus. In Four Volumes*, Vol. II (London: D. Appleton, 1880), 221.

78 He was probably referring to four cycles of the sun, two moving from west to east and two from east to west, all contained within the period of 341 generations. Egyptian sources tell of nothing comparable.

79 See Donald B. Redford, *Pharaonic King-Lists, Annals and Day Books* (Mississauga: Benben 1986). On the pride of the late-age Egyptians in their past, see Jan Assmann, "Die Entdeckung der Vergangenheit. Innovation und Restauration in der ägyptischen Literaturgeschichte," in Gumbrecht and Link-Heer (eds.), *Epochenschwellen und Epochenstrukturen*, 484–499 (see chapt. 1, n. 17).

80 Herodotus II 142–143, Rawlinson, *History of Herodotus*, 221–223.

of how the world came into being, and of the mechanisms, rituals, and institutions whose task it is to ensure that the time never fades and that further changes and discontinuities are prevented from ever happening.

Things were much the same in Mesopotamia. C. Wilcke actually begins his analysis of the Sumerian list of kings with the following generalization: "The past was very important to the people of the Ancient East; their Now and Today was based on past events" (Wilcke 1988, 113). However, these people used the past similarly to the Egyptians; that is, the past was used to confirm the present, and everything was always as it is now unless it went back to the "founding age" of the gods. The lists of kings are a means of orientation and control, not of creating meaning or importance. We may therefore conclude that this intensive preoccupation with the past, as practiced in the calendars, annals, and lists of kings in the Ancient East, served to halt history and strip it of any semiotic value.

Absolute and Relative Past

"Hot" societies, according to Lévi-Strauss, "resolutely internal[ize] the historical process and mak[e] it the moving power of their development."[81] We now know enough about the Egyptian and Mesopotamian methods of recording to be able to say with certainty that this is not "internalized" history. Memory in the sense of an "internalized past" refers to mythical and not historical time, because only the mythical age is the age of "becoming," whereas historical time is nothing but the continuation of what has already become. As such – I am indebted to Aleida Assmann for this parallel – this scenario corresponds precisely to the "eternal present" of the totalitarian regimes Orwell describes. The internalized – to be more precise, remembered – past finds its form in narrative, and this has a function. Either it becomes the driving force of development or it becomes the basis of continuity. In neither case, however, is the past remembered purely for its own sake.

---

[81] Lévi-Strauss, *La pensée sauvage*, 309f.; Engl. *The Savage Mind*, 234 (see chapt. 1, n. 33); "intériorisant résolument le devenir historique pour en faire le moteur de leur développement."

Foundational stories are called "myth," and the term is usually used in contrast to history. There are two pairs of opposites involved here: fiction (myth) as opposed to reality (history), and purpose-oriented evaluation (using the past for an argument – myth) as opposed to pure objectivity (studying the past for the past's sake – history). These conceptual pairs, however, have been long due for the scrap heap. If there is such a thing as texts presenting an uncontaminated past, free from all reconstructive imagination and subjective values, then we cannot expect to find them in Antiquity and they would be irrelevant to the purposes of this study.[82] The forms of the remembered past entail myth and history without any distinction between them. The past that is fixed and internalized as foundational history is myth, regardless of whether it is fact or fiction.

The classic example of history transformed into myth, and of experience made into memory, is the Exodus (M. Walzer 1988). Although the historicity of the events recounted in the Second Book of Moses cannot be demonstrated by archaeology or epigraphy, an example of historical authenticity that is beyond doubt is available: the fall of the fortress at Masada (Pierre Vidal-Naquet 1981 and 1989).[83] This has become a foundational story for the modern state of Israel. The ruins of Masada were not only laid bare in accordance with all the rules of archaeology, but they were made into a holy site, where new recruits to the Israeli army must swear their oath of allegiance. The story is told by Josephus Flavius in Book VII of *The Jewish War*. Its interest lies not in the objectivity of the account or in the archaeological verification of the latter,[84] but in its foundational importance. The story is essential because it illustrates through a religious and political martyrdom precisely those virtues to which young Israeli soldiers are made to commit themselves. Myth is a story one tells in order to give direction to oneself and the world – a reality of a higher order, which not only

---

[82] This objection applies particularly to John Van Seters, *In search of history* (New Haven: Yale University Press, 1983).

[83] See now also Yael Zerubavel, *Recovered Roots. Collective Memory and the Making of Israeli National Tradition* (Chicago: University of Chicago Press, 1995); Nachman Ben-Yehuda, *Masada Myth: Collective Memory and Mythmaking in Israel* (Madison: University of Wisconsin Press, 1995); id., *Sacrificed Truth. Archaeology and The Myth of Masada* (New York: Prometheus Books Amherst, 2002).

[84] Which has proved impossible; see the critical interventions by Y. Zerubavel and N. Ben-Yehuda.

rings true but also sets normative standards and possesses a formative power. The annihilation of European Jewry, for instance, is an historical fact and as such is the subject of much historical research, but in modern Israel it has also become a foundational story under the heading of "The Holocaust"; it is thus also a myth from which the state draws an important part of its legitimation and its orientation. It is solemnly commemorated by public monuments and national institutions, is taught in schools, and constitutes a central element of Israel's official "mythomotor."[85] Only an important past is remembered, and only a remembered past can become important. Remembering has always been an act of semioticizing, of giving meaning to something, and this still applies today, even if the concept has fallen somewhat into disrepute in relation to history. One must simply bear in mind that memory has nothing to do with the study of history. You cannot expect a history professor to "fill the memory, coin the terms, and interpret the past."[86] This does not alter the fact that the process is continuously going on; but the process does not denote the task of the historian – it is a function of social memory,[87] and unlike the historian's work it is a basic anthropological feature. Although it transforms the past into foundational stories (myths), this does not in any way dispute the

[85] Concerning problems relating to the official commemoration of the Holocaust in Israel, see the illuminating essay by Ouriel Reshef, "Une commémoration impossible: l'holocauste en Israel," in P. Gignoux (ed.), *La commémoration. Colloque du centenaire de la section des sciences religieuses de l'EPHE* (Louvain-Paris: Peeters, 1988), 351–367. See also James E. Young, "Memory and Monument," in G. Hartman (ed.), *Bitburg in Moral and Political Perspective* (Bloomington: Indiana University Press, 1986), 103–113.

[86] Michael Stürmer, "Geschichte in geschichtslosem Land," *FAZ*, April 25, 1986. See Hans-Ulrich Wehler, "Geschichtswissenschaft heutzutage: Aufklärung oder 'Sinnstiftung'," in A. Honneth (ed.), *Zwischenbetrachtungen. Im Prozeß der Aufklärung* (Frankfurt: Suhrkamp, 1989), 775–793. I also consider the term "*Orientierungswissen*" (knowledge of orientation), which Wehler prefers to "*Sinnstiftung*" (giving meaning) in the study of history, to be an exaggeration. The term "orientation" presupposes precisely the same concept of meaning that is rejected by "giving meaning." If study is cut off from questions of value (in the Max Weber sense of the word), it can only produce knowledge; how far one wants and is able to orient oneself by this knowledge is a matter of pedagogics, politics, and didactics – depending on how the knowledge is to be applied. Certainly no one would expect "orientation" from a subject like Egyptology.

[87] In modern theories of history, this distinction has been largely done away with, see Burke, "Geschichte als soziales Gedächtnis" (see chapt. 1, n. 35). Historiography is now regarded simply as a particular genre of group memory.

reality of the events but emphasizes their future "binding" qualities as something that must not under any circumstances be forgotten.

This insight, however, should not lead us into disregarding certain important distinctions. The term "foundational story" indicates something functional, and the question arises as to what this function is. It makes all the difference whether the story takes place in a time of its own, from which the progressive present never distances itself and can therefore always be made present through rituals and festivals, or it occurs in historical time and so stands at a measurable and increasing distance from the present and can be brought to life not through ritual reenactment (*Vergegenwärtigung*), but only through memory (*Erinnerung*).[88] The fact that the Exodus and the Conquest form part of the foundational history of Israel does not make these events into *myths* in the sense of recurrent events in the world of the gods, such as Eliade describes (1953 and 1966). In Israel's case, the function of the foundational story has changed, and although neighboring cultures are based on cosmic myths, Israel takes an historical myth and through it internalizes its own historical becoming.[89] Lévi-Strauss's expression could not be more apt: it is the "driving force of development."

Myth is the past condensed into foundational narrative. The distinction with which I am concerned lies between an "absolute" and an historical past. In the former (E. Cassirer 1923, 130) – that is, the other time from which the progressive present always maintains the same distance and therefore constitutes a kind of eternity (the Australians call it dream time) – myth provides the foundation for a cold society's worldview. This past is made present by cyclical repetition. With the historical past, myth underlies the image a hot society has of itself when it internalizes its *devenir historique* (historical "becoming").

---

[88] Cf. Klaus Koch, "Qādām. Heilsgeschichte als mythische Urzeit im Alten (und Neuen) Testament," in J. Rohls and G. Wenz (eds.), *Vernunft des Glaubens* (Göttingen: Vandenhoeck & Ruprecht, 1988), 253–288.

[89] Using the terms introduced by Michael Fishbane, one could describe the difference as the transition from myth as "historia divina" to myth as "historia sacra;" see my article "Myth as 'historia divina' and 'historia sacra,'" in D. A. Green and L. S. Lieber (eds.), *Scriptural Exegesis. The Shapes of Culture and the Religious Imagination*, Essays in Honor of Michael Fishbane (New York: Oxford University Press, 2009), 13–24.

Eliade has drawn the distinction as succinctly as one can: a semioticized cosmos is replaced by a semioticized history.

The Mythomotor of Memory

Foundational and Contra-Present Memory. Hot memory not only measures out the past, as an instrument of chronological orientation and
control, but it also uses past references to create a self-image and to
provide support for hopes and for intentions. This is called myth.
The most preferred form is narrative, and as these past glories shed
luster on the present, they actually fulfill two different and opposing functions. The first is foundational and it makes the present into
something meaningful, divinely inspired, necessary, and unchangeable. The Osiris myth served this purpose for the Egyptian kings;
likewise the Exodus story for Israel. In Chapter 7, we see how Homer's
Iliad did the same and study the foundation of a Pan-hellenic consciousness. I call the second function the "contrapresent" (G. Theissen
1988). This proceeds from deficiencies experienced in the present,
and conjures up memories of a past that generally takes the form of
an heroic age. Such tales shed a very different light on the present by
emphasizing what has gone wrong, what has disappeared, or become
lost or marginalized, and thus there is a deliberate break between then
and now. Instead of being given a solid base, the present now finds
itself dislocated or at the very least falling short of the great and glori-
ous past. Homer's epics are also a good example for this. If this analysis
is correct, the epics were written during a period of transition, when
the world of the Greeks was changing and the free and expansive way
of life of the horse-breeding aristocracy was giving way to the narrower
and more communal lifestyle of the Polis. This created deficiencies
that brought about the vision of a heroic age beyond the age of decline
and fall. The two functions, then, are by no means mutually exclusive,
although it still seems advisable to separate them as concepts. There
are memories that are clearly contrapresent – that is, they relativize
the present and are therefore under certain circumstances undesir-
able, such as those memories of the Roman Republic during the early
days of the Emperors (H. Cancik-Lindemaier and H. Cancik 1987);
but there are others that are just as obviously foundational, like that
of Golgotha during the early stages of Christianity or the Masada cult

in modern Israel. There are also memories in mythical form that can be both at the same time. In principle, any foundational myth can change into a contrapresent one, and so the two attributes are not integral to the myth as such, but arise according to the context of image and action required for a particular present for a particular group in a particular situation. Each of them, however, provides a directional impetus that I call the mythomotor.[90]

In cases of extreme deficiency, a contrapresent mythomotor may become subversive, for instance under foreign rule or oppression. Then traditional memories no longer support the existing situation but on the contrary throw it into question and call for total change. The past to which they refer appears not as an irrevocably lost heroic age but as a social and political Utopia toward which one can direct one's life and work. Thus memory turns into expectation, and the "mythomotored" time takes on a different character. The circle of eternal recurrence now becomes a straight line leading to a distant goal. Circular revolution (as the Earth revolves round the sun) turns into political revolution in the sense of overthrow, and such movements can be observed all over the world: ethnologists subsume them under names such as "messianism," or "millenarianism," or "chiliasm," and thus relate them back to the Jews' anticipation of the Messiah, although they do not wish to postulate any genetic connection. Indeed it would seem that under structurally similar conditions, and more or less unconnected with Christianity, such movements – sharing the main features of messianism and millenarianism – arise quite spontaneously all over the world. They occur most typically in situations of oppression and suffering.[91] The Jewish Apocalypse is therefore unlikely to be the source of this historical phenomenon, but should

---

[90] The term "*mythomoteur*" was coined by Ramon d'Abadal I de Vinyals, "A propos du Legs Visigothique en Espagne," in *Settimane di Studio del Centro Italiano di Studi sull' Alt. Medioevo* 2 (1958), 541–85 and taken up by John Armstrong, *Nations before Nationalism* (Chapel Hill: North Carolina University Press, 1983) and Anthony D. Smith, *The Ethnic Origins of Nations* (Oxford: B. Blackwell, 1986).

[91] See Vittorio Lanternari, *Movimenti religiosi di libertà e di salvezza dei popoli oppressi* (Milano: Feltrinelli editore, 1960); Engl. *The religions of the oppressed. A study of modern messianic cults*, trans. by Lisa Sergio (New York: Knopf, 1963); Peter Worsley, *The Trumpet Shall Sound. A Study of `Cargo'-Cults in Melanesia* (New York: Schocken Books, 1968); Wilhelm E. Mühlmann, *Chiliasmus und Nativismus: Studien zur Psychologie, Soziologie und historischen Kasuistik der Umsturzbewegungen* (Berlin: Reimer, 1961).

be seen simply as the earliest known evidence of a cultural, anthropological universal.[92] The Book of Daniel, which is the oldest example of a millenaristic form of contrapresent mythomotor, was written in just such a situation. Today it is generally dated as coming from the time of Antiochus IV Epiphanes, that is, the time of the first religiously motivated resistance movement known to history: the Maccabean Wars.[93]

In Egypt, too, we can clearly see the change from foundational to contrapresent mythomotor (J. Assmann 1983). It remains open to question if and when the shift to revolutionary mythomotor actually took place. The only overtly revolutionary texts date from the late phase of Egyptian culture, and they are certainly no older than the Book of Daniel. They deal with the *Potter's Oracle* (transmitted in the Greek language) and the Demotic *Prophecies of the Lamb*, and they foretell the return of a messianic king who, after a long period of oppressive foreign rule, will establish a new time of glory by restoring the Pharaohs. This, unquestionably, is a mythomotor of hope and expectation.[94]

---

[92] On the Jewish Apocalypse see the anthology by David Hellholm, *Apocalypticism in the Mediterranean World and in the Near East* (Tübingen: Mohr, 1983) (2nd ed. 1989) with bibliography. On the Mesopotamian background, see Helge S. Kvanvig, *Roots of Apocalyptic. The Mesopotamian Background of the Enoch Figure and the Son of Man* (Neukirchen: Neukirchener Verlag, 1988). This deals with mythical themes that come from Mesopotamia but do not involve the dynamic, revolutionary element until they enter the context of Early Judaism.

[93] J. C. H. Lebram, "König Antiochus im Buch Daniel," *Vetus Testamentum* 18 (1968), 737–773; Klaus Koch et al., *Das Buch Daniel*, EdF (Darmstadt: Wissenschaftliche Buchgesellschaft, 1980). The date (165 BCE) has already been pointed out by Porphyry in his pamphlet *Against the Christians*. The Maccabean Wars have by now come to be seen, however, as the first religiously motivated civil war disguised as a resistance movement against forced assimilation. Martin Hengel, *Judentum und Hellenismus. Studien ihrer Begegnung unter besonderer Berücksichtigung der Situation Palästinas bis zur Mitte des 2. Jh. v. Chr.*, 3rd ed. (Tübingen: Mohr, 1988); see also Erich Gruen, *Heritage and Hellenism. The Reinvention of Jewish Tradition* (Berkeley: University of California Press, 1998); Steven Weitzman, "Plotting Antiochus's Persecution," *JBL* 123.2 (2004), 219–234.

[94] Alan B. Lloyd, "Nationalist Propaganda in Ptolemaic Egypt," in *Historia* 31. *Zeitschrift für Alte Geschichte* (Wiesbaden, 1982), 33–55, interprets the *Potter's Oracle*, as well as the Sesostris Romance, the *Demotic Chronicle*, and the Nektanebos episode in the Alexander Romance, as an expression of "nationalistic" resistance to the rule of the Macedonians. For details, cf. my book *The Mind of Egypt. History and Meaning in the Time of the Pharaohs*, trans. Andrew Jenkins (New York: Metropolitan Books, 2002), 384–388.

The *Potter's Oracle*, however, shows detailed parallels with a text that is 2,000 years older, the *Prophecies of Neferti*, and the question arises as to whether this text too is not proof of a messianic movement with a corresponding contra-present, revolutionary mythomotor. It is, though, a prophecy that did not arise out of deficiency but, on the contrary, represented a present situation as marking the solution to previous problems. The text prophesies that King Amenemhet I, founder of the 12th Dynasty, will be a messianic figure. After lengthy verses describing the catastrophic period without pharaonic rule, the conclusion reads:

> A King will come from the south, Ameni by name,
> The son of a woman from Ta-Seti, a child from Upper Egypt [...]
> Ma'at (truth-justice-order) will return to its rightful place,
> While Isfet (lies-injustice-chaos) is driven away.

This king, however, will not establish a "thousand-year empire." He will simply restore normality. By Ma'at the Egyptian did not mean some kind of Utopia, but an order without which the world was uninhabitable and peaceful coexistence impossible. The concept of Ma'at only became contrapresent in the Late Period; only then it no longer meant the straightforward normality of the status quo that every king was expected to maintain, but instead a "Golden Age."

> Ma'at had come from heaven to its time
> and united with the earthly.
> The land was watered, the stomachs were full,
> There was no year of hunger in either country.
> The walls had not yet fallen, the thorn did not yet prick
> In the time of the divine forefathers.[95]

Only by way of this phase, in which foundational turns into contrapresent, is it possible to conceive of further development into revolutionary mythomotor. The *Prophecies of Neferti* are still contained within the foundational category, because the restoration of the Ma'at does not entail the overthrow of the existing order – it is simply a return

---

95 Eberhard Otto, "Das 'Goldene Zeitalter' in einem ägyptischen Text," in *Religions en Égypte hellénistique et romaine* (BCESS) (Paris: Presses universitaires de France, 1969), 92–108. See also J. Assmann, *Ma'at*, 225 f., (see chapt. 1, n. 11) and J. Assmann, *The Mind of Egypt*, 386, (see chapt. 1, n. 94).

to order. Therefore one cannot interpret this text as an expression of hope or expectation, whereas the *Potter's Oracle* is revolutionary in precisely this sense. It foretells the coming of a royal savior who arouses hopes and expectations that can only be fulfilled by the overthrow of the existing political order.

The fact that this text stems from the same time as the Book of Daniel gives much cause for thought. Direct influence is highly improbable, because the two are very different.[96] Their similarities lie only in the structure of the revolutionary mythomotor. And so the most likely explanation is that they were written under similar historical circumstances – that is, at a time of national resistance movements that were happening in Judea as well as in Egypt.

There are, of course, far more recent illustrations of this form of mythomotor. All nationalistic movements mobilize memory in order to conjure up a past that stands in stark contrast to the present – a time of liberty and self-determination that can only be restored by shaking off the yoke of foreign rule. What we call folklore and take to be age-old tradition largely arose or at least was given its fixed form during the 18th and 19th centuries to support such nationalistic resistance movements (E. Hobsbawm and T. Ranger 1983). Scottish tartan provides a fitting example of such "invented traditions."[97] This is a theme I return to in Chapter 3.

Memory as Resistance. In addition to the Book of Daniel, the Book of Esther is a typical example of contrapresent or contrafactual memory. What is described here is the exact inversion of an anti-Jewish pogrom in that here it is not the Jews but their persecutors who are killed. Although King Ahasveros can no longer revoke his orders – given at

---

[96] Lebram, "König Antiochus im Buch Daniel," (see chapt. 1, n. 93) believes that there is Egyptian influence in the Book of Daniel. He thinks that Egyptian traditions concerning the Persian King Kambyses – the embodiment of a godless ruler – may have been the model for King Antiochus. The Coptic Kambyses Romance, however, derives from a much later period. Contemporary accounts of the Persians' rule in Egypt tend to be quite favorable to the Persians; see Alan B. Lloyd, "The Inscription of Udjahorresnet, A Collaborator's Testament," *Journal of Egyptian Archaeology* 68 (1982), 166–180.

[97] See Hugh Trevor-Roper, "The Invention of Tradition: The Highland Tradition of Scotland," in E. Hobsbawm and T. Ranger (eds.), *The Invention of Tradition* (Cambridge: Cambridge University Press, 1983), 15–42.

the instigation of the villainous Haman – he is able to warn the Jews and encourage them to defend themselves; thus the day ends with the slaughter of the persecutors. Here is a reversal of the diaspora experience. To my knowledge, however, it did not go so far as to become a revolutionary mythomotor. Instead, the Esther scroll became the liturgy for the carnival-like festival of Purim, which stages Utopia as a topsy-turvy world. This is a typical case of counter-history, in which the past is represented from the viewpoint of the victims in such a way that today's oppressors look pitiful and today's vanquished seem to be the true conquerors of yesteryear. Similar stories arose in Egypt at the same time and under the same conditions (A. B. Lloyd 1982).

Generally, it appears that religion tends to go together with the foundational function. In relation to Judaism, it appears that the link with contra factual and contrapresent memory is much more striking than elsewhere, and in any case one can certainly argue that "the general function of religion is to convey non-simultaneity through memory, visualization and repetition" (Cancik and Mohr 1990, 311–313, quotation 311). This nonsimultaneity can, in certain contexts, assume the character of the other time and then memory becomes an act of resistance.

The requirements of everyday life aim at coordination and communication, and hence at "establishing simultaneity."[98] The inhabited, colonized, measured, and controlled time in which all actions fit in with one another and can be effectively, communicatively interwoven is one of the great achievements of civilization, but this has often been described and need not concern us here. Our focus is more on the institutions that work in the direction of heterogenizing time and establishing nonsimultaneity; until now these have attracted considerably less attention. Their roots are in festivals and rituals, and during the evolution of literate cultures they have taken a large variety of forms. All the same, the establishment and communication

---

[98] The concept of "simultaneity" here is to be understood as "homogenized time" in the sense of Luhmann's "time dimension." Nikolas Luhmann, "Sinn als Grundbegriff der Soziologie," in J. Habermas and N. Luhmann (eds.), *Theorie der Gesellschaft oder Sozialtechnologie* (Frankfurt: Suhrkamp, 1971), 25–100; Luhmann, "Gleichzeitigkeit und Synchronisation," *Soziologische Aufklärung* 5 (1990), 95–130 uses a much more generalized idea of simultaneity, which does away with all the distinctions that we are concerned with here.

of nonsimultaneity seem to constitute the essence of religion, to whose decline in the western world the unmistakable trend toward "one-dimensionality" is undoubtedly linked. Through cultural memory, human life gains a second dimension or a second time, and this remains through all the stages of cultural evolution. The heterogenization of time, the production of nonsimultaneity, the possibility of living in two times, is one of the universal functions of cultural memory or, to be more precise, of culture as memory

"The nightmare vision of humanity without memory . . . " writes T. W. Adorno, "is no mere waste product . . . , but it is inextricably bound up with the progression of the bourgeois principle. Economists and sociologists such as Werner Sombart and Max Weber have attributed the principle of traditionalism to feudal society, and that of rationality to middle-class forms of society. This, however, means no less than the fact that memory, time, and remembrance of the developing bourgeois society itself are eliminated as a kind of irrational relic."[99] According to H. Marcuse, this elimination leads to the "one-dimensionality" of the modern world, which without memory is reduced by the other dimension of its reality.[100] This criticism points emphatically to the contrapresent function of cultural memory: that of freedom through memory.

One-dimensionality is not confined to the modern world. It generally occurs throughout everyday life. Because of the demands of workaday life, we structure the world into foreground and background; consequently, most of the time the big issues are obscured. We concentrate on routine matters, pushing aside the more fundamental decisions and reflections; otherwise we would not be able to attend to our immediate needs. This does not, however, mean that the excluded perspectives are simply forgotten or suppressed. They form a background that is kept at the ready by cultural memory. This, together with its objectivized forms, has no place in our daily concerns, which is why H. Marcuse objects to hearing Bach on the transistor in the kitchen, or classics being sold in the department store. He complains

---

99 Theodor W. Adorno, "Was bedeutet Aufarbeitung der Vergangenheit?," in *Bericht über die Erzieherkonferenz am 6. u. 7. November in Wiesbaden* (Frankfurt: Deutscher Koordinierungsrat, 1959), 14, quoted by Herbert Marcuse, *The One-Dimensional Man* (Boston: Beacon Press, 1964), 102.

100 Ibid.

that this robs the classics of their "antagonistic power" (H. Marcuse 1964, 64), because culture is not meant to be the "background" of our everyday world but rather it presents a contrast – "air blowing from another planet" (ibid. 85). Cultural memory gives us this fresh air in a world that, in the "reality of daily life," becomes too narrow for us. This is also, and especially true of memory: "Remembrance of the past may give rise to dangerous insights, and the established society seems to be apprehensive of the subversive contents of memory. Remembrance is a mode of dissociation from the given facts, a mode of 'mediation' that breaks for short moments the omniscient power of the given facts. Memory recalls the terror and the hope that passed" (ibid., 98).

Tacitus complained about the destruction of memory under totalitarian rule: "We would also have lost our very memories, together with freedom of speech, if it were equally in our power to forget as well as to be silent"[101] "Dictatorship," H. Cancik-Lindemaier and H. Cancik have commented on this passage, "destroys speech, memory and history."[102] On the other hand, memory can be a weapon against oppression. The text that illustrates this most strikingly is G. Orwell's *1984*.[103] In extreme cases of totalitarian ruthlessness, the innate liberating power of cultural memory may come to the fore.

In a world where the government forces all its subjects to toe the party line, memory offers access to a different world, facilitating detachment from the absolutism of the present "given reality." In a more general and less political context, the same applies to the pressures exerted by everyday chores and social constrictions – pressures that always lead us in the direction of uniformity, simplification, and one-dimensionality.

---

[101] Tacitus, *Agricola* 2, 3. See Tacitus's *Agricola, Germany*, and *Dialogue on Orators*. trans. with an introduction and notes by Herbert W. Benario (Norman: University of Oklahoma Press, 1991), 26.

[102] See Cancik-Lindemaier and Cancik, "Zensur und Gedächtnis," 182 (see chapt. 1, n. 48).

[103] See A. and J. Assmann, "Schrift, Tradition und Kultur," 35 f. (see chapt. 1, n. 47).

2

Written Culture

FROM RITUAL TO TEXTUAL CONTINUITY

Ancient Egyptian culture had a very definite concept of what was needed to keep the world in motion. The main features were activities of a ritual or spiritual nature through which a whole edifice of knowledge was passed on whose foundations were laid far more by rites than by books. If the rituals were not properly performed, the world would fall apart, and correctness was a matter of knowledge – an *officium memoriae*. Similar ideas can be found in China where everything depended on ritual and on those who were assigned to carry it out by keeping the world in their heads and by not forgetting anything. In Judaism, things were different. The Jews detached themselves from such rituals, concentrating instead on the interpretation of texts. This guaranteed – in the words of Peter Schäfer – "harmony between Heaven and Earth."[1]

The language in the sources and the particular concepts of each culture can be subsumed under the single heading of "continuity"[2] – a continuity that is ritual in Ancient Egypt and China, and

---

[1] See Peter Schäfer, "Text, Auslegung und Kommentar im rabbinischen Judentum," in J. Assmann and B. Gladigow (eds.), *Text und Kommentar* (Munich: Fink, 1995), 163–186, quote 171.

[2] Although the term used for this in the German original can be literally translated as "coherence," "continuity" seems more apt in this context. "Coherence" refers to simultaneous connection, whereas "continuity" renders better the idea of diachronic cultural identity as a connection stretching over the sequence of time.

textual in rabbinical Judaism as the ritual continuity was lost with the destruction of the temple in 70 AD. From then on the seat of knowledge was no longer the performance of sacred actions and recitations, but the scholarly study of the written, foundational word. In the context of cultural history, we can call this the transition from ritual to textual continuity. Hölderlin's poem *Patmos* provides an extraordinarily succinct summary of this movement from cosmic rites to textual interpretation:

> Without awareness we've worshiped
> Our Mother the Earth, and the Light
> Of the Sun as well, but what our Father
> Who reigns over everything wants most
> Is that the established word be
> Carefully attended, and that
> Which endures be interpreted well.[3]

Although I am not trying to suggest that Hölderlin was actually thinking of the transition from ritual to text, there can be no doubt that he was referring to a shift from historical and cosmic phenomena to holy writings and their interpretation. This may not be in the sense of a cultural shift, but it is certainly a shift from nature to poetry, as is made clear by a later line: *Dem folgt deutscher Gesang* ("German song must accord with this"). Nevertheless, Hölderlin's verses shed a somewhat surprising light on my thesis. One could hardly find a more apt expression for the principle of looking after the words (*Textpflege*), than "the established word be/Carefully attended"; "and that / Which endures be interpreted well" is a precise instruction to also look after the meaning (*Sinnpflege*).

Repetition and Interpretation

The past does not just emerge of its own accord; it is the result of a cultural process of construction and representation. This process is always

---

[3] Hölderlin "Patmos" in Friedrich Hölderlin, *Poems of Friedrich Hölderlin*, trans. James Mitchell (San Francisco: Ituriel's Spear, 2004), 39–45, here 45. See also Cyrus Hamlin, "Hermeneutische Denkfiguren in Hölderlins Patmos," in P. Härtling and G. Kurz (eds.), *Hölderlin und Nürtingen* (Stuttgart, Weimar: Metzler, 1994), 79–102, esp. 90.

guided by particular motives, expectations, hopes, and aims, each of which takes its form from the referential frame of the present. The insights provided by Halbwachs act as a constant point of reference. He demonstrated that social reconstructions of the past represented group-related fictions of continuity. In this section of the book, I examine how such continuity is imagined, not only through memory figures but also during the cultural procedures. What actually happens during cultural reproduction? The following statement is a good point of departure: repetition and interpretation are functionally equivalent processes in the production of cultural continuity.

As cultural memory is not biologically transmitted, it has to be kept alive through the sequence of generations. This is a matter of cultural mnemotechnics, that is, the storage, retrieval, and communication of meaning. These mnemotechnics guarantee continuity and identity, the latter clearly being a product of memory. Just as an individual forms a personal identity through memory, maintaining this despite the passage of time, so a group identity is also dependent on the reproduction of shared memories. The difference is that the group memory has no neurological basis. This is replaced by culture: a complex of identity-shaping aspects of knowledge objectified in the symbolic forms of myth, song, dance, sayings, laws, sacred texts, pictures, ornaments, paintings, processional routes, or – as in the case of the Australians – even whole landscapes. Cultural memory circulates in forms of commemoration that were originally bound up with rituals and festivals. As long as these rites were predominant, the knowledge that was all-important for identity was handed down through repetition. It is the very essence of all rites that they follow a given, unchanging order. Thus each performance is consistent with its predecessors, so that in illiterate societies time typically follows a circular pattern; it is therefore fair to talk of this cultural circularity in terms of "repetition compulsion." This, indeed, is what guarantees ritual continuity, and this is what societies free themselves from as they move over to textual continuity.[4]

---

[4] This has been stressed by such anthropologists as E. A. Havelock, W. Ong, and J. Goody. On the repetitiveness of oral cultures, see especially Walter Ong, "African Talking Drums and Oral Noetics," *New Literary History* 8.3 (1977), 409–429.

Ritual Repetition and Interpretive Presentification
(Vergegenwärtigung[5])

As already mentioned earlier, ritual is not solely confined to the repetition of a fixed procedure. It is far more than an ornamental structuring of time, which, similar to wallpaper with its recurrent figures, simply reconstructs a series of actions in order to preserve a pattern. Ritual also realizes a meaning. This was clear from the example of the Jewish festival of Seder, with its fixed order ("seder" actually means "order") repeated every year in identical fashion. But Seder Night also "presentifies" the Exodus from Egypt through songs, homilies, anecdotes, and discussions. Every element of the ritual order is geared to this one event that can only be captured through the form of memory (Hebrew: "zikaron"). Everyone eats the bitter herbs to remind them of the bitterness of serfdom, the "Charoset" is meant to recall the clay with which the Children of Israel made the bricks to build the cities of Egypt. In fact, each detail of the meal serves a memory function. The Christian Last Supper, which clearly derives from the Jewish Seder, has preserved exactly the same form of remembrance. Bread and wine are the zikaron of the Crucifixion, which for Christians has the same element of redemption and liberation as the Exodus has for Jews. What is more surprising is that exactly the same structures can be found in Ancient Egyptian rituals. Every element is part of a precise order and refers to a meaning, although the setting of this lies in the *absolute past* of divine myth and not in the *relative past* of the people's own history. All the same, we learn – much as we do in relation to the Last Supper – that this is (or means) "Osiris" (or something similar). The whole Egyptian cult rests on the two dimensions of ritual repetition and mythical presentification through sacramental interpretation.[6] Ritual

---

5 The French term "présentification" as coined by J. P. Vernant, "De la présentification de l'invisible à l'imitation de l'apparence," in *Image et signification*. Rencontres de l'École du Louvre (Paris: Documentation française, 1983), 25–37. It seems to provide the most adequate rendering of what is meant by "Vergegenwärtigung" (literally, "making something present").

6 See my articles "Semiosis and Interpretation in Ancient Egyptian Ritual," in S. Biderstein and B.-A. Scharfstein (eds.), *Interpretation in Religion*, Philosophy and Religion 2 (Leiden: E. J. Brill, 1992), 87–110 and "Altägyptische Kultkommentare," in J. Assmann and B. Gladigow (eds.), *Text und Kommentar*, 93–109 (see chapt. 2,

repetition is only a form to contain the meaning that is to be preserved and made present. If this dimension of reference and presentification were not present, then we would not be dealing with rites as such, but with ritualized routines – mere actions that are prescribed for purely rational, practical purposes.

The element of repetition recedes, as ritual changes to textual continuity; now we have a different container for meaning. The question arises, however, as to whether this meaning that provides the basis for a group's *connective structure* does not actually have a much firmer and more secure foundation through rituals than through texts. Meaning can only retain its life through circulation, and that is provided by the shared communication of rites. But texts in themselves do not automatically circulate – they must *be* circulated[7] – and if this ceases to happen, they become a grave for, rather than the bearer of, meaning. Only an interpreter, with all the arts of hermeneutics and the skills of communication, can revive that meaning. Of course the meaning of a ritual can also pass into oblivion, and another meaning may inevitably take its place. Texts are simply a riskier form of transmitting meaning. There is always the potential danger that they will be removed from circulation and communication, which is not the case with ritual.

The transition from ritual to textual continuity fundamentally changes the time-structure of cultural memory. All the forms of ritual circulation depend on time and place, on temporal recurrence, and/or spatial translocation. You have to wait for a feast to return or a rite to be performed, and you have to go to an image, a monument, a sacred place in order to reconnect with its meaning.[8] To reconnect

n. 1). On the various devices of "sacramental interpretation" see my book *Death and Salvation in Ancient Egypt*, trans. D. Lorton (Ithaca: Cornell University Press, 2005), 349–368.

7 This is the reason why N. Luhmann does not classify writing as a medium of communication; see his essay "The Form of Writing," *Stanford Literature Review* 9/1 (1992), 25–42. Interestingly, the Egyptian word *sphr* for "putting into circulation" also means "to write." This, however, does not exhaust the function of writing. Together with its preceding systems of notation it opens up a "metacommunicative" space beyond that of communication that serves as a storehouse for messages that have been excluded. We have discussed this idea already in the Introduction.

8 The ritualized form of institutionalizing the extended situation in oral societies creates that particular time structure that Jan Vansina has described as "floating gap" and that Maurice Bloch characterized as a combination of sacred cyclical time and profane linear time. Time gets divided, on the one hand into a mythical past that

with the meaning of written cultural texts, you do not have to wait for the next performance; you simply have to read them. The difference between ritual and textual reiteration may be illustrated by a quotation from Flavius Josephus in which he opposes Jewish and Gentile forms of cultural participation (I am quoting the text in a translation of the 18th century by William Warburton):

That high and sublime knowledge, which the Gentiles with difficulty attained unto, in the rare and temporary celebration of their Mysteries, was habitually taught to the Jews, at all times. (...) Where, in any place but in this, are the whole People, by the special diligence of the Priests, to whom the care of public instruction is committed, accurately taught the principles of true piety? So that the body-politic seems, as it were, one great Assembly, constantly kept together, for the celebration of some sacred Mysteries. For those things which the Gentiles keep up for a few days only that is, during those solemnities they call "Mysteries" and "Initiations," we, with vast delight, and a plenitude of knowledge, which admits of no error, fully enjoy, and perpetually contemplate through the whole course of our lives.[9]

Whereas the Gentiles have to wait until the next celebration of their mysteries, the Jews are in constant and continuous possession of their cultural texts, because they are "habitually taught," by "public instruction." Their "mysteries" are permanent. Their form of community or "body politic" coheres and reproduces itself not by way of ritual but by means of teaching and learning. When Josephus speaks of "teaching," he does not just think of teaching how to read and write, but of interpretation or "exegesis." To ensure the continuous readability of written cultural texts over a long stretch of time that can effect changes in language use and historical reality, the meaning of the texts must be kept alive by constant adaptation to changing circumstances; otherwise this meaning gets lost within the three or four generations of communicative memory. In a literate culture such as the Jewish

is cyclically repeated and "re-presentified" in the various ritual performances and that remains always at the same distance to the linearly proceding present, and on the other into a recent past that moves along linearly with the present. Where the cultural texts are predominantly codified in written form, the floating gap tends to disappear and the time-structure of the "extended situation" changes ritual repetition to permanent presence.

9 Flavius Josephus, *Contra Apionem* II 22, trans. William Warburton, *The Divine Legation of Moses*, Vol. 1 (London: J. and P. Knapton, 1738), 192–193.

society that Josephus describes, continuous exegesis fulfills the function of institutionalizing cultural continuity that in the pagan world is fulfilled by ritual repetition.

Early Written Cultures: The Stream of Tradition

Writing developed in Mesopotamia out of preliminary forms in the context of everyday life and not out of ceremonial communication. It only began to play a role in the functional areas of cultural memory later. Ceremonial forms of communication remained, because their multimedia complexities could not be recorded, thus the domain of ritual repetition, which continued to provide the backbone of cultural continuity. Gradually, however, alongside the practical texts of daily communication, a collection of normative and formative texts came into being that were not just written versions of the oral traditions but that emerged from the spirit of writing itself. This literature, about which I use the felicitous expression coined by the Assyriologist Leo Oppenheim, formed the "stream of tradition" incorporating those texts that were destined to survive.[10] This stream is an organic flow that cuts out its course and then carries greater or lesser quantities of material along with it; as some texts disappear, some enter the flood, and others are extended, shortened, revised, or anthologized in ever changing combinations.[11] Gradually, different structures are formed

---

[10] Leo Oppenheim, *Ancient Mesopotamia. Portrait of a Dead Civilization* (Chicago: University of Chicago Press, 1964). W. W. Hallo distinguishes within the Mesopotamian tradition between three categories: "canonical," "monumental," and "archival." The "canonical" category seems to correspond to Oppenheim's "stream of tradition." However, because we are using the word "canon" here strictly in relation to texts that survive not as individual writings but as parts of a closed and sanctified tradition, it seems more appropriate to stick to terms like stream of tradition or great tradition (R. Redfield).

[11] This fluid structure is best illustrated by the Bible, which represents a thousand-year stream of tradition that suddenly came to a standstill at a particular moment in time. Initially, there was an increase in and a continuation of the writing of texts – Deutero- and Tritojesaja (second and third Isaiah) – linking up with different traditions, juxtaposing variations, combining older and newer layers of text, anthologizing, collecting, etc., and above all there was a vast range of different genres: laws, genealogies, family histories, historical accounts, love songs, drinking songs, songs of praise, confessions, laments, prayers, hymns, proverbs, lyrics, manuals, prophecies, educational books, romances, short stories, myths, fairy tales, sermons, biographies, letters, apocalypses. This was a flowering tree with many branches, which in the

from the center or the periphery. Some assume central importance because they are copied and quoted more often than others; thus they eventually become classics that embody normative and formative values. The school of writing played a vital role here; it created an institutional framework for the copying, circulation, and archiving of texts, thereby ensuring that the texts and their values remained present and accessible. In this way a "great tradition"[12] emerged that created a repository of knowledge and, more importantly, education that extended back over hundreds and then thousands of years. The Mesopotamian "house of tablets" and the Egyptian "house of life" were the bearers of this most extensive text-supported form of cultural memory.

The emergence of the classics altered the tense of culture. The "festive" distinction between primal time and the present was now joined by another division – that between past and present, the ancient and the modern. The past was the time of the "classics." It was not a primal age that always remained the same distance away from the progressive present – a distance that was not temporal but ontic; this was an historical past, whose distance from the present was observable and measurable. In Mesopotamia during the 1st millennium, there were already early forms of past-related historiography (J. v. Seters 1983); at the same time in Egypt there was a profound conservationist and archival interest in old monuments, texts, and archaism, as well as a lively awareness of ancient traditions.[13] Libraries and book culture

process of canonization was transformed into the rigid architecture of a house with many rooms on many floors although it remained uniform and for ever closed. The Old Testament history of tradition had frozen under the spell of the "Ur-text," and thus the work of passing on, and hence the history of the cultural memory contained in those texts, was no longer of prime importance. In more recent times, however, there has been a change of attitude. Michael A. Fishbane, *Biblical Interpretation in Ancient Israel* (Oxford: Clarendon Press, 1986) is particularly illuminating in this respect.

[12] Robert Redfield, *Peasant Society and Culture* (Chicago: University of Chicago Press, 1956).

[13] See J. Assmann, "Die Entdeckung der Vergangenheit," (see chapt. 1, n. 17); Redford, *Pharaonic King-Lists*, (see chapt. 1, n. 10); Peter Der Manuelian, *Living in the Past. Studies in the Archaism of the Egyptian Twenty-sixth Dynasty* (London: Kegan Paul International, 1994), and my book *The Mind of Egypt: History and Meaning in the Time of the Pharaohs* (New York: Metropolitan Books 2002), 335–364 (see chapt. 1, n. 94). For Mesopotamia see Gerdien Jonker, *The Topography of Remembrance. The Dead, Tradition and Collective Memory in Mesopotamia* (Leiden: E. J. Brill, 1995) and

grew and flourished in the environment of temple scriptoria, palaces, and schools. However, as before, festivals and rituals still constituted the basic principle of cultural continuity.

Canonization and Interpretation

The decisive change from ritual to textual continuity did not come about through writing but through damming the stream of tradition so that it stopped flowing. The running river became the canonized lake, and originally it was not the "sacred" but the "canonical" text that required interpreting. This was the starting point of the hermeneutic culture, as I now try to explain.

C. Colpe has suggested that there are only two, completely independent forms of canonization in human history: the Hebrew *Tanakh* and the Buddhist *Tripithaka* (C. Colpe 1987). All other forms – in the West: the Alexandrian canonization of the Greek classics (although personally, I would regard the question as to which actually depended on which to be open), the Christian Bible, and the Koran; in the East: the Jaina canon, and Confucian and Taoist texts – derive from these initial starting points. A rich library of interpretive literature that itself becomes canonical is connected to these examples of canonization. Thus cultural memory organizes itself into canons of the first, second, and sometimes even third order, as primary and secondary literature, or texts and commentaries. The most important step toward canonization is the act of "closure." This draws a definitive line between the canonical and the apocryphal, and between the primary and the secondary. Canonical texts cannot be changed – this marks the crucial difference between them and the stream of tradition. They are sacrosanct, and must be handed down word for word. "Ye shall not add unto the word which I command you, neither shall ye diminish ought from it, that ye may keep the commandments of the Lord your God which I command you" (Deut. 4:2). It is clear from this passage that the Hebrew canon was born out of the spirit of the covenant that God

Stefan Maul, "Altertum in Mesopotamien. Beiträge zu den Sektionsthemen und Diskussionen," in D. Kuhn and H. Stahl (eds.), *Die Gegenwart des Altertums. Formen und Funktionen des Altertumsbezugs in den Hochkulturen der Alten Welt* (Heidelberg: edition forum Heidelberg, 2001), 117–124.

made with his chosen people.[14] The canonical text has the binding force of a treaty.

A closer look at the difference between sacred and canonical texts shows that the former also exist outside canonized traditions. They exist in oral (the most impressive example being the Veda) as well as written form (e.g., the Egyptian *Book of the Dead*). Sacred texts also demand word-for-word reproduction, which is why the Veda are not written down – the Brahmins have less faith in writing than in memory. A sacred text is a kind of speech-temple, a presentification of the holy[15] through the medium of the voice. It does not require any interpretation, but simply a ritually guaranteed recitation that scrupulously observes all of the prescriptions relating to time, place, and accuracy. A canonical text, however, embodies the normative and formative values of a community. It is the absolute truth. These texts must be taken to heart, obeyed, and translated into real life. That is why they need interpretation rather than recitation. They appeal to the heart, not to the mouth or ear. But such texts do not speak directly to the heart. The route from the listening ear and the reading eye to the understanding heart is as long as that from the graphic or phonetic surface to the formative, normative meaning. And so the canonical text requires the presence of a third party – the interpreter – to mediate between the text and the reader/listener, and to clarify the meaning hidden within the words. That meaning can only emerge through the three-way relationship between text, interpreter, and listener.[16]

In this way, institutions of interpretation, and thus a new class of intellectual elites, emerge around traditions of canonization: the Israelite *sofer*, the Jewish *rabbi*, the Hellenistic *philologos*, the Islamic *sheikh* or *mullah*, the Indian *Brahmin*, and all the sages and scholars of Buddhism, Confucianism, and Taoism. These new bearers of cultural memory are a class apart – they are the spiritual leaders, and they remain relatively independent of the institutions of political and economic power (Chr. Meier 1987). They are only able to represent the

---

[14] On the history of the canon formula, see the second section of this chapter.

[15] Cf. Vernant, "De la présentification de l'invisible," 293–295 (see chapt. 2, n. 5).

[16] See the astonished response of the Chamberlain, when Philip asks him: "Understandeth thou what thou readest?" "How can I, except some man should guide me?' (Acts. 8:30,31; *hodegesei*,' hence the term *hodegesis* meaning showing the way through explanation of a text).

various demands made by the canon if they maintain an independent position, as their task is both to embody and to spread its authority and its revealed truth. In the early written cultures, the bearers and guardians of the stream of tradition were also administrators, healers, dream interpreters, diviners, and prophets – in all cases, people who either received or gave orders within the existing political structure. There was no traditional, central point from which this organization with its own normative, formative values could have been opposed. The canonization process was therefore also one of social differentiation, as it produced a position independent of the political, administrative, economic, legal, and even religious authorities. The task of its representatives was (to use Hölderlin's expression) to ensure that the "established word be/Carefully attended," that is, to interpret it and look after its meaning. There was always a gap between fixed text and a changing reality because the letter could not be changed one iota, but the human world was constantly subject to change; this gap could only be bridged by means of interpretation. The latter therefore became the central principle of cultural continuity and identity, and the norms of cultural memory could only be extrapolated from renewed study of their textual sources. Interpretation became the expression of memory, and the interpreter the remembrancer of a forgotten truth.

With the increasing production of texts, however, a situation very swiftly arose that Aleida Assmann describes as a separation of cultural memory into "working and storage memory"– or "canon and archive"(A. Assmann 1999, 2006). The mass of primary, secondary, and tertiary texts – of canonical, semi-canonical, and apocryphal writings – far exceeded the capacity of what any society of a particular era could remember and internalize. But as more and more texts sank into the archival background, the written word grew increasingly into a form of forgetting, a graveyard of meanings that had once emerged from live interpretation and communication. And so gradually areas of discarded or obsolete or forgotten knowledge developed within a cultural tradition, blurring the borders between "us" and "them," or "self" and "other."

It is obvious that in the history of the *connective structure*, it was the invention of writing that caused the deepest break. Writing divided this history into two phases: one of ritual repetition and one of textual interpretation. The watershed is well known and well documented.

Jaspers's famous concept of the "Axial Age" describes this revolution perfectly,[17] even though he strangely ignored the role of writing – an omission that was soon corrected by others.[18]

Repetition and Variation

The main difference between textual and ritual continuity lies in the fact that the latter is based on repetition (i.e., variations are not allowed), whereas the former not only allows but even encourages variation. This may not be immediately obvious. One would have supposed that it would be the world of oral tradition, of rites and myths, that would be full of variations, because the words are not fixed and every performance actualizes things in its own way. The written text, however, is fixed for all time and therefore can only be repeated with each copy and each reading. I am not referring to the text itself but to that which the text converts into language, that is, not the written form, but the message it contains. In the world of oral tradition, the potential for innovation and hence for new information is small. This only remains in the cultural memory if it gives expression to something familiar. In the world of written tradition, the reverse is true, as is known from the famous lament of Khakheperre-sonb, an Egyptian author from the time of the Middle Kingdom:

> Had I unknown phrases,
> Sayings that are strange,
> Novel, untried words,
> Free of repetition;
> Not transmitted sayings,
> Spoken by the ancestors!

[17] Karl Jaspers, *Vom Ursprung und Ziel der Geschichte* (Zürich: Arternis, 1949); Engl. The Origin and Goal of History, trans. Michael Bullock (New Haven: Yale University Press, 1953); Shmuel N. Eisenstadt (ed.), *Kulturen der Achsenzeit. Ihre institutionelle und kulturelle Dynamik*, 3 vols. (Frankfurt: Suhrkamp, 1992), (see Introduction, n. 9); J. P. Arnason, S. N. Eisenstadt, and B. Wittrock (eds.), *Axial Civilizations and World History, Jerusalem Studies in Religion and Culture* 4 (Leiden: E. J. Brill, 2005). The historical syndrome of the "Axial Age" refers not only to textual continuity but also to the facilitation of "the evolution of ideas." We return to this subject in Chapter 7.

[18] In this context, the name of E. A. Havelock stands out. His life's work was devoted to studying this transition within the framework of Ancient Greek culture. See Chapter 7.

> I wring out my body of what it holds,
> In releasing all my words;
> For what was said is repetition,
> When what was said is said.
> Ancestor's words are nothing to boast of,
> They are found by those who come after.
> Not speaks one who spoke
> There speaks who one who will speak
> May another find what he will speak!
> Not a teller of tales after they happen,
> This has been done before;
> Nor a teller of what might be said,
> This is vain endeavor, it is lies,
> And none will recall his name to others.
> I say this in accord with what I have seen:
> From the first generation to those who come after,
> They imitate that which is past.[19]

This is a powerful lament on the pressure for innovation and variety that is inherent to written culture – a problem unique to the writer. The public expects the bard to deliver the familiar, and the writer to give them something new. In the world of oral tradition, the rank of the singer is determined only by the extent of his knowledge, for example, if he can recite 7, 20, or 300 tales. The more he knows, the higher he goes (in some memory cultures, he could even achieve the rank of prince). The singer's memory is the only means of storing knowledge. There are no other forms of accessing that knowledge, other than the prescribed forms of his performance. Repetition is therefore not a problem but a structural necessity. Without it, the tradition would break down. Innovation would mean forgetting.

Repetition only appears to be a problem when it no longer has any structural importance for the process of tradition, or when the preservation of and the access to knowledge have become independent of the singer and his ritualized performance. This is the case with

---

[19] Tablet BM 5645 rto. 2–7 ed. A. H. Gardiner, *The Admonitions of an Egyptian Sage* (Leipzig: J. C. Hinrichs, 1909), 97–101; Miriam Lichtheim, *Ancient Egyptian Literature I: The Old and Middle Kingdoms* (Berkeley: University of California Press, 1973), 146 ff.; B. G. Ockinga, "The Burden of Khackheperrecsonbu," *JEA* 69 (1983), 88–95.

writing. It is surprising that this problem reared its head so early. It was already apparent in Egypt during the very beginnings of literary culture. However, it was only in Greece that it began to influence the formation of structure, because it was the Greeks who developed a literature based on the principles of variation and innovation, thus making it a medium for the evolution of ideas and the revolution of knowledge.

Perhaps the most astonishing thing of all about Khakheperre-sonb's lament is the fact that we hear the voice of an author who regards tradition as something external, alien, and threatening, and who is in despair about his task of establishing and legitimizing his own language as something new and individual in the face of this inherited authority. Tradition for the oral poet was not external; it permeated everything he said, and it came from within him. The writing poet, on the other hand, saw it as something external; he felt the need inside to express himself in opposition to what had come down to him. Khakheperre-sonb calls his text: *The collection of words, the picking of sayings, the quest for songs in searching the heart*, and he addresses his lament to his own heart:

> Come, my heart, I speak to you,
> Answer me my sayings!
> Unravel for me what goes on in the land.

He is the first known *scrittore tormentato* (Italo Calvino) in the history of literature. His torment lies in the isolation that accompanies the act of writing. The writer, alone with himself and his heart, must "wring out" his inner self in order to find something new and individual to distinguish him from tradition. The past, as noted earlier, arises out of a break in the flow of time and out of the attempt to bridge the gap. Here we come to one of the most common and typical conditions that give rise to the past – the written record of tradition. Once it takes on the form of the written word, of the objectified text, and once its bearer is no longer filled with a spiritual stream that flows from within, there is already a break and at any time this can find its way into the conscious mind as the difference between old and new, then and now, past and present. Of course, this detachment from a tradition objectified through writing need not mean the torment, alienation, and isolation felt by Khakheperre-sonb – it may also be taken as a liberation, and then it's a very different story. Only in its written form does tradition take on a concrete shape toward which the bearer may adopt a critical approach.[20] In turn, it is only through writing that the bearer gains the necessary freedom to introduce something new, even unprecedented to the old, familiar material:

> Had I unknown phrases,
> Sayings that are strange,
> Novel, untried words,
> Free of repetition [...]

The break that writing causes in the process of tradition manifests itself in the opposition between old and new. This now becomes dramatic, in the sense that each new text must establish itself against the old and old texts run the risk of becoming obsolete. This need not be the case, however, because frequently texts are like wine – many are suitable for storage, and as the years go by, their taste and value may actually increase with age. In the written tradition, "old" carries connotations of nobility. The oral tradition could not be stored, and thus age was an alien concept for it. The particular authority and preciousness associated with old texts were recognized very early on in the written cultures of Mesopotamia and Egypt. Access to knowledge could be acquired through books, and especially through *old* books:

> Justice comes to him distilled,[21]
> Shaped in the sayings of the ancestors.
> Copy your fathers, your ancestors,
> [...]See, their words endure in books,
> Open, read them, copy their knowledge,
> He who is taught becomes skilled.[22]

Old texts, then, increased in value and in the power to illuminate, but of course they could only survive if they could be stored. From now

---

[20] This view is particularly prominent in E. A. Havelock and, following on from him, N. Luhmann. We return to this subject in connection with Greece.

[21] Literally strained or filtered, as in beer brewing.

[22] Lichtheim, "The Instruction Addressed to King Merikare," in *Ancient Egyptian Literature I*, 97–109, here 99 (see chapt. 2, n. 19). Hellmut Brunner, *Altägyptische Weisheit* (Zürich: Arternis, 1988), 142.

on, the process became the natural one of the survival of the fittest, but this did not always mean survival of the best. Decisions were often taken that had nothing to do with quality. Unquestionably the two most important texts of Egyptian literature, *The Dispute between a Man and his Ba*,[23] and *The Sun Hymn of Akhnaton*,[24] are attested to only in a single manuscript or inscription and they evidently never found their way into the stream of tradition. In the *Sun Hymn*, the reason is clear: it fell victim to the ruthless elimination of all memories connected with the Armana period. The reasons for its neglect in *The Dispute*, however, are not so clear. An astonishing number of texts that are just as important to us as the recognized classics – including *The Shipwrecked Sailor*, the papyrus Westcar, *The Admonitions of Ipuwer*[25] – can only be found in one single manuscript.[26] Obviously the formation of tradition was bound up with processes of selection, and the aging of texts with their accompanying increase in value and authority depended on the criteria underlying these processes. Writing – and this for me is a crucial point – does not in itself provide continuity. On the contrary, it brings with it the risk of oblivion, of disappearance under the dust of time; thus it may often break the continuity that is integral to oral tradition.

Textual continuity entails a framework of references that cancel out the break inherent in writing – a framework within which the texts may remain present, effective, and accessible even over thousands of years. One can distinguish between three forms of intertextual connection: commentary, emulation, and critique. Generally, commentary applies to canonical texts. Because these cannot be changed, extended,

---

[23] Berlin papyrus 3024, trans. Lichtheim, *Ancient Egyptian Literature I*, 163–169, (see chapt. 2, n. 19).

[24] Miriam Lichtheim, *Ancient Egyptian Literature II, The New Kingdom* (Berkeley: University of California Press, 1976), 96–100.

[25] All of these texts have been translated by Lichtheim, *Ancient Egyptian Literature I* (see chapt. 2, n. 19).

[26] The history of Khakheperre-sonb's reception is not much better. He is, however, represented by at least two witnesses who show that he was part of the school tradition and therefore counted as one of the "classics." Both Ipuwer and Chacheperreseneb are mentioned as "classics" on an inscribed tombstone of the Ramesside period from Saqqara; see J. Assmann, "Die Entdeckung der Vergangenheit," 488 f. (see chapt. 1, n. 17).

imitated, or criticized but stand forever fixed in their wording, variation can only take place on another level that will leave them intact. This is the level of commentary. What can be imitated, however, are classical texts. Of course these can also be interpreted or "treated" as the Alexandrian philologists might say. But a text is only classic when it becomes the model for new texts, as Homer was for Virgil, Virgil for Milton, and so on. Within the framework of scholarly discourse, criticism is directed against foundational texts. This was how Aristotle dealt with Plato, and Mencius with Confucius; it represents a rather different form of intertextual connection that I call "hypolepsis" and that will be dealt with in more detail later in the chapter on Greece. All three forms of intertextuality deal with foundational texts. In the context of written culture and textual continuity, cultural memory organizes itself around these texts, interpreting, imitating, learning, and/or criticizing them. What should be emphasized, however, is that sacred texts are in this sense not foundational, because they are not open to development or to any kind of intertextual variation. Sacred texts belong to the realm of ritual continuity and repetition.

Rituals help people to achieve a form of coherence and continuity that fits in with Nature. "Nature revolves but man advances." This basic distinction between Nature and history – as formulated by the 18-century English poet Edward Young in his *Night Thoughts* – is removed through the principle of ritual continuity. Strict repetition enables man to adapt to the cyclical structure of Nature's regeneration processes, and thus to participate reverentially in the eternal divinity of cosmic life.[27] The distinction between repetition and variation – drawn by Aristotle in *De Anima* to distinguish between man and the world of plants and animals[28] – can, however, be used recursively within the term of variation characteristic of the human world to distinguish between ritual and textual continuity:

---

[27] See J. Assmann, "Das Doppelgesicht der Zeit im altägyptischen Denken," in A. Peisl and A. Mohler (eds.), *Die Zeit* (München: Oldenbourg, 1983), 218 f., which also shows William Blake's illustration of these lines, depicting the "revolving nature" of the Egyptian symbol of the Ouroboros – the snake biting its own tail.

[28] Aristotle, *De Anima II*, 4.2. We will be looking more closely at this in Chapter 7. That there is variation also in the world of plants and animals has been shown by evolution theory, but this form of variation takes place on a much larger time scale.

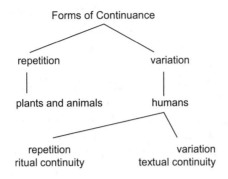

THE CANON — CLARIFYING A CONCEPT

The Classical History of Meaning

The term "canon" refers to the kind of tradition in which the content and form are as fixed and binding as they can possibly be. Nothing may be added, nothing may be taken away, and nothing may be altered. The history of this "canon formula"[29] goes back to various spheres of social action: the *true-to-life* reproduction of an event ("witness formula"), the *faithful-to-word-and-meaning* reproduction of a message ("message formula," Quecke 1977), the *word-for-word* reproduction of a text ("copyist" formula),[30] and the *literal* compliance with

---

[29] Willem C. van Unnik, "De la règle mäte prostheinai mäte aphelein dans l'histoire du canon," *Vigiliae christianae* 3 (1949), 1–36. The classical location of this in the history of the Christian canon is the 39th Easter epistle of Athanasius with the list of holy scriptures culminating in the statement: "These are the sources of salvation . . . Let no-one add (anything) to them, and let no-one take (anything) away." On the functions of the term, see Aleida Assmann, "Fiktion als Differenz," *Poetica* (1989), 242–245.

[30] In this functional context, the expression first appears in Babylonian colophons and, just as in Deuteronomy, it is in the form of an imperative: "Add nothing and take nothing away!" This is one of the measures taken as a *sauvegarde des tablettes*; see G. Offner, "A propos de la sauvegarde des tablettes en Assyro-Babylonie," *RA* 44 (1950), 135–143. Hubert Cancik, *Mythische und historische Wahrheit*, Stuttgart Bibelstudien 48, 1970 and Michael Fishbane, "Varia Deuteronomica," *ZAW* 84 (1972), 349–352 also draw attention to parallels with Deuteronomy. This function is the earliest recorded, in the *Plague Prayers of Mursilis*, a Hittite text from the 13th century BCE. It is the text of a treaty, and Mursilis declares:

[But] to this tablet
I have added no word
Nor did I take any away.

(E. Laroche, *Collection des textes Hittites* No. 379 = KUB XXXI 121).

laws or contracts ("contract formula").[31] One should not, however, draw too sharp a distinction between the last two in this list, because evidently the process of tradition in the Ancient Orient was viewed in terms of laws and contracts. There was no major difference between the word-for-word copying of a text and literal compliance with its content. The Babylonians developed an acute sense of protectiveness towards the written text, and there was sometimes a profusion of colophons – consisting of blessings or curses – to defend them against damage or against corruption (Offner 1950). The same formulae were used to seal contracts. Just as the blessing and the curse obliged the signatories to keep an agreement, the copyists were obliged to copy texts faithfully. The ethics of their vocation were in the same category as those of compulsory laws. Their task of "handing down" entailed an obligation that has the character of a binding contract to be faithful to the text – even if the text itself was not a contract but, for an example, an epic poem.[32]

This legalistic concept of textual tradition, starting in Babylon, spread to the West, and persisted until Late Antiquity. Thus we read, for example, in the *Letter of Aristeas* about the successful completion of the Hebrew Bible into Greek (the *Septuagint*): After the books had been read, the priests and the elders of the translators and the Jewish community and the leaders of the people stood up and said, that because so excellent and sacred and accurate a translation had been made, it was only right that it should remain as it was and no alteration should be made in it. And when the whole company expressed their approval, they bade them pronounce a curse in accordance with their custom upon any one who should make any alteration either by adding anything, or changing in any way whatever any of the words that had been written, or making any omission. This was a very wise precaution to ensure that the book might be preserved for all the future time unchanged.[33]

---

[31] Cancik, *Mythische und historische Wahrheit*, 85 ff. (see chapt. 2, n. 30), sees it differently, and believes the expression here and in Deuteronomy refers to the copyist's formula. The original function relating to agreements should be added to the four listed by A. Assmann "Fiktion als Differenz," 242–245 (see chapt. 2, n. 29): messenger, copyist, canon, and witness.

[32] In connection with the Erra Epic, the canon formula appears for the first time in a colophon cf. Fishbane, "Varia Deuteronomica" (see chapt. 2, n. 30).

[33] *The Letter of Aristeas*, ed. R. H. Charles (Oxford: Clarendon Press, 1913), §§ 310–312.

This textual canonization by way of contractual obligation even extended to the reading and interpretation of a text. The Gnostic Gospel *The Ogdoad and the Ennead* (Nag Hammadi Codex VI No. 6) ends with lengthy instructions about the writing and protection of the text. Here, also encountered is the legalistic curse formula; but it applies to the reader and not the copyist: "Let us write a curse upon the book, so that the name will not be misused for evil purposes by those who read the book, and so that they shall not oppose the works of fate!" (Mahé 1978, 84 f.)

The link between faithfulness and reproduction acts as the common denominator for the different uses of the formulae. The attitude of a following second party (*secundus* and *sequi* [= follow]), who must stick rigidly and resolutely to what has gone before, is repeatedly described. This approach even applies to the musical canon: voices must "follow" one another and emulate precisely what has been sung by their predecessors. The canon therefore refers to the ideal of zero deviation in the sequence of repetitions. The proximity to what I have described as *ritual continuity* is self-evident. The canon may therefore be defined as "the continuance of ritual continuity through the medium of written tradition."

The history of the canon formula, however, does not derive from ritual but from the law. The earliest records by far go back to documents that demanded the utmost faithfulness in following the laws and contractual obligations. Such instructions are to be found in Deuteronomy[34] and, earlier still, in the Hammurapi Codex and in Hittite texts.[35] Thus the canon may also be defined as the transposition of an ideal, rooted in the sphere of the law, concerning binding obligation and faithful rendition throughout the central field of written tradition. Ritual and the law have in common the fact that they pin human conduct down to a prescribed set of rules, and the people affected are put in the role of the secundus whose duty it is to follow. A glance at basic texts of the Jewish canon will show that they cover both ritual and law, and the same link can be seen throughout the history of Jewish canonization, because the two decisive phases – the

---

[34] Deuteronomy 4.2; see Johannes Leipoldt and Siegfried Morenz, *Heilige Schriften. Betrachtungen zur Religionsgeschichte der antiken Mittelmeerwelt* (Leipzig: Harrassowitz, 1953), 57 f.

[35] I look at this more closely in Chapter 6.

Babylonian exile and the destruction of the Second Temple – meant a loss not only of legal sovereignty and political identity, but also of ritual continuity. Both could only be saved through the form of the canon that survived these two ruptures. The original canon and the original Deuteronomy as a kind of "portable Fatherland" (Heine) rescued Israel as a connective structure through 50 years of exile, despite the loss of land and temple (Crüsemann 1987).[36] After the destruction of the Second Temple in 70 AD, the three-part, twenty-two or twenty-four-book canon of the Tanakh[37] – which had already emerged during the Hellenic period – was finally concluded (Leiman 1976). At last the canon replaced those institutions within whose framework and indeed within whose foundation the accepted traditions had first arisen: the temple and the synedrium.[38]

The concept of the canon is so important for the mechanisms and media of cultural continuity that we should take a closer look at its history. Here, we clearly have an inseparable combination of a Greek word and a Hebrew situation. The first thing to note, however, is that the Greek word itself is derived from a Semitic term[39] that was imported, along with its subject matter, into the world of the Greeks. *Kanôn* is connected to *kanna* that means reed or cane, and this in turn goes back to the Hebrew *qaneh*, Aramaic *qanja*, Babylonian/Assyrian *qanu*, and, finally, Sumerian *gin*: the genus of reed *arundo donax* that (similar to bamboo) is used in the production of sticks and poles. This is the basic meaning of *kanôn*. It is in fact a building tool and means "straight pole, rod, level, ruler" (with measurements).

From this very concrete starting point, the word took on a variety of associated meanings that grouped themselves around four main

---

[36] See Moshe Halbertal, *People of the Book. Canon, Meaning, and Authority* (Cambridge MA: Harvard University Press, 1997).

[37] The Hebrew term "Tanakh" is an abbreviation for the three parts of the Jewish Bible: T(orah: Pentateuch) – N(evi'îm: Prophets) – Kh(etuvîm: hagiographies).

[38] See Arnold Goldberg, "Die Zerstörung von Kontext als die Voraussetzung für die Kanonisierung religiöser Texte im rabbinischen Judentum," in A. and J. Assmann (ed.), *Kanon und Zensur*, 200–211, (see chapt. 1, n. 48).

[39] The Semitic etymology has been disputed (in my view incorrectly) by Hjalmar Frisk, *Griech. Etymol. Wörterbuch* (Heidelberg: Winter, 1973), I, 780. For the basic history of the term, see Herbert Oppel, *Kanon. Zur Bedeutungsgeschichte des Wortes und seinen lateinischen Entsprechungen (regula – norma)* (Leipzig: Dieterich, 1937).

categories that I am designating by letter a, b, c, or d, and corresponding to the next four subheads in this book:

- measure, ruler, criterion (a)
- model (b)
- rule, norm (c)
- table, list (d)

Measure, Ruler, Criterion (a). Around the middle of the 5th century
BCE, the Greek sculptor Polykleitos wrote a treatise under the title
Kanon, setting out the ideal proportions of the human body.[40] According to later accounts, he also made a statue to which he gave the same
name, putting these figures into practice and thereby providing a
model – my category (b). This concept of the canon continues to be
used today in art history, indicating "a metric system that allows us to
deduce from the measurements of one section those of the whole, and
from those of the whole to deduce those of the smallest part."[41] Polykleitos, however, also had something else in mind. The parts are not
only proportionate to the whole so that they can be calculated down
to the last detail[42] (this is the Egyptian principle[43]), but they also form

---

[40] Diels, *Vorsokratiker* 28B1 and 2. The following quotation is a good illustration of the
meaning of this canon in the context of the quest for precision (akribeia): "Success
depends on many numerical ratios, whereby one tiny detail may be decisive." On
Polykleitos's canon see Jörg Weber, *Kanon und Methode. Zum Prozeß zivilisatorischer
Begründung* (Würzburg: Königshausen and Neumann 1986), 42–49 and also Adolf
Borbein, "Polyklet," *Göttinger Gelehrte Anzeigen* 234 (1982), 184–241. Tonio Hölscher,
"Tradition und Geschichte. Zwei Typen der Vergangenheit am Beispiel der griechischen Kunst," in J. Assmann and T. Hölscher (eds.), *Kultur und Gedächtnis*, 140 f.
(see chapt. 1, n. 17) connects Polykleitos's work and with it the Greek theory of
art to the overall intellectual situation at that time, as a revolutionary period of lost
traditions and radically liberated possibilities of action. The new latitude gave rise to
an increased need for orientation, and so the overthrown traditions were replaced
by the rational canon.

[41] Oppel, *Kanon*, 48–50 (see chapt. 2, n. 39). After Galen, Polykleitos himself named his
statue "Canon," to provide a model illustration of his theory. According to Pliny, *N.H.*
34, 55 ("Polyclitus . . . doryphorum fecit et quem canona artifices vocant liniamenta
artis ex eo petentes veluti a lege quadem") it was the artists of the Imperial Age
that named Doryphorus "Canon," because they regarded the statue as a normative
model.

[42] *Dictionnaire de l'académie des Beaux Arts III* (Paris: Firmin Didot, 1858), 41.

[43] See the monograph by Whitney Davis, *The Canonical Tradition in Egyptian Art*
(Cambridge: Cambridge University Press, 1989), with a detailed bibliography.

a functional or animated whole, a "system" (*systema*). The body must seem as if animated from within. The invention of the *contrapposto* served this purpose; it made stillness visible as potential movement.

The structure that we encounter here is quite typical, namely: the special connectability (*Anschliessbarkeit*) or imitability of something that has been constructed according to new rules that combine strictness of form with practicality. The same applies to all those works of art that have become models for their genre and hence are called *classic* – such as Corelli's trio-sonatas, and Haydn's string quartets op. 33 (L. Finscher 1988). The canonical principle only fulfills its function as a form of cultural memory through imitative, neoclassical reversion in the form of *mimesis, aemulatio, imitatio* (E. A. Schmidt 1987, 252 ff.): it becomes the focal point of the restrospective search for orientation. Polykleitos was canonized because he had created a canon. Canonization is not an arbitrary matter of reception, but it is the fulfillment and release of a potential contained within the work itself, using a strict form and a binding set of rules.[44]

The philosopher Democritus wrote a book with the same title around the same time as Polykleitos, and Epicurus also wrote a book with the same title at a later date (Oppel 1937, 33–39). This book was about measuring reliable knowledge – criteria for distinguishing between true and false, reality and illusion. Euripides used the term "canon" to differentiate "straight" from "crooked" in a moral sense.[45] The link with the concrete "ruler" is clear here. One of the more technical uses can be found in sophist stylistics, in connection with "isokolia," with carefully calculated prose, using colons of exactly the same length.[46] In the musicology of the Pythagoreans (also known as

---

[44] One must distinguish between "connectability" (*Anschliessbarkeit*) and "repeatability." Egyptian art is based on repetition, and it belongs to the category of "ritual continuity" in which there is no compulsion to vary the pattern. Western art, on the other hand, is geared toward connectability (i.e., to imitation conditioned by variation). Thus, the classical work is not only strict in form but it is also formally autonomous and reflexive. Haydn's string quartets op. 33 are like a treatise on the art of composition, and Polykleitos's Doryphoros was actually accompanied by just such a treatise.

[45] Oppel, *Kanon*, 23–25 (see chapt. 2, n. 39); Electra 50 ff. ("Canon of Reason").

[46] Ibid., 2–23. See Aristophanes' parody in *The Frogs* on Euripides' verse rhythms (797 ff.):

> They bring plumb lines and rules for the verses,
> And forms of bricks to fit in,
> And set squares and circles, Euripides
> Will measure the tragedies line by line.

"canonicians"), the "harmonic canon" indicates a monochord used to measure tonic intervals according to the length of the string (Oppel 1937, 17–20).

The quest for absolute precision (*akribeia*) – the idea of an *instrument* that can provide *correct norms* both for knowledge and for production of art works, sounds, sentences, and actions – acts as the common denominator for the technical and the intellectual use of the canon. Architecture provided the original site for this ideal of precision. This was the living context of the instrument of the canon, and it supplied the *tertium comparationis* for all its transferred meanings. *Akribeia* entails the most exact plans, calculations, and realizations through form and measurement, including numbers, directions, perfect straightness, or perfect curves. Everything is geared to order, purity, and harmony, so that chance is eliminated and there is no unchecked sloppiness, corner cutting, or deviation from the norm.

"'Rulers [*kanosi*], weights [*stathmois*] measures, and numbers [*metrois kai arithmois*], are everywhere in use, so that the random and haphazard [*to eike kai hos etyche*] may find no place in any production."[47]

Model (b). The application of the concept of the canon to a person or type of person who acts as a model for correct behavior originally goes back to Aristotelian ethics. The "sensible" person (*phronimos*) is characterized as the "canon of conduct" (*Protreptikos* fr 52 Rose; Oppel 1937, 40). The modern use of the word dates from the Augustan era, when it was applied with exactly the same meaning to the classical theory of mimesis. Lysias was regarded as the canon of the purest Attic language – that of the law courts, "dihegesis"; Thucydides was the canon of historiography, and so forth (Oppel 1937, 44–47). Related terms in this context are *horos* (boundary) and *paradeigma* (example). The model sets out the boundaries of a particular genre or an ethical norm, and the *classics* embody these timeless norms in their purest form. They provide the criteria for both artistic production and aesthetic judgment.

---

47 Plutarch, *De Fortuna*, 996, in Plutarch's *Moralia*, in Fifteen Volumes, II, trans. by F. C. Babbitt (London: William Heinemann, 1962), 85.

The notion of measurement acts as a common denominator for (a) and (b), (a) being more concerned with precision, and (b) with norms. The idea of normative works by normative authors is also part of the contemporary understanding of the canon, and all judgmental aesthetics refer to the great works as objectifications of perfection. *Index* [the pointing finger] is the name of a similar canon established by Quintilian. Other terms used are *ordo* and *numerus* (see (d)).

Rule, Norm (c). This meaning is only one short step away from (b). The model illustrates the norm, but the latter itself can only be established by way of rules. Thus the law itself is a canon, that is, the prescriptive basis for communal life and behavior, as opposed to the arbitrary will of rulers in monarchies and oligarchies.[48] In this sense, the Decalogue is also described by Philon and other Jewish writers as a canon.[49] Panaitios uses the same word in relation to ethics, when he speaks of the *kanón tes mesótetos = regula mediocritatis* (Oppel 1937, 88). This is the language of the early church, whose *kanón tes aletheías = regula veritatis, regula fidei* denotes the essence of faith – the norm against which everything else should be measured.[50] All synodal decisions – for example, fixed rules concerning penance – form part of "canon law" (Oppel 1937, 71 f.) In all these contexts, the term is related to rules and norms that govern different aspects of life; thus, the earlier use that referred to grammatical rules during the Augustan era gradually began to disappear (Oppel 1937, 64–66).

Table, List (d). In Imperial Rome, canon was the name given to the tables of astronomers and chroniclers, which were meant to provide a sound basis for reckoning time and for writing history, respectively. In the 2nd century, the mathematician Claudius Ptolemaios (known

---

[48] For further documentation, see Oppel, *Kanon*, 51–57 (see chapt. 2, n. 38).

[49] Ibid., 57–60. In Philon, the "canon" refers to the Decalogue and not to the whole Torah. Elsewhere, all individual laws are referred to as *kanones*.

[50] Kurt Aland, *Das Problem des neutestamentlichen Kanons*, in E. Käsemann (ed.), *Das Neue Testament als Kanon* (Göttingen: Vandenhoeck & Ruprecht, 1970), 145 f.; A. M. Ritter, "Die Entstehung des neutestamentlichen Kanons," in A. and J. Assmann (eds.), *Kanon und Zensur*, 93–99, 97 f., (see chapt. 1, n. 48).

to us as Ptolemy) called his time-reckoning tables *prócheiroi kanónes*; these included the "Kings' Canon" (*kanón basileíon*) – a list of kings' names beginning with the Babylonian King Nabonassar. The term is still used in English to denote the Egyptian and Mesopotamian lists of kings, but this usage generally tends to be confined to binding, normative contexts; in other contexts, words such as "list," "catalogue," "inventory," and so on are used.

The lists of classic, "model" authors, orators, historians, playwrights, philosophers, and others, as established for Alexandrian and Imperial grammarians, were not called canon in those times. Nor were the lists of sacred texts so hotly debated[51] by the early church with regard to their suitability for religious services (E. A. Schmidt 1987).[52] This fact alone emphasizes how the concept has changed its meaning since Antiquity.

All the original uses of the word "canon" were linked to concrete meanings, and therefore, if we are looking for common features, we ought to consider their actual function. It would seem that the architectural term – and here the crucial factor is the pole that serves as a level to ensure that the stones in a wall are properly aligned – underlies all the metaphorical applications. If this canon is provided with a scale of measurements, it can also serve as a ruler.[53] In other words, initially the canon was an *instrument* used for the particular purpose of architectural aligning and measuring – a meaning that can be extended to that of normative action. Such an instrument not only registers what is but it also prescribes what has to be, in terms of straight lines and precise distances.

It is characteristic of these early uses of the concept that they always involve measurements of some sort:

Because of this metaphorical reference, the instrumental aspect was decisive in Antiquity. However, because it denoted the right lines to follow, there was a natural progression toward tables or lists. Initially of

---

[51] See E. Käsemann's collection *Das Neue Testament als Kanon* (see chapt. 2, n. 50), and elsewhere.

[52] In the oldest known list of canons, the Muratori fragment, canonical books are defined as "se publicare in ecclesia populo...potest"; those "which make things known to the people in the community" (i.e., that may be read out during the service).

[53] A *kanon tes analogias*, or "measure for proportions."

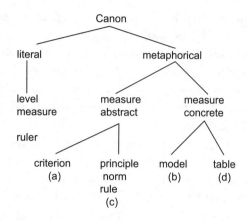

minor importance, the Church's use of this concept in relation to the list of "canonical" texts made these a central element in the modern meaning. As seen earlier, the tables of the astronomers and chroniclers were used as instruments to calculate time, and these followed the pattern of intervals marked out by architectural and musical devices. The astronomical canon offered chronological scales based either on natural events like the circulation of the stars or on historical events like games, festivals, reigns, and regimes. Conversely, in the absence of this instrumental context, the term was not applied to the lists we use it for today: those drawn up by the Alexandrian grammarians to name the classical poets, authors, orators, philosophers, and so forth. Such lists did not provide model proportions or measurements, and in the classical meaning of the word they were not canonical; only individuals could qualify, not groups. If you wanted to make a speech, you would choose Lysias or Isocrates as your model, not the list of the top ten speakers. The latter was not a canon but in Greek *choros*, in Latin *ordo*, *numerus*, or *index*. This is also why such groupings were not linked to exclusivity in Antiquity, and those not on the list were not consigned to some "apocrypha."[54] Today, the term has been reversed and is applied to groups and never to the individual work or author. Thus the list may be the canon, but not Lysias or Thucydides.

---

[54] Emphasized by E. A. Schmidt, "Historische Typologie der Orientierungsfunktionen von Kanon in der griechischen und römischen Literatur," in A. and J. Assmann (eds.), *Kanon und Zensur* 246–258, 247 (see chapt. 1, n. 48).

The More Recent History of the Term

If we disregard those meanings of canon that were already specialized in Antiquity and have come down to us unchanged – for
example, canonical law, Polykleitos's ideal proportions, the lists of
kings – we can clearly see that the term underwent a complete transformation that arose from its metaphorical sense. How did this come
about?

The prime cause of the reversal was the Church's use of the word.[55]
The dispute over which of the sacred texts should be authoritatively
recognized as such went on for more than two hundred years, though
the term "canon" was never used. At the time, it was mainly confined to
(c), that is, the Mosaic Law, individual synodal decisions, or the basic
principles of life and faith (*kanón tes alethaías, regula veritatis, regula
fidei*). But in the 4th century AD, the discussion was ended through
binding resolutions passed by the synod (canons), and the list was
fixed for good. It was given the name "canon," but not as a table in
the sense of (d); this was a binding decision with all the force of law,
as in (c), which represented a strange merger between the list, as in
(d), and the obligatory, foundational, and formative principle of (c).
Thus, the idea of the *textual canon* was born; this constitutes the most
concrete and so, to a degree, the most literal meaning of the word
today:

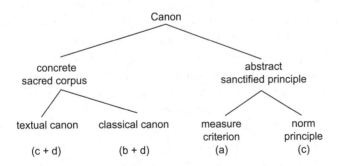

55 Oppel, *Kanon*, 69f., (see chapt. 2, n. 39); Rudolf Pfeiffer, *History of Classical Scholarship
from the Beginnings to the End of the Hellenistic Age* (Oxford: Clarendon Press, 1968),
207. The first documentary evidence is probably that of Eusebius's *History of the
Church* (*hist. eccl.* 6.25,3).

Canon and Code. If we ignore for the moment the meaning "ruler, measure, criterion," we can see at a glance that the term has become far more concrete in terms of its content and its values. When we see the word "canon," we immediately think of holy scriptures or binding norms, and not of gauges or rulers. The instrumental meaning, related to astronomical and chronological tables and grammatical rules, disappeared, as the term was enriched by the categories of norms, values, and general applicability. These astronomical and chronological tables and grammatical rules do not involve norms or values. They only refer to what is, rather than to what ought to be. That is why, in contradistinction to Antiquity, we distinguish between canons and rules. The latter are a necessary precondition for communication and hence to all forms of society and meaning, and you will find them wherever people form a community. For these rules, we have the term "code." By contrast, canon does not denote any anthropological universal, but it does stand for a special case – that of a principle, norm, or value that is far more binding than an individual code such as the grammatical rules of a language. The only time we might possibly speak of canon in such a context would be in relation to a highly normative grammar, that is, an aesthetically or ideologically conditioned form of language. The point here is that the term is never applied to natural norms (like those of grammatical acceptability), but is used for the not self-evident norm of a particular kind of perfection. It is what we might call a code of the second degree, in so far as it comes to us from outside, or from above, in the form of a rule imposed on and additional to the internal (and hence natural or self-evident) systems of discipline that govern our social communication and our formation of meaning. We only speak of a canon when the code of the first degree, that is, that which underlies all our social communication, is made subject to a value-oriented code of the second degree.

In this context, the civil code is not a canon, whereas a constitution is. The latter lays down principles that must be observed and so, to a certain extent, may be regarded as sanctified. These principles underlie all further laws but they are not open to processes of decision because they themselves must provide the basis for all decisions. D. Conrad (1987) therefore defines the canon as a "norm of the second degree."

The Principle of Sanctification: A Unifying Formula, or Autonomous Laws.
This brings us to the norm of norms – into which the original meaning of abstract measurement finally evolved. We can now speak of
the canon as a principle of sanctification, linking diverse elements
together in a single unit. We have seen that it has derived its sense
of rule or norm from its use by the Church, which was the first to
lay claim to such binding canonical (i.e., based on the truth) and
indisputable authority, and which, by tying its members to the canon,
produced a monocentric culture. Characteristic of such cultures is
their all-embracing guidance; they come up with a unifying formula
that brings all the different codes of cultural communication together,
leaving no space for independent thought or discussion.

At this point, we must return to the category of "measure, criterion,"
in order to focus on a paradox within the modern terminology. The
canon need not only refer to the single, overriding formula for cultural
unity; it may also work the other way round, referring to the basis of
particular orders that go against the overall authority of state, church,
or tradition.

By invoking a canon, as for instance Stalinism invoked Socialist
Realism, the state authority in the form of its censors may persuade its
artists to toe the line;[56] but by invoking a different canon, for example,
that of "pure reason," it is possible to think independently of state,
church, and so forth.[57] One is the principle of cultural heteronomy
that subjects individual cultural practices to an overriding discipline or
dogma; the other is the principle of cultural autonomy that promotes
differentiation of discourse, independently of the general cultural
context. This kind of canon guarantees that principles may be freed
from the authority of decrees and diktats, and instead be subject to
independent testing of the evidence. The norms are also canonical
here, because they are not up for discussion. However, they are not
authoritarian and imposed by force; in this case they are rational and
they gain consensus by proving their own validity.

---

[56] Hans Günther, "Die Lebensphasen eines Kanons - am Beispiel des sozialistischen
Realismus," in A. and J. Assmann (eds.), *Kanon und Zensur*, 138–148 (see chapt. 1,
n. 48).

[57] Kathleen Wright, "Kant und der Kanon der Kritik," in A. and J. Assmann (eds.),
Kanon und Zensur, 326–335 (see chapt. 1, n. 48).

It is this latter concept of the canon that lies at the basis of scholarship and provides the roots of new disciplines. Kant talks of the canon in philosophy, J. S. Mill of the canon in logic, and the "canon of the four rules of interpretation" plays an important role in jurisprudence (Conrad 1987, 51). Polykleitos's future-oriented treatise entitled *Kanon* may perhaps also be classified as marking the basis and boundaries of artistic autonomy. With every imposition of canonical norms in spheres such as philosophy, ethics, logic, philology, art, and so forth, culture loses part of its coherence and correspondingly increases in variety and complexity.

The paradox of the modern concept lies, then, in the fact that it can be used to engender both autonomy and uniformity. Whereas the classical and modern enlightenment called on the canon of truth as a principle with which to differentiate between codes, the medieval church and modern totalitarian regimes invoke the canon of authority in order to coordinate all codes. In both cases – and I call this the common denominator – it is not simply a matter of norms, but of the norm of norms, the foundation, the ultimate criterion, the "principle of sanctification."

The Sanctified Corpus: The Canon and the Classics. In the 4th century AD, when the church began to use the term "canon" to denote those writings it considered to be sacred, the term underwent the decisive changes that led to its present meaning. From that time onward, it was linked to the idea of a holy heritage, "holy" in the sense of an absolute and binding authority as well as something untouchable – nothing should be added, altered, or taken away. Of course the texts that we now call the canon go much further back than the 4th century, and indeed the debate over what constituted the Holy Writ began as early as the 2nd century, and that in turn would have been unthinkable without the precedent set by the Jews and the canonization of the Hebrew Bible in the 1st and 2nd centuries.[58] There were, however, major differences between the Jewish and the Christian concepts of

---

[58] Sid Z. Leiman, *The Canonization of Hebrew Scripture: The Talmudic and Midrashic Evidence* (Hamden: Archon Books, 1976); Frank Crüsemann, "Das 'portative Vaterland.' Struktur und Genese des alttestamentlichen Kanons," in A. and J. Assmann (eds.), *Kanon und Zensur*, 63–79 (see chapt. 1, n. 48).

what was binding in the sacred texts and of what should therefore be legitimately handed down. For the Jews, the main criterion was verbal inspiration,[59] whereas for the Christians it was apostolic status, that is, the authority of witnesses. The Jews viewed the text as direct revelation; the Christians, however, saw it as the path to revelation that through the preaching of the Gospels was essentially oral. In terms of the literalness of the texts and the legitimacy of tradition, there are further differences between Catholic and Protestant theology. However, the concept of the theological canon is broad enough not only to cover such differences but also to be applied to every other collection of sacred texts, so long as they are considered by their adherents to be authoritative and untouchable. The Muslim Koran and the Buddhist (Hinayana) Pali canon are two obvious examples.

The modern theological concept of the textual canon now occupies the place that in Antiquity was held by the builder's gauge – the most vivid and concrete usage, and therefore an excellent metaphor for the more figurative use of the term. What we have before us now when we talk of fixed lines and traditional ideas is not a measuring instrument but the Bible, although we relate the concept not to the sacred but to the classic in the sense of the model that provides us with norms, measurements, and values. It embodies our veneration of the old that in Asia and also in Egypt takes the form of ancestor worship, and in Western countries relates to an intertextual dialogue between authors of the past and present. If it is linked to a definitive and unalterable piece of tradition, either sacred (i.e., religious) or classical (i.e., literary, philosophical, or scientific), it can be said that the religious and the classical canon both function in the same way.

However, the classical canon has still other roots than the theological. The former links up with the old meaning of measure and criterion, both for the production and, especially, for the judgment of art. It answers the question, What can we use as a guide?

59 There is no word in Hebrew for canon; there are only expressions that denote canonical texts. A particularly important and illuminating expression is the one used by the Jamnia synod: canonical texts [as] "dirty the hands" (i.e., they are as untouchable as sacred objects). See Goldberg, "Die Zerstörung von Kontext," 209, n. 4, (see chapt. 2, n. 38).

The canon defines the proportions of what is beautiful, great, or important, and it does so by pointing to works that embody and exemplify the relevant values. But it not only points backward to the reception of a selected work; it also looks forward to an expanding array of possible connections. It encompasses the idea of the sacred together with guidelines for production and for judgment, and creates a "principle of sanctification."

Any selective acceptance of a tradition, that is, any act of reception, also entails recognition of a specific set of values. Reception and values condition each other, and thus the concept of canon naturally refers to both at the same time. This is the basis of its terminological fertility. In its reference to an unchangeable body of sacred texts, it automatically evokes the directional, normative force of those texts, and by highlighting the criteria and obligatory values behind the production of art, it also draws attention to the works that exemplify those values.

On the other hand it is this double meaning – which is not inherent but only developed through its theological application to the canon of Holy Writ – that gives it a degree of ambiguity. This becomes clear if we examine a different, narrower meaning of the term, that is, if we apply the distinction recursively and set it within its opposing contexts. In the broader sense, it opposes tradition; in the narrower it opposes the classics:

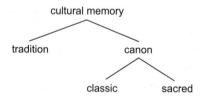

The decisive criterion for the distinction between tradition and canon is the exclusion of alternatives and the "fencing-in" of what has been selected. For the distinction between classic and canon, the vital factor is the evaluation of what has been excluded. The exclusion, however, does not in any way condemn the nonclassic as bad, inferior, or "heretical." Judgment is only a question of authority, connectability, and decisiveness. Above all, classical selections are not absolute or binding. Other eras, other schools, will make other selections. The canon of the classics and of classicism is always open to change, and

every period has its own canon.[60] Such shifts are only possible when
that which has been excluded remains dormant in the cultural memory and does not disappear under the weight of total condemnation.
The latter represents the other end of the canonical spectrum, in
which whatever is excluded is the subject of negative discrimination.
Even under these conditions, Christian tradition has managed to preserve an astonishing number of apocryphal texts (including pseude-
pigraphic Syrian, Ethiopian, and Slavic scripts and heretical writings
explicitly opposing the Church Fathers). In the rabbinical tradition
on the other hand, every item of Hebrew literature that has not made
it into the canon has been systematically expunge from memory.

Summary

The intrusion of the Church brought about a dramatic change in
the meaning of the canon, but even this was not so absolute as to
completely eliminate the original roots of the term. The history of
the canon is a kind of palimpsest, in which Judeo-Christian culture
superimposes itself on Greco-Roman and the two merge into an inseparable unit. We can see how, from a cultural point of view, the universal,
instrumental principle evolved through a series of enhancements and
restrictions that resulted in giving the original potentialities of the
concept a quite new turn.

The Accentuation of Invariance: From the Precise to the Sacrosanct. There is
a common factor in the different ancient and modern uses of the word
"canon," and that is invariance. No matter which meaning is adopted,
it offers a secure point of reference, providing uniformity, precision,
and coherence, and at the same time excluding arbitrariness, chance,
and disunity. Invariance is achieved through guidance either by way
of abstract rules and norms or through concrete models (people, art
works, texts). It may be applied to different cultural spheres – literary
genres, rhetoric, philosophy – or to practical realities such as socially
binding laws or sacred texts.

The history of the word *kanón* has already revealed to us a whole
range of different situations, in which classical culture "opted for

---

[60] E. A. Schmidt, "Historische Typologie" (see chapt. 2, n. 54) draws attention to this
point.

invariance," and in which the term took on ever greater complexity. During the Greek enlightenment of the 5th century BCE, it embodied precision of thought as opposed to the richly varied imprecision of mythical thinking; at the same time, through the rise of democracy it took on the task of expressing law-based continuity, in opposition to the arbitrary will of tyrants and oligarchs. Then came Alexandrian and especially Imperial classicism and, during these periods, it embodied the selective and normative model of tradition. Finally, the early Church, especially because of the proliferation of revelatory literature, found itself having – after centuries of prevarication – to take a binding decision with regard to what should and should not be chosen as its Holy Writ; this transformed the canon into the embodiment of a closed and invariable collection of texts of the highest authority, imposing the most rigid obligations as opposed to the ever flowing stream of new revelations in an ever open tradition.

We must, however, distinguish between the quest for invariance through precision and the quest for security through stabilization. The former requires recourse to rational norms, but this is prevented in the latter. The finality of an authoritative decision (e.g., by a committee) guarantees invariance, although this can only remain firm if the subject matter is taboo and acts as proof against any further test or decision. In this sense, invariance means sanctification. Thus the meaning of canon shifts from what is right to what is sacrosanct. Norms are then removed from the forum of reasoning and public consensus, and are subject to a higher authority.[61]

Controlling Variance: The Binding Force of Reason. The question, "What can we use as a guide?," which the canon answers, becomes pressing when conventional measures are no longer adequate to deal with a given situation. This occurs especially when there is a dramatic increase in the number of possible actions open to us. Already considered, the most far-reaching instance of this increase is the transition from repetition to variation as embodied in the switch from ritual to textual continuity. In the framework of written

---

[61] In this context, the distinction between legality and authority is particularly important, as elaborated by Dieter Conrad, "Zum Normcharakter von 'Kanon' in rechtswissenschaftlicher Perspektive," in A. and J. Assmann (eds.), *Kanon und Zensur*, 46–61, 55f. (see chapt. 1, n. 48).

culture, tradition lost its no-alternative self-evidence and in principle became open to change. The same, however, applies to other spheres: an important technological or artistic discovery, or on the negative side the disappearance of traditional norms (like tonality in music), opens up a vast new range of possibilities, and this in turn creates the need to rein in the principle of "anything goes." We fear loss of meaning through entropy. In the 5th century BCE, Greece experienced a whole complex of far-reaching political, technological, artistic, and intellectual innovations. As a result, tradition lost its binding force, creating a need for some kind of "precision" (*akribeia*), that is, for a "generalisation of semantic orientation that made it possible to fix an identical meaning for different partners in different situations, and from this to draw the same or similar conclusions" (Luhmann). And so the Greeks, having lost their traditional forms of orientation, looked for universally binding rules and norms in order to compensate for the insecurity that arose from the decline of casuistry, particularly in art[62] (Polykleitos), ethics (Euripides), philosophy (Democritus), and politics (Archytas of Tarent). This led to the foundation of new disciplines and hence to an increased cultural complexity through forms of discourse that set their own rules. In the context of canonization, this was a movement of innovation with new laws and axioms, and not one of tradition that would have entailed reinforcing the old laws and sanctifying existing conventions.

Accentuating the Borders: Polarization. As a general, independent guide, the "plumb-line" of the canon draws a clear line between what is "A" and what is not "A." This is its prime function. It separates the straight from the crooked, the conventional from the deviant, the good from the bad, the beautiful from the ugly, the true from the false, the just from the unjust. The whole idea of the border (*horos*) that Oppel rightly considers to be at the heart of the canon is geared to this binary schema that prestructures all possible operations into two values. The code that governed 5th-century Greece was precisely this binary principle or criterion.

---

[62] In this context, the distinction between legality and authority is particularly important, as elaborated by Conrad, ibid., 55 f.

The borders drawn by the intellectual canon have their equivalent in social and historical realities. The evolution of the term "canon" and of the historical phenomena connected with it – the Hebrew Bible, the Buddhist Pali canon, and so on. – can be divided into different periods that were marked by intense areas of conflict between and even within cultures. In relation to the concept first put forward by the Greek sculptor Polykleitos, T. Hölscher has reconstructed the 5th-century battlefront between the old and the new that was formed as a result of radical innovations that departed from tradition. The Hebrew Bible is another paradigm, as it was also fixed during a time of deep cultural conflict – initially between Hellenism and Judaism, which we can call an intercultural clash that followed earlier intercultural clashes (whose memory is preserved in ancient texts): between Israel and Egypt, Assyria, and Babylon – in short, between Israel and "the peoples." This was followed by internal cultural conflicts between the Sadducees and the Pharisees, the Samaritans, the Essenians, the Qumran community, and later the Christians – with the Pharisees eventually emerging as the winners. There were similar clashes during the early history of the Christian Church. Such internal, cultural schisms result in the formation of a canon.

In this context, the semantic expansion of the term led to a wide range of consequences. One can and should draw an historical line to distinguish between the canonical and the apocryphal (initially as a value judgment separating the essential from the non essential); this divides orthodoxy and heresy, which is not a matter of us and them, but of friend and foe. As this guideline was no longer confined to objects and situations, but was extended to people as well, decisions now had to be made in relation to existence itself, that is, to matters of life and death.[63]

Accentuating Values: The Creation of Identity

Times of internal cultural polarization, when traditions are broken and people must decide which order to follow, result in the formation

---

[63] I deal with this dynamics in *Moses the Egyptian. The Memory of Egypt in Western Monotheism* (Cambridge, MA: Harvard University Press, 1997), and *The Price of Monotheism* (Stanford: Stanford University Press, 2010).

of canons. In such situations, the canon embodies each competing order, and each canon lays claim to being the best or indeed the only true tradition. Whoever subscribes to it, automatically subscribes to a normative definition of one's self or to an "identity" that will be in harmony with the demands of reason or of revelation. In this respect, canon and "conversion" belong together.[64]

The distinction between A and "non-A" is far from being the end of the canonical story. To become a canon, A must be linked to a set of incontrovertible values towards which people must aspire. It therefore also incorporates a motivational force, the ultimate goal of which is truth, justice, beauty, uprightness, communality, love, and so on. Without this motivational perspective, no one would subject one's self to the normative restrictions. If we use the canon to answer the question "What can we use as a guide?," we present a one-sided depiction that reduces it to a kind of relief, to the solution to a problem. The concept of the canon also embodies aspirations and values.

The canon is a movement "towards greatness, towards the categorical, towards the aspirational" (Gehlen 1961, 60). This claim of the canon arises from its degree of generalisation, and the more general it is, the wider the gap between the demands and the contingencies that each concrete case will be. Whoever subjects himself to the canon must renounce the casuistic flexibility of adaptation to different situations, and therefore the greater the demands, the greater the renunciation. In turn this means that the foundational motivating structure of the canon must be all the stronger and the reward for adhering to it must be all the richer. The laws of Deuteronomy that set out to govern Jewish life right down to the last detail do not fall into the category of relief, of problem solving; they set standards that can only be achieved by enormous effort. And so, wherein lies the motive for making such a collective and continuous effort?

If you give up smoking, you make a sacrifice that is based on reasons of health and hygiene. You do not announce to the world that you have joined the community of nonsmokers. The canon, on the other hand, requires values that transcend matters of pure habit or practicality or

---

[64] Thomas Luckmann, "Kanonisierungsstile," in A. and J. Assmann (eds.), *Kanon und Zensur*, 28–37, (see chapt. 1, n. 48). For Antiquity, see especially Arthur D. Nock, *Conversion* (Oxford: Clarendon Press, 1963).

idiosyncratic preferences. The identity-giving category of belonging plays a special role here, and the sanctified texts, rules, and values create the foundation and the form of a (collective) identity. The whole history of the concept revolves round the increasing importance of this category, and certainly it provides the key to the motivational structure. The sanctification of a particular tradition always leads to the sanctification of a particular community. From being a neutral measuring instrument, the canon grew into a survival strategy in the establishment of cultural identity. The Jews, in bowing to the severity of their laws, did so in the knowledge that they were the "chosen" and therefore the sanctified people (Exod. 19:6).

The canon, then, is the principle underlying the establishment and stabilization of a collective identity that also provides the basis for individual identity as the medium of individualization through socialization, or as Habermas puts it, self-realization through incorporation into "the normative consciousness of a whole people."[65] It connects the first-person singular to the first-person plural, at one and the same time representing the collective social body and a system of meanings and values through which the individual becomes part of the whole, thereby signaling his identity as a member.

As a new form of cultural continuity, the canon distinguishes itself both from traditionalism as an unalterable obligation to the past and from anti-traditionalism as a mode of changing norms, rules, and values under the sign of autonomous reason. The fact that the metaphor derives originally from architecture[66] is highly significant, because it not only posits the idea of the world as a construction in which man is the architect of his own reality, his culture, and himself but it also emphasizes the need for defining and binding principles that this construction must adhere to, if the "house" is to survive.

The emergence of the canon, however, does not by any means mark the end of the evolution of written culture. We would not even be able to reflect on these processes if we could only think and write within its

---

[65] Jürgen Habermas, "Können komplexe Gesellschaften eine vernünftige Identität ausbilden?," in *Zur Rekonstruktion des Historischen Materialismus* (Frankfurt: Suhrkamp, 1976), 92–126, here 107.

[66] Weber, *Kanon und Methode* (see chapt. 2, n. 40) justifiably places great emphasis on this.

borders, and indeed it represents a principle that has long since given way to quite different forms of cultural memory. The very existence of a subject like Egyptology presupposes that our research and teaching have freed themselves from the normative and formative diktats of foundational texts. The borders of cultural memory have now become fluid and whole new areas have opened up beyond the scope of those texts from whose ceaseless study the modern humanities – including Egyptology – have emerged. The humanist is an interpreter who no longer focuses exclusively on the meaning of foundational texts. According to Wilamowitz, the true scholar must consider the (Greek) particle "án" to be as important as the dramas of Aeschylus. This, most people would agree, is somewhat over the top, but the opposition the statement aroused showed clearly the influence still exercised by the absolute values of the foundational texts over a period that had included the Enlightenment and historicism.

There were three main arguments against historicism. One pointed to the danger of "unbridled relativism" (A. Rüstow) and opposed it with a new, canonical system that is related to values and identity. This incorporated the "third humanism" of Werner Jaeger and his school that explicitly rejected Wilamowitz's historical positivism.[67] The second, more subtle approach regarded historical criticism as a kind of refining that would bring out the kernel of truth (or in theological terms the "kerygma" of the text) all the more brightly. This approach was adopted by H. G. Gadamer's hermeneutics[68] and R. Bultmann's project of "de-mythologizing." The third and most recent approach discovered in historicism itself a hidden canon as a background of values and self-images: the "exotic" is nothing other than a bestowal of identity with inverted symptoms.[69] The idea of a "value-free" discipline as proposed by Max Weber has shown itself to be highly problematical, because in itself it also implies values. This applies just as much to the

---

[67] Werner Jaeger, *Das Problem des Klassischen und die Antike*, Naumburger Conference (Darmstadt: Wissenschaftliche Buchgesellschaft, 1930).

[68] Hans Georg Gadamer, *Wahrheit und Methode. Grundzüge einer philosophischen Hermeneutik* (Tübingen: Mohr 1960), 269 ff. (see 270 f. on Jaeger); Engl. *Truth and Method*, trans. Garrett Barden and John Cumming (New York: Seabury Press, 1975).

[69] See, for instance, Fritz Kramer, *Verkehrte Welten* (Frankfurt: Synidcat, 1977) and Edward Said, *Orientalism* (New York: Pantheon, 1978).

removal of the boundary between memory and history that was so important to Halbwachs.[70]

The 20th century went through various forms of recanonization in the form of Nationalist-Fascist and Marxist-Leninist concepts, the anti-Communist and anti-Nationalist restoration of a Roman-cum-West-European "West" in the postwar era, different brands of fundamentalism (Christian, Jewish, Islamic, and so forth), and secular movements and counter-movements in the service of particular minority identities and histories, such as feminism, black studies, gay rights, and others. It seems that we can never extract ourselves from the network of normative, formative values, and thus the task of the historian can no longer be seen as deconstructing or "undermining" (Gadamer) the barriers of the canon; instead it analyzes their structure and brings the processes to light that have put them in place.

[70] Burke, "Geschichte als soziales Gedächtnis" (see chapt. 1, n. 35); Pierre Nora, *Zwischen Geschichte und Gedächtnis* (Berlin: Wagenbach, 1990).

3

Cultural Identity and Political Imagination

IDENTITY, CONSCIOUSNESS, AND REFLEXIVITY

Identity is a matter of consciousness, that is of becoming aware of an otherwise unconscious image of the self. This applies both to individual and to collective life.[1] I am only a person to the extent that I know myself to be one, and in exactly the same way, a group – whether it be a tribe, race, or nation – can only be itself to the degree in which it understands, visualizes, and represents itself as such. In this chapter, I examine forms and categories of collective self-image and self-presentation in ethnic rather than individual terms and consider the role played by cultural memory in this process.

---

[1] Around 1980, "identity" was a major subject of interdisciplinary research and discussion. Examples include Claude Lévi-Strauss, *L'identité, séminaire interdisciplinaire* (Paris: B. Grasset, 1977/1983); Guy Michaud (ed.), *Identités collectives et relations interculturelles* (Bruxelles: Éditions Complexe, 1978); Hans Mol (ed.), *Identity and Religion. International Cross-Cultural Approaches* (London: Sage Publications, 1978); Jacques Beauchard (ed.), *Identités collectives et travail social* (Toulouse: Privat, 1979); Odo Marquard and Karlheinz Stierle (eds.), *Identität (Poetik und Hermeneutik VIII)* (Munich: Fink, 1979); *L'identité. Actes de la recherche en sciences scoiales No. 35* (Paris, 1980); Burkart Holzner and Roland Robertson (eds.), *Identity and Authority. Exploration in the Theory of Society* (Oxford: B. Blackwell, 1980); *Identité et régions*, Union des Associations Internationales (Bruxelles, 1981); Anita Jacobson-Widding, *Identity: Personal and Socio-Cultural* (Uppsala: Academiae Upsaliensis, 1983).

Personal and Collective Identity

There is a strange, seemingly paradoxical relationship between the two forms of identity. I would like to define this by way of two theses that seem to contradict each other:

1. A self grows from the outside in. It builds itself up individually by participating in the interactive and communicative patterns of the group to which it belongs and by contributing to that group's self-image. Therefore, the "we" identity of the group takes precedence over the "I" of the individual – in other words, identity is a social phenomenon, or what we might term "sociogenic."

2. The collective "we" identity does not exist outside of the individuals who constitute and represent it. "We" is a matter of individual knowledge and awareness.[2]

The first of these arguments puts the whole before the part, and the second reverses the relationship. This runs parallel to what is known in linguistics as the dialectic between dependence and constituency (or descendance and ascendance). The part depends on the whole and only assumes its identity through the role that it plays within the whole, but the whole only emerges from the interplay between the parts. The combination of the two arguments endows the term "sociogenic" with two meanings: individual consciousness is sociogenic not only through socialization (from outside in) but also because it creates community by being the bearer of a collective self-image, or awareness of the "we." My focus will be precisely on this active meaning of sociogenesis, that is on how a community acquires its collective or sociocultural identity.

First, it will be helpful if we replace the simple "I versus we" dichotomy with a triad, by dividing "I" into "individual" and "personal":

---

[2] This argument supports the "methodological individualism" of Hans Albert, "Methodologischer Individualismus und historische Analyse," in K. Acham and W. Schulze (eds.), *Teil und Ganzes. Zum Verhältnis von Einzel- und Gesamtanalyse in Geschichts- und Sozialwissenschaften* (Munich: Deutscher Taschenbuchverlag, 1990), 219–239.

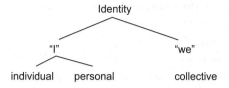

Individual identity is the coherent self-image that builds itself up in the consciousness of the individual through features that (a) distinguish them significantly from everyone else and (b) remain constant across the various phases of their development. It is the awareness, beginning with the constant motif of one's own body, of an irreducible self that is unmistakable and irreplaceable. *Personal identity*, on the other hand, is the embodiment of all of the roles, qualities, and talents that give the individual his own special place in the social network. Individual identity relates to the contingencies of life, incorporating such key elements as birth and death, physical existence, and basic needs. Personal identity relates to social accountability and recognition. Both aspects of the "I" identity are determined sociogenically and culturally, and both processes – individuation and socialization – follow culturally prescribed paths. They arise from a consciousness that is formed and determined by the language, ideas, norms, and values of a particular time and culture. Thus, in the sense of the first thesis, society is not a powerful opponent for the individual; instead it is a constitutive element of the self. Society is not a dimension mightier than the individual, but represents a constituent element of the self. Identity, including that of the "I", is always a social construct, and as such it is always cultural.

The distinction between first-person singular and first-person plural identities should therefore not be seen as one between natural growth and cultural construction. There is no such thing as an identity that grows naturally. There is, however, a difference in so far as the collective identity – unlike the personal – has no link with such natural factors as the body; and what we call the "social body" does not exist as a visible, tangible reality. The elements of collective identity are underpinned by factors that are purely symbolic, and the social body is simply a metaphor – an imaginary construct. As such, however, it has its own position in reality. The collective or "we" identity is the image that a group has of itself and with which its members associate themselves. It therefore has no existence of its own, but comes into being through recognition by its participating individuals. It is as strong or as weak as its presence in the consciousness of its members and its motivating influence on their thoughts and actions.

This book focuses on the link between social self-image and social memory (i.e., awareness of history). Groups base, in the words of the ethnologist Rüdiger Schott (see Chapt. 1, n. 67), their awareness of their unity and uniqueness particularly on events that take place in the past. Societies need the past mainly for the purpose of self-definition. In the words of the Egyptian writer Muhammad Husayn Haykal, "a nation only lives by reviving its past."[3] Or as J. G. Droysen put it, every group possesses in its past "the explanation and awareness of itself – a common property of all participants, which makes their community all the more solid and all the more internal the richer it is."[4] The imagined national community is based on an imagined continuity that reaches back into the depths of time.

Basic Structures and Forms of Enhancement

The concept of collective identity is still subject to the same criticism leveled at the Durkheim School in 1925 by M. Bloch: that it merely adds the word "collective" to such terms of individual psychology as representation, conscience, mentality, and memory. This use of language, he says, is "convenient, but rather fictive." However, in this case it really does refer to something fictive – a product of social imagination. The fictive or metaphorical element of the collective identity consists first in the totally symbolic reality of membership and second in the fact that it lacks the factor of irreducibility. A collective identity can be renounced (as long as such renunciation is not hindered or prevented by external forces) – for example, through emigration or conversion – or it may fade into insignificance. In both of these cases, life goes on unhampered; if, however, the "I" identity is eroded,

---

[3] Muhammad Husayn Haykal (1888–1965), quoted by Hinrich H. Biesterfeldt, "Ibn Haldun: Erinnerung, historische Reflexion und die Idee der Solidarität," in Assmann and Harth, *Mnemosyne*, 177 (see chapt. 1, n. 2).

[4] Johann G. Droysen, *Historik*, ed. P. Leyk (Stuttgart Bad-Cannstadt: Frommann-Holzboog, 1977), 10, 45.

undermined, or damaged, there will be pathological consequences. Collective identities belong to the category known as the social and political *imaginaire* (Castoriadis 1975; Anderson 1983; Baczko 1984; Elwert 1989).

Culture and society are basic structures, that is, irreducible conditions of our humanity. Without this foundation and framework, human existence as we know it would be unthinkable. Even a hermit who might renounce both is still marked by them and, by simply turning his/her back on them, (s)he acknowledges his/her fundamental role. Through this, culture and society convey or generate an identity that is always personal though not necessarily collective. The individual's self-awareness is influenced by them, but this does not mean that (s)he will automatically have a sense of belonging to a particular society and its culture. This sense tends to be taken for granted as something that lies below the surface of the conscious, motivational self-image. Membership is only enhanced by reflection into the articulate form of a "we" identity when it is deliberately brought to the surface – for example, through initiation rites – or when it rises spontaneously, for instance through a confrontation with different societies and other ways of life. According to our understanding, a collective identity is a reflexive form of social belonging, whereas cultural identity correspondingly entails conscious participation in or recognition of a specific culture.

The difference between a basic structure and its enhancement through reflection can be illustrated by the example of feminism. Every human belongs almost irrevocably to one or other of the sexes. But talk of a male or female identity only becomes meaningful (in our context) if this simple categorization is linked to a "we" consciousness, that is a sense of belonging or solidarity, and the motivational force of a particular self-image. This is precisely what feminism produces: a collective female identity. Marx did the same for social class when he talked of a "collective subject." By making people conscious of a particular, shared situation, belonging can be changed into homogeneity and the mass can be transformed into a collectively acting "subject" whose capacity for action will be tied to its identity. In both cases, this occurs through contrastive or even antagonistic solidarity – in this instance, respectively against men and against the upper classes. Antagonism is one of the most common conditions that gives rise to reflection and to the enhancement of basic structures into collective identities.

Personal and individual identity also emerges and develops through reflection. Here, though, the process through which the individual is connected into a social and cultural network is essential and unavoidable. We can call this "anthropological reflexivity." It is the process that G. H. Mead (1934) described as "mutual reflection" (Thomas Luckmann) – the formation and stabilization of identity through identification with both "significant others" and with the image of oneself mirrored by these others (T. Luckmann, in Marquard/Stierle 1979). Experience of oneself is always mediated; only experience of others is direct. Just as we are unable to see our face except in a mirror, we are unable to see our inner self other than by reflection, and it is the latter that creates awareness. Contact with others also entails contact with ourselves, and the self of personal identity is simply not available to us without communication and interaction. It is an awareness of oneself that at the same time involves awareness of the expectations of others and our resultant obligations and responsibilities.

If contact with others is to lead to the formation of identity, the person concerned must live with them in a shared world of symbolic meaning. This does not necessarily imply, however, that this shared world has to represent a collective identity. It only does so when the identity has been consciously formed and preserved. In its basic or (if one might be permitted to use such a paradoxical term) natural state, culture in fact works the other way, because with all its norms, values, institutions, and views of life of the world, it becomes a given, that is, a world order that is taken for granted and brooks no alternative, thus rendering its uniqueness and its conventionality invisible to the individual.[5] For that reason, it cannot endow the individual with an awareness of "we" or with an identity. Once again, it cannot be emphasized sufficiently enough that identity presupposes other identities. Without the plural, you cannot have the one, and without otherness

---

[5] See Peter R. Hofstätter, *Einführung in die Sozialpsychologie* (Stuttgart: Kröner, 1973), 57–73, who gives a precise definition: "The sum of self-evidences in a social system is what we call its culture" (93).

you cannot have individuality. It is one of the strange features of cultural formations that on the one hand (at least until now, when we are still a long way away from building a global society with a global culture) they only exist in the plural, whereas on the other hand it comes naturally to us to forget this fact. It would never occur to anybody, under normal circumstances, that they are alone in the world, that is, that they are surrounded by beings whose similarity to themselves they would not recognize as such. And yet for societies, this is precisely what *is* normal. The most widespread principle of ethnic self-definition is the use of the term "human being" (for example, Bantu, Inuit, or the Egyptian *remetj*). This, however, is just one obvious example of the much wider tendency of every culture to modify its own black-and-white system of position and negation, which underlies the construction of all meanings, into the invisibility and intangibility of a "gray area" of implicit rules and meanings that render the system inaccessible to questioning and hence to change (Mary Douglas 1966, 1970, 1975). Reality would not be reality if those who lived in it were aware that it is a "social construct."

All cultures share this tendency to draw a veil of forgetfulness or self-evidence over their conventionality and contingency (that is, the fact that their constructed realities could be differently conceived) because this is part of our natural human dependence on culture. Even if humans continue to see it as their task and indeed as their God-given opportunity "to cast off savagery and put on humanity" (*humanitatem induere feritatem deponere*), as Petrarch once put it in a letter (R. Pfeiffer 1976, 15f.[see Chapt. 3, n.20]), they have never found themselves objectively placed in such a situation. Countering their culture, they have, on the one hand, their children, who along with every generation are born into it as "young barbarians" (although they are not "savage" but simply in need of "cultivation"), and on the other different cultures whose nature, seen from their own ethnocentric perspective, will appear to be savage. People do not decide in favor of culture and against savagery. Because we are dependent on culture, it comes to us as our (second) nature. Animals adapt instinctively to their particular environment. We lack these instincts and adapt instead to culture as a symbolic world of meaning that makes the world accessible and habitable. We have no other choice. There is no savagery to be cast off; there is only a deficiency that must be compensated for. Thus, we learn what we depend on and which of our elements are dependent.

Nevertheless, it frequently happens that cultures see their own aims and effects as the overcoming not of deficiencies but of actual savagery. They articulate themselves through fictions of chaos (G. Balandier 1988). Culture is seen as the conquest and reversal of a natural state in which man is wolflike, might is right, there are no laws, and everyone is free to pursue their own ends and the needs and desires of the moment. Culture sees itself as a means of distancing people from the turmoil of nature. Living with its symbolic meanings, its norms, institutions, and so forth, implies an external and internal detachment from both the world and from one's self, in the sense that one is no longer a slave to one's instincts. In this way, space is cleared in which one can reflect and act of one's own volition. This is a precondition for identity. "Deliberately creating distance between oneself and the outside world can be called the basic act of human civilization," writes A. Warburg in the Introduction to *Mnemosyne* (Gombrich 1984, 382). Culture institutionalizes that distance. It produces familiarity and confidence – in oneself, in the world, in society. It frees us from being inundated with stimuli, with the urgency of decision making, from doubts and scruples, and therefore creates the latitude that is unique to human existence.[6]

This latitude is what makes personal and individual identity possible. It facilitates the processes of communication and interaction, the "reciprocity of perspectives" (H. Plessner) that underlie the freedom of action and of self-experience that go to establishing identity. Freedom of action is not just a matter of decision making but also involves the whole surrounding complex of meanings, and it is against this background of shared meanings that intersubjective action, or interaction takes place.

---

[6] See Nikolas Luhmann, *Vertrauen. Ein Mechanismus der Reduktion sozialer Komplexität* (Stuttgart: Enke, 1973). Cf. also the Greek term *pistis*, which Christian Meier interprets as "the self-evident interweaving of expectation and fulfilment" (Christian Meier, "Die politische Identität der Griechen," in Marquard and Stierle [eds.], *Identität*, 371–496, 375 [see chapt. 3, n. 1] referring to Peter Spahn, *Mittelschicht und Polisbildung* [Frankfurt: P. Lang, 1977]).

The fact that not only an "I" but also a "we" identity emerges from these shared experiences requires a further degree of consciousness.[7] As long as the symbolic world of meanings appears to its inhabitants as a given, unalterable order, we find that consciousness of a collective identity is scarcely possible in naïve ethnocentrism. I act like this, and in no other way, because I am a human being, and not just because "we" (in contradistinction to others) act like this and in no other way.

In the following, I try to describe some of the typical conditions that make crucial elements of these meanings reflexive, open to examination, and hence explicit, non-self-evident, and thus symbolically expressive of a first-person plural identity.

Identity, Communication, and Culture

If we look again at the problem of identity from the perspective of communication, we must once more start out from some fundamental facts of human existence. Aristotle defined man as *zoon politikon* – the social animal that lives amid groups, communities, and political systems. Man is by nature dependent on social living, as has been confirmed by behavioral research. The drive to form groups is therefore part of our basic human equipment, as are community-forming actions and attitudes (Eibl-Eibesfeldt). However, this social instinct is shared with certain animals that also live in groups, herds, packs, and so on – for example, wolves or bees. But following on from Aristotle, we can say that man distinguishes himself from all other social animals by his use of language. He is the *zoon logon echon*, the animal in possession of language, and indeed these two definitions go together, because language is the outstanding tool for the formation of groups. It is the basis of communication that, in turn, is the basis of human bonding.

Symbolic Forms / Symbols of Identity. Consciousness of social belonging, also called "social identity," depends on shared knowledge and shared

---

[7] In a way, this is a second stage of detachment, not only from the world but also from the specific symbolic meanings already brought about by the first step (i.e., away from the "world"). See also Meier, "Die politische Identität," 373 ff., who interprets the 7th and 6th-century crisis in Greece as one of confidence, leading to a "detachment from the existing order."

memory; and these are both articulated by a common language or communicated by way of a common system of symbols. It is not just a matter of words, sentences, and texts here, because communication may also take place, as we have seen, through rites and dances, patterns and decorations, costumes, tattoos, food and drink, monuments, pictures, landscapes, and so on. Everything can become a symbol to denote community. It is not the medium that decides, but the structure and function of the signs. This complex of shared symbols might be called "cultural formation," and when this has been established and, above all, passed on, it corresponds to a collective identity. The cultural formation, then, is the medium through which collective identity is created and preserved down through the generations.

It is because of their symbolic – not biological – base and self-definition that human groups are to be found in such huge diversity. Man is capable of living in communities that may vary in scale from a tribe of a few hundred to a state of millions or even billions. He can even belong to more than one group at a time: family, political party, trade union, religion, nation.[8] Cultural formations are therefore varied, polymorphous, and polysystemic. Within the macro-formation of one culture you will find an array of cultural micro-formations. A tribal culture is liable to be much less polymorphous, that is, far more monolithic than a post-traditional written culture. The more complex a culture becomes, with its many subformations and subcultures, the more essential the functions and institutions of internal communication will be.

Circulation. Along with identity, we might define culture as a kind of immune system for the group, and examine how this system functions. The parallel to the biological immune system is quite striking, particularly with regard to circulation. Just as the interaction between fixed and mobile cells creates and maintains (or reproduces) a physical identity by ceaselessly producing coherence and organic integration through innumerable contacts, so too is social identity built up

---

[8] The multilayered and heterogeneous character of any social and personal identity has been stressed by Amartya Sen, *Identity and Violence. The Illusion of Destiny* (New York: W.W. Norton, 2006).

and preserved by way of interaction.[9] What is circulated here is cultural meaning that is coded and articulated through shared language, knowledge, and memory; it is a store of common values, experiences, expectations, and interpretations that create the symbolic world picture view of a society.[10]

The circulation of a common meaning gives rise to a sense of community. Within every individual group member an awareness arises of the paramount importance of the group; individual desires, instincts, and goals are subordinate to this. The cardinal sin in Egyptian, as in all primal codes of ethics, was greed – self-enhancement at the expense of others. Even this has an extraordinary parallel in microbiology. In certain respects, the greedy avaricious person is the "cancer cell" in society, and the following extract from a research paper on cancer strikingly makes the point: "Normally every cell strictly subordinates itself to the interests of the complete organism. Independent actions are far from easy, because a tight network of controls ensures that every cell works in harmony with the rest of the organism."[11] This network of controls is also present in society, ensuring that the common good has predominance over individual agendas.

At the level of simple societies, or what we might call "face-to-face communities," the most important form of social circulation is

---

9 For the interpretation of the immune system see Francisco J. Varela, "Der Körper denkt. Das Immunsystem und der Prozess der Körper-Individuierung," in H. U. Gumbrecht and K. L. Pfeiffer (eds.), *Paradoxien, Dissonanzen, Zusammenbrüche. Situationen offener Epistemologie* (Frankfurt: Suhrkamp, 1991), 727–743 (with bibliography). I am using an analogy here and am not, of course, suggesting any kind of biological foundation of group identity. All groups are "imagined communities" (Benedict Anderson, *Imagined Communities: Reflections on the Origin and Spread of Nationalism* [London: Verso, 1983]). I refer to systems theory that treats both the (biological) immunity system and the (cultural) identity system as self-referential systems, processing information on the distinction between inner and outer, system and environment, own and foreign, and providing self-definitions.

10 In J. Habermas's terminology of identity theory, both approaches would come under the heading of "conventional identity." "Post-conventional," on the other hand, would entail action according to general norms of reason. However, it is not clear how such action can be linked to the concept of identity. An element of the irrational always seems to be inherent in collective identities. See Jürgen Habermas, "Können komplexe Gesellschaften" (see chapt. 2, n. 64).

11 Barbara Hobom, "Darmkrebs – Ende einer stufensweisen Erbänderung," *FAZ*, Feb. 14, 1990.

dialogue. Language is the most common means of constructing and fueling social reality,[12] although the media that are used to circulate meaning are not exclusively linguistic. The earliest and most effective vehicles for creating social networks and identities were economics and kinship. M. Mauss (1966) and following on from him M. Sahlins (1972) emphasized the communicative importance of trading that drew individuals into a system of social give-and-take with all of its concomitant interdependence and responsibility. C. Lévi-Strauss (1948) drew attention to the social and cultural significance of kinship systems and rules relating to marriage. He regarded the ban on incest as the central achievement of culture. Here too, through the prevention of small-scale autarchies and by the imposition of broader alliances and interdependencies, a group is established that reaches beyond the confines of the family thus establishing a socio cultural identity. The sense of community circulating within that group is also a practical process.

The identity-securing knowledge that we have here subsumed under the term "sense of community" embraces two very different complexes that we may call "wisdom" and "myth." On the level of simple forms we can say they correspond to proverbs and narratives. Proverbs promote the "sense of community" in the form of common sense.[13] Their core is the practice of solidarity, so that "every cell works in harmony with the rest of the organism." They are concerned with values and norms, with the rules that lead to functional coexistence, and with the axioms that underlie successful communication. These functions can be called "normative." Normative texts answer the question, "What should we do?" They provide us with guidance to assist our decisions and judgments. "The path of life" is a common metaphor

---

[12] For further information on this "social-constructionist" theory of language, following on from Wittgenstein and also from Alfred Schütz, see John Shotter, "The Social Construction of Remembering and Forgetting," in D. Middleton and D. Edwards (eds.), *Collective Remembering* (London: Sage, 1990), 120–138, who provides additional references.

[13] See Clifford Geertz, "Common Sense as a Cultural System," in C. Geertz, *Local Knowledge* (New York: Basic Books, 1983), 73–93, and also essays by Bernhard Lang, "Klugheit als Ethos und Weisheit als Beruf. Zur Lebenslehre im Alten Testament," 177–192, and Theo Sundermeier, "Der Mensch wird Mensch durch den Menschen. Weisheit in den afrikanischen Religionen," 117–130, both in A. Assmann (ed.), *Weisheit. Archäologie der Literarischen Kommunikation III* (Munich: Fink, 1991).

in Ancient Egypt for instructional literature, and the Chinese *Tao* ("the way") points in the same direction; the Jewish term *halakhah*, the principle of normative, instructive textual interpretation, is connected with *halakh*, meaning "to go."[14]

The other functions can be called "formative," and these texts – tribal myths, epic songs, genealogies, and so forth – answer the question, "Who are we?" They define and reinforce the group identity and motivate communal action by narrating a shared history.[15] These foundational, motivational tales are what we subsumed under the term "mythomotor."

Tradition: Ceremonial Communication and Ritual Coherence. Myth and identity are linked by the fact that they both answer questions about who we are, where we come from, and what our place in the cosmos is. They preserve the sacred traditions on which any group bases its consciousness of unity and particularity (R. Schott 1968). Whereas normative wisdom shapes and justifies the formal aspects of life (customs and conventions), formative myth provides it with meanings. The most striking distinction between wisdom and myth, however, emerges when we consider their manner of circulation. Wisdom uses the forms of everyday communication, whereas myth uses ceremony. The latter's sole concern is to promulgate the knowledge that establishes and preserves identity, and because this knowledge cannot spread or reproduce itself of its own accord it has to be staged and circulated. In this sense, ceremony may be viewed as the institutionalization of circulation.

In the context of identity, we must therefore return to the rituals that we have already discussed in relation to memory culture (ritual as the medium of cultural, as opposed to communicative memory) and written culture (ritual, as opposed to textual coherence). Rites exist in order to keep a group's identity system working. They enable

---

[14] In 1977, at the yearly AJS conference in Boston, the Assyriologist T. Abush was able to demonstrate *A Babylonian Analogue of the Term Halakha*. See also Fishbane, *Biblical Interpretation*, 91–280, (see chapt. 2, n. 11).

[15] In light of the narrative nature of the formative function, particularly in its early, original form, it should be considered alongside the other principle of Jewish exegesis, the (H)aggadah, which relates to these stories. See Fishbane, *Biblical Interpretation*, 281–442 (see chapt. 2, n. 11).

participants to share the knowledge that makes their world go around, thus constituting and reproducing the identity of the group. For so-called primitive people, the cultural sense is synonymous with reality or order, because order is not a given – it needs ritual staging and myth-ical articulation to counter the ubiquitous disorder and decay that mark the world around us. Myths express order, and rites produce it (G. Balandier 1988). There are in fact two forms of order here: one is that of everyday living that is shaped and governed by common sense, and the other is the festival that incorporates the store of common knowledge relevant to identity – the ceremonially communicated cul-tural memory. In illiterate societies, rites or ceremonies have the task of reproducing and circulating this common knowledge, and therefore they are systematically and inextricably linked to the establishment of identity. They are the infrastructure providing the canals or arter-ies along which the elements that form identity flow. Connected to a detached and ceremonial form of communication, social identity is separate from everyday life. In illiterate societies and in societies that – similar to Ancient Egypt – are based on the continuity of ritual coherence despite their written culture, the coherency of the group depends on ritual repetition that is both synchronic and diachronic.

ETHNOGENESIS AS THE ENHANCEMENT OF BASIC STRUCTURES OF COLLECTIVE IDENTITY

Earlier in this chapter I have shown that identity is a matter of knowl-edge, consciousness, and reflection, and I asked to what this knowl-edge referred. Its substance and form relate specifically to culture.

On a basic structural level, there is perfect congruence between social (ethnic), political, and cultural formations. Provided people are settled, they live and communicate face to face, and their social communion is regulated by marriage rules.[16] However, there is a limit to the size of such communities – they seldom extend beyond a few thousand. Even today, most linguistic, cultural, and ethnic formations

---

[16] See also Robert Redfield, *The Little Community* (Chicago: University of Chicago Press, 1956). Friedrich H. Tenbruck, *Geschichte und Gesellschaft* (Berlin: Duncker & Hum-blot, 1986), 253 ff., refers to this form as the *Lokalitätsprinzip*.

conform to this general, natural pattern.[17] Anything that extends beyond it is the result of enhancements, but these are for the most part unstable and need new forms of stabilization. The result is a typical starting point for the establishment of collective identities. Broadly speaking, it is mainly a lack of congruence between ethnic, cultural, and political formations that sets off the process of reflection, and this leads to a loss of given values and a growing consciousness of the need for a binding cultural sense. As society becomes more complex, the primary alliance between ethnic, cultural, and political formations begins to disintegrate and to create problems that may be divided into two categories: those of integration and those of distinction.

Integration and Centrality

When an ethnic unit merges with another ethnopolitical group through alliance, migration, or conquest, there are bound to be problems of integration and acculturation. The dominant culture takes on transethnic validity, thereby acquiring the status of the more advanced civilization and thus marginalizing the cultural formations of the other group. The establishment of early civilizations always coincided with the creation of new forms of political organization that far exceeded the natural dimensions of human socialization. The symbolic meanings of such enhanced groupings were then no longer confined to the primary anthropological functions of communication, interaction, and detachment from the everyday world, but they had the additional task of stabilizing a highly volatile political formation and integrating a range of more or less heterogeneous sociocultural formations. Within this framework of a culture that was extended geographically and ethnically, split into high and low plus central and peripheral, socialization took place along different lines and on different levels. It was no longer parents and primary social constellations that were in charge of cultural knowledge, but institutions; and the acquisition of knowledge became a long and difficult task. Culture ceased to be the embodiment of self-evidence, as defined by the social psychologist

[17] Of course nowadays there are far more people living in so-called civilized states than in tribal cultures, but there are still more tribal cultures than states.

Peter R. Hofstätter, or of sophistication, as the social anthropologist Arnold Gehlen sees it:

It is firm and always limiting, inhibiting forms – worked on slowly over hundreds and thousands of years – like law, property, the monogamous family, precise division of labor – that have bred and nurtured our initiatives and attitudes, making them into the lofty, exclusive, selective aspirations to which we may give the name of culture. Such institutions as the law, the monogamous family, and property are not in themselves natural in any sense of the word and they can be very swiftly destroyed. Just as unnatural is the culture of our instincts and ways of thinking, which have to be supported, maintained, and controlled from outside by those institutions. And if you take away the supports, we very soon revert to primitivism (A. Gehlen 1961, 59).

What Gehlen has in mind here is not culture as such, but rather integratively enhanced culture. This is not simply the creation of dependency or compensation for a deficiency, but culture on a higher level, compared to which primitive cultural formations do indeed seem savage and therefore need to be set aside in order to advance humanity. Gehlen's culture is a movement "towards the great, the aspirational and the categorical," and it is always "forced, difficult and improbable." He does not seem to realize that he is in fact describing culture at one particular historical stage, and he seems equally unaware that this culture has to stabilize not only people in all the fragility of their instincts and attitudes but also the political organization that carries and is borne by it. What he describes here is virtually the same as the Ancient Egyptian concept of culture, whose fundamental problem from its inception was integration. (It was not until the advent of Hellenism that distinction became at least as great a problem as integration.)

One can scarcely avoid the thought that the aspirational character of integratively enhanced culture, with its movement "towards the great and [. . .] the categorical," found its expression in the colossal size and style of the symbolic forms used by these early civilizations. The more than life-sized manifestations, achieved only through huge effort and technological mastery, correspond precisely to the equally more than life-sized, painstakingly achieved greatness of the political formation. The most impressive example of this syndrome of "nationhood, state-building, and colossality" is the Egyptian pyramids of the

4th Dynasty (ca. 2600 BCE). "Here in truth faith moved mountains," writes the Egyptologist Wolfgang Helck, "but it also gave the decisive impetus for the creation of the Egyptian nation. Only now, at last, through this common task, did the Egyptian State emerge as an organized entity in which everyone had his place" (W. Helck 1986, 19).

The pyramid as a sign and symbol of community and of a political identity (embodied by the living Pharaoh) may sound anachronistic. Nowadays we might think of the Lenin mausoleum in Moscow, or especially the Mao mausoleum in Beijing, which was built by 700,000 people from every region in China as an integrative strategy to counter the danger of political collapse after Mao's death (L. Ledderose 1988). In the same vein, William Wood suggested in 1800 that a giant pyramid be erected in London, "to delight, astonish, elevate, or sway the minds of others through the medium of their senses." Clearly he believed that only the extraordinary dimensions of a pyramid could inspire the English to engage in the concept of a motherland, and to visualize and perpetuate the nation as a collective identity.[18] Similar significance is attached to the colossal architecture of early empires,[19] even in the Bible. The well-known story of the Tower of Babel (Genesis 11) relates that:

And they said, Go to, let us build us a city and a tower, whose top may reach unto heaven; and let us make us a name, lest we be scattered abroad upon the face of the whole earth.

What could a name signify, if not the embodiment and symbol of an ethnopolitical identity? And what is the fear of being scattered abroad if it is not a desire for integration (as well as an awareness of the fragility of the existing structure)? Here, too, the longed-for ethnopolitical greatness is given visible expression through the construction of a great building. As we learn from the end of the story, Jahweh thwarts this ambition not only by destroying the tower but also, and especially,

---

[18] W. Wood, *An Essay on National and Sepulchral Monuments*, quoted by R. Koselleck, "Kriegerdenkmale als Identitätsstiftungen der Überlebenden," in Marquard and Stierle (eds.), *Identität*, 255–276, 261 (see chapt. 3, n. 1).

[19] On the political significance of the colossal, see H. Cancik, "Größe und Kolossalität als religiöse und ästhetische Kategorien. Versuch einer Begriffsbestimmung am Beispiel von Statius, Silve I 1: Ecus Maximus Domitiani Imperatoris," in *Visible Religion VII, Genres in Visual Representations* (Leiden: E. J. Brill, 1990), 51–68.

by creating a confusion of languages. The theme of identity could scarcely be made more apparent. As the sociolinguist Joshua Fishman rightly asks, "What better symbol system than language do we possess to convey and foster such identity?" (in A. Jacobson-Widding 1983, 277, [also, see here Chapt. 3, n. 1]). Fishman's remark was in reference to "modern ethno-cultural identity, but the problem is far from being confined to modern times. As Aristotle pointed out, a common language is the earliest medium for forming human groups."

Integration, then, brings about a large-scale ethnopolitical identity that transcends the natural formations of human socialization that it stabilizes by means of a comprehensive and binding set of symbolic meanings. Inevitably, however, this process leads to the reflectiveness of cultural formations. Acculturation entails transition from one culture to another: even from the standpoint of the superior "target" culture, this transition means "abandoning savagery and embracing humanity."[20] Whatever happens, there will be a cultural pluralism that requires a kind of culture consciousness, just as knowledge of several languages sharpens the awareness of language generally. A meta-level of cultural reflection is formed, providing a platform from which culture itself (or various aspects of it) may be thematized and made explicit. Thus implicit norms, values, and axioms turn into codified laws and conventions. This is not only a consequence of the invention of writing but also an effect of the need for explanation that arises out of the problem of integration. Knowledge that can be made explicit and available for scrutiny is *ipso facto* changeable and open to criticism; the same may be said of plurality and complexity, because they are the exact opposite of self-evidence, which allows no alternative.

Culture, however, does not by any means always work as an integrating, unifying force. It can also stratify and separate to at least the same degree. The Indian caste system represents the most obvious example of this. The distinctive features of each caste are defined in purely cultural terms, by way of specific areas of competence. Within a shared ethnic identity – foreigners are by definition without a caste – this

---

[20] Petrarch uses the terms *feritas* and *humanitas* in a letter of dedication; see Rudolf Pfeiffer, *History of Classical Scholarship. From 1300 to 1850* (Oxford: Clarendon Press, 1976), 1981, 15f.

system creates a culturally induced inequality. The starting point for such developments is typically linked to literacy,[21] and in the early civilizations of Mesopotamia and Egypt scribes were members of an elite that united cognitive, political, economic, religious, ethical, and legal competences. Writing and knowledge, writing and administration, writing and government all went hand in hand. And so an ever widening gap opened between the writing, administrating, and ruling elite on the one hand, and the working, producing masses on the other. The question arises as to whether there was a self-image that encompassed both levels. Did they still see themselves as members of a single group? The more complex the culture, the wider the gap within the group, because there were never more than a few specialists able to master the required knowledge and put it into practice (E. Gellner 1983).

The stratifying power of culture, with its creation of inequality, can lead in two different directions: (1) a sociological, educational distinction that separates experts and specialists from the illiterate masses, and (2) an ethological distinction, with the refined lifestyle of the educated upper classes in stark contrast to the "rough and ready" lives of their inferiors. Culture thus becomes an upper class phenomenon. This is generally not a matter of elite culture as opposed to lower class culture, but of culture itself, which is simply mastered and realized more fully by the elite than by ordinary people. And so one section of society (the elite) claims to be representative of the whole. An Egyptian official, for example, would not have seen himself as the bearer of a specific official culture – for example, technology professional or class ethics – but as the bearer of culture itself. Being a bearer of culture is a demanding job, and it can only be done by someone whose personal prosperity allows him to disregard the immediate problem of having to earn a living. This approach to culture was common to all ancient societies. The lower classes were part of culture only in so far as they were targeted by it. Good deeds and care of the needy were central principles of Egyptian, Oriental, and also biblical ethics (Bolkestein 1939). The solidarity that was inculcated

---

[21] In India, Vedic-Brahman mnemotechnics fulfill the function of writing.

into each individual also included the poor and the underprivileged – the proverbial "widows and orphans."[22]

The imperial culture in which the center dominates the periphery was always borne by a small elite. This tiny minority, however, symbolized the social identity of the whole. It was possible to gain access to the elite through scholarship (in Babylon, Egypt, and China) and state examinations (China). Culture conveys a sense of belonging that is something very different from a natural, ethnocultural awareness. A consciously communicated and acquired sense of belonging connects with a different consciousness than the sense of belonging into which one is born. This culture makes people aware that they belong to a higher level of humanity. This is very different from the sort of awareness engendered by the problems of distinction, but in a somewhat weaker sense it is also a form of cultural identity.

We must therefore differentiate between a representative and an exclusive elite culture. The latter, for example, that of the elite French-speaking aristocracy of 18th-century Europe, never regarded itself as representative in an ethnic sense. A Polish aristocrat of that time felt far more akin to his French counterparts than to the peasants of his own country. He would probably not even have understood the term "fellow countryman." Poland then was an aristocratic nation (in the sense of a nation formed by the nobility). A. D. Smith distinguishes between "lateral" and "vertical" ethnic groups. Lateral groups are aristocracies in which culture is elite and stratified, so that by the time it reaches the lower levels it is either weak or completely absent. Vertical societies are demotic, that is, permeated by a single ethnic culture – although to various degrees, according to circumstances – at all levels of the population (A. D. Smith 1986, 76–89). The dichotomy here, though, is overly simplified; it does not take into account the important distinction that we have drawn between "exclusive" and "representative." Egypt and Mesopotamia belonged

---

[22] See the bibliography in J. Assmann, *Ma'at* (see chapt. 1, n. 11). Also, H. K. Havice, *The Concern for the Widow and the Fatherless in the Ancient Near East. A Case Study in O.T. Ethics*, PhD thesis (Yale University, 1978).

to the lateral group with an elite culture that was to be seen as representative but not exclusive. Culture can still bridge the social gaps it creates and act as a unifying force through the ideology of "vertical solidarity."[23]

Integratively enhanced cultural formations, whose integrative powers hold an empire together internally, also tend to exert an extraordinary outward power of assimilation. The classic example of this is China. Foreign conquerors consistently forgot their own origins, and as rulers of the country became more Chinese than the natives themselves – they were "Sinicized" (i.e. assimilated to Chinese culture).[24] Exactly the same process took place in Babylon and Egypt. "He who drinks from the waters of the Nile will forget where he came from." Well-known examples of cultural assimilation in the Ancient World were those of the Assyrians to the Babylonians[25] and the Romans to the Greeks. In the modern world, until comparatively recent times France was the country that exerted particular powers of cultural assimilation. In order to develop such powers, a culture has to move out of its own habitual self-evidence, and make itself prominently visible by exposing, explaining, and stylizing itself. Once it has revealed its inner strength, only then it can become the target of conscious identification and the symbol of a collective cultural identity.[26]

Distinction and Equality

It may perhaps seem pointless to differentiate between integration and distinction as two separate elements in the enhancement of basic cultural structures. After all, are they not simply aspects of one and

---

[23] On the term "vertical solidarity," see J. Assmann, *Ma'at*, (see chapt. 1, n. 11).

[24] See Wolfgang Bauer (ed.), *China und die Fremden. 3000 Jahre Auseinandersetzung in Krieg und Frieden* (Munich: C. H. Beck, 1980).

[25] On the Assyrian-Babylonian "culture war," see Peter Machinist, "Literature as Politics. The Tukulti-Ninurta Epic and the Bible," *Catholic Biblical Quarterly* 38 (1976), 455–482. P. Machinist, "The Assyrians and their Babylonian Problem," *Jahrbuch des Wissenschaftskollegs zu Berlin* (1984/85), 353–364.

[26] This is the act of identification for which Aleida Assmann, "Opting In und Opting Out," in H. U. Gumbrecht and K. L. Pfeiffer (eds.), *Stil. Geschichten und Funktionen eines kulturwissenschaftlichen Diskurselements* (Frankfurt: Suhrkamp, 1986), 127–143, coined the term "opting in."

the same phenomenon? If culture must become visible in order to exert its powers of integration and assimilation, does that not automatically make it distinctive? What does stylization mean, if it is not distinctive particularity made visible? And does identity not always entail unity and peculiarity at the same time? One might ask if there is any point in distinguishing between one identity that emphasizes unity and another that emphasizes peculiarity – or indeed if it is possible to emphasize one without the other. Such objections are justified. Whereas culture produces identity internally, it also produces alienation externally. The psychologist E. H. Erikson has called the process "pseudospeciation,"[27] and the ethologist I. Eibl-Eibesfeldt sees this as one of the prime causes of human aggression (I. Eibl-Eibesfeldt 1975, 1976).[28] Culturally induced alienation can and does lead to xenophobia, genocide, and war. This ambivalence is also part of the phenomenology of cultural memory. Love and hate are two sides of the same cultural coin.

There can be no doubt that enhanced unity strengthens the boundaries between the group inside and the world outside. The most striking example of this is the Great Wall of China, built by the imperial unifier Shih Huang-ti.[29] The same mechanism can be observed in Egypt. Modern excavations have shown that the foundations of prehistoric cultures in Upper and Lower Egypt had extensive links – the former with Africa, the latter with the Near East (J. Eiwanger 1983,

---

[27] Erik H. Erikson, "Ontogeny of Ritualization in Man," *Philosophical Transactions of the Royal Society*, 251 B (1966), 337–49; Konrad Lorenz, *Die Rückseite des Spiegels* (Munich: Piper, 1977); Engl. *Behind the Mirror: A Search for a Natural History of Human Knowledge*, trans. Ronald Taylor (New York: Harcourt Brace Jovanovich, 1977).

[28] On the somewhat perilous proximity of this ethological theory to the political theory of the constitutional lawyer Carl Schmitt ("Gruppenbildung über Feindbilder"), see A. and J. Assmann, "Kultur und Konflikt. Aspekte einer Theorie des unkommunikativen Handelns," in J. Assmann and D. Harth (eds.), *Kultur und Konflikt* (Frankfurt: Suhrkamp, 1990), 11–48.

[29] This "Great Wall" is not yet the structure that is still partly preserved today, which took on its present form during the early 15th century, but it served the same purpose – see H. Franke and R. Trauzettel, "Das Chinesische Kaiserreich," *Fischer-Weltgeschichte*, vol. 19 (Frankfurt: Fischer, 1968), 75. Interestingly, the building of the first Chinese Wall, and with it the first imperial-scale political identity, coincided with a large-scale burning of books that in the style of Orwell's *1984*, set out to eradicate the cultural memory by getting rid of Confucianism, thus clearing the way for something radically different.

61–74). With the unification of the kingdom – the creation of an all-embracing political formation bringing together the different ethnic and cultural groups in the Nile Valley – these far-reaching links disappeared. Mesopotamia provides another example. In earlier times, along with the Near East, it was the center of a cultural network that extended to Anatolia and Egypt in the west, and the Indus Valley in the east.

The process is reversed with enhanced distinction, in so far as distinction from the outside inevitably leads to increased unity on the inside. Nothing binds people more tightly than the need to defend themselves against an external foe. The best means of coping with internal political problems is to pursue an aggressive foreign policy.[30] There can be no denying this link between integration and distinction; however, I would still like to differentiate between these two forms of cultural formation according to which of them gives rise to the factors of enhancement. Egyptian culture, for instance, gained distinctiveness as an inevitable by-product of its internally evolving power of integration. The Jews, on the other hand, gained their unique power of integration through having to maintain their distinctiveness externally.[31] In both cases, the one could not be gained without the other, but all the same one can see that the different problems gave rise to different forms of cultural enhancement.

Just as Gehlen generalizes integratively enhanced culture, the ethnologist Wilhelm E. Mühlmann sees the essence of culture as its distinctively enhanced form. He introduces the term *limitische Struktur* ("limitic structure"): Evidently a boundary is present, but it does not have to be (at least not in the first instance) marked in the 'soil.' It defines itself rather through the person himself, who becomes the bearer of the 'boundary marker.' This boundary denotes itself by means of tattooed patterns, body painting, scarring, decoration, costume, language, cuisine, lifestyle – in short, through 'culture' as possessions, traditions, myths, and so forth. Mats, sarong patterns,

---

[30] See the chapter on "Military Mobilization and Ethnic Consciousness" in Anthony D. Smith, *The Ethnic Origins of Nations* (Oxford: B. Blackwell, 1986), 73 ff.

[31] M. Weber noted that the idea of "the chosen people" emerged from the principle of distinction and kept recurring under similar conditions. "And behind all ethnic diversities there is somehow naturally the notion of the 'chosen people'" (Max Weber, *Economy and Society*, (Berkeley: University of California Press, 1978), 391.

and the design of weapons can mark boundaries, and even songs and dances can do the same. None of these things are simply 'there' – they provide a separation from 'others,' and are linked to concepts and ideologies of preference and superiority. For the boundary concept of primitive people, this kind of marking (Latin *margo*) is much more important than the existing demarcation of fields – which may *also* be present – because it belongs to something more comprehensive and more intrusive on human existence: a 'limitic structure.' (. . .)

"In its ideal form, the 'limitic' structure demarcates culture not as *one* way of living – as opposed to others that might also be called cultures – but as *the* way, as the true cosmos against which others are viewed as subhuman. They may count as 'cultures' in the eyes of the scholar with his broader, casuistic view, but not for the native. Only slowly and painfully is the lesson learned that the 'other' is also something similar to human" (W. E. Mühlmann 1985, 19).

Mühlmann too seems unaware that what he is describing is not a universal basic structure but a specific form of enhancement. He does not see that enhanced distinction, an upgraded "limitic structure," is not directed against an outside world that is deemed to be cultureless and subhuman, but on the contrary opposes a culture that is felt to be superior. Mühlmann himself offers us an excellent example: Scottish tartan. We know that this is an invented tradition (E. Hobsbawm and T. Ranger 1983) that does not go further back than the 18th century and, just like Macpherson's *Ossian*, was designed to upgrade and empower the periphery against the integrative central culture of the English realm. Distinctive enhancement does not apply to the essence of a culture, but refers to the special case of "identity systems that can adapt to contrasting environments" (E. H. Spicer 1971). The birth of such (collective) identity systems, which are marked by a particular degree of persistence, is always – according to Spicer – linked to a principle of opposition or antagonism. Distinctively enhanced identity is a "counter-identity" – a resistance movement.[32] It arises and persists as a counter not to cultureless chaos, but to another, dominating culture and is typically to be found among minority groups.

---

[32] Smith, *The Ethnic Origins*, 50–58, 92 (see chapt. 3, n. 30) calls this "ethnicism," which he defines as "a movement of resistance and restoration."

Thus, the persecution of minority cultures (for example. Jews, blacks etc.) by majority cultures has resulted in these oppressed peoples clinging to their identity for dear life. Spicer cites the cases of the Catalans, Basques, and Galicians in Spain, however there are hundreds of examples all over the world, for example, the French-speakers in Canada, the Breton-speakers in France, and so forth. It is this oppositional principle that constitutes one of the common threads in both personal and group identity. Just as there can scarcely be a concept of oneself without a concept of others, [...]there can be no sense of group without some other group.[33]

Alan Dundes justifiably singles out folklore as a typical system of symbols that defines this counter-identity, as long as folklore does not denote cultural formations in general but those that have been peripherally preserved in contact with – and in contrast to – other, dominant cultural systems. Folklore is a subcultural, regionally specific formation that has the same relationship to a dominant culture as local dialect to the standard language. However, because Dundes overlooks this important distinction, he also makes the mistake of generalizing a special case. In a situation of cultural suppression, alienation, and marginalization, as virtually all those European customs and traditions that are called folklore have undergone, their usage becomes established as a symbolic way of expressing a counter-identity "that can adapt to (and resist) contrasting environments."

Intracultural antagonisms or dualisms may also lead to the distinctive enhancement of cultural formations by upgrading their limitic structure. Seventeenth and 18th-century Russia represents a good example of this. Here the drive toward modernization that was common to all European countries during that period resulted in a clash between the old culture and the new, with the symbolism of the one representing the negation or reversal of the other. Thus culture takes on a primary, distinctive (limitic) sense: one does something in a particular way mainly because other people do it differently, and one wishes to show that one does not belong to that other group. The style of beard, "walking against the sun," touching the cross with two instead of three fingers – for the old school these were all symbols of deep

---

[33] A. Dundes, in Jacobson-Widding, *Identity*, 239 (see chapt. 3, n. 1.)..

significance, because the reformers did them the other way round.[34] The modernizing impulses of the Enlightenment led everywhere to a similar dualism of old versus new. Not even Judaism, which had to maintain its counter-identity against all the contrasting environments of its many host countries, was exempt from it.[35]

Distinction is not confined to the movement from below to above, or from the periphery to the center. It also occurs the other way around. It is not by chance that the word itself carries connotations of excellence (again separating it from that which is inferior), and this additional meaning brings me back to the exclusivity of elite cultures that I have already touched on. The upper classes always set great store by visible expression of their superiority, and so they tend to have special ways of symbolizing their distinctive force or limitic structure.[36] These include, for instance, the shining white robes and long-haired wigs of the Ancient Egyptian "literocracy" – the literate class that was also the ruling one – or the brightly polished shoes, dark suits, white cuffs, and long fingernails that count as distinguished even today in parts of some eastern countries. If *noblesse oblige*, then it does so mainly to an often uncomfortable stylization involving a deliberately cultivated, theatrical lifestyle. We can call this sort of vertical distinction "elitism" in contrast to ethnicism and nationalism that are both based on lateral distinction.

Distinctive or limitic cultural enhancement is inextricably bound up with a particular consciousness of belonging and of togetherness. This is the "we" identity that is intensified by its alienation from "them" and finds its support and its expression in a primary limitic symbolism. "They" may be the upper or the lower classes, the reformers or the

---

[34] Jurij Lotman and Boris Uspenskij, "Die Rolle dualistischer Modelle in der Dynamik der russischen Kultur (bis zum Ende des 18.Jahrhunderts)," *Poetica* 9 (1977), 1ff.; Renate Lachmann, "Kanon und Gegenkanon in der russischen Kultur," in A. and J. Assmann (eds.), *Kanon und Zensur*, 124–137 (see chapt. 1, n. 48).

[35] On the conflict between traditionalism and enlightenment (*haskalah*) in Judaism, see for example B. J. Fishman, in Jacobson-Widding, *Identity*, 239 (see chapt. 3, n. 1.), 263 ff.

[36] Pierre Bourdieu, *La distinction. Critique social du jugement* (Paris: Éditions de Minuit, 1979); Engl. *Distinction: A Social Critique of the Judgement of Taste*, trans. Richard Nice (London: Routledge & Kegan Paul, 1986). See also Thorstein Veblen, *A Theory of the Leisure Class* (New York: Macmillan, 1899).

traditionalists, the oppressors or the inhabitants of a neighboring vil-lage – there are innumerable challenges that will demand the visible manifestation of one's allegiance. But this is always a matter of cultural counter-stylization, or contradistinction, and it is always a response not to the problem of chaos but to that of another culture.

When culture undergoes limitic upgrading, it changes its status to that of religion – not in the case of elitism (although there are also typical upper class religions),[37] but in the case of ethnicism and nationalism. The religious element of distinctively enhanced identity lies in the claim to exclusivity that underpins the consciousness of "we." This element sets out to take hold of every individual, and of every aspect of every individual. All other distinctions fade to nothing against the one overriding distinction: "I do not know parties anymore, only Germans."[38] The first and simultaneously most impressive exam-ple of this limited upgrading in the face of danger can be found in the Bible, with the story of Josiah's reforms (2 Kings chapters 22f.), which I examine in more detail in Chapter 5. Both these reforms themselves and in particular the recollection of them in deuteronomic histori-ography can be viewed as ethnic renewal. After a period of Assyrian dependence and then a far more radical break with tradition during Babylonian captivity, a people reflects on its true identity.[39] Today we would speak of it as the birth of a nationalist movement. This awaken-ing is described as the unexpected reappearance of a forgotten book. But what sort of forgetting, of identity loss is this?

The loss of land, temple, and political identity, for instance as expe-rienced by the Kingdom of Juda in 587 BCE, normally coincides with a loss of ethnic identity (this is what happened about 140 years earlier to the ten tribes of the North that were deported by the Assyrians). Such ethnic groups forget who they are or were, and they merge into other groups (A. D. Smith 1986). Sooner or later, that was the fate

---

[37] See Peter Anthes and Donate Pahnke (eds.), *Die Religion von Oberschichten* (Marburg: Diagonal, 1989).

[38] Speech delivered by the German emperor Wilhelm II in 1914 before the parliament at the outbreak of World War I.

[39] The account was revised several times. Essential for our argument is the *post-exile* version, which views tradition in light of what was experienced during the catastrophe and the period of exile. For details, see Hermann Spieckermann, *Juda unter Assur in der Sargonidenzeit*, FRLANT 129 (Göttingen: Vandenhoeck & Ruprecht, 1982).

of all of the ethnic groups in the Ancient World. The Jews were the only ones to resist forgetting their identity. This was due to the exiled community in Babylon that clung with all its might to the memory of the normative, formative self-image that had come down to it through the generations and had formed the foundations of its ethnic identity.

The special feature of this identity was the pact that God had made with the Jews, "that he may establish thee today for a people unto himself, and that he may be unto thee a God" (Deut. 29:13). This idea is constantly repeated and forms the basis of the identity,[40] which must not be just a matter of outer display but also must become part of consciousness and memory – an affair of the heart. Josiah summoned all the people, "small and great," to assemble in Jerusalem. "And he read in their ears all the words of the book of the covenant (*sefer ha'-b⁽e⁾rît*) which was found in the house of the Lord. And the King stood by a pillar and made a covenant before the Lord, to walk after the Lord and to keep his commandments and his testimonies and his statutes with all their heart and with all their soul [...] And all the people stood to the covenant." "With all one's heart and with all one's soul" and "all the people" are set phrases that show this is a movement of awakening, in which a latent or even forgotten normative and formative self-image breaks through once more into a new consciousness. Hence the repetition of "with all your heart and with all your soul" (Deut. 4:29; 6:5; 10:12; 11:13; 26:16; 30:2; 30:6; 30:10).[41]

Religion and ethnicity are now inseparably conjoined. A confederation of tribes promotes itself to become a "people," the people are "holy" (Exod. 19:6; Deut. 26:19), and finally they become "the

---

[40] This is particularly common in Jer. (11:4; 24:7; 30:22; 31:33; 32:38). Sometimes, it is linked to circumcision (4:4, and also Deut. 10:16; for renewal of the heart, see esp. Ezekiel 11:19). Circumcision is the ethnic *katexochen*, denoting distinction from the heathen, polytheists and idolaters, with whom all contact is forbidden.

[41] The solemn oath (*adê*) that Asarhaddon makes all his people swear, to be loyal to his successor Ashurbanipal, frequently mentions the expression *ina gummurti libbikunu* (with the whole heart) – see, for example, Kazuko Watanabe, *Die adê-Vereidigung anlässlich der Thronfolgeregelung Asarhaddons*, Baghdader Mitteilungen vol. 3 (Berlin: Gebr. Mann, 1987), 160–163. It has often been pointed out that the Assyrian contracts for vassals were a model for the Israelite covenant with God (see H. Tadmor and also M. Weinfeld in L. Canfora, M. Liverani and C. Zaccagnini [eds.], *I Trattati nel Mondo Antico. Forma, Ideologia, Funzione* [Rome: "L'Erma" di Bretschneider, 1990]).

congregation of the Lord."[42] Every individual must know and never forget that he is part of a nation and that his membership obliges him to follow a strictly regulated (by contract) way of life, clearly separated from that of all other peoples. The ethnic term "Jew" thus becomes a "normative self-definition' (E. P. Sanders 1980 ff.), and this is an identity that has to be maintained even at the cost of one's own life.

The book of Deuteronomy is the manifesto and the constitution of an ethnic resistance movement. The model used is that of distinction and resistance through sacralization of identity, which is typical of such movements. In Egypt, too, the development of distinctive identity enhancement followed a similar direction. During the Persian era, a period of foreign rule, Egypt came under the pressure of an alien political and cultural code against which it had to mobilize forces of "national" contradistinction (A. B. Lloyd 1982). This is the background to the massive building program undertaken by King Nektanebos and continued by the Ptolemy dynasty. In my view, this was a distinctive identity enhancement that functioned in the same way as that of the Israelites, even though it used a completely different cultural method. There was no written canon in Egypt, but in its place there were temples. These, however, should be seen as a form of canonization. They all followed the same groundplan-layout, they were all covered in writing, and so they codified tradition in monumental form. Their high walls also provided barriers against the outside world, thus providing a solidly visual equivalent of the "iron barrier" that the law constituted for the Jews. The walls of the Egyptian temples encompassed not only rituals, images and writings but also a practical guideline for a way of life. Within the temple there were strict rules, for instance, about cleanliness. Nektanebos's temple-building program is yet another example of a distinctively enhanced, sanctified national identity. The temple became an identity symbol for Late Period Egypt that saw itself as the holy, or indeed "the holiest land" (*hierotáte chóra*) and as the "temple of the whole world."[43]

---

[42] Deut. 23:1–8 states explicitly who will be allowed to enter the "congregation of the Lord" (*qehal JHWH*).

[43] See now Hubert and Hildegard Cancik, "'Tempel der ganzen Welt' – Ägypten und Rom," in S. Appel (ed.), *Egypt – Temple of the Whole World* (Leiden: E. J. Brill, 2003), 41–57.

The solution found in Judea and Egypt is what we have called the canonization of the cultural memory. Canonization means that everything regarded as alien or irrelevant is excluded, whereas everything significant (in the sense of formative and normative) is sacralized, that is, given the status of binding obligation and unchangeability. These admittedly extreme examples show that ethnic identity and durability depend on cultural memory and the form of its organization. The disappearance of ethnic groups (apart from rare exceptions like the Inca Empire) is not a matter of physical annihilation but of collective and cultural forgetting. If we bear in mind all of the ramifications of this observation, it will be clear that any change in the organization of cultural memory – for example, through innovations in the manner of recording it (writing), of circulating it (printing, radio, TV), or of transmitting it (canonization, decanonization) – may bring with it the most radical alterations in collective identity.[44]

That is why, in all seriousness and for good reasons, the modern phenomenon of the nation-state has been linked to the invention of the printing-press (B. Anderson 1983). Striking enhancements of collective identity are to be found wherever there are particular advances in cultural technology: writing in early civilizations, writing and mnemotechnics in Israel and Greece, and mnemotechnics in Brahman India. Even with the Assyrians, whose accomplishments were initially military and only subsequently cultural, empire building was associated with a cultural institution that they are believed to have invented and the importance of which can scarcely be overestimated: the Palace Library (today it would be called National[45]). This was a collection containing the complete, written cultural memory of Assyrian-Babylonian society, linked to a consistent codification and incipient canonization of and commentary on the stream of tradition. The idea of a national library (unlike the specialized libraries of the temples and houses of tablets, and the houses of life in Egypt) should also be

---

[44] The concept of a transnational and transcultural identity that is common to all "world-religions" (except Judaism) always implies a collection of canonized scriptures. This illustrates the strong connection between the organization of memory (canonization, in this case) and the formation of identity.

[45] The decisive difference between a "palace" and a "national" library is public accessibility. It is striking that the famous library of Alexandria that followed the model of the oriental palace library was already open to the public.

seen as a mobilization of cultural memory in the sense of limitic or integrative upgrading. What has shown itself, however, to be by far the most effective means of giving permanence to an ethnic identity is religion. Every instance of unusual durability quoted by A. Smith, from the Samaritans to the Basques, shows the same pattern in which ethnic identity merges with a particular religion (A. D. Smith 1986, 105–125).

PART II

CASE STUDIES

Preliminary Remarks

Among the cultures of the Ancient World, there were two that gave their traditions a form that was so time-resistant and influential that their identity has remained in effect even today: Greece and Israel. The link between the two has provided the foundation not only for the Christian West but also for Islam. In the former, it is the Greek classics – literature and philosophy – that together with the Hebrew Bible and the New Testament rest at the heart of cultural memory, whereas in Islam it is Greek scholarship that has triumphed, although the Hebrew Bible has been superseded by the Koran. Nevertheless, there is no doubt that both the western and the Islamic culture are each based, in their different ways, on Greek and Judeo-Israelite heritages. Their heritage has not only endured through these connections, they also exist in a kind of "pure state" – Israel in Judaism and Hellas in humanism.

How did this come about? How did these two particular streams of tradition – unlike Babylon, and unlike Egypt – survive the decline of the Ancient World? This question takes us back to the origins of the semantic formations from which the two cultures emerged. In both Israel and Greece, simultaneously although for the most part independently, two crucial stages in the process fixed these meanings: (1) the production of foundational texts from the 8th to the 5th century, and (2) the canonization of these texts, together with the development of an interpretive culture in Hellenism. Both are also characterized by a break. The Judaism of the Second Temple and of the Diaspora looks back at Israel; the Hellenistic world (including Rome and all subsequent forms of Classicism and Humanism) looks back at Homeric and classical Hellas. Judaism developed the institution of the *sofer*, of written scholarship as the organ of its canonizing hindsight,[1] whereas Hellenism fulfilled this role through Alexandrian philology.[2] The Alexandrian reworking of the Greek tradition that became the starting point for western classics, coincided both temporally and geographically with the Jewish reworking of sacred texts that provided the starting point for the textual canon. Both movements were unquestionably connected to the fixing of a national identity. During those centuries, the intellectual climate in the world of the Eastern Mediterranean was dominated by the desire to codify, systematize, and definitively establish tradition. As a reaction to the expansion of a Greco-Oriental culture of unification, each of the affected individual cultures looked back to its past in an endeavor to fashion and keep a national identity of its own: in Mesopotamia, they turned to the extensive collections of ancient literature in the institutions of the Palace Library, which had been initiated in the 8th century under the neo-Assyrian Empire; in Egypt, they canonized the *Book of the Dead*[3]; in Persia, they examined the old Avestan records. This is the general historical background against which one may set these two otherwise very distinct cases – the Jewish scriptures and the Greek classics. In the context of this book, however, it is not the historical comparison that is of interest so much as the underlying concept of a national written culture that embraces both the textual canon of sacred texts and the classical canon of literature. This concept seems to me to be characteristic of what in more recent times has constituted the central element of the canon.

I do not need to discuss the now familiar processes of canonization again; for our purposes, it is more interesting to juxtapose these

---

[1] See, for example, Stadelmann 1980, and the essays by B. Lang and G. Theissen in A. Assmann 1991, as well as my book *Of God and Gods*, chapter 5.

[2] Rudolf Pfeiffer, *History of Classical Scholarship from the Beginnings to the End of the Hellenistic Age* (Oxford: Clarendon Press, 1968).

[3] During the 7th and 6th centuries, the *Book of the Dead* developed from a pool of unconnected spells out of which every individual funerary papyrus chose its own specific selection into a real book with a selection of 167 spells in a fixed order.

processes with traditions that did not survive. Babylon and Egypt are two cases that immediately spring to mind. Their written traditions reach much further back into history than those of Greece and Israel, as far as the beginning of the third millennium BCE, and they continued to provide the dominant political and cultural context when the Greek and Israelite cultures were emerging.[4] They finally disappeared with the spread of Christianity and then of Islam. Clearly, then, these streams of tradition could not continue to flow in comparable fashion, and I examine the case of Egypt in order to find out why.

Mesopotamia was unique: its bilingualism (Sumerian and Akkadian), its changing rulers (Sumerian, Akkadian, Cassite, Assyrian, Babylonian, Chaldean, and others) and the spread of its writings, religion, and culture to other tribes and peoples (Elamites, Amorites, Hurrites, Hittites, Canaanites, and so forth) made it the exact opposite of the virtually monolithic Egyptian culture and society. Such internal variety offers very favorable conditions for the establishment of traditions, and every major phase of political upheaval was accompanied by an effort to codify and fix them. The process began with a record of the Sumerian kings toward the end of the third millennium, and continued with the great canonization of Sumerian and then Akkadian texts in the Ancient Babylonian period (18th to 17th century BCE) and in the Cassite period (15th century), reaching its zenith in the libraries of the new Assyrian rulers of the 8th and 7th centuries (Lambert 1957). Mesopotamia had forms of written, textual, and book culture that were then continued by Greek and Jewish traditions; therefore Babylonian culture seemed to have had a more profound influence on later and more enduringly successful traditions than Egyptian culture. This seems to suggest that the establishment of cultural meaning has to take place along the lines of "logocentrism" (i.e., through language, texts, books, and so on). It seems scarcely conceivable that there might once have been traditions that were not written and that could even have been at the heart of the most venerated form of cultural memory, but Ancient Egypt offers the most impressive example of exactly this kind of culture. If we begin to query the processes of canonization, and the different media and organizational forms of cultural memory,

[4] On Greece, see Burkert 1984.

we encounter a very special phenomenon: the Late Egyptian temple. In this Chapter I argue that, similar to the Israelites and the Greeks, during the same period and probably under the same historical conditions, the Egyptians also produced their own canon. This did not take the form of a collection of books, but rather the temple.

4

Egypt

The Mythomotor of Integration

The Egypt of the Pharaohs did not have a national historiography that was even remotely comparable to that of the Bible. The first tentative beginnings were made during the period of the Ptolemies (Manetho). The lists of kings, which date back to the New Kingdom, were not meant to be history; they were used instead to measure time (i.e., "cold" memory). This does not mean that the Egyptian self-image did not incorporate any specific memories or solid forms of reconstruction. Such forms, however, were not narrative as we might expect, but they were condensed into a symbol, and in linguistic terms this was: "The unification of the two lands" (in Egyptian *zmȝ tȝwj*). "The two lands" was the name that Ancient Egyptians normally gave to their country, and this referred to Upper and Lower Egypt – in Egyptian *Shemaᶜ* and *Mehu*, two totally different words. The Egyptian king had two titles: *njswt* for King of Upper Egypt, and *bjt* for Lower. His two crowns symbolized his dual rule, and they were assigned to two crown goddesses and two crown cities, which were the capitals of earlier, mythical (possibly even historical) states that were united into the Pharaonic Empire (E. Otto 1938).[1] This central political symbol is

---

[1] See Hubert Roeder, *Mit dem Auge sehen: Studien zur Semantik der Herrschaft in den Toten- und Kulttexten* (Heidelberg: Heidelberger Orientverlag, 1996).

illustrated on the side panels of the royal throne. Horus and Seth are pictured tying and entwining the armorial plants of Upper and Lower Egypt in a longitudinal pattern that forms a hieroglyph meaning *zm3* [to unite]. The state over which the king reigned was the result of a unification brought about in mythical times by the two gods, and renewed by every king on his accession to the throne and throughout his period of rule.[2]

The tale of Horus and Seth gives narrative form to the foundational duality myth of the Egyptian state. But the feuding brothers represent more than just the geographical division into Upper and Lower Egypt. Horus embodies civilization, justice, and order, whereas Seth stands for barbarism, violence, and chaos.[3] Unity is only possible through a reconciliation of these opposing principles; however, this will only be possible if the one is subjugated to the other. Justice, culture, and order must fight and win, but they cannot do so of their own accord. Nor can they drive out chaos, barbarism, and violence – they can only subdue them. Myth, therefore, does not set up a definitive condition – it creates a never-ending project: controlling chaos and establishing order through unity, according to the principle "*ab integro nascitur ordo.*" Unity is always a potential problem, for it is never given but is something that must be always established and maintained.

The myth is not recounted simply for educational or entertainment purposes. It accomplishes two things. First, it describes a world divided into two that, as mentioned earlier, can only survive if the two parts are combined into a unit that allows order to triumph over chaos; second, it mobilizes the energy needed to establish and to maintain this unity. Such memory figures are almost like a call to arms, exerting a normative, formative power that helps to create a self-image and to inspire action. The dynamic nature of this symbolized identity is

---

[2] On this symbolism, see Henri Frankfort, *Kingship and the Gods* (Chicago: University of Chicago Press, 1948); J. Gwyn Griffiths, *The Conflict of Horus and Seth* (Liverpool: Liverpool University Press, 1960); see also the highly relevant comments by Barry J. Kemp, *Ancient Egypt. Anatomy of a Civilization* (London: Routledge, 1989), 27–29.

[3] On Seth, see Herman te Velde, *Seth, God of Confusion*, trans. G. E. van Baaren-Pape (Leiden: E. J. Brill, 1967); Erik Hornung, "Seth. Geschichte und Bedeutung eines ägyptischen Gottes," in *Symbolon* N.F. 2 (1975), 49–63; Hellmut Brunner, "Seth und Apophis – Gegengötter im ägyptischen Pantheon?," *Saeculum* 34 (1983), 226–234.

what I mean by the term "mythomotor."[4] The myth of Horus and Seth converts the memory of the original duality into the driving force that will bring about unity. The true secret of the unique coherence of the Egyptian state may lie in this mythomotor. It is not simply a matter of durability; instead, it is the power to repeatedly renew identity in a process of constant structural self-reproduction, even after the most disastrous ruptures.[5]

Egyptian mythodynamics clearly served to enhance a collective consciousness of identity through integration. This did not entail shutting off the external world, but was brought about by establishing an inner unity through combining the parts into a whole; the single unit was then thought of as all-embracing, and thus it had no need to distinguish itself from other, outside units. The borders of identity were seen as the borders of humanity and of the orderly world. Dominion over the two lands thus meant dominion over everything – in Egyptian *nb tm* (ruler of everything) or *nb w^c* (sole ruler) – which in effect meant that the two lands had become the world as created by the sun-god and entrusted to the king.

"Monumental Discourse": The Writing of Power and of Eternity

Unlike in Mesopotamia, writing in Egypt did not evolve exclusively in the context of economics, but also in that of political organization and representation: it recorded events of special political significance. The first written monuments were political manifestos in service of the emerging state, and one might categorize them as "prospective memory." They relate to the present as if to a "future past," formulating a record that is meant to preserve the present in the cultural memory to come. This clearly had two main purposes: the first, to guarantee the durability of the outcome of these actions by capturing them in stone and housing them in a sacred setting that would be permanent and would be open to the world of the gods; the second was to create a means of chronological orientation by recording the main event of a year, and then naming the year after it. Herein lies the origin of both Egyptian annals and historiography, and of Egyptian monumental

---

4 See Chapter 1.
5 See J. Assmann, *The Mind of Egypt* (see chapt. 1, n. 94).

architecture and art, whose sole function was to provide a visible and permanent link between the world of humans and that of the gods. This is also the origin of the hieroglyph, which is a form of pictorial art and, as "the words of the gods" (the meaning of the Egyptian word for "hieroglyphs"), was used only to record what was to be housed in the "sacred space of eternity."[6]

Thus "monumental discourse" arose as the medium through which the state made both itself and its eternal order visible. The dual references of writing, plus art and architecture, reflected the special relationship between the concepts of state and eternity (or immortality) in Egypt. The state was not only an institution to ensure peace, order, and justice; it also made immortality – or at least survival beyond death – possible.[7] Every hieroglyphic monument makes reference to this connection. It serves to immortalize the individual, and it acknowledges its debt to the state. As the state in Ancient Egypt had a monopoly on all crafts, it alone could make them accessible to the individual, thereby maintaining control of the only medium for collective identity and social self-promotion, and the only medium for survival in the social memory after death. Monumental discourse, then, was not only a means of communication but also a road to salvation. By opening up the possibility of communicating with posterity over thousands of years, it offered the individual the opportunity for equal longevity that would last –in the words of Diodor or Hecataeus – for as long as he "remained in the memory because of his virtue." Monumental discourse was indeed one of virtue (Egyptian *Ma'at*, which also means justice, truth, and order), of eternity, and of political belonging.[8] As such, it was the most important means of organizing cultural memory in Egypt.

Of course writing did not remain limited to its original function as a central element of monumental discourse. Indeed, the change from its hieroglyphic (i.e., pictorial) nature was so fundamental that one can

---

[6] On the origin and early history of hieroglyphic writing, see Adelheid Schlott, *Schrift und Schreiber im alten Ägypten* (Munich: C. H. Beck, 1989) and her references to other literature.

[7] For more details, see J. Assmann, *Ma'at*, (see chapt. 1, n. 11) and *Death and Salvation in Ancient Egypt*, trans. David Lorton (Ithaca: Cornell University Press, 2005).

[8] I have discussed this function of monuments and hieroglyphs in more detail elsewhere; see J. Assmann, "Stein und Zeit" (see chapt. 1, n. 47) and "Gebrauch und Gedächtnis. Die zwei Kulturen Ägyptens," in Assmann and Harth (eds.), *Mnemosyne*, 135–152 (see chapt. 1, n. 2).

almost talk of two separate media. Within the framework of monumental discourse, writing never deviated in the slightest from its original pictoriality, right up until the end of Ancient Egyptian culture. Outside that framework, however, it evolved into a cursive form in which the original images were simplified to the point of being unrecognizable. Thus, two forms of writing developed: the hieroglyphic inscription and cursive handwriting. Only the latter is what is now called writing in the normal sense of the word, and this of course is what was taught to Egyptian schoolchildren. The other, inscriptive form was classified as art; it was only taught to those pursuing a career as chief draftsman. As a form of art (or monumental discourse), inscriptive writing was subject to binding rules that were so specialized and rigid that they were rightly regarded as a canon. Thus in Egypt, too, cultural memory is associated with canonization, although here it relates to the visual medium and not to written texts. The exclusion of variation is absolute – a fact that was apparent even to Plato, and is still regarded as the characteristic feature of Egyptian art. "The most striking visual fact about Egyptian images is their sameness – one work is more or less like another" (Davis 1989, 3).

Plato's reflections on the Egyptian temple in his *Laws* were actually based on a misunderstanding that was fruitful and also very revealing in relation to the self-image of Late Egyptian society. He reports that the Egyptians kept the models or standard forms – the Greek term is *schemata* – which recognized and recorded for all time the ideal beauty in their temples. For the Egyptians, it was

"necessary for the young in the cities to practice fine postures and fine songs. They made a list of these, indicating which they were and what kind they were, and published it in their temples. Painters and others who represented postures were not allowed to make innovations or think up things different from the ancestral. And they are still not allowed to – not in these things or in music altogether. If you look into this you will find that for ten thousand years – not 'so to speak' but really ten thousand years – the paintings and sculptures have been in no way more beautiful or ugly than those that are being made, with the same skill, by their craftsmen now" (*Laws* 656d-657a).[9]

9 "The Laws of Plato," trans. with notes by Thomas L. Pangle (New York: Basic Books, 1979), 36–37.

What Plato was referring to here, and what must be seen as the very heart of this story, was the truly astonishing uniformity of the architectural and artistic forms used in Egypt. This was one of the most important features of the Late Egyptian self-image. Of course, a law was never passed during the first or fourth dynasty that specified that there should never be any deviation from the current state of the arts for the rest of time. It was the Late Period that insisted on the need to adhere strictly to the art of former epochs. The walls of the tombs were faithfully copied, ancient forms of architecture revived, and statues sculpted just as they had been 1,500 years before.[10]

Furthermore, the whole evolution of Egyptian art reveals a principle that Jacob Burckhardt described as a "hieratic immobilization"or sacred fixation ("hieratische Stillstellung").[11] A good deal of research and scholarship was devoted to this principle within the context of the Egyptian canon. It lost none of its binding force even during the period of Hellenism (in fact, the temples of the Ptolemies were much closer in form to those of the two-thousand-year-old past than they were to the forms of Hellenism).[12] In recent times, it has become increasingly clear that J. Burckhardt had intuitively hit the nail on the head with

[10] See J. Assmann, *The Mind of Egypt*, chapter 5 (see chapt. 1, n. 94).

[11] "Only art is not merely kept at a particular level over the course of time, but it is even held up on high, i.e. further, loftier developments are temporarily cut off by hieratic freezing, and what was once achieved with enormous effort is taken as sacred, we learn this especially from the beginning and end of the ancient cultural worlds of Egypt and Byzantium" (Jacob Burckhardt, *Die Kunst der Betrachtung. Aufsätze und Vorträge zur bildenden Kunst*, ed. H. Ritter [Köln: DuMont, 1984], 195).

[12] Initially, the Egyptian canon refers to a system of proportions of the human body that is incorporated into a "square grid"; see Erik Iversen, *Canon and Proportions in Egyptian Art*, 2nd, ed. (Warminster: Aris and Phillips, 1975). More recently, however, a much more comprehensive concept of the Egyptian canon has begun to establish itself, which relates not only to the rules of Egyptian art but also to the whole social and economic framework; see for example the work of Whitney M. Davis, *The Canonical Tradition in Egyptian Art* (Cambridge: Cambridge University Press, 1989); "Canonical Representation in Egyptian Art," *Res 4: Anthropology and Aesthetics* (1982), 20–46; "The Canonical Theory of Composition in Egyptian Art," *Göttinger Miszellen* 56 (1982), 9–26. I have tried to separate these rules into five complexes: (1) proportion (canon in its narrower sense); (2) projection (two-dimensional representation of space); (3) representation (iconic forms and conventions); (4) exclusion (what is *not* represented programmatically, particularly the space-time abstractness of the Egyptian image); (5) syntax (especially the hypotactic structure of the image). See J. Assmann, "Viel Stil am Nil? Ägypten und das Problem des Kulturstils," in Gumbrecht and Pfeiffer (eds.), *Stil*, 522–524 (see chapt. 3, n. 26) and "Sepulkrale Selbstthematisierung im Alten Ägypten," (see chapt. 1, n. 14).

his concept of "writing of giants" (*Riesenschrift*). Art and writing were so intricately interwoven that one cannot even talk of a close relationship; they were one and the same thing (Fischer 1986, 24). Writing was a form of art, and art was an extension of writing. This explains the detailed and realistic pictoriality that remained consistent at all times in Egyptian hieroglyphics, similar to the strictly uniform types and forms of Egyptian art. The pictorial, artistic character of monumental writing and the written character of art conditioned each other. And so the constrictions of Egyptian art were caused not by an inability to progress, but by a prescribed bond between the signifier and the signified, the loosening of which would have meant "modifying the moorings of their existence" (Lacan 2001, 192).[13]

I would like to now examine the hieratic immobilization, or ten-thousand-year uniformity that so impressed Plato. The hieroglyphic system of writing, at least in its late form, seems, conversely, to be characterized by a degree of openness that would be difficult to find in other writing systems. It was not the content that was frozen, or canonized, but the generative principle, that is, that of iconicity. The characters always had to be icons. The openness of the portfolio that facilitated the constant introduction of new signs and meanings nevertheless depended on the iconicity of those signs, which – even if the reference to a word or group of sounds may have remained obscure – were always recognizable as the image of something. For the most part, it was therefore possible to extrapolate from the icon a reference that could be put into language. Once hieroglyphic writing began to make use of its inherent openness to new graphic forms, the pictorial nature of its signs ceased to be purely aesthetic, and it belonged to the systemic rationality of writing that would not have been legible without it. Therefore that which is in place here is not, in fact, a hieratic but a systemic or structural immobilization required by the rationality of the system rather than by religious commands.

Egyptian hieroglyphs are a complex system because they simultaneously denote both language and the world. They have a dual nature:

---

[13] It is feared that such loosening would also destroy the binding quality of the laws of communal life; thus, for instance, Confucius argued that everything depended on round being called "round" and square, "square," and in the 5th century BCE the musicologist Damon – quoted approvingly by Plato – maintained that the laws of the state would crumble if one made any changes to musical keys.

their elements function both as *signs*, relating to language, and as *icons*, reproducing forms from the outside world. With this latter function, they do the same as art and belong to the schemata mentioned by Plato. These schemata are sacred because, according to Late Egyptian belief, they were designed by the gods, as were the temple plans and the rituals and everything else that was to be preserved by the Late Egyptian temple. Hieroglyphic script was comprehensive because it encompassed everything that could be illustrated, forming a kind of encyclopedic pictorial dictionary (*orbis pictus*) that gave presence to the whole world within the confines of the temple. And it was holy because pictures as such were holy. All illustratable figures were the products of the divine creator, and were articulated (i.e., fashioned pictorially) in forms – Plato's schemata – by the god Thoth, the inventor of writing. To use Friedrich Junge's striking expression, the world was "the hieroglyphs of the gods" (Junge 1984, 272).

Canon and Identity

There can be no doubt that the Egyptians succeeded in creating a lasting cultural identity that was unique in the Ancient World. Equally evident is that the means they used to institutionalize their durability and their exclusion of change was precisely that which is called the canon – a new form of cultural continuity or connective structure arising out of writing. In Egypt, however, this was not textual continuity, which is far from being a given factor in the formation of a written culture. What is decisive in the latter is the emergence of a culture of interpretation, and this is precisely what was missing from the Egyptian handling of texts. They were copied, and they were varied, but they were not interpreted.

In a very general, anthropological sense, commentary is one of the basic forms of human communication, along with narration, argumentation, description etc., and so of course it can be argued that, strictly speaking, Egyptian written culture also contained forms of commentary, but these seem to have been confined to two kinds of text: cultic and medicinal. These might be described in terms of sacramental interpretation (J. Assmann 1977)[14] and professional literature. The former was connected to a separation of meaning into two

---

[14] See now J. Assmann, *Death and Salvation*, chapter XV, 348–368 (see chapt. 4, n. 7).

levels of signification – rather like allegory. The style of commenting naturally arose from this semantic split, combining the surface meaning and deep meaning, sense relating to the world of the cult and sense referring to the divine world, worldly meaning and the deeper, divine meaning. The practice of commenting in "specialist prose" or "professional literature," on the other hand, grew out of the need for precision, exhaustiveness, and completeness. In both cases, the commentary was immanent in the discourse, in the sense that the text and the commentary were not separated into two distinct forms of discourse. In fact the commentary grew on the basic text almost parasitically in the course of its passage from one generation or copy to another – the text not yet being subject to the canonic rule by which nothing might be added, taken away, or changed. Tradition and interpretation are inextricably bound together (on Israel, see Fishbane 1986). The step toward commentary in its own right took place when a line was drawn in one way or another under the production of texts and people became aware that anything worth saying and everything worth knowing were preserved in the "great texts" – so that the culture from then on, in the late stage (*Späthorizont*) of posthistory, was limited to interpreting them in order to prevent the link with wisdom and truth from rupturing. This form of closure manifested itself in different written cultures in a variety of ways. For the Alexandrians, Homer was the pinnacle, and the classics were regarded as unmatchable models; for Chinese scholars, everything that could be known was contained in their own classics although, in view of their notorious obscurity, all comprehension remained incomplete; for Averroes, Aristotle had definitively marked out the boundaries of knowledge – a figure of speech that anticipated Alexandre Kojève (who coined the term *posthistoire*), who saw in Hegel the end of the history of thought, and who could only imagine a future form of philosophy in the Hegel exegesis. Jews speak of the "end of prophecy," which defines the boundaries of the Hebrew canon, whereas Muslims talk of Muhammad as the "seal of the prophets" and of the "closing of the gate of interpretation," with regard to the deuterocanonical tradition. In a strict sense, it might be said that commentary presupposes finality, because the very act of interpreting indicates that the text is durably fixed, and not open to revision or to replacement by new texts. For philologists, the term "text" itself is relative and stands in contrast to commentary. A poem, a law, a treatise, and so on, will only become a text in this strict sense once it has been made the object of a commentary – that is, the commentary is what makes a text a *text*.

It appears that in Egypt – with the possible exception of the 17th chapter of the *Book of the Dead* – such "texts" did not exist. Although old works were faithfully preserved, the new ones never took a stance on the commentary in the old ones but simply continued the form along the same lines. Thus the classic teachings of Ptahhotep were followed by a succession of new teachings, right into the Hellenist period, and the *Book of the Dead* – canonized in the Persian period at the latest – was joined by newer Books of the Dead such as *The Book of Breathing* and *The Book of Traversing Eternity*. Commentary needs a dividing line that dams the stream of tradition and divides it into center and periphery. None of these conditions for the division into text and commentary existed in pre-Hellenistic Egypt.[15]

As a consequence, Egyptian culture, despite the major role played by writing, owes its unique continuity more to ritual than to textual coherence. The canonization of pictorial art and its underlying syntax was intended to serve the cause of repetition, not of development or of regulated variation. This is a very special case of a ritual culture that was supported by writing and by text, and that is why, in the Late Period, when the culture had to defend itself against assimilation by the foreign cultures of the Persians and the Macedonians, it did not do so using the form of a book – as in Israel – but using that of a temple. It was the temple as the fortress of ritual continuity that provided the basis for the continuation of this culture, and in the following section I examine how this was done.

THE LATE PERIOD TEMPLE AS A "CANON"

Temple and Book

Concerning the Hathor Temple of Dendera, we are told that its "great ground-plan together with the inventory of this city is engraved on

---

[15] See the essays by Jan Assmann, "Text und Kommentar. Einführung," in J. Assmann and B. Gladigow (eds.), *Text und Kommentar*, 9–34 (see chapt. 2, n. 1) and Ursula Rössler-Köhler, "Text oder Kommentar," ibid., 111–140. BD 17 is interspersed with glosses in the form of questions and answers. Rössler-Köhler interprets these glosses, which are written in red in carefully written manuscripts, as a commentary. I, however, view this text as an initiatory interrogation, in which the initiate has to recite a sacred text and is examined on its meaning.

the wall at the appropriate place, without anything having been taken away or added because it is perfect in relation to [the wisdom] of the forefathers."[16] And, referring to the Horus Temple in Edfu, we learn that Ptolemy's new building was based on a plan "as begun by the forefathers and as stands in the great plan of this book, which fell from heaven north of Memphis."[17] The concepts of book and temple are obviously not all that different. In fact, the temple is nothing other than the three-dimensional, monumental transposition of a book and has all of the characteristics of a canon: similar to the Koran, it is a revelation that fell from heaven, and similar to the Torah it must have "nothing added and nothing taken away."[18]

The sources constantly talk of such a book, the realization of which is seen as the Late Egyptian temple. On one occasion it is described as the work of Imhotep, a vizir and sage of the 3rd Dynasty, who, as the architect of King Djoser's necropolis, and as such the inventor of stonemasonry and of the pyramid in its earliest form (the step pyramid), was not only documented by his contemporaries but also remained alive in cultural memory and was honored by the gods (Wildung 1977). Elsewhere, it is said to be the work of the god Thoth himself, the Egyptian equivalent of Hermes, who was known as the god of writing, mathematics, and wisdom.[19] The book is the basis of the

---

[16] A. Mariette, *Dendérah* III 1872, plate 77 a, b; also E. Chassinat and F. Daumas, *Le temple de Dendérah* VI, 152, 1–3.

[17] E. Chassinat, *Le temple d'Edfou* VI, 6.4; see also Dietrich Wildung, *Imhotep und Amenhotep. Gottwerdung im Alten Ägypten* (Munich: Deutscher Kunstverlag, 1977), 146, § 98.

[18] On the history of the canon formula, see Chapter 2.

[19] See Patrick Boylan, *Thoth, the Hermes of Egypt* (London, New York: Oxford University Press, 1922), esp. on Thoth as the author of the temple books: 88–91. Some of the "42 indispensable (*pány anankaîai* = canonical) books of Hermes," which according to Clemens Alexandrinus, *Stromat.* VI.4.3 5–7, were mastered by the Egyptian priests, deal with the construction of the temple. On Clemens's information about Egypt, see Albert Deiber, *Clément d'Alexandrie et l'Égypte* (Cairo: l'Institut français d'archéologie orientale, 1904). Joachim F. Quack discovered in many hundreds of fragments in hieroglyphic, hieratic, demotic writing, and even Greek translation the remains of a lengthy composition that he dubbed "The Book of the Temple" and that also contains instructions about the contruction of the temple; see Joachim F. Quack "Der historische Abschnitt des Buches vom Tempel," in J. Assmann and E. Blumenthal (eds.), *Literatur und Politik im pharaonischen und ptolemäischen Ägypten*, BdÉ 127 (Cairo: l'Institut français d'archéologie orientale, 1999), 267–278; "Das Buch vom Tempel und verwandte Texte. Ein Vorbericht," *ARG* 2 (2000), 1–20; "Le manuel du temple. Une nouvelle source sur la vie des prêtres égyptiens," *Égypte Afrique & Orient* 29

temple, and the temple in turn preserves the book along with other books in its library. The bond between the two is unmistakable.

The nature and meaning of this bond are immediately obvious if one views the Late Egyptian temple as a cultural phenomenon *sui generis*. There are four clear features that the temple shares with sacred literature and that it brings together as a unit:

1. the *architectural* aspect: the temple as the realization of a "ground-plan" (Egyptian *snt*);[20]
2. the *epigraphic* aspect: the ornamental element of the temple as the realization of a "model" (Egyptian *sšm*);
3. the *cultic* aspect: the temple as the stage for the cult of sacrifice, and the realization of a directive according to a "prescription" (Egyptian *sšm, tp-rd, nt-ᶜ* etc.),[21] and
4. the *ethical* aspect: the temple as a place for a way of life and for the fulfillment of divine laws.[22]

If the Late Egyptian temple is seen as a combination of all these factors, then there is clearly good reason to call it a cultural phenomenon in its own right rather than call it the last remnants of an architectural tradition that went back thousands of years. In light of our search for ways in which cultural memory found expression, the Egyptian temple of the Late Period is unquestionably a great deal more than just a building.

But even if we look on it simply as a piece of architecture, it will be obvious that this temple is not the mere continuation of a tradition – it represents something quite new. It follows a unified architectural concept or a canonical plan much more strictly than the temple construction of earlier eras had done. All the great temples of the Greco-Roman era can be seen as variations on a single archetype, and the

(2003), 11–18; "Organiser le culte idéal. Le Manuel du temple égyptien," in *BSFÉ* 160 (2004), 9–25.

[20] This is dealt with by Clemens under the 10 "hieroglyphic" books about the construction of the temple.

[21] This is covered by the books Clemens mentions under "The Art of Sacrifice."

[22] This is covered by the books Clemens mentions under "Education" as well as by the ten "hieratic books about laws, gods and the whole of priesthood education." Jan Quaegebeur, "Sur la 'loi sacrée' dans l'Égypte gréco-romaine," *Ancient Society* 11/12 (1981/82), 227–240, has convincingly identified the concept of a "sacral law" – frequently mentioned in Greek sources – with such codifications.

Horus Temple of Edfu may be regarded as the most perfect and best preserved example of this. The plan of the Late Period also differs from those of the past in the nature of its layout. The vital new element here is the box structure of the outer cover. In the Edfu Temple the sanctuary is protected from the outside world by no fewer than five walls with corridors and rooms between them. The fact that this was a central concept for the Late Egyptian temple can be seen from the two-dimensional reproductions with up to seven interlinking portals. Each portal symbolizes a zone that mediates between interior and exterior. The meaning is clear: this layout denotes the idea of an inner sanctum that must be protected against the profanities of the outside world with every possible means. The architecture is permeated by security measures that indicate a profound awareness of danger – the fear of profanation. This in turn indicates the degree of sanctity that must be preserved and that evidently goes far beyond the need for inaccessibility and secrecy that was traditionally associated with holy places. The main coordinates in Late Egyptian temple architecture, then, were security versus danger, interior versus exterior, sanctity versus profanity.

All this reflects certain elements of the Late Egyptian mentality, which are recorded not only by Egyptian but also, and especially, by Greek sources. First of all, one can clearly see a deeply ingrained xenophobia, accompanied by the fear of profanation and a desire for seclusion. The story of Joseph illustrates that the Egyptians never sat at the table with foreigners: "And they set on for him by himself, and for them by themselves, and for the Egyptians, which did eat with him, by themselves: because the Egyptians might not eat bread with the Hebrews; for that is an abomination unto the Egyptians" (Gen. 43:32).[23]

Herodotus reported that the Egyptians avoided adopting the customs of the Greeks and of all other peoples.[24] Classical authors

[23] In the late classical romance *Joseph and Aseneth*, this is reversed: "For Joseph did not eat with the Egyptians, because that was an abomination to him" (7.1). Gerhard Delling, *Die Bewältigung der Diasporasituation durch das hellenistische Judentum* (Göttingen: Vandenhoeck & Ruprecht, 1987), 12.

[24] Herodotus, *Hist.* II, 91 cf. 49 and 79. Herodotus also says that, compared to other people, the Egyptians do everything backward (II, 35). This is obviously a reference not only to his own observations but also to an image that would have corresponded

constantly complained about the arrogance, reserve, and exclusive-
ness of the Egyptians.[25] Moreover, Egyptian texts condemned foreigners as being unclean – they were not allowed to come anywhere
near the temples or any sacred ceremonies. Seth was made God
of foreigners and was insultingly nicknamed "the Mede," becoming
the "counter-god"; and, foreigners were dubbed "typhonic beasts"
(Brunner 1983; Helck 1964). Seth's new nickname indicated that
this development took place during the Persian period, and this is
confirmed by other historical observations. There can be little doubt
that the xenophobia and fear of profanation arose during this time of
foreign rule, and Egyptian culture began to withdraw into the temples
in order to protect itself against the incursions of the outer world.
In this late phase we can see how the culture changed from integrative to distinctive. Under foreign rule the Egyptians, similar to the
Jews, developed defensive strategies for their cultural system that were
anachronistically termed nationalism.[26]

If we take a closer look at the forms and inscriptions, we see that the
architectural, epigraphic, cultic, and ethical aspects of the Late Period
temples are joined by a fifth feature that is of vital importance to our
understanding of cultural memory: the temple as a representation
of the past and as the expression of a specific awareness of history.
In simple terms, the Late Period Egyptian temple is "built memory."
This is all the more striking in Hellenism: Greek forms of art were
adopted everywhere else in the Mediterranean and the Near East

---

to the Egyptians' own view of themselves, though naturally from a different perspective. This is the self-image of orthopraxy, which believes itself to be the only rightful
way.

[25] See the relevant passages in Garth Fowden, *The Egyptian Hermes. A Historical
Approach to the Late Pagan Mind* (Cambridge: Cambridge University Press, 1986),
15 f.

[26] Lloyd, "Nationalist Propaganda," (see chapt. 1, n. 94); Ramsay MacMullen, "Nationalism in Roman Egypt," *Aegyptus* 44 (1964), 179–199; J. Gwyn Griffiths, "Egyptian
Nationalism in the Edfu Temple Texts," in J. Ruffle et al. (eds.), *Glimpses of Ancient
Egypt: Studies in Honour of H. W. Fairman* (Warminster: Aris and Phillips, 1979), 174–
179. The term "enclave culture" proposed by Mary Douglas to refer to minority
movements such as the Jewish sects in Hellenistic Palestine seems more appropriate.
See Mary Douglas, *In the Wilderness: The Doctrine of Defilement in the Book of Numbers*
(Oxford: Oxford University Press, 2001), esp. chapter 2, "The Politics of Enclaves,"
42–62. See also J. Assmann, *Of God and Gods: Egypt, Israel and the Rise of Monotheism* (Madison: Wisconsin University Press, 2008), chapter 5; and *The Mind of Egypt*,
chapter 26, 389–408 (see chapt. 1, n. 94).

culture. Only in Egypt, culture adhered to the canon of traditional forms. The reason for this is that those forms had an iconic meaning: with their tori, cornices, and sloping walls, the temples rendered a monumental, stone version – fifty times larger – of the reed hut that was the original, prehistoric shrine. These new structures, built (or at least financed) by foreign, Macedonian rulers, appeared from the outside to be the embodiment of traditional Egyptian architecture, and indeed they represented a renaissance in the shape of a return to the past – a renewal of tradition. This could also count as a typical method of fixing meaning through canonization. The significance and the reason why these buildings can be rightly and justifiably seen as the expression of a particular consciousness of history and identity (or as architectural memory) can be gauged from some of the countless inscriptions with which they are covered.

The outstanding feature of the Egyptian Late Period temple is probably its richness of décor. Not only the walls but also the ceilings and even the columns are inscribed with scenes and texts. It is clear that many of the books kept in the temple libraries were used as models for the stone decorations. This was not exactly a new development; from the Old Kingdom to the Late Period one can see a steady increase in the degree of decoration. However, the difference here lies in the quality, a shift that goes back to the Persian period. Until then, the decorative element was always related to the function of the room concerned: for example, it symbolically represented and preserved cultic procedures. The Late Period saw the introduction of something new, namely the codification of knowledge.[27] What was now eternalized in stone went far beyond the reaches of ritual.

---

[27] Hermann Kees, *Der Götterglaube im alten Ägypten* (Leipzig: Hinrichs, 1941), 416 f. is very revealing on this subject: "At historic turning points, groups like to store collected works. Fear of losing the heritage outweighs creativity. And so in Egypt the most creative period, also in the intellectual field, the Old Kingdom, was also the most barren in terms of writing. Only the epigones began to put together the intellectual heritage in permanent form. The late temples also set out to be effective through the mass of their knowledge. Their records of rituals, festivals, and of the gods themselves were kept in scholarly fashion." In this context, Kees speaks of a "fear of forgetting" that took hold of Egypt in the Late Period (p. 415). Certainly the experience of foreign rule, and particularly the culture shock of Hellenism, led to a loss of tradition's self-evidence, which in turn brought with it a need for explanation.

There were cosmographical, geographical, theological, and mytho-logical texts and images, along with extensive inscriptions, ethical precepts for the priests, inventories, lists of sacred objects, instruc-tions, and proscriptions for individual temples and for all temples and for different regions – in short, a veritable encyclopedia such as had never before been seen in the temples of former times. The writing itself also took on encyclopedic dimensions, with a huge, even explo-sive increase in the number of signs, from ca. 700 to ca. 7,000. Each temple developed its own system of writing. This was based on the pictorial iconicity inherent in the hieroglyph system that – unlike the cursive writing derived from it – allowed for the introduction of an endless stream of new signs because the world of objects was itself an endless source of new images. The concept of writing as an iconic encyclopedia of images (or *orbis pictus*) developed from this, in which the whole world and the corresponding idea of the world as a "hiero-glyphs of the gods" (Junge 1984, 272) could be illustrated. During the time it absorbed the world into itself, so to speak, the Egyptian temple also closed itself off from the world. This claim to totality is another typical element of canonization. For the Jews, Christians, and Muslims, it is the Tanakh, the Christian Bible, and the Koran, respectively, that contain and explain everything that is knowable and worth knowing.

The Egyptian Late Period temple, however, contains more than just the sum of knowledge – it actually contains *the world*. This is "cosmothe-ism" rather than monotheism.[28] If I may talk in Wittgensteinian terms, with this type of religion the meaning of the world lies most emphat-ically inside rather than outside itself. The world itself is a whole that is full of meaning and is therefore divine. This is what the Late Period temple seeks to illustrate. Its base is the primal waters, its columns are the plant world growing out of the waters, its roof is the heavens. Friezes of gift-bearers and gods of the Nile symbolize the individual regions of the country. Thus each temple is a representation of the whole world (D. Kurth 1983).

The cosmic representation also takes in the dimension of time. This is a particularly significant point in relation to cultural memory,

---

[28] See J. Assmann, "Magische Weisheit. Wissensformen im ägyptischen Kosmotheis-mus," in A. Assmann (ed.), *Weisheit*, 241–258, 241 ff. (see chapt. 3, n. 13) and J. Assmann, *Moses the Egyptian. The Memory of Egypt in Western Monotheism* (Cambridge, MA: Harvard University Press, 1997), 142 f.

because the cosmos is not only seen as space but first and foremost as a process. What the temple illustrates through its symbolic forms and icons is therefore (1) the cosmogonic process by which the "primeval hill" emerged from the "primeval waters," and (2) the daily cycle of the sun's course, to the regular rhythm of which the life of the divine and eternal cosmos unfolds. The temple is therefore at one and the same time the "primeval hill," the place of origin from which the creator fashioned the world, and the "luminous place" (*akhet* in Egyptian, commonly rendered as "horizon") where the sun rises and sets. It is this latter aspect to which the astronomical ceilings, solar friezes, and architraves refer, whereas the primeval hill is the subject of the elaborate myths of "temple-origin" to be seen in the inscriptions and "monographs" (Reymond 1969; Finnestad 1985).

The myths of temple-origin link the building's construction history to cosmogony, in much the same way as official Egyptian historiography links the latter with the dynastic history of Egypt. This leads us to the concept of the preexistence of power. In the beginning was power. The gods practiced it by bringing forth a world out of the primal waters, furnishing it, and making it habitable. With the transfer of power from the gods to demigods and human dynasties, the cosmogonic process was also transferred to the heavens, and in the form of the sun's course, it no longer served the purpose of creation so much as that of keeping the world going – and humans also played their part in this process. The site of their work was the temple. Here is a form of historical consciousness that Erik Voegelin (1974) called "historiogenesis" – a combination of cosmogony (i.e., genesis) and history. The cosmogonic process continues into history, with the kings seeing themselves as the successors, deputies, and sons of the creator god. Creation was not separated from history with a simple break on the seventh day; instead, history was viewed as a continuation of creation under the changed conditions of the fallen world. According to Egyptian and indeed many other interpretations, the fall consisted in the separation of heaven from earth and of the gods from men.[29] The process of transition, however, was not quite as seamless as Voegelin would have us believe. Nor can we talk here

---

[29] Willibald Staudacher, *Die Trennung von Himmel und Erde. Ein vorgriechischer Schöpfungsmythos bei Hesiod und den Orphikern* (Diss., Tübingen, 1942); te Velde, *Seth,*

of a directed, linear history (as in the philosophy of history), which Voegelin would like to contrast with the conventional interpretation by eastern and other mythical histories. The emphasis on the "cosmogonic phase," when the gods themselves were still in power and lived here on Earth, cannot be ignored. This *historia divina* is the true and meaningful history that alone is to be narrated and is what the myths that are immortalized in the temple refer to. If the temple is indeed built architectural memory, that memory is concerned with the mythical, primeval time.

Voegelin is right, however, when he insists that the Egyptians and Babylonians had a very different approach to this mythical time than that of primitive people and even that of the Greeks. The lists of kings gave Egyptians and Babylonians an instrument that enabled them to measure precisely the distance between their present and the primeval time, and even permitted the division of that primeval time into historical periods (Luft 1978). In terms purely of form, this would seem to remove the distinction between mythical time and the historical present, but the lists of kings and the annals were not history as such – they were an instrument of chronological orientation. They served to measure a space whose importance was nowhere near comparable to that of the cosmogonic primeval time narrated by the myths. The Egyptians were able to gaze back over thousands of years of events – sometimes the inscriptions in the Late Period temples even give precise details of preceding buildings from the 18th to the 12th Dynasty – and yet it was the mythical primeval time that they regarded as being the true history and source of reality, by comparison with which their own human history was mere repetition and ritual conservation. This approach that concentrated on origin and circulation found expression in the architecture, images, cults, and language of the Late Period temple.

In brief, then, we have seen that the temple was regarded as the earthly realization of a heavenly book: as a *building*, it embodied a divine ground-plan; its *decorations* reproduced a whole library in stone;

(see chapt. 4, n. 3); László Kákosy, "Ideas of the Fallen State of the World in Egyptian Religion: Decline of the Golden Age," *Studia Aegyptiaca* VII (1981), 81–92. See also Erik Hornung, *Der ägyptische Mythos von der Himmelskuh. Eine Ätiologie des Unvollkommenen*, OBO 46 (Göttingen: Vandenhoeck & Ruprecht, 1982).

its *rituals* followed divine prescriptions; as a "*built architectural memory*," that is, as the visualization of historical consciousness, it linked the present with the mythical, primeval time of origins. By adding its own postscript to what the gods had prescribed, the temple also became a model of the world because the latter was "built" according to the same principles. There is, however, one more immensely important aspect that we have yet to consider, namely the temple as the house of a particular way of life.

The "Nomos" of the Temple

I call this way of life the *nomos* of the temple that linked cultic purity with social morality. Cultic purity entailed scrupulous adherence to a whole range of instructions, which were predominantly in the form of proscriptions, especially relating to food.[30] These instructions varied from temple to temple, and from region to region. Each region had its own forbidden foods (Montet 1950) and each temple its own proscriptions, according to the theology of the god who was worshiped there. For example, in the Temple of Osiris, raising one's voice was forbidden; in the "Abaton" (i.e. prohibited place, sacred to Osiris) of Esna, blowing a trumpet was not permitted, and so on. The first vow a priest had to take on ordination was: "I shall not eat that which is forbidden to priests."

The following list of priests' vows has come down to us in Greek and, as will be seen, all of them are in negative form:

> I shall not cut [...],
> I shall not instruct anyone to [...],
> I have not cut off the head of any living creature,
> I have not killed any human, [...]
> I have not slept with any boy,

---

[30] See Michel Muszynski, "Le droit égyptien à travers la documentation grecque," in *Le droit égyptien ancien*. Colloque organisé par l'Institut des Hautes Études de Belgie (Bruxelles: Institut des hautes études de Belgique, 1974), 163–180; Quaegebeur, "Sur la 'loi sacrée'," (see chapt. 4, n. 22). In Greek sources there is often talk of a *hieratikos nomos* or *hieros nomo*, which probably indicates a codification of binding rules relating, above all, to the priests. Such collections of laws, of which a whole series of fragments have come down to us in Greek and in Egyptian-Demotic, were part of the "books of the gods" (*tmᶜ n ntr*, transcribed into Greek as *Sem(e)nouthi*) – the sacral literature that was edited, copied, and preserved in the temples.

I have not slept with the wife of another, [...]
I shall neither eat nor drink what is forbidden or is listed in books [as
   forbidden].
I shall not make long fingers.
I shall not make any measurements on the threshing floor.
I shall not take any scales in my hand.
I shall not wrongly measure any land.
I shall not enter any unclean place.
I shall not touch any sheep's wool.
I shall not grasp any knife, until the day I die.[31]

These vows, which the novice had to swear at his ordination, bear an
extraordinary resemblance to the famous "negative confession" that
counts as chapter 125 in the Egyptian *Book of the Dead*. There, the dead
man must take a test before being accepted in the Great Beyond. While
his heart is being weighed on a scale against a figure of the Goddess of
Truth, he has to list eighty-two sins that he swears he has *not* committed.
With every lie – and this presumably is the basic principle behind the
procedure – his heart becomes heavier. This chapter, with its detailed
list of sins, is known to have been in existence in the New Kingdom,
that is, since the 15th century BCE, and the idea of such a day of
judgment goes even further back.[32] It has therefore been suggested
that the Late Egyptian *nomos* of the temple is actually derived from the
much older "*nomos* of the beyond." However, the reverse is more likely:
the law of the beyond, although it occurs in much earlier texts, is only
secondary and illustrates the taboos and moral proscriptions (which
are rooted in the cult) in the Underworld, which is thus conceived as
a sacred place in close proximity to the gods.[33] And so, the "negative

---

[31] Reinhold Merkelbach, "Ein ägyptischer Priestereid," *Zeitschrift für Philologie und Epigraphik* 2 (1968), 7–30; see Reinhard Grieshammer, "Zum 'Sitz im Leben' des negativen Sündenbekenntnisses," *ZDMG Supplement II* (1974), 19ff. For the Egyptian original (from "The Book of the Temple") see Quack, "Das Buch vom Tempel und verwandte Texte" (see chapter 4, n. 19).

[32] Joachim Spiegel, *Die Idee des Totengerichts in der ägyptischen Religion*, LÄS 2 (Glückstadt: Augustin-Verlag, 1935); Jean Yoyotte, "Le jugement des morts dans l'Égypte ancienne," in *Sources Orientales* 4 (Paris, 1961); Samuel G. F. Brandon, *The Judgment of the Dead* (New York: Weidenfeld & Nicolson, 1967); Reinhard Grieshammer, *Das Jenseitsgericht in den Sargtexten* (Wiesbaden: Harrassowitz, 1971); J. Assmann, *Death and Salvation*, chapter 3 (see chapt. 4, n. 7).

[33] Grieshammer, *Das Jenseitsgericht*, (see chapt. 4, n. 32); J. Assmann, "Death and Initiation in the Funerary Religion of Ancient Egypt," in W. K. Simpson (ed.), *Religion and Philosophy in Ancient Egypt*, YES 3 (1989), 135–159.

confession of sins" that everyone including nonpriests had to swear to contains typical temple taboos, such as:

> I have not trapped the birds from the preserves of the gods,
> I have not caught the fish of their marshlands,
> I have not diverted water at its season,
> I have not built a dam on flowing water,
> I have not quenched the fire when it is burning,
> I have not neglected the dates for offering choice meats,
> I have not withheld cattle from the god's-offerings,
> I have not opposed a god in his procession.[34]

There are further vows that refer not to the cult but to the administration of the temple:

> I have not diminished the aurora,
> I have not encroached upon fields,
> I have not laid anything upon the weights of the hand balance,
> I have not taken anything from the plummet of the standing
> scales [...].

There are other very general negative sins referenced:

> I have done no wrong in the Place of Truth,
> I have not learnt that which is not,
> I have done no evil,
> I have not daily made labour in excess of what was due to be done for
> me, my name has not reached the offices of those who control slaves,
> I have not deprived the orphan of his property,
> I have not done what the gods detest [...],
> I have not made hungry,
> I have not made to weep,
> I have not killed,
> I have not commanded to kill,
> I have not made suffering for anyone [...].[35]

The same three forms occur in the priest's oath and, finally, also in a group of texts that list the *nomos* of the temple *in situ* – namely, at the

---

[34] *Book of the Dead 125*, trans. by R. O. Faulkner, ed. by Carol Andrews (London: British Museum Publications, 1985), 31.
[35] Ibid., compiled from various extracts.

side entrance through which the junior priests entered the temple in the morning[36]:

> Lead [no one] into falsehood,
> do not enter into uncleanness,
> tell no lies in his house!
> Do not be greedy, do not slander,
> do not accept bribes,
> do not distinguish between poor and rich,
> add nothing to weights and measures and take nothing away,
> add and subtract nothing[37] from a bushel [...][38]
> Use no swearwords,
> do not place lies above truth in talking!
> Guard against doing something else during the time of (religious) services,
> no-one who talks then will remain unpunished.
> Make no music in his house, inside the temple,
> do not go near the place of the women [...]
> do not arrange the service according to your own wishes,
> but look into the books and into the instructions of the temple,
> which you should pass on as a lesson to your children.[39]

And at the main entrance in the Pronaos, through which the high priest entered as envoy of the king, we read:

> [...]
> [I have come] on the path of God,
> I have not judged partially,
> I have not made common cause with the strong and I have not disadvantaged the weak,
> I have stolen nothing,
> I have not reduced the parts of the Horus eye,

---

[36] Known as "temple entrance texts," see Grieshammer, "Zum 'Sitz im Leben'," 33 ff (for a list of such inscriptions see 22, n. 14) (see chapt. 4, n. 31); Maurice Alliot, *Le culte d'Horus Edfou au temps des Ptolemées*, Bibl.d'Étud. 20 (Cairo: Institut français d'archéologie orientale, 1949), 142 ff., 181 ff.; H. W. Fairman,, "A Scene of the Offering of Truth in the Temple of Edfu," in *Mitteilungen des Deutschen Archäologischen Instituts*, Cairo 16 (1958), 86–92; J. Assmann, *Ma'at*, 140–149, (see chapt. 1, n. 11).

[37] "*jtj jnj*" – the same turn of phrase as earlier, with reference to the temple plan. See J. J. Clère, "Deux statues 'gardiennes de porte' d'époque ramesside," *Journal of Egyptian Archaeology* 54 (1968), 135–148, esp. 140 f.

[38] From the inscription Edfou III 360–361 = Kom Ombo II, 245.

[39] From the inscription Edfou III 361–362.

> I have not [cheated] with the scale,
> I have not violated that which belongs to the eye of God.[40]

If one reads these texts as a series of temple and cultic rules, it is astonishing to see how far they go beyond the rules actually laid down for priests; they seem in fact to form the basis for a whole way of life, a "general priestly moral code."[41] Conduct in the temple as prescribed by these rules includes admonitions against actions that would not even take place in the temple. Whoever enters must be clean, but cleanliness does not just mean steering clear of anything the particular god might dislike when inside the temple – it also means abstaining from such activities outside the temple. Thus priesthood becomes a way of living that models lifestyle on strict orthopraxy.

On the other hand, if the texts are read as a general code of conduct, the many rules stipulated seem rather surprising; these only take on any real meaning in the context of a particular cult and in relation to the particular "abominations" of a particular god (e.g., music or loud voices). One will search in vain for such instructions among the many lessons of life that have come down to us from Ancient Egypt, whereas conversely warnings against partiality, corruption, dishonesty with weights and measures, wrongdoing, greed, and violence play a fundamental role in Ancient Egyptian "wisdom literature" (H. Brunner 1988). And so here is a unique mixture of rules concerning purity, class, and morality that could be called the *nomos* of the temple, and whose first appearance in chapter 125 in the Egyptian *Book of the Dead* shows just how old the whole concept is. Its recurrence in the decorations of the Late Period temples bears witness not only to its longevity but also to its canonization as orthopraxy.[42] When Herodotus and others speak of the *nomoi* – the laws and customs of the Egyptians – they are in fact referring to the *nomos* of the temple that in the Late Period had become, if not the universally binding then certainly *the*

---

[40] Edfou III 78–79, see Alliot, *Le culte d'Horus*, 142 f. (see chapt. 4, n. 36); Fairman, "A Scene of the Offering," 91 (see chapt. 4, n. 36).

[41] This is the expression used by Walter Otto, *Priester und Tempel im hellenistischen Ägypten II* (Leipzig, Berlin: Teubner, 1908), 239, in an attempt to characterize the inscriptions.

[42] I use this term as an analogy to orthodoxy. While the latter is concerned with the conformity of teaching and interpretation to rules and canons, orthopraxy entails conforming to the rules of conduct.

representative form of Egyptian life. Just as in the earlier times of pharaonic culture the official-cum-scribe had been the embodiment of "Egyptianness," in the Late Period the priests took over that role.

Plato and the Egyptian Temple

My interpretation of the Late Egyptian temple as an organized form of cultural memory, with the permanence and enhanced binding qualities that were subsumed under the term "canon" goes back mainly to Plato. He saw the Egyptians as the people with the longest memory. Periodic catastrophes had destroyed tradition everywhere else in the world but the Egyptians had been spared this traumatic amnesia. They were able to preserve such memories as Atlantis that had been lost even to those most closely affected, like the Greeks themselves.[43] Plato calculated the length of this memory as being ten thousand years, in accord with Herodotus, who based his figures on Hekataios of Miletus. It was said that the latter had been shown 345 statues of priests in the temple at Thebes, where the office of high priest had been handed down from father to son over succeeding generations.[44] The 345 generations were the basis of the ten-thousand-year calculation, and this was in stark contrast to the length of Greek memory, whose generations of nobility (like that of Hekataios himself) went back a mere 16 generations before arriving at a god or mythical hero.[45] The tale of the statues is based on a misunderstanding that may have suggested itself precisely through the overpopulation of statues at the Temple of Karnak, but there can be little doubt that the misunderstanding was of Egyptian origin. During the Late Period the Egyptians regarded temples as the storehouses and treasure chambers of a tradition that reached back through precise, historically defined periods as far as creation itself. One can well imagine the pride with which they showed off their history to Greek travelers in the form of the temples and other monuments that recorded a myth-free past stretching over so many thousands of years. For the true meaning of these monuments

---

[43] Plato, Timaios 22b.
[44] Herodotus Hist. II, 143
[45] See Fritz Schachermeyr, *Die griechische Rückerinnerung* (Wien: Oesterreich. Akad. d. Wiss., 1984). On the principle of a genealogically organized concept of history, see Schott, "Das Geschichtsbewußtsein schriftloser Völker" (see chapt. 1, n. 67).

had never faded to the extent that it could be turned into legend that would have attributed their construction to mythical beings. On the contrary, the inscriptions were still there to be read, the time gaps were measurable, the formal language familiar, and every Egyptian knew that these things all bore witness to one's own long past. "Egyptian monuments," wrote the clear-sighted J. Burckhardt in 1848, "are the books of their history written in the script of giants."[46]

Plato's writing in his *Laws* about the temples was based on another misunderstanding that was equally productive in relation to the self-image of Late Egyptian society. He saw them as what might – to use the terminology of Russian semiotics – be called an "iconic grammar of culture" or the explicit formulation of a system of rules, adherence to which generated the well-formed "sentences" (i.e., attitudes, opinions, and actions) of culture, but crafted in pictorial and not linguistic form. The knowledge that stands like a revelation at the very beginning of Egyptian culture and that unites all statements about life in a uniquely impressive manner is expressed not through words but through iconic forms. This is a fundamental feature of the temples, even if everything else – especially their pedagogic function – must be relegated to the realm of fantasy. Plotinus wrote something similar about the function of the images:

The wise men of Egypt, I think, also understood this, either by scientific knowledge or innate knowledge, and when they wished to signify something wisely, did not use the form of letters that follow the order of words and propositions and imitate sounds and the enunciations of philosophical statements, but by drawing images [agalmata] and inscribing them in their temples, one beautiful image for each particular thing, they manifested the non-discursiveness of the intelligible world. Every image is a kind of knowledge and wisdom and is a subject of deliberation. And afterwards [others] deciphered [the image] as a representation of something else by starting from it in its concentrated unity, already unfolded and by expressing it discursively and giving the reasons why things are like this.[47]

---

[46] In: Franz Kugler, *Handbuch der Kunstgeschichte*, 2nd ed. with additional material by Dr. Jacob Burckhardt (Stuttgart: Ebner Seubert, 1848), 39.

[47] Plotinus, Enneades V, 8, 5, 19 and V, 8, 6, 11, Cf. A. H. Armstrong, "Platonic Mirrors," *Eranos* 1986 Vol. 55 (Frankfurt: Insel, 1988), 147–182. On Plotinus's concept of non-discursive thinking see Richard Sorabji, *Time, Creation and the Continuum. Theories in Antiquity and in the Early Middle Ages* (Ithaca, NY: Cornell University Press, 1983), 152 f.

This once again illustrates that in Egypt the medium of cultural memory is pictures and not speech. The temple provides the setting for these pictures – and hence the central institution of cultural memory. Here, too, one can see the basic concept of the Late Period temple as a codification and canonization of the *forms* of a reality that has been created, regulated, and preserved by the gods. There is no clearer illustration of this principle than Late Egyptian hieroglyphics. The Late Period saw a veritable explosion of innovations that, as has already been mentioned, increased the number of signs from approximately 700 to about 7,000. This was all part of the comprehensive process of renewal embodied by the temples of that time, because each one strove to create its own writing system and to establish its own repertoire of signs and meanings. The hieroglyphic script therefore became a mark of the competence of the priests, and thus it was now the sacerdotal (*hiero-*) script. As such it was as esoteric as the knowledge it codified.

With the progression into a more clerical structure of culture as it withdrew into the temples came its sanctification. And to the degree in which cultural meaning became sanctified its forms became frozen because of the fear of losing contact with one's origin and one's identity – the "fear of forgetting," to use Hermann Kees' expression. Behind this is the reflective element of tradition that I have already discussed as a typical starting point for enhanced forms of collective identity, that is, for the transition from cultural formations to cultural identities. One's own culture loses its self-evidence and is no longer to be regarded as the unquestionable order of the world. What for the individual had appeared to be fixed boundaries and bonds, laws and norms, are no longer effective as "implicit axioms" (D. Ritschl 1985) whose validity is guaranteed by a natural social and cosmological framework, and instead they demand explicit formulae. This gives rise to cultural metatexts, or "self-thematizations of the social system" (N. Luhmann). This is what lies behind Plato's interpretation of the temples: they provided a definitive system of norms for beauty as well as for the social and political order for the rest of time.

From this point of view, the Late Egyptian temple joins those other cultural metatexts that at around the same time and under a similar pressure of general upheaval arose elsewhere in the Ancient World. There, too, the reflective element of tradition led to comprehensive codifications and manifestations of cultural identity based especially on an intensive preoccupation with the people's own past. In Babylon and particularly Assyria there were the palace libraries, in Israel were the great works of law and history, and in Greece was Peisistratus's definitive version of Homer's text (U. Hölscher 1987) and the beginnings of historiography.[48] In Egypt there are even earlier signs of archaism and restoration, culminating in the Ethiopian and Saite periods (25th and 26th Dynasties, 8th–6th century) and the "Saite Renaissance" (H. Brunner 1970; I. Nagy 1973).[49] But only in the Late Egyptian temple does one find this single, representative, all-embracing canon. This one form of all forms expressed everything that linked the Egyptians to their origins.

There are two further points worth noting about this organizational form of cultural memory:

1. The Identification of Culture and Cosmos

Every culture tends to equate its own order with that of the world in general. Normally, this ethnocentric self-image begins to weaken in the course of those experiences of change that lead to reflection on tradition and to enhanced forms of identity. Then the cultural identity ceases to be the same as the world order. But in this instance Egypt provides an exception. The conviction that there had been a seamless continuation from creation right through to the present survived even the major upheavals of the first millennium BCE; not only was it not weakened but it was even enhanced to a very special awareness of a unique identity. The Egyptians had no doubt that if their culture disappeared, so too would the world order (if not the world itself), its meaningful structure, and its integral role in life, disappear: "But the whole of Egypt's cultural and social life, like the configuration of the land itself, was unique. So too was the Egyptian mind, with its immovable conviction that the cultural identity of Egypt and the stability of the physical universe itself were one and the same thing" (Fowden 1986, 14).

The temples were the centers that kept the world going. Thus the preservation of Egyptian culture and the continuance of the world were simply aspects of the one task allotted to the priests, whereas the

---

[48] See the important work of van Seters, *In Search of History*, (see chapt. 1, n. 82).

[49] See also J. Assmann, *The Mind of Egypt*, chapt. 23, 335–364, (see chapt. 1, n. 94).

temple was not only a container of the world but was also a monumental and explicit expression of it.

2. The Compactness of Cultural Symbolism and the Nondifferentiation of the Word

At the time when the temple was becoming the central organizational element of Egyptian cultural memory, there were similar processes of cultural stabilization going on in other centers of the Ancient World and even further afield in India and China. This coincidence, already noted as long ago as the 18th century, has been designated by Karl Jaspers as the "Axial Age. The common feature of these "axial age cultures" (Eisenstadt 1987, [see Introduction, n. 9]) is the differentiation and privileging of language as the central organizing form of cultural memory. In all of them, cultural meaning was fixed and traditions revived through a return to the great foundational texts and through the institutionalization of an educational culture that ensured that the vision of reality encoded in these texts would remain present and normative through every age. This movement, however, did not take place in Egypt. Here the vision of reality was not codified principally in texts but in visual forms (schemata) of writing and art, ritual, and ways of life. By canonizing and institutionalizing this compact organization of cultural memory in its Late Period temples, Egyptian culture succeeded in surviving the massive cultural upheaval brought about in the Ancient World as early as the Persian period by the onset of Hellenization; and as the monument to a past cultural era it was able to go on well into the post-axial world. But it was not in a position to create those forms of interpretive culture that were predominant in the axial cultures and were thus able to preserve their semantic formation right up to the present day.

5

Israel and the Invention of Religion

RELIGION AS RESISTANCE

While the state was Egypt's great achievement, religion was Israel's. Inevitably, of course, there were and are religions all over the world that are normally an element of the culture within which they are born and within which they die. In Israel, however, religion was created in a completely new and radical way that made it independent of the general culture and enabled it to survive through every cultural change, subjugation, and assimilation. Religion became a kind of "iron wall" that Israelites used to separate themselves from the surrounding "alien" culture. However, this radical version was not yet completely identical with the ancient Israelite religion, which was inextricably embedded in the political structures of David's kingdom and the preceding, pre-state forms of organization. Only the religion of the Second Temple that emerged from the experience of exile, and then of course Judaism itself, constituted religion in its absolute distinctness and with its unshakable core.[1] As an autonomous unity it then became the basis and the medium for resistance against the cultural and political structures of a hostile outside world.

[1] My interpretation follows that of Yehezkel Kaufmann, *Golah ve-Nekhar*, 2 vols. (Tel Aviv: Devir, 1929/30), whose arguments were made accessible to me by C. W. Ephraimson's partial translation: Y. Kaufmann, *Christianity and Judaism. Two Covenants* (Jerusalem: Magnes Press, 1988). The motif of the "iron barrier" plays a central role in Kaufmann.

The Erection of the "Brazen Wall"

Israel and Egypt's Route to Orthopractical Separation. In Late Period Egypt, the orthopractical sacralization of the country corresponded to that of its way of life, with a vision of Egypt as the "holiest land" (*hierotáte chóra*)[2] and of a *templum mundi*[3] – all of which entailed an awareness of absolute uniqueness, based on a special proximity to the gods, or a "living community of the whole of Egypt with the gods."[4] The closest parallel to this development is the Israel of the Second Temple. Here, too, the orthopractical sanctity of life (in Hebrew, *halakhah*) as set down in the 613 commandments and proscriptions of the Torah, is linked to a special awareness of uniqueness. Uniqueness is also based here on a relationship with God, although this is not conceived in terms of living together,[5] because that would be unthinkable for the transmundane Jewish God. This relationship stems from the idea of the Jews as "chosen" and from the covenant they had made with God. Orthopraxy means "adaptation to God." "And ye shall be holy unto me: for I the Lord am holy" (Lev. 17–26, passim).[6] However, it is also distinction, seclusion, and uniqueness – in other words, a very

---

[2] Garth Fowden, *The Egyptian Hermes. A Historical Approach to the Late Pagan Mind* (Cambridge: Cambridge University Press, 1986), 14 refers in this context to Theophrastus, *De pietate*, ed. W. Pötscher (Leiden: E. J. Brill, 1964), 2f.; Porphyrius, *De abstinentia*, ed. J. Bouffartigue and M. Patillon (Paris: Les Belles Lettres, 1977), II, 5,1; Engl.: *On Abstinence*, trans. Thomas Taylor (London: Centaur Press, 1965); Eusebius v. Cäsarea, *Praeparatio evangelica*, 1, 9, 7.

[3] Asclepius 24, Nag Hammadi Codex II, 5, 122–123, see H. H. Bethge, *Vom Ursprung der Welt: die fünfte Schrift aus Nag Hammadi Codex II* (Diss. Berlin Ost, 1975).

[4] Julian, ep. 111, 433 b (en koinonía mèn pròs theoús Aigýptō te pásē).

[5] In fact, the same idea is to be found in those traditions that talk of the tent, temple, or home (*mishkan*) of Yahweh (e.g. Exod. 25:8): "And let them make me a sanctuary; that I may dwell among them." The Egyptians could make a similar case. They could show, with good reason, that the concept of a community of gods and men denoted not the present reality but a primal time, a kind of golden age, and the present world was the result of that original community breaking up (see J. Assmann *Ma'at*, chapter 6 [see chapt. 1, n. 11]). According to the Egyptian view, the break was healed by precisely those institutions of symbolic mediation and divine representation that the Bible condemns as "idolatry." Herein lies the crucial difference between Israel and Egypt. Yahweh's "dwelling" (*shekhinah*) is never symbolic but always directly present, though changeable and inaccessible. According to the reformed theology of Deuteronomy, it is not God but his *name* that dwells in the temple. See Moshe Weinfeld, *Deuteronomy and the Deuteronomic School* (Oxford: Clarendon Press, 1972), 191–209.

[6] Henning Graf Reventlow, *Das Heiligkeitsgesetz, formgeschichtlich untersucht*. WMANT 6 (Neukirchen: Neukirchener Verlag, 1961).

special form of identity. Living according to the law implies a conscious declaration of belief in a "normative self-definition" (E. P. Sanders). In this context, Israel and Egypt followed parallel paths in the Persian kingdom and Hellenism, respectively, even though the one path led to a history that changed the world, while the other ended if not in total oblivion, then at least in the subterranean countercurrents.

The Late Egyptian temple, with its fortress-like appearance, represents the most striking embodiment of seclusion – of a way of life sheltered by its high, thick walls from the profane outside world. It was, however, a Jew who used this image in order to illustrate the idea of seclusion:

When therefore our lawgiver, equipped by God for insight into all things, had surveyed each particular, he fenced us about with impregnable palisades and with walls of iron, to the end that we should mingle in no way with any of the other nations, remaining pure in body and in spirit, emancipated from vain opinions, revering the one and mighty God above the whole of creation. [...] And therefore, so that we should be polluted by none nor be infected with perversions by associating with worthless persons, he has hedged us on all sides with prescribed purifications in matters of food and drink and touch and hearing and sight.[7]

Written in Egypt by an Alexandrian Jew of the diaspora during the time of Ptolemy, the text uses an Egyptian image. The "brazen wall" initially referred to the king, who as commander-in-chief protected his country, his soldiers, and his vassals.[8] As long ago as the 14th century BCE, a Canaanite prince used the same image in his correspondence with the Egyptian court:

> Thou art the Sun-god who rises over me,
> and a brazen wall which is reared for me (!)
> and because of the mighty power of the king my lord
> I am tranquil.[9]

---

7 *Letter of Aristeas*, 139 and 142, in Moses Hadas (ed. and trans.), *Letter of Aristeas* (New York: Ktav Pub. House, 1973), 157.

8 Initially applied to Thutmosis III.: Urk IV 1233. On Akhnaton, see Maj Sandman, *Texts from the Time of Akhenaten*, Bibliotheca Aegyptica 8 (Bruxelles: Éd. de la Fond. Égyptol., 1938), 84; Ramses II: A. Mariette, *Abydos* I, 52, 16 ff. and *Rec. de Travaux* 35, 126 on Hornacht Prince of Mendes in the 3rd Intermediate Period. See also Albrecht Alt, "Hic murus aheneus esto," *ZDMG* 11 (1932), 33–48.

9 Letter from Abimilki of Tyrus, ed. Knudtzon, *Die El-Amarna-Tafeln* (1907–15), No. 147, see William F. Albright, "The Egyptian Correspondence of Abimilki, Prince of Tyre," *The Journal of Egyptian Archaeology* 23 (1937), 190–203, here 199.

At the same time, however, the heretic king Echnaton was proclaiming the sun-god Aton as his only god, describing him as his "wall of a million cubits."[10] This image persisted. A tablet from the 13th century BCE (now in London) calls Amun:

> Thou wall[11] of bronze
> That taketh to thyself those that stand in thy favour.[12]

And in the Cairo papyrus 58033, the "credo of the Amun religion" from the time of the "Theban Theocracy"[13] (11th century BCE), we read:

> He created a wall of bronze for him who "is on his water."
> No evil shall touch him who wanders along his path.[14]

This brings together two vital concepts: the brazen wall and "God's path." The wall is not yet conceived of as a boundary for exclusion, but is simply for protection against evil. The path, however, is already laid out, and it is the route along which Egyptian culture will, in the next few centuries, retreat from foreign rule into the shelter of the temple walls, shutting itself off in order to pursue its own fixed, orthopractical way of life in defiance of an unclean outside world.

The Jewish path of the orthopractical *halakhah* led the Jews not only through foreign rule but also, and especially, through exile and the diaspora. The decisive stations along this route were:

1. The catastrophe of the Northern Kingdom, 722 BCE, and the deportation of the ten tribes of Israel by the Assyrians.
2. The prophecy of disaster and religious opposition under increasing pressure from the Assyrians, culminating in the "discovery of the book" under Josiah, 621 BCE.

---

[10] Sandman, *Texts from Akhenaten*, 111 (see chapt. 5, n. 8).
[11] The Egyptian text says "portal," but the words for "portal" (*sbht*) and "wall" (*sbtj*) sound similar, and the scribe probably mixed them up.
[12] Tablet BM 5656, see J. Assmann, *Ägyptische Hymnen und Gebete* (Zurich: Artemis, 1975), No. 190, vol. 18–19.
[13] E. Meyer, "Gottesstaat, Militärherrschaft und Ständewesen in Ägypten," in *Sitzungsberichte der Preussischen Akademie der Wissenschaft* (Berlin, 1928).
[14] On this text, see J. Assmann, *Ägyptische Hymnen und Gebete*, No. 131, 312 (see chapt. 5, n. 12).

3. The destruction of the Temple, 586 BCE; deportation, exile, and return of the *bene haggolah* in 536 BCE.
4. The persistence of the deuteronomic religion, tolerated under Persian sovereignty.
5. Resistance against Hellenization and the Maccabean Wars.
6. Resistance against Rome and the destruction of the Second Temple, 70 AD.
7. Hadrian's crushing of the Bar-Kochbah rebellion and the expulsion of the Jews from Palestine in 135 AD.

This list illustrates the number of factors that needed to come together to produce the stabilization of Jewish tradition and identity. One thing is clear: this was far from being the normal evolution of a culture. But the sequence of internal tensions and schisms that characterized Israel's history during the period of the Second Temple and had already been prefigured in the prophets' opposition to almost all the kings was even more decisive than these intercultural confrontations that also affected cultures like Babylon and Egypt. Schisms of that nature do not seem to have occurred in Babylon or Egypt.

The Exodus as a Memory Figure

The history narrated by tradition itself starts with an exceptional situation. Exile and diaspora are both at the beginning. Under the leadership of Moses, a diverse band of Hebrews had fled from the forced labor camps of Egypt, wandering for forty years through the wilderness; and, in place of the Pharaoh, God dictated to them the text of a completely new covenant that was to free them from political oppression by subjecting them to the commandments of God and his prophets. All the vital elements of Israel's subsequent history that led to a unique stabilization of tradition are already prefigured in this one act of identity-giving: the exile or diaspora of the children of Israel in Egypt, the situation of the minority, oppression, resistance against the pressure to assimilate into a physically superior culture with its "fleshpots" – and in addition to all of this, polytheism, the worship of images, sorcery, the cult of the dead, idolization of rulers, and especially the concepts of liberation and extraterritoriality. As the origin of a nation and of a way of life, Israel's experience could scarcely have been more different from Egypt. There, the images of origin rested on the principle of autochthony.[15] The temple – whose walls protected the god and those who followed his path against the threatening, unclean world outside, ultimately becoming an image for the whole of Egypt as the home of the gods and the pious – stood on the primal hill, the first place to have arisen out of the primal waters. The Exodus and the revelation on Mount Sinai as Israel's central images of origin rested on the principle of extraterritoriality. The covenant was sealed between an ultramundane God, who had no temple or place of worship on Earth, and a people wandering between Egypt and Canaan in the no-man's-land of the Sinai Desert. The covenant preceded the acquisition of a homeland, and that was the crucial point. The bond was extraterritorial, that is, independent of any territory, which meant that it remained universally valid no matter where in the world the Jews might find themselves.

What we have in mind with this account is the Exodus, not as an historical event but as a "memory figure." Thus, it occurs on a different level from that of the seven stations along Israel's path to pharisaic and rabbinical Judaism, which were to crystallize its traditions into the canon of the Hebrew Bible. These stations are of interest because they provide the historical background, but the historicity of the Exodus is a matter of extreme controversy. On the Egyptian side, there is virtually no evidence on offer.[16] The only mention of Israel in an Egyptian text refers to a tribe in Palestine, and certainly not to a group of immigrants or "guest workers" in Egypt itself.[17] What matters here, however, is not the historical accuracy but the importance of this story for Israelite memory. One simply cannot overestimate its significance. The Exodus of the Israelites from Egypt was the foundational act that provided the basis for the identity not only of the people, but also of God himself. Wherever the Lord of the Covenant appeared, calling on

---

[15] On the spreading of this motif, see Klaus E. Müller, *Das magische Universum der Identität. Elementarformen sozialen Verhaltens. Ein ethnologischer Grundriß* (Frankfurt: Campus, 1987).

[16] For an account of the research on this subject, see Helmut Engel, *Die Vorfahren Israels in Ägypten* (Frankfurt: Knecht, 1979) and James Hoffmeier, *Israel in Egypt. The Evidence for the Authenticity of the Exodus Tradition* (Oxford: Oxford University Press, 1999).

[17] The famous "Israel stele" from the time of Merenptah, end of the 13th century BCE. This first mention of Israel in Egypt's history is an announcement of its destruction!

the Israelites to obey him, they were referred to as "my servants whom I brought forth out of the land of Egypt" (Leviticus, 25, 55). In other words, right from the start, the people were defined by emigration and segregation.

The "Yahweh-Alone Movement" as a Community of Memory

If we look back on the theory of memory as based on Halbwachs, and ask ourselves which group might use the memory of the Exodus to support its self-image, its aims, and its hopes, and which historical situation would be most suited to place this memory at the center of its reconstruction of the past, the first that would come to mind would certainly be the Jewish diaspora. Egypt, as the foreign culture, is everywhere, and upholding the law of God opens up the path to liberation from slavery and persecution, and will lead to the Promised Land, wherever that may be. One could scarcely imagine a more suitable or more significant story to keep alive a scattered nation's will to survive through thousands of years of dispersion and oppression. The Exodus tradition is – both historically and as the central memory figure in the identity of Israel – of course, older than the diaspora situation and the Babylonian exile, which in all probability could not have been endured without the loss of identity had it not been for this tradition. On the other hand, it is difficult to imagine that the Kingdom of David would have placed the Exodus and Sinai tradition at the center of Israel's self-image.

This entire process could be interpreted rather differently. In 1971 Morton Smith proposed the theory that the carrier of monotheistic religion had not been the state but, initially, a small group of dissidents who had formed the "Yahweh-alone movement."[18] One should view the Israel of earlier times, from its beginnings until well into the 7th

---

[18] This thesis was taken up and developed by Bernhard Lang (ed.), *Der Einzige Gott* (Munich: Kösel, 1981); "The Yahweh-Alone Movement and the Making of Jewish Monotheism," in *Monotheism and the Prophetic Minority* (Sheffield: Almond Press, 1983), 13–59; "Vom Propheten zum Schriftgelehrten. Charismatische Autorität im Frühjudentum," in H. v. Stietencron (ed.), *Theologen und Theologien in verschiedenen Kulturkreisen* (Düsseldorf: Patmos, 1986), 89–114; Crüsemann, "Das 'portative Vaterland'" (see chapt. 2, n. 57); Manfred Weippert, "Synkretismus und Monotheismus. Religionsinterne Konfliktbewältigung im alten Israel," in J. Assmann and D. Harth (eds.), *Kultur und Konflikt* (Frankfurt: Suhrkamp, 1990), 143–73, and others.

century, as polytheistic, in the sense of a *summodeistic* state.[19] Yahweh
was the god of the State, like Assur in Assyria, Marduk in Babylon,
or Amun-Re in Egypt, but he was the head of a pantheon (however
small) and not the one and only god. Cultural life then was open to the
Canaanite world; intermarriage with Midianites, Moabites, Gibeonites,
and even Egyptians (e.g., Solomon) was common; and Baal was worshiped all over the land. Israel's religion was only a regional variant
among the many cults and concepts of the Near East.

The first signs of change can be seen in the 9th century. Under King
Asa (died ca. 875) there appears to have been a puritan reform, continued by his son Jehoshaphat and the prophet Elijah with persecution of
the priests of Baal. Here we have the beginnings of the Yahweh-alone
movement; during the centuries that followed, this movement waged
a bitter struggle against the surviving and at times strengthening cult
of Baal and against the continuing practice of polytheism. Because
after the victory, the transmission was restrospectively one-sided, the
polytheistic-syncretistic culture of Ancient Israel is seen only through
the negative perspective of its opponents (heathen religions were deni-
grated similarly – in records that have been much better preserved – by
the Fathers of the Church). What the texts describe as an endless conflict between the notoriously rebellious and forgetful people of Israel
and the demands of their own religion, was in historical reality a conflict between a monotheistic minority and a polytheistic-syncretistic
majority. It should be emphasized that this majority also believed in
Yahweh, and the kings certainly made themselves the special patrons
of the cult of Yahweh. But for them, Yahweh was the highest and not
the *only* god. This was what the prophets condemned as apostasy.

In the second section of this chapter, I describe the conflict from
the inner perspective of Deuteronomy, which may be seen as the central text of the Yahweh-alone party. If viewed from inside, so to speak,
the battlefronts seem very different. It is not the party that forms the
canon, but vice versa. The canon stands at the beginning, and its insistence on monotheism is what sparks off the schisms and conflicts.
The Mount Sinai revelation and the Jordan covenant represent the

---

[19] Eric Voegelin, *Order and History*, vol. 1 (Baton Rouge: LSU Press, 1956) coined this
expression with reference to worship of the god of the empire in early civilizations.

beginning, and subsequent disasters stem from the Israelites' forgetfulness of their original vows and promises. This inner view also has
an historical foundation. The post-exile conflicts between the exiled
community and those who had stayed, between the Jews and the
Samaritans, between the Babylonian and the Egyptian Golah, and
later between the Hellenized and the orthodox branches of Judaism,
were all the result of the canon and its normative demands.

Religion as Resistance. The Emergence of Religion from Opposition to One's Own Culture

Centuries of struggle brought forward something completely new in
world history – namely, religion in the sense of a distinct set of values,
meanings, and actions that are quite separate from the spheres of
culture and politics. This distinction can only be explained if it is
translated from the conceptual sphere back into social reality and
then interpreted as antagonisms between groups; what we in fact have
here is one dissident group that seceded from the rest of society. In
our context, the denunciation of the common culture as alien and
the claim that the only true Israelite was the one who shared the
monotheistic convictions of the dissidents were decisive. This was how
religion arose in the context of – and in opposition to – culture, but it
was not a foreign culture; it was their own that they branded as alien,
rebellious, and forgetful.

The boundary drawn here between the inclusive, assimilatory culture and the exclusive religion committed to the concept of purity
found its symbolic expression in the brazen wall that was now built
around (1) the identity and (2) the traditions of the group that
regarded itself as the true Israel. The process had one feature that
was also typical of Mesopotamia, Egypt, and elsewhere: the conflict
with a culture seen as stronger and therefore as threatening led to
the construction of a barricade to protect tradition and identity. But
this did not lead to internal schisms in Egypt or in Mesopotamia. That
which is established as "self," as opposed to the "other" culture, always
embraced religion and culture as an inseparable unit. With the "true"
Israelites, however, the uniqueness of the process lay in the exclusion
of their own culture, and in the separation of religion, culture, and

political power.[20] It was this vital separation that found its symbolic form in the memory figure of the Exodus story. The journey away from Egypt becomes the equivalent of the journey away from a profane, impure, oppressive, assimilatory, godless environment that in fact constitutes the world. This ideology prefigures the borderline between the secular and the spiritual, which is central to the new form of religion.

In a world that did not know any difference between religion and culture, cultural life in all spheres was shaped by religion in a manner inconceivable to us today, so that all dealings and communications were either explicitly or implicitly linked to some kind of recognition of the gods involved. The group that insisted, however, on recognizing only one god cut itself off from the inter-ethnic community and set itself up as a separate people; it was no longer possible to enter into this separate, closed community through immigration, marriage, or any other form of application for membership; belonging could only be secured through conversion.[21] The *shemaͨ Jisra'el* became a declaration of commitment to an identity, and one had to be prepared to die for it.[22] Conversion, commitment, and martyrdom were all facets of the brazen wall with which this new nation separated itself from its surroundings, and they were constituent parts of a religion that now began to crystallize into a completely new combination of semantic formation and identity.

---

[20] One might ask whether Akhnaton's monotheistic reforms were not also directed against his own culture, thus leading to a similar structure. If these reforms had found followers outside the court and if, through this, the reintroduction of the former cult had led to continuance through a dissident "Aton-alone movement," one might have been able to talk of a comparable, religiously defined identity in the framework of opposition to the existing culture. This, however, was not the case.

[21] See Morton Smith, *Palestinian Parties and Politics That Shaped the Old Testament* (New York: Columbia University Press, 1971), 30: "any group which insisted on worshiping only one god thereby made themselves a peculiar people [...] and made the joining of their group a matter of *conversion*, not mere adherence."

[22] In Jewish Bibles and prayerbooks, the last letters of the first and last words of this expression (the Ajin of *shemaͨ* ["hear"] and the Daleth of *echad* ["one"]) are emphasized by large print, and these letters form the word *'ed'* (witness) = *martys* as indicating a truth that is evidenced by death. See also the section on "Sterben für die patrioi nomoi," in Hans Kippenberg, "Die jüdischen Überlieferungen als patrioi nomoi," in R. Faber and R. Schlesier (eds.), *Die Restauration der Götter. Antike Religion und Neo-Paganismus* (Würzburg: Königshausen and Neumann, 1986), 45–60.

The wall would not have been so high and the borderline so rigid, if all this had not taken place within the people's own culture, because the definitive way of living had to impose itself against the self-evident daily routine of that culture. It therefore needed the basis of an elaborate set of laws, which would have been totally unnecessary in a self-evident culture. Whoever lived according to these laws could not forget for one minute who he was or where he belonged. Such a distinctive way of life was so difficult that it could only be pursued through ceaseless learning and awareness. Basically, it was a kind of professional art that could only be practiced by specialists with nothing else to worry about apart from mastering an extremely complex repertoire of priestly taboos and prescriptions. These now became the nucleus of a general legal code, and thus the principle of priestly separation – which was the case particularly in Egypt – now applied to the whole people: "for thou art an holy people unto the Lord thy God."[23]

The Babylonian exile lifted this holy people out of the cultural context with which they had been in vehement conflict for centuries, forming a community in exile (*golah*) in what had now really become an alien culture, away from their native kingdom, from the cult of sacrifice, and thus from all forms of competition from any alternative beliefs. In this group it was therefore all the easier to carry on the Yahweh-alone movement, since events had completely confirmed the prophecies of disaster. The wall around tradition and identity now, for the first time, became a protection. Consequently, this group was the only one of the many deported by the Assyrians and Babylonians to preserve its identity over fifty years and then, in 537, after a change of power, finally to return to Palestine.

The Restoration of Tradition as a Persian Cultural Policy

The Persian Empire that ruled the East including Israel and Egypt for two centuries (545–323 BCE) stabilized its power in the provinces

---

[23] Deut. 14:2; 14:21; see also especially the holy laws laid down in Lev. 19 (and forward) and Exod. 19:6; see Frank-Lothar Hossfeld, "Volk Gottes als 'Versammlung,'" in J. Schreiner (ed.), *Unterwegs zur Kirche. Alttestamentliche Konzeptionen* (Freiburg: Herder, 1987), 123–142.

by making itself the authority on and guardian of local tradition.[24] In Egypt a commission was set up "to record the earlier law that had been in force until the 44th year of the reign of Amasis."[25] A certain Udjahorresne was commissioned to restore the "life houses" – the scriptoria adjoining the temples – which were the most important institutions of tradition (A. B. Lloyd 1982a). The temple that Darius I built in el-Khargeh can be regarded as the first representative of the new type, with decorations that were no longer related solely to the cult but also recorded an accumulation of important knowledge; this was what I described as the symbolic expression of fencing off and stabilizing tradition and identity in Egypt. Persian rule entailed the restoration and codification of traditions in Egypt. There is therefore good reason to suppose that only now did the *Book of the Dead* take on its definitive form in regard to the number and sequence of chapters. Until then, it had been a pool from which the scribes had compiled more or less individual collections of spells. The late version of the *Book of the Dead*, known as the *Saite Recension* but in fact first attested to in manuscripts from the Persian period, fixed this stream of tradition, thus creating something like a canon.

At the same time, the Hebrew canon was taking shape in Palestine, and it was not merely tolerated by the Persians but actually commissioned by them. The "Book of Laws" (presumably Deuteronomy), which, in the words of the philosopher and Judaist Jacob Taubes, Ezra brought from Babylon "on the points of the Persian bayonets,"[26]

---

[24] Hans G. Kippenberg sees this process as a general principle of imperialist politics: "If colonizers want to create an empire out of their conquered territories, then they must make themselves into the protectors or even the inventors of the traditions of the subjugated races." In Kippenberg, "Die jüdischen Überlieferungen," 51 (see chapt. 5, n. 22) with reference to Jan-Heeren Grevemeyer (ed.), *Traditionale Gesellschaften und europäischer Kolonialismus* (Frankfurt: Syndikat, 1981), 16–46; Gérard Leclerc, *Anthropologie und Kolonialismus* (Munich: Hanser, 1973). See also Peter Frei and Klaus Koch, *Reichsidee und Reichsorganisation im Perserreich*, OBO 55 (Freiburg: Fribourg University Press, 1984).

[25] Wilhelm Spiegelberg, *Die sogenannte Demotische Chronik* (DemSt 7) (Leipzig: J. C. Hinrichs, 1914), 30–32; E. Meyer, "Ägyptische Dokumente aus der Perserzeit," in *Sitzungsberichte der Preussischen Akademie der Wissenschaft* (Berlin, 1915), 304 ff.

[26] In Persian, Ezra is called the "writer of the laws of the God in Heaven"; Hans H. Schaeder, *Esra der Schreiber. Beträge zur historischen Theologie 5* (Tübingen: Mohr, 1930) thought that Ezra was a Persian state secretary with special responsibility for Jewish affairs.

was now fashioned into a canon. The end of prophecy is a precondition of the canon,[27] because – to use the Islamic expression – the gate must be shut[28] through which any new and binding meanings might enter. Prophecy had no place in the depoliticized province of Jehud, which was part of the satrapy of Transeuphratene. The prophets normally spoke to the king and people in the name of Yahweh, but now the satrap was far away, and the king, even farther. Thus instead of prophets, there were now scholars who codified, canonized, and interpreted the traditions.

The depoliticized spiritual climate in which this work took place testifies in particular to that stratum of biblical tradition known as the "priestly code." Here, the concepts of legitimate kingship and expectations of the Messiah, which played such a central role in the prophetic and deuteronomic tradition, virtually disappeared.[29] The monotheistic religion of the Yahweh-alone movement, which had been formed as a counterculture before the exile, now became the inner culture within the mighty union of the Persian Empire, concerning itself solely with clean living, and teaching and interpretation, while delegating all worldly matters to the occupying Persian power.

The process of depoliticizing public life began to take effect generally during the Persian period. In Egypt and Babylon was seen the clericalization of culture, during which time the role of representing culture shifted from scribe-officials to scribe-priests; in Israel the transition was from prophets to scholars. Religion stabilized and distinguished itself as a genuine alternative method of creating an identity only in Israel. It was only here that a people emerged that defined its outer boundaries and its inner unity in a manner that was

---

[27] Joseph Blenkinsopp, *Prophecy and Canon* (Notre Dame: University of Notre Dame Press, 1977); Lang, "Vom Propheten zum Schriftgelehrten" (see chapt. 5, n. 18); see also Leiman, *The Canonization of Hebrew Scripture* (see chapt. 2, n. 57).

[28] In Islam, it is not the gate of prophecy but that of independent searching and judgment (*iğtihad*) that is closed. See Tilman Nagel, *Die Festung des Glaubens. Triumph und Scheitern des islamischen Rationalismus im 11. Jh.* (Munich: C. H. Beck, 1988), 9 ff. Prophecy is closed by Muhammad himself, who is called "the seal of the prophets."

[29] I am referring here to conversations with the late Georg Christian Macholz, to whom I am indebted for a great deal of information. See now Mary Douglas, *Leviticus as Literature* (Oxford: Oxford University Press, 1999).

completely independent of political and territorial constrictions and that adhered solely to the bond of "the Law and the Prophets."[30]

Later on, however, this self-definition became repoliticized whenever the dominant political power attempted to interfere in the way of life of God's "holy people." The first spectacular case of this kind was when Antiochus IV Epiphanes took measures to introduce Hellenization (e.g., the ban on observing the Jewish laws), which led to the Maccabean Wars.[31] This culture war was a programmatic confrontation between *Ioudaismós* and *Hellenismós* (2 Macc. 2, 21, see E. Will and C. Orieux 1986).[32] This was the first time that Jewish identity was conceptualized as a way of life founded on religion,[33] and the non-Jewish, Hellenist life was correspondingly branded as heathen.[34] There were further violent clashes under the Romans, and the mythomotor formulations of political aspirations were strengthened into apocalypticism and messianism.[35] The apolitical antizealotry of the

---

[30] Outer boundaries: these were not territorial but consisted in the "limitist" symbolism of a way of life regulated by laws that made it difficult to have contact with any non-members (the day of rest, a ban on intermarriage and on sharing food, etc.). Inner unity: this was achieved by emphasizing membership, as evinced by the many new identity markers, such as "the children of exile" (*bene haggolah*), "the rest," "the men of the covenant," "the assembly" (*qahal*), "the community" (*jahad*), "synagogue," etc. See E. P. Sanders, *Jewish and Christian Self-Definition, 3 vols.* (Philadelphia: Fortress Press, 1980ff.); *vol. 2: Aspects of Judaism in the Graeco-Roman Period* (Philadelphia: Fortress Press, 1981); Schreiner, *Unterwegs zur Kirche,* (see chapt. 5, n. 23)

[31] Steven Weitzmann, however, is skeptical about the historicity of this edict, see: "Plotting Antiochus' Persecution," *JBL* 123.2 (2004), 219–234.

[32] But see now Erich Gruen, *Heritage and Hellenism. The Reinvention of Jewish Tradition* (Berkeley: University of California Press, 1998), who holds that the Jewish opposition was not against "Greek" but "common" culture (ho koinos bios, "the common way of life").

[33] See Martin Hengel, *Judentum und Hellenismus: Studien zu ihrer Begegnung unter besonderer Berücksichtigung Palästinas bis zur Mitte des 2. Jh. v. Chr.,* 2nd ed. (Tübingen: Mohr, 1973); *Juden, Griechen und Barbaren. Aspekte der Hellenisierung des Judentums in vorchristlicher Zeit* (Stuttgart: KBW Verlag, 1976); Fergus Millar, "The Background to Maccabaean Revolution," *JJS* 29 (1978), 1–21, takes a different view.

[34] On the emergence of this opposition, see Carsten Colpe, "Die Ausbildung des Heidenbegriffs von Israel zur Apologetik und das Zweideutigwerden des Christentums," in Faber and Schlesier (eds.), *Restauration der Götter* (see chapt. 5, n. 22), and also Gerhard Delling, "Die Ausbildung des Heidenbegriffs von Israel zur Apologetik und das Zweideutigwerden des Christentums," in Faber and Schlesier (eds.), *Restauration der Götter* (see chapt. 5, n. 22).

[35] Michael Stone, *Jewish Writings of the Second Temple Period* (Assen: Van Gorcum, 1984); Hellholm, *Apocalypticism,* (see chapt. 1, n. 92). On the political aspect, see Pierre Vidal-Naquet, *Les juifs, la mémoire et le présent* (Paris : F. Maspero, 1981), 17–42.

rabbinate only won out after the destruction of the temple in 70 AD and, above all, after Hadrian's crushing of the Bar-Kochbah rebellion in 135 AD.

The history of this process, which culminated in the canon of the Hebrew Bible and the identity of rabbinical Judaism, was a series of confrontations that were handed down in the form of Exodus traditions as the central memory figure:

Memory figures of confrontation:

Egypt	Israel
	The founding of "God's people" by Moses
Worshipers of the Golden Calf	The Levites (Exod. 2)
'The inhabitants of the land'	Immigrants: ban on making any covenants and on interbreeding (*amixia*)[36] (Exod. 34)

Historic confrontations

Royalty seeking assimilation	Prophets, puritan reforms
Syncretic cultic practices	attempted by the dissident Yahweh-alone movement (internal opposition)
Assyrian pressure to assimilate	Israelite resistance (external opposition)
Babylonian foreign culture	Community in exile
"am ha-ares": those who stayed, Samaritans[37]	"bene haggolah": returning exiles Jews
Egyptian Golah	Babylonian Golah[38]
"Hellenismós"	"Ioudaismós"

---

[36] "*Amixia*": of course, it was only the classical writers who gave this name to the situation, see Delling, "Die Ausbildung des Heidenbegriffs," 15 ff. (see chapt. 5, n. 34). In the language of the Pentateuch, the ban on mixing with the local inhabitants was justified by the "jealousy" of the Lord. In Antiquity, the Jews' *amixia* was negatively associated with a general misanthropy (Philon, *virt.* 141; Diodorus, *bibl.* 34, I, 2 and 40, 3, 4; Josephus, *c. Ap.* 2, 291, etc.; see also Jan N. Sevenster, *The Roots of Pagan Anti-Semitism in the Ancient World* [Leiden: E. J. Brill, 1975]). See now Peter Schäfer, *Judaeophobia: Attitudes toward the Jews in the Ancient World* (Cambridge: Harvard University Press, 1997).

[37] The Samaritans (Hebrew *kuttim*) saw themselves as the descendants of the northern tribes of Israel. They were regarded as heretics as they recognized only the Torah and not the prophets or hagiographers as Holy Writ.

[38] Bernd-Jörg Diebner, "Gottes Welt, Moses Zelt und das Salomonische Heiligtum," in T. Römer (ed.), *Lectio Difficilior Probabilior? Mélanges offerts à Françoise Smyth-Florentin, Dielheimer Blätter zum Alten Testament und seiner Rezeption in der Alten Kirche Beiheft 12* (Heidelberg: Wissenschaftliches Theologisches Seminar, 1991), 127–154. 130 f., draws attention to this area of conflict.

	Sadducees,
	Pharisees,[39] and other "puritanical"
	groups (Essenes), zealots[40]
Various foreign cultures	Jewish Diaspora.

The decisive thread running through this network of confrontations is the interweaving of external and internal opposition. This can already be seen in the Exodus tradition. The foundation of God's people was accompanied by the destruction not only of countless Egyptians through the ten plagues and in the Red Sea in persecution of the Israelites but also of a whole section of the Jewish people themselves, who were subjected to the harshest penalty for their recidivism and their obstinacy. From the very beginning it was made clear that membership was not only a matter of blood, descent, and inborn rights. A sharp distinction was drawn between the ethnic and the religious identity, that is, between Israel and the "true" Israel. And so the Exodus traditions took on the form of a memory figure that threw and even today continues to throw into relief all the historic confrontations, not only with the foreign cultures of the Assyrians, Babylonians, Persians, Greeks, Romans, and others but also with the majority of the Israelite group that sought to assimilate the Hellenist culture.

Israel's exclusive quest for purity was directed against their own people, and individually against their own souls. The ban on *amixia* – mixing with the inhabitants of the land – would not have been so rigid, and the commandment to "drive out before thee the Amorite, and the Canaanite, and the Hittite," and so on (Exod. 34) would not have been so harsh they it had not been directed against the Canaanite residing within their own hearts. The whole ideology of exclusion

---

[39] The clash between the Sadducees and the Pharisees was between the professional scholars of the clerical establishment (Sadducees) and a lay movement that promulgated a way of life strictly in keeping with the Torah (Pharisees). The Pharisees insisted on the divinely sanctioned authority not only of the scriptures but also on the time-honored tradition of their interpretation, which they traced back genealogically from their own teachers to the revelation on Mount Sinai. This later led in rabbinical Judaism to the doctrine of the oral Torah as a second revelation derived from Sinai and developed over the millennia. The Sadducees, on the other hand, disputed the authority of this oral tradition. See Jacob Lauterbach, "The Sadducees and the Pharisees," in *Studies in Jewish Literature*, in Honour of K. Kohler (Berlin, 1913).

[40] On the political battlegrounds within early Judaism, see especially Vidal-Naquet, *Les juifs, la mémoire et le présent*, 17–72 (see chapt. 5, n. 35).

is given sharp focus by the metaphor of marriage and the taboo on adultery and seduction. Apostasy is giving in to seduction, and the fear of seduction motivates separation. This fear corresponds to the "jealousy" of Yahweh, who wishes to lock his people in and keep them away from the rest of the world, similar to a patriarchal husband. The violent potential of this memory figure, it must be stressed, was never exploited by the monotheistic movements of Israel or of Judaism itself (except for the Maccabeans), but it played a substantial role in the movements of secession, liberation, and, especially, land acquisition – a role that in later times (e.g., with the Puritan migrants to North America and the Boers in South Africa) drew its self-image and legitimacy from this memory figure.

RELIGION AS MEMORY: DEUTERONOMY AS A PARADIGM OF CULTURAL MEMORY

The following section on cultural memory presents a slightly controversial thesis that requires a few preliminary explanations. I am going to examine one of the foundational texts of both Judaism and Christianity from a purely cultural perspective, independently of religious history and theology. My focus will be on the fifth Book of Moses, Deuteronomy, as the basis of a form of collective mnemotechnics that was completely new at the time and that established a kind of cultural memory and identity along with a new kind of religion. Viewed in the context of cultural memory, what was new in this religion was not so much the content (monotheism and iconoclasm) as the form. It created an all-embracing framework that made the comparatively natural settings of collective and cultural memory dispensable. These settings comprised kingdom, temple, and territory – the representative institutions that were normally regarded as integral and necessary stabilizations of the collective memory, or *lieux de mémoire*. With the aid of the new mnemotechnics, all these places were now transferred from the exterior to the interior and from the material to the imaginary, so that a spiritual Israel now emerged that could be situated wherever a group assembled to study the sacred texts and revive memory. In the preceding section, I described this process of internalization as one of writing and canonization from the outside, and through historical reconstruction I tried to set it within the

political and social history of Israel. The biblical texts shed a great deal
of light on this process, and Deuteronomy is a particularly explicit
example. This book develops an art of memory that is based on the
separation of identity from territory. What we have here is an exhor-
tation in the land to remember the bonds that were sealed outside
the land, which were situated in an extraterritorial history: Egypt,
Sinai, wilderness, Moab, and so forth. The truly foundational *lieux de
mémoire* lay outside the Promised Land. This, then, was the basis of
the mnemotechnics that made it possible for people to remember
Jerusalem when they were away from it, for example, in Babylon: "If
I forget thee, O Jerusalem, let my right hand forget her cunning"
(Psalm 137:5). If one could be in Israel and think of Egypt, Sinai, and
the wandering in the wilderness, then one could be in Babylon and
think of Israel.

Old Testament scholars agree that Deuteronomy was the manifesto
of a group, "movement," or "school" (Weinfeld 1972), which was the
bearer of a new, spiritual form of identity that was based solely on
the Torah, and through this one foundation possessed everything that
other societies had to build up in visible form – territories, institutions, monuments and the trappings of power. Heinrich Heine aptly
called the Torah a "portable fatherland" (Crüsemann 1987). Thus the
borders between the homeland and foreign territory were not drawn
geographically, but rather, in that "spiritual space" that Hugo von Hofmannsthal described in a speech made in 1927 when he referred to
the "*Schrifttum*" [literature] of a nation. "Not through our living on
home ground," the speech begins, "and not through our personal
contact in our everyday dealings, but above all through a spiritual
attachment we are bound to the community."[41] The Israelites seem
to have been the discoverers or inventors of this spiritual attachment,
and it was made possible through their writings. Among the much
discussed consequences of the written culture, the development of an
extraterritorial or spiritual living space is probably the most significant.
Deuteronomy is the text that focuses on and illuminates this process
by developing mnemotechnics that help to keep all the decisive bonds

---

[41] Hugo von Hofmannsthal, "Das Schrifttum als geistiger Raum der Nation, Rede,
gehalten im Auditorium maximum der Universität München am 10.1.1927," in
Gesammelte Werke in zehn Einzelausgaben. Reden und Aufsätze III, ed. by B. Schoeller, I.
Beyer-Ahlert, and R. Hirsch (Frankfurt: Fischer, 1980), 24–41, 24.

alive in the collective memory, irrespective of the indispensable and thus, in this sense, natural framework.

The term "natural" is a vital one for me. Here we are dealing with mnemotechnics whose relation to the natural forms of collective memory – as analyzed by Halbwachs – is exactly the same as that of the antique *ars memoriae* to natural, individual memory. Religion in the deuteronomic sense is an artificial enhancement[42] of collective memory. Nothing would be more natural in the Promised Land than to forget the wilderness, or in Babylon to forget Jerusalem. The remembering that is demanded in Deuteronomy is something unlikely, even paradoxical, and so it can only be activated by daily practice and concentration.

The Shock of Forgetting: The Foundational Legend of Cultural Mnemotechnics[43]

For the western art of memory[44] there is a foundational legend that describes something similar to a primal scene. This is the much quoted tale of the poet Simonides, as told by Cicero (see ch. 1, p. 15f.). Simonides is said to have had the good fortune to have survived the collapse of a festival hall, which killed all the other participants, disfiguring them to such an extent that they were unrecognizable. The poet, however, was able to identify all the dead bodies, because he had memorized the seating positions. The crucial point of this story is the localization of memory. The memory artist was able to arrange all the data in an imaginary space, recalling the participants in the context of this image.[45]

---

[42] It goes without saying that, in this usage, the term "artificial" does not have any negative connotations. Terms like "uprooting" and "homelessness," however, have in fact been used to criticize the Jews, because the sense of nationalism was unable or unwilling to go beyond a territorial representation of home and identity.

[43] A more expanded version of the following section was published earlier in Assmann and Harth, *Mnemosyne*, 337–355 (see chapt. 1, n. 2).

[44] See Frances Yates, *The Art of Memory* (London: Routledge & Kegan Paul, 1968); Anselm Haverkamp and Renate Lachmann (eds.), *Gedächtniskunst: Raum, Bild, Schrift. Studien zur Mnemotechnik* (Frankfurt: Suhrkamp, 1991).

[45] Cicero, *De Oratore* II, 86, 352–387, 355 (and onward). See also text, German translation, and detailed commentary by Renate Lachmann, *Gedächtnis und Literatur* (Frankfurt: Suhrkamp, 1990), 18–27; Engl.: *Memory and Literature*, trans. Roy Sellars (Minneapolis: University of Minnesota Press, 1997). Regarding location as a form of mnemotechnics, see also Part I, Chapter 1, Section 3 (of the present book).

There is also a foundational legend and primal scene for the memory culture of the Judeo-Christian world.[46] It is the story of how the Book of Deuteronomy was found and of how Josiah's reforms developed it. As in the Simonides story, the story begins with a catastrophe and a loss of identity. The catastrophe here, however, befell the entire nation, and it was not the cause but the consequence of forgetting.

According to the report in 2 Kings 22:2–13, during repair work on the Temple, the High Priest Hilkiah found an evidently forgotten "book of the Torah" (*sefer ha-torah*) or "Book of the Covenant" (*sefer ha-bᵉrît*). When it was read to the king, he was horrified and "rent his clothes." This book not only contained the "commandments, testimonies and statutes" of the covenant that the Lord had made with Israel but it also detailed the terrible curses that would fall on those who disobeyed. All the hardships and disasters of the past and present were now revealed as divine punishment because the religious and political practices of the country had been in gross violation of what had been set out in the covenant.

The deuteronomic history can be understood as a codification of memory based on the principle of guilt. It set out to explain and to cope with the catastrophes of the present in terms of the work of Yahweh (G. v. Rad 1958). In Chapter 6 I examine the link between guilt, memory, and historiography in more detail. In discussing the story of Josiah's reforms[47] as a foundational legend, we need not concern ourselves with its historicity. Even if the reforms do not correspond to any historical reality – a suspicion that arises from the fact that neither Jeremiah nor Ezekiel make any detailed reference to them – they are nevertheless of central importance as a memory figure. For our purposes, there are three significant aspects in this story:

1. The intention to break with tradition: the monopolization of the cult in Jerusalem made deep and far-reaching inroads into the religious life of the country, which were of a severity that can hardly be overestimated.[48]

---

[46] Concerning the difference between this term and "memory art," see Chapter 1, Preliminary Remarks.

[47] For a more comprehensive analysis of the account of Josiah's cultic reforms, which obviously underwent several revisions, see Spieckermann, *Juda unter Assur* (see chapt. 3, n. 39).

[48] The closest parallel to this was the Armana Revolution in Egypt, with its closure of all the temples in the country and the focus of religious life exclusively on Armana.

2. The legitimation of this break with tradition through the unexpected appearance of a book, that is, of a forgotten truth.

3. The resultant dramatization of the theme of memory.

In this story, the unexpected discovery of the book plays a role similar to that of Simonides: in a disastrous situation of complete forgetfulness, it is the only witness to a forgotten and unrecognizable identity. If we examine this book closely – tradition and research have identified it as the fifth Book of Moses[49] – we shall see very clearly that the motifs of forgetting and remembering form a constant thread.[50]

The text is Moses's legacy. It begins with information about time and place. The scene is the eastern bank of the Jordan, and the time is the period of preparation for the crossing into the Promised Land after forty years of wandering. All of the themes are significant: the border, the preparations to cross it, the end of the forty years. If we begin with the last of these, this span of forty years marks the end of a generation of eyewitnesses. Those who had firsthand experience of the Exodus from Egypt, when they were aged between twenty and thirty, had now grown old and, with their death, the living memory of the Exodus, the covenant on Mount Sinai, and the wanderings in the wilderness also disappeared.

In the account, their testimony is constantly invoked: "Your eyes have seen what the Lord did because of Baal-peor" (4:3).[51] "Thine eyes have seen all that the Lord your God hath done unto these two kings" (3:21). It all leads to the warning, "lest thou forget the things which thine eyes have seen" (4:9), "... for I speak not with your children which have not known, and which have not seen the chastisement of the Lord your God, his greatness, his mighty hand, and his stretched out arm, And his miracles, and his acts, which he did in the midst

---

49 Some Church Fathers, as well as Hobbes and Lessing, had already made this identification, but the historical and critical foundation was first laid by de Wette in his *Beiträge zur Einleitung in das Alte Testament* I (1806), and has since been universally accepted by Old Testament scholars.

50 See also Willy Schottroff, *'Gedenken' im Alten Orient und im Alten Testament. Die Wurzel zakar im semitischen Sprachkreis* (Neukirchen: Neukirchener Verlag, 1964), esp. 117 ff. "*Zkr*" (to remember) in Deuteronomy; Brevard S. Childs, *Memory and Tradition in Israel*, SBT 37 (Naperville, IL: A.R. Allenson, 1962).

51 See Numbers 25:4 (Jerusalem Bible): Yahweh said to Moses, "Take all the leaders of the people. Impale them facing the sun, for Yahweh, to deflect his burning anger from Israel."

of Egypt unto Pharaoh the king of Egypt, and unto all his land; And what he did unto the army of Egypt, unto their horses and to their chariots, how he made the water of the Red Sea to overflow them as they pursued after you, and how the Lord hath destroyed them unto this day; And what he did unto you in the wilderness, until ye came into this place [. . .] But your eyes have seen all the great acts of the Lord which he did. Therefore shall ye keep all the commandments which I command you this day . . . " (11, 2–8).

This speech was addressed to the eyewitnesses, who had personally seen and experienced the miracle of the Exodus. They are now told to preserve and pass on this history, which is why 2 Kings 23:3 speaks not only of commandments and statutes but also of "testimonies," and why the letters *'ajin* and *Dalet* in the first sentence of the *Shema*^c prayer forming the word *'ed* (witness) are emphasized in large writing in Jewish Bibles and prayer books:

s^ema^c Jisrael, adonaj elohênu adonaj aechad
Hear, O Israel: the Lord our God, is one Lord. (Deut. 6:5)

The last eyewitnesses of the Exodus are told again and again not to forget what they have seen.

Forty years represent a critical incursion into the collective memory, and if this account was not to be lost, it had to be transformed from biographical to cultural memory. The means used were collective mnemotechnics, and Deuteronomy names no fewer than eight different techniques of cultural memory:

1. Awareness: learning by and taking to heart.
   "And these words, which I command thee this day, shall be (written[52]) in thine heart" (6:6).
   "Therefore shall ye lay up these my words in your heart and in your soul" (11:18).

---

[52] The Hebrew text does not in fact speak of writing, but see Jeremiah 31:33: "I will put my law in their inward parts, and write it in their hearts."

2. Education: passing on the commandments to future generations by communication, circulation, and conversing about them at all times and in all places.[53]

"And thou shalt teach them diligently unto thy children, and shalt talk of them when thou sittest in thine house, and when thou walkest by the way, and when thou liest down, and when thou risest up" (6:7).

3. Visibility: markings on the body [*tefillim*].

"And thou shalt bind them for a sign upon thine hand, and they shall be as frontlets between thine eyes" (6:8, also 11:18).

4. Limitic symbolism: inscriptions on doorposts (*mezzuzôt*).

"And thou shalt write them upon the posts of thy house, and on thy gates" (6:9, also 11:21).

5. Storage and publication: inscriptions on whitewashed stones.

"And it shall be on the day when ye shall pass over Jordan unto the land which the Lord thy God giveth thee, that thou shalt set thee up great stones, and plaister them with plaister; And thou shalt write upon them all the words of this law, when thou art passed over [. . .] Therefore it shall be when ye be gone over Jordan, that ye shall set up these stones, which I command you this day, in mount Ebal, and thou shalt plaister them with plaister [. . .] And thou shalt write upon the stones all the words of this law very plainly" (27:2–8).[54]

Ebal is the mountain on which "to curse" (27:13–26). Curses were read from this mountain against all those who could not be reached by the arm of the law. The stones with the text of the covenant stand as witnesses to the forgotten commandments.[55]

---

53 See also the Lord's warning to Joshua after the death of Moses: "This book of the law shall not depart out of thy mouth; but thou shalt meditate therein day and night..." (Josh. 1:8). The law must be not only in the heart but also in the mouth. On "Conversational Remembering" from a psychological perspective, see Middleton and Edwards (eds.), *Collective Remembering*, 23–45 (see chapt. 3, n. 12). Shotter's essay in the same volume, 120–138, is important for our understanding of the role of speech in the construction of common memory.

54 The fulfillment of this commandment is reported in Josh. 8:30–35.

55 On the function of the inscription as a witness, see Josh. 24:26–27: "And Joshua wrote these words in the book of the law of God, and took a great stone, and set it up there under an oak, that was by the sanctuary of the Lord. And Joshua said unto all the people, Behold, this stone shall be a witness unto us; for it hath heard all the

6. Festivals of collective remembrance: the three great festivals of assembly and pilgrimage, at which all people, great and small, must appear before the Lord.[56]

"*Mazzot*" (= Pesach, or Passover) – the feast that commemorates the Exodus from Egypt, "that thou mayest remember the day when thou camest forth out of the land of Egypt all the days of thy life" (16:3).[57]

"*Shavuot*" – The Feast of the Weeks, in commemoration of the time in Egypt: "And thou shalt remember that thou wast a bondman in Egypt" (16:12).[58]

"*Sukkot*" – the Feast of the Tabernacles, when every seventh year the whole text of the book is to be read (see number 8, below).

Part of this festival entails bringing "the first of all the fruit of the earth," and the person who makes the sacrifice must make a prescribed speech before God (in Deut. chapter 26; see Gerhard von Rad 1958, 11–20). This speech, which G. von Rad calls a "little historical credo," is in effect a short account of the history of the Exodus, extended by reference to the fathers and to the conquest of the land (26, 55–59).

7. Oral tradition: poetry as a codification of historical memory.

Toward the end of the book, there is a great song of warning against the terrible consequences of unfaithfulness and forgetting, expressed in a densely poetic form. This song is to remain alive in the oral tradition of the people, so that they will be

---

words of the Lord which he spake unto us: it shall be therefore a witness unto you, lest ye deny your God."

[56] Originally, all three festivals were connected with harvests (*Mazzot* for barley, *Shavuot* for wheat and other cereals, *Sukkot* for autumn crops). It is assumed that festivals only changed to being commemorative when the Israelites lost their land and the diaspora began, so that the link between the festivals and the agricultural cycle was broken. The role that memory played in the texts that gave rise to festivals is of particular interest here.

[57] On the festival of *Mazzot* as a *Zikkaron* (commemorative feast), see Exod. 12:14; Lev. 23,: 4–8. See Cancik and Mohr (eds.), "Erinnerung/Gedächtnis," notes 73–77 (see chapt. 1, n. 31).

[58] It was after the Bible was written that the feast of Shavuot changed to commemorating the revelation on Mount Sinai and the handing over of the Torah. See Max Dienemann, "Schawuot," in F. Thieberger (ed.), *Jüdisches Fest und jüdischer Brauch*, reprint (Königstein: Jüdischer Verlag, 1979), 280–287.

permanently reminded of their obligations: "Now therefore write ye this song for you, and teach it to the children of Israel: put it in their mouths that this song may be a witness for me against the children of Israel. For when I shall have brought them into the land which I sware unto their fathers, that floweth with milk and honey; and they shall have eaten and filled themselves, and waxen fat; then will they turn unto other gods, and serve them, and provoke me, and break my covenant. And it shall come to pass, when many evils and troubles are befallen them, that this song shall testify against them as a witness; for it shall not be forgotten out of the mouths of their seed . . ." (31:19–21).

8. Canonization of the text of the covenant (Torah) as the basis for literal observation.

"And Moses wrote this law [. . .] And Moses commanded them, saying, At the end of every seven years, in the solemnity of the year of release, in the feast of tabernacles . . . thou shalt read this law before all Israel in their hearing" (31:9–11).[59] The obligation to stick to the letter of the law is repeated many times: "thou shalt not add thereto, nor diminish from it" (12:32; see also 4:2).[60]

---

59 This corresponds to the common practice among the Hittites of reading the texts of agreements at regular intervals; see Viktor Korošec, *Hethitische Staatsverträge. Ein Beitrag zu ihrer juristischen Wertung.* Leipziger rechtswissenschaftliche Studien 60 (Leipzig: T. Weicher, 1931), 101 f.; George E. Mendenhall, *Law and Covenant in Israel and in the Ancient Near East* (Pittsburgh: Biblical Colloquium, 1955), 34; Klaus Baltzer, *Das Bundesformular,* 2. ed. (Neukirchen: Neukirchner Verlag, 1964), 91 f. For the Assyrians, see Ernst Weidner, "Hof- und Haremserlasse assyrischer Könige," *AfO* 17 (1954–1956), 257–293. During the Feast of the Tabernacles, Ezra read the Torah aloud to the people from beginning to end (Nehemiah 8:1,18; see also Baltzer, *Das Bundesformular,* 91–93). See also the stipulation at the end of the testament of the Hittite king Hattusilis I (16th century BCE): " . . . and this tablet is to be read [by his successor] every month; thus you will remember my words and my wisdom again and again." Laroche, *Catalogue des textes Hittites,* No. 6, quoted by Cancik and Mohr (eds.), "Erinnerung/Gedächtnis," 314, (see chapt. 1, n. 31).

60 On the "canon formula" and its different forms, see Chapter 2, the beginning of section 2. In Deuteronomy we find a combination of formulae connected with covenants and with copying, commanding that every single detail of the covenant must be adhered to literally, and nothing must be changed in the form of the text. This obligation reflects the fact that tradition too was seen as binding, and hence as a kind of contract drawn up between author and scribes. Adherence to a contract also entails its being handed down intact, and the characteristic curses that protect

The synagogal reading from the Torah where it is read out in its entirety in a yearly cycle is derived from the rotational reading of the covenant. The reading of the Word of God, including Christian services, followed on from an institution that was devised as an organ of collective memory.[61]

Of these eight forms of collective mnemotechnics, the eighth was the most significant. It entailed an incursion into tradition that subjected the fluid mass of conventions to a rigid process of selection, which stabilized and sanctified the elements selected – that is, that enhanced them to the level of final authority and forever brought to a standstill the stream of tradition. From that time on, nothing could be added, and nothing could be taken away. The covenant had become a canon.[62]

In the light of the distinction between communicative and cultural memory, we can now see more precisely the basic problem underlying Deuteronomy – the transformation of communicative memory (live and embodied by eyewitnesses) into cultural memory (formed and supported by institutions) or into mnemotechnics. Memory that is no longer embodied by or alive in the communicative memory of a generation inevitably forms a contrast to the progressive present, and so it becomes contrapresent (G. Theissen 1988).

Endangered Memory and Socially Conditioned Forgetting

Anyone who reads fairy tales will be familiar with the subject of the admonition under no circumstances to forget a particular thing; one

---

the covenant also apply to the protection of its wording. The formulae used in the colophons of Babylonian cuneiform tablets have the same imperative form as in Deuteronomy. But here the warnings are clearly directed at the copyists. See G. Offner, "A propos de la sauvegarde des tablettes en Assyro-Babylonie," *RA* 44 (1950), 135–43; Cancik, *Mythische und historische Wahrheit* (Stuttgart: Bibelstudien 48, 1970), 85 ff.; Michael Fishbane, "Varia Deuteronomica," *ZAW* 84 (1972), 349–52.

[61] See Baltzer, *Das Bundesformular,* 91 ff. (see chapt. 5, n. 59); also Gerhard von Rad's interpretation of Deuteronomy as "Gesetzpredigt" (law sermon), *Deuteronomium-Studien*, FRLANT N.F.40 (Göttingen: Vandenhoeck & Ruprecht, 1947), 36 f.

[62] See A. and J. Assmann (eds.), *Kanon und Zensur* (see chapt. 1, n. 41). On the emergence of the Hebrew canon and the importance of Deuteronomy as a kind of crystallization of the biblical canonization process, see the essay by F. Crüsemann. For a more general view of the importance of the canon principle, see the essays by C. Colpe and A. and J. Assmann. Cf. now, in much greater detail, *Of God and Gods,* chapter 5.

always knows for certain then that the particular thing is about to be forgotten. Fairy tales are partial to warnings against the transgression of certain boundaries or against entering a mysterious room. It is always the framework of the unfamiliar, and this is particularly applicable to food, that encourages forgetting.

The journey into the unknown or the transgression of a border represents a prime example and model for the process of forgetting. The child forgets his parents, the envoy, his message, the prince, his noble birth, the soul, its heavenly origin, because there is nothing in the new world to bear or support memory. It has lost its frame of reference, and thus, it becomes unreal and disappears.

This is precisely the situation presupposed by Deuteronomy. Its "words" (*d͡ebarîm* [the Hebrew title of the book] based on its beginning: "These be the words which Moses spake unto all Israel . . .") are spoken at the border. A more radical change of framework than the one that confronted the people of Israel at the end of their wanderings is simply unimaginable. Once they had crossed the Jordan and eaten of the "milk and honey" of their new home, they would forget their identity and their mission, or covenant.

Reading Deuteronomy, one is given the impression that nothing could be less natural or self-evident than remembering a story that has all the signs of being absolutely unforgettable, and that nothing could be more natural and self-evident than forgetting the experiences of the last forty years. How does the text justify this pessimistic appraisal of the durability of the past and of collective memory? There are two recurrent themes: contrast and temptation. The land that is now to be Israel's home will present them with conditions that are completely different from the ones that they have previously had to endure:

" . . . a land of brooks of water, of fountains and depths that spring out of valleys and hills; A land of wheat, and barley, and vines, and fig trees, and pomegranates; a land of oil olive, and honey; A land wherein thou shalt eat bread without scarceness, thou shalt not lack any thing in it; a land whose stones are iron, and out of whose hills thou mayest dig brass. When thou hast eaten and art full, then thou shalt bless the Lord thy God for the good land which he hath given thee. Beware that thou forget not the Lord thy God, in not keeping his commandments, and his judgments, and his statues, which I command thee this day: Lest when thou hast eaten and art full, and hast built goodly houses, and dwelt therein; And when thy herds and thy flocks multiply, and thy silver and thy gold is multiplied, and all that thou hast is multiplied; Then thine heart be lifted up, and thou forget the Lord thy God, which brought thee forth out of the land of Egypt, from the house of bondage [. . .] And thou say in thine heart, My power and the might of mine hand hath gotten me this wealth. But thou shalt remember the Lord thy God [. . .] And it shall be, if thou do at all forget the Lord thy God, and walk after other gods, and serve them, and worship them, I testify against you this day that ye shall surely perish . . . " (8:7–19).

"And it shall be, when the Lord thy God shall have brought thee into the land [. . .] to give thee great and goodly cities, which thou buildedst not, And houses full of all good things which thou filledst not, and wells digged, which thou diggedst not, vineyards and olive trees, which thou plantedst not; when thou shalt have eaten and be full; then beware lest thou forget the Lord, which brought thee forth out of the land of Egypt, from the house of bondage . . . " (6:10–12).

Forgetting was caused by changes in the framework of living and social conditions. Food functioned as the symbol and embodiment of the new reality to which the old had had to give way. The experience of forty years in the wilderness was reduced to the astonishing fact that man does not live on bread alone – "And he humbled thee, and suffered thee to hunger, and fed thee with manna, which thou knewest not, neither did thy fathers know; that he might make thee know that man doth not live by bread only, but by every word that proceedeth out of the mouth of the Lord doth man live" (8:3). If the surrounding reality were to change, it is quite probable that what used to be valid will swiftly be forgotten, because it now would run counter to external conditions and would no longer be confirmed or supported by them.

Memory, however, is not only exposed to a natural fading when external conditions change; it can also be subject to destruction from outside. There is constant reference in the passages to snares and temptations. The land into which Israel is to move will exercise all its powers of seduction, and so the future will depend on the Israelites not mixing with the inhabitants, but on their erection of an insurmountable barrier to keep themselves separate.

" . . . thou shalt make no covenant with them, nor shew mercy unto them: Neither shalt thou make marriages with them; thy daughter thou shalt not give unto his son, nor his daughter shalt thou take unto thy son. For they will turn away thy son from following me, that they may serve other gods [. . .] But thus shall ye deal with them; ye shall destroy their altars, and break down their images, and cut down their groves, and burn their graven images with fire" (7:2–5). " . . . thine eye shall have no pity upon them; neither shalt thou serve their gods; for that will be a snare unto thee" (7:16).

Israel must not forget, and must not give way to temptation: " . . . thou shalt not learn to do after the abominations of those nations" (18:9). The motif of temptation refers to polytheism and idolatry, the religious conventions of the land across the Jordan. The way of life laid down for Israel was diametrically opposed to these conventions: there could be no other god than the Lord, no idols, no shrines other than the Temple in Jerusalem, no prophets, no "observer of times, or an enchanter, or a witch, or a charmer, or a consulter with spirits, or a wizard, or a necromancer" (18:10–11),[63] or even the smallest attempt at adaptation to the laws and customs of this land. That would be an abomination to the Lord.[64]

What Israel must not forget, once it moved into the Promised Land and was living in prosperity, was the covenant sealed with the Lord in the wilderness. Past and future in this story were divided up into wilderness and fertile land, wilderness and civilization. Yesterday did not continue into today; on the contrary, the two were as sharply divided as could be. Nevertheless, yesterday must be preserved for today. A work of memory art was demanded of the people, but there would be no encompassing framework of present reality to support it. This meant that they must remain strangers in their own homeland and in their own present, because adaptation would lead to forgetting. The extent of the stakes can be seen in the story of the discovery of this book outlined in 2 Kings 22–23. In light of what is prescribed in Deuteronomy, it is all too clear that the entire system of worship that had been flourishing in the land at that time was precisely what the Lord had condemned as an abomination, and so there had to be a nationwide cleansing operation of unparalleled severity and even cruelty in order to destroy its root and branch. Here, memory has a shocking and destructive effect.

Josiah's reforms are represented as a revolution coming from on high, and they were implemented by way of a forgotten truth. The

---

[63] See also Lev. 19:26; 19:31; 20, 27.

[64] On the conflict between monotheism and polytheism in Israel, see M. Weippert, "Synkretismus und Monotheismus" (see chapt. 5, n. 18).

shock of a restored memory, a *mémoire involontaire* on a collective level, set lawmaking in motion. Only such a forgotten truth that, in contrast to continuous tradition, had come down untarnished through the ages could have imposed itself with such revolutionary force. From the outside, through the eyes of an historian, one can discern a strategy that is typical of many reforms. The new is represented as a return to the original. The Morton Smith School, to which we also subscribed in the first section of this chapter, views Josiah's reforms as the triumph of the "Yahweh-alone movement," which prophets and individual groups mounted in opposition to the official policies and practices of the kingdom (M. Smith 1987, 11–42). According to this interpretation, the concept of monotheism did not emerge from something forgotten; instead it surfaced from the underground, branding the existing conventions as a relapse and an act of forgetting. The biblical account proceeds from the fact that the religious customs of the kingdom had been preceded by pure monotheism, which in the days of the empire had been overwhelmed by a process of assimilation into the cultural environment and therefore had in actual fact been forgotten. But the knowledge once inculcated into the people could not be eternally repressed, and during a phase that, incidentally, was politically highly charged,[65] it forced its way back via a comprehensive and radical cleansing or "purge" (Ezek. 20, 36–38).[66] In this reconstruction, religious history manifests itself as a drama of memory, along exactly the same lines as Freud's theory. Memory of the Exodus is the linchpin of this reform, the success of which can only be explained if understood in terms of a memory drama, of the return of the repressed that assumes that there was "something" that could be supplied by the memory figures of the Exodus, Sinai, and the Promised Land.

During the ordeal of their exile in Babylon, the Jews had laid the foundations of a form of cultural mnemotechnics that had and has had no parallel in human history. This memory art was unique and also "artificial" as it was based on a memory that, within the frame of

---

[65] During Josiah's reign, there was a rapid decline in the power of Assyria, which had taken control of the northern kingdom 100 years earlier, and had subjugated the southern kingdom both politically and culturally as a vassal state. Its grip then loosened, creating an opportunity for greater self-determination. Deuteronomy was the result of this quest for autonomy. On the historical background, see Spieckermann, *Juda unter Assur*, 227 ff. (see chapt. 3, n. 39).

[66] See Michael Walzer, *Exodus and Revolution* (New York: Basic Books, 1985), 68 f.

reference of the existing reality, not only lacked any confirmational evidence but in fact constituted the direct opposite of that reality: the wilderness against the Promised Land, Jerusalem against Babylon. However, with the aid of these mnemotechnics, the Jews were able – across a gap of almost two thousand years and despite being scattered to all four corners of the Earth – to keep alive their memory of a land and a way of living that was in stark contrast to their present, whatever and wherever that was: "This year slaves, next year free, this year here, next year in Jerusalem." Such a utopian memory, which was not supported by their existing circumstances, is what G. Theissen (1988) felicitously described as contrapresent.

Although the cultural mnemotechnics of Deuteronomy are concerned with a very specific phenomenon that can only be understood in the context of Israel's particular historical situation, the principle of contra-present memory is a general one. Admittedly, Judaism represents an example of extreme enhancement; in every society, however, there are "anachronistic structures" (Erdheim 1988) and institutions that are devoted to preservation rather than progress. Religion is a typical instance of such structures. Within the culture that shapes the present, religion keeps alive a past that must not be forgotten. Its "function is to convey the non-contemporaneous through memory, revival and repetition" (Cancik and Mohr 1990, 311). Retrospective obligation, memory, and preservation are primal acts of religion.[67] Deuteronomy gave a narrative form to this structure, solidifying it into a vivid memory figure. Life is not confined to today any more than man can "live by bread only" (Deut. 8:3). Religion, in the form first laid down by Deuteronomy, that became the yardstick for all later religions, meant holding fast to a bond that had been sealed under completely different and extreme conditions even though that bond did not find the slightest confirmation in the contemporary situation.

[67] On the problematical etymology of *religio* (from *religere*, "to observe carefully," or from *re-ligari*, "to tie back," "to reconnect"), see Hans Zirker, "Religion," in G. Bitter and G. Miller (eds.), *Handbuch religionspädagogischer Grundbegriffe* 2 (München: Kösel, 1986), 635–643. The vital element in both cases is the prefix "*re*," conveying the meaning of "backwards." See Heinz-Josef Fabry, "Gedenken und Gedächtnis im Alten Testament," in Gignoux (ed.), *La commémoration* (see chapt. 1, n. 85).

6

The Birth of History from the Spirit of the Law

SEMIOTIZATION OF HISTORY UNDER THE SIGNS OF REWARD AND PUNISHMENT

In the context of cultural memory, Israel provides us with a paradigm for two equally important phenomena: damming the stream of tradition by canonization, and initiating historiography. The two are closely related. The common ground here is provided by the ethno-genetic process through which a collective identity is established with the support of a canonized tradition driven by the mythomotor of an internalized history. This theoretical interpretation corresponds to the classical paradigm, which also brings canon and history together in the closest possible fashion. We read, for instance, in Josephus: "Our books... are only 22 in number and contain a report on all times. 5 of these are the books of Moses, which contain the laws and traditional history from the origin of man to the death of the law-giver. History from Moses to Artaxerxes was written by the prophets in 13 books. The remaining 4 books contain hymns to God and precepts for the conduct of human life." (See Chapter 7, Section 2 for further comment on this passage.) The first and most important parts of the Tanakh – the Torah and the Prophets – are subsumed here under the heading of history. "Damming the stream of tradition" is the task of historiography, which must decide on the one binding memory. The prophets are the bearers of this memory, and the end of prophecy is also the end of historiography: "From Artaxerxes to our own time there has been a tradition, but this does not enjoy the same esteem because the sequence of the prophets was broken." The prophetic or "charismatic" history reached from Moses to Nehemiah, and their memories were set down in thirteen books. The special duty of memory that the Israelites were bound to fulfill had its origin in law. This was derived from the covenant Israel had made with God, and such a covenant made the strongest demands on the memory: every detail had to be memorized, preserved, and obeyed, and woe to him who left anything out, added anything, or changed anything. Both the famous canon formula[1] and the imperative *zakhor ve shamor!* (Remember and keep!) originally had a legal meaning.

In the previous chapter, I dealt with the historical framework of canonization, and now I turn my attention to the framework of history and historiography. Our main thesis is that both of these were closely related to the work of the legal institutions in the Ancient Near East.

I begin by defining history in terms that I suggested in a different context: "History is the result of action and memory. History does not exist for us other than through memory, and we cannot remember events other than through action."[2] Action presupposes the existence of a degree of flexibility (*Handlungsspielraum*), and this must be *legally* structured through obligations and liberties. In other words, action takes place within a legally structured space. It would be easy to show – although it would take one beyond the scope of this study – how a historical space developed out of the legally regulated, interstate relations between the Sumerian city-states through the medium of cuneiform writing, which spread across Mesopotamia in the third millennium BCE and in the Late Bronze Age incorporated the whole of the Ancient World, Egypt, and the Aegean into a single "ecumenism."[3] Here, however, my aim is to show that the genesis of the Ancient World

---

[1] See 103 ff.–201 as well as 236 f. J. Assmann, "Stein und Zeit," 105 (see chapt. 1, n. 47).

[2] On the link between concepts of history and action, see Rüdiger Bubner, *Geschichtsprozesse und Handlungsnormen* (Frankfurt: Suhrkamp, 1984).

[3] The studies by P. Artzi, "The Birth of the Middle East," *Proceedings of the 5th World Congress of Jewish Studies* (1969), 120–124; "Ideas and Practices of International Coexistence in the 3rd Mill. BCE," *Bar Ilan Studies in History* 2 (1984), 25–39; Munn-Rankin, "Diplomacy in Western Asia in the Early 2nd Mill BC," *Iraq* 18 (1956), 68–110, are of particular interest in this context.

and the Ecumenical Age[4] with its foreign policy ramifications created a structural change not only in the areas of action but also in the memory – namely, the memory linked to longterm covenants and to the acceptance of binding agreements and laws. The obligations, both internal and external, imposed on people through state-organized communities also applied to the future, and together with the resultant area of action, they formed the "world" and also the socially conceived time in which remembered history took place.[5]

This reconstruction, in which the law takes a central position in the connective structure of early societies, is in keeping with the language of the sources. What we are calling the connective structure of a culture and society, and which constitutes the subject matter of this study, is covered in early cultures by such terms as "right," "law," "justice," "faithfulness," "truthfulness," and so on.[6] Trust in the world, which makes memory and action possible through a "reduction of complexity" (Luhmann [see chapt. 3, n. 6]) is based on the validity of legal obligations.

It is no coincidence that the title of this chapter is connected to Nietzsche; the thesis that memory was born from the spirit of the law forms the second treatise and the main argument of his *On the Genealogy of Morals*. Here, however, I do not develop the argument from the standpoint of morality or individual obligations, but from that of history and collective obligations. "Beware that thou forget not...!": this cultural imperative is also addressed to the collective in Israel. The connection between memory and the law affords an

---

[4] This expression was coined by Eric Voegelin, *Order and History IV. The Ecumenic Age* (Baton Rouge: LSU Press, 1974), although it was in relation to a later period that extended from the Persian Empire to the end of the Roman Empire. However, political unity in a kingdom is not the decisive factor for the term "ecumenism." It is more important to be conscious of the fact that there are other orders outside one's own, and that despite all the differences in language, customs, and laws, all orders and peoples share the same world and are capable of intercultural understanding. This gives rise to the concept of the "inhabited Earth" as a shared but multicentered place of history.

[5] Friedrich H. Tenbruck, "Gesellschaftsgeschichte oder Weltgeschichte?," *Kölner Zeitschrift für Soziologie und Sozialpsychologie* 41 (1989), 417–439, 436 highlights that in the introduction to his historical work Polybios identified the process whereby events become increasingly interlinked, and he established the link between "ecumenism" and "history."

[6] I have tried to show how this applied to Egypt, in J. Assmann, *Ma'at* (see chapt. 1, n. 11).

opportunity to examine cuneiform cultures, at which I have barely glanced so far, in more detail.

Iustitia Connectiva

The meaning of events presents itself as a connection between actions and consequences, which is usually called "causality." For earlier societies, however, this terminology would be inappropriate. The concept of causality suggests an automatic and a natural progression from one event to another, but this is the exact opposite of what we find in ancient texts. There, it is a matter of powers, instances, and institutions that guard the connection between action and cause, ensuring that good is rewarded and evil punished. In all cases, the focus is on requital, not on causality.[7] However, the manner in which this principle functions is imagined in different ways.

Instead of requital, the sources speak of justice.[8] This is the central concept that binds law, religion, and morality together. Justice directs the judgment of the judges and the actions of kings, it guides people along their different paths, and it links deed to consequence. Meaning and justice are therefore synonymous, for in a just world, good triumphs and evil perishes. This was the basis of ancient Near Eastern wisdom, whose principal concern was to prevent people from taking their own revenge and also from seeking personal happiness in their own way. The concept of connective (i.e., binding) justice seems appropriate for the following reasons:

1. It binds people together, thereby creating a basis for social cohesion and solidarity.

---

[7] Causality is a fiction, or construct – what Hayden White calls "poetry." H. Gese distinguishes between "sequence" and "consequence" as theoretical connectors. Even the concept of consequence goes too far. Just like "causality," "consequence" suggests something natural, logical, and automatic. This would be inappropriate for earlier ways of thinking, as Hans Kelsen, *Vergeltung und Kausalität* (Den Haag: W. P. van Stockum, 1947) has shown.

[8] See Hans H. Schmid, *Gerechtigkeit als Weltordnung* (Tübingen: Mohr, 1968), as well as unpublished typescript; J. Assmann, "Der leidende Gerechte im alten Ägypten. Zum Konfliktpotential der ägyptischen Religion," in C. Elsas and H. G. Kippenberg (eds.), *Loyalitätskonflikte in der Religionsgeschichte* (Würzburg: Königshausen and Neumann, 1990), 203–224, 203–214. Now Bernd Janowski, *Die rettende Gerechtigkeit. Beiträge zur Theologie des Alten Testaments* 2 (Neukirchen-Vluyn: Neukirchener Verlag, 1999).

2. It links success to good deeds, punishment to crime, thus ensuring meaning and coherence in what would otherwise be an aimless, free-flowing stream of events.

Both social (1) and temporal (2) dimensions meet in the term "obligation," which contains the root *ligo* – to bind. Both the social and the temporal horizons of validity for legal norms are significant here. An obliging or binding norm obliges people and time by placing its claims to validity on a limited or unlimited future.

In this manner, justice creates a space of memory in which that which is valid today was also valid yesterday and will remain valid tomorrow. The commandment not to forget is therefore of the utmost importance, since it is the strongest and the earliest incentive for memory.

The connective structure can be visualized in four different ways:

a) The simplest and most widespread concept of interconnected action and consequence is that of an automatism by which good "pays off" and evil "comes back" to haunt one. This principle of an "immanent providence"[9] does not presuppose divine or state intervention, but is based on everyday experience of an orderly, communal life. It suggests a self-regulated circulation of good and evil that finds expression in the "golden rule,"[10] but also in the concrete casuistry of proverbs ("Truth will come to light"; "Cheaters never prosper").

This straightforward wisdom was given more specific expression in the civilizations of the Ancient Near East as I demonstrate in my forthcoming discussions of social, political, and religious justice.

b) *Social* justice based the relation of doing and faring on a powerful concept of solidarity and reciprocity. The reward for good and punishment of evil was not automatic; it depended on "thinking of one another" and "acting for one another" (the fundamental Egyptian precepts of social justice). Meaning relies on a shared act of memory that runs counter to the egotistical instinct for forgetting. Egyptians placed great emphasis on

[9] Aleida Assmann, "Was ist Weisheit: Wegmarken in einem weiten Feld," in A. Assmann (ed.), *Weisheit*, 15–44, 19 (see chapt. 3, n. 13).

[10] Albrecht Dihle, *Die Goldene Regel* (Göttingen: Vandenhoeck & Ruprecht, 1962).

order being maintained through solidarity, in particular with their concept of *Ma'at*; the Arab historian Ibn Haldun uses the term *'asabiyya*, which places more emphasis on the emotional aspect of solidarity.[11] The ethnologist Meyer Fortes (1978) uses the term "amity."

c) *Political* justice made the state responsible for the functional link between deed and consequence. Egypt – obviously through political application of the social justice characterized under "b," here – and India are classic examples of this interpretation of reality. According to this view, if the state collapses, there will be chaos. Meaning and order will disappear from the world. Good will no longer be rewarded, evil will no longer be punished, the great will devour the small, and sons will kill their fathers.

d) *Religious* justice placed the functional link between deed and consequence in the hands of the gods. Reward and punishment were no longer the automatic, self-regulating results of people's actions, but depended on divine intervention. This presupposed a "theology of will," which ascribed an intentionality to the gods as far as the fate of human beings was concerned.

The concept of connective justice only functioned as an incentive for memory in this form. Divine justice and the corresponding idea of human responsibility filled events with meaning, and everything depended on knowing what this was. One might call this process "semioticizing through theologizing."

The country in which the theology of the will originated was Mesopotamia. This is the source of the earliest texts by far that attribute events to the will of the gods. Bertil Albrektson (1967) showed that the Mesopotamian gods were at least as prone to interfering in human affairs as the God of the Old Testament. What he failed to spot, however, was the fact that most of the texts he alluded to were of legal character: agreements whereby potential transgressors would be subject to divine retribution. The formula of the curse expressed most

---

[11] Hinrich H. Biesterfeldt, "Ibn Haldun: Erinnerung, historische Reflexion und die Idee der Solidarität," in Assmann and Harth (eds.), *Mnemosyne*, 284 ff. (see chapt. 1, n. 2).

clearly what was expected of the gods, namely the imposition of connective justice.[12] The future, into which these texts would extend their powers of obligation, lay in the hands of the gods, whose duty it was to ensure that the laws were not forgotten and that those who violated them were punished. The oldest text of this kind is a stela on the border between Lagash and Umma. The transgressor is warned that Enlil and Ningirsu will destroy him through a political disaster: his people will refuse to obey him and they will kill him.

The law constitutes a sphere of action regulated by norms, and even a ruler is subject to them. Just as his subjects are under his authority so, too, is he under the authority of the gods. If a king violates the norms, he will suffer the consequences; memory of such punishment also helps to strengthen the norms. This is the theme of lamentation literature and of moral legends about kings – especially Naram-Sin. Under the title *The Curse on Aggade*, the well-known tale relates how King Naram-Sin destroyed the Temple of Enlil in Nippur, and so Enlil sent the Gutians into the land:

From the distant mountains he made them come down, who are like no other (known) people, and cannot be counted among people. The Gutians, who know no ties like a true people, who have the form of humans, but whose words are of the nature of the voice of a dog, Enlil made come down from the mountains. In masses upon masses they covered the earth like locusts.[13]

This form of narrative – not documentary but highly poetic – is based on a preconceived meaning or semioticization. This is the principle of *iustitia connectiva*, the legal sphere that was protected by the gods to whom the entreaties were made, with whom contracts were sworn

---

[12] The curse is the strongest form of connection between action and consequence. If all social and political institutions fail, the curse will still ensure that the evildoer will be punished. The converse is also true of the blessing. Curse and blessing presuppose religious justice, because they involve the gods (or God) as agents of the action-consequence process, even when they appear to be acting independently. Unfortunately, no one has yet put together a comprehensive account of the ancient curse. On the Bible and the Ancient Near East, Willy Schottroff, *Der altisraelitische Fluchspruch*, WMANT 30 (Neukirchen: Neukirchener Verlag, 1969) is still the leading authority.

[13] Adam Falkenstein, "Fluch über Akkade," *Zeitschrift für Assyriologie* 57 (NF 23) (1965), 70; Bertil Albrektson, *History and the Gods. An Essay on the Idea of Historical Events as Divine Manifestations in the Ancient Near East and in Israel* (Lund: Gleerup, 1967), 25 f. Engl. trans. Kramer, in ANET Suppl. 210–215.

and who would link punishment to guilt or, in more general terms, consequence to deed.[14]

Hittite Historiography around 1300 BCE

In the great historical writings of the Hittites, a striking link between guilt, law, and justice is demonstrated. The classic scenario leading to punishment by the gods is an oath, the breaking of the oath, and the violation of an agreement. The case of Suppiluliuma, which I now look at in some detail, offers a clear example of this. After consultation with the oracle, two "tablets" were specified containing binding agreements that Suppiluliuma was accused of having broken. One concerns a sacrifice to the River Mala (Euphrates), and the other and much more important one, a treaty with Egypt. With reference to this treaty, Mursilis declares:

> But to this tablet
> I added not a word,
> Nor did I take one away.
> See, Gods, my Lords!
> I do not know! But earlier,
> Which kings were there –
> Whether then someone added
> Or took away,
> I know nothing of that,
> And afterwards have heard nothing
> Of the matter.[15]

This declaration, which H. Cancik (1970, 85 f.) takes to be the first use of the formula "take nothing away, add nothing," does not refer to an accurate copying of a text but to the literal fulfillment of the conditions of a contract.[16] It is striking that the formula is used here in exactly the same sense as in Deuteronomy (4:2). Even its precursor in the

---

[14] For guidance through the extensive field of Ancient Near Eastern and Greek contracts and oaths, see the anthology by Canfora et al. (eds.), *I Trattati nel Mondo Antico* (see chapt. 3, n. 41).

[15] E. Laroche, *Collection des textes Hittites* No. 379=KUB XXXI 121; see Dietrich Sürenhagen, *Paritätische Staatsverträge aus hethitischer Sicht* (Pavia: Iuculano, 1985), 11.

[16] See 103 ff. and 121. "Literal" and "faithful" are closely related concepts in ancient eastern thinking; see Offner, "A propos de la sauvegarde" (see chapt. 5, n. 60).

epilogue of the Hammurabi Codex has less to do with documentary faithfulness – as Cancik argues – than with the faithful fulfillment of the duties set out. In Egypt too, all the documents containing this formula (though it was not known as such) refer to the virtue of faithfulness. Officials boast that they have neither subtracted nor added (*jnj jtj* – bring, take), by which they do not mean the work of copying but of fulfilling commissions and carrying out duties.[17]

In addition to the annals and lists of kings used as instruments of chronological direction (on Egypt, see Redford 1986), which we have classed as the media of cold memory, other genres developed in the Ancient East (earlier in Mesopotamia, later in Egypt) that, even if they are not historiography as such, can be classified as historical texts: accounts of the deeds of the rulers in Mesopotamia, royal "novellas" and inscriptions in Egypt (Hermann 1938). What they have in common is that they do not look back on the past, but record present events for remembering in the future. In Mesopotamia there are a host of other genres, such as stelar boundary markers (*kudurru:* Steinmetzer 1922), omina, pseudo-stelae, letters to the gods, inscriptions on buildings, and so forth, far transcending the range of things found in Egypt. The difference between these two cultures regarding the experience and recording of history lies in the fact that Mesopotamia had a culture of divination, whereas Egypt did not. I address the consequences of this in due course. Mesopotamia therefore led the way in matters pertaining to forms of history and the beginnings of historiography. But these were indeed only the beginnings.

The second half of the second millennium BCE, that is, the Late Bronze Age, was to provide a dramatic turning point in this context. The texts became richer, looked back further into the past, gave more precise details, and constructed broader connections. The pinnacle was reached with the Hittite texts, including three works that were all written around the same time: *The Deeds of Suppiluliuma, The Ten Year Annals,* and *The Great Annals* of Mursilis. In these works, all written around 1320, Mursilis II gives an account of not only his own reign but

---

[17] One use of this formula that comes very close to the sphere of law is in the context of weights and measures. Here, too, the official is sharply reminded that he must take nothing away and must add nothing (Chapter 125 of the Egyptian *Book of the Dead,* see J. Assmann, *Ma'at,* chapter 5 [see chapt. 1, n. 11]).

also that of his father Suppiluliuma. This is unique, and is of particular interest to us because here for the first time the past is made the subject of historiography.[18] However, for the most part this Hittite history is not concerned with any sort of critical view. This is not "history for its own sake," and the Hittites were "more interested in using the past than in recording it" (J. van Seters 1983, 122). But although historical memory was indeed a matter of using rather than documenting the past, the important thing in our context was the fact that the Hittites differed from their neighbors and their predecessors in that they were able to make something out of their past, extrapolating more meaning from the events that had already taken place. Instead of the cold memory of the Mesopotamian and Egyptian lists of kings and annals, which were mere chronological records,[19] they dealt with hot memories of important past events that enabled them to gain a better understanding of the present. *The Deeds of Suppiluliama* represent the zenith of Hittite historiography, and within this text the VII tablet is the unmistakable highlight[20]:

While my father sojourned in the land of Kargamis, he sent Lupakki and Tarhunta-zalma into the land of Amka. They went, attacked the land of Amka, and brought back deportees, cattle (and) sheep to set before my father.

[18] See H. Cancik: "A tale of the past that is free from any directly political aim." The suggestion that there is no political aim, which also plays an important part in Grayson and v. Seters, seems to me unjustified. It suggests a humanist, Greek-style objectivity linked to theoretical curiosity, and indicates an idealism that is foreign to most forms of historiography. The concept of cultural memory, however, gives a central position to the functional context, and to the motives and aims underlying references to the past.

[19] In this context, it is worth mentioning that the Hittites did not have lists of kings, which v. Seters appears to hold against them (113): "Can there be a real historiography without chronology?" What lists of kings did Thucydides have to rely on?

[20] In fact, there are many elements of Hittite historiography in Mesopotamian texts Ivan Seters's examples are from more modern texts, especially the Tukulti-Ninurta epic; see Peter Machinist, "Literature as Politics. The Tukulti-Ninurta Epic and the Bible," *Catholic Biblical Quarterly* 38 (1976), 455–482, from the second half of the 13th century, and Sargon III's letter to God. The fact that Mesopotamia took its full part in the development that began in the Late Bronze Age and first became evident on a large scale in the texts of the Hittites is much more important. However, this was not an exclusively Hittite phenomenon, as it affected the entire civilized world at that time. The Babylonian and Assyrian texts that v. Seters quotes to oppose Cancik all came later. They show that the development was continued here, and that Hatti, Egypt, Mesopotamia, Israel, and finally Greece (Herodotus) all participated in a uniformly spreading concept of history.

But when the Egyptians heard of the attack on Amka, they became afraid. Since furthermore their Lord Piphururijas had died, the Queen of Egypt Tahamunzu (wife of the King) sent an envoy to my father with the following message:

"My husband is dead, and I have no son. The people say that you have many sons. If you send me one of your sons, he could become my husband. I shall never take one of my servants to be my husband."

When my father heard that, he summoned the great ones to council and said: "Since days of yore nothing like this has ever happened to me!" He went and sent Hattu-zitis, the chamberlain, saying: "Go and bring me reliable information! They might be trying to deceive me. Whether perhaps they do have a prince – of this bring me reliable information!" . . .

The Egyptian envoy, Lord Hanis, came to him. Because my father had told Hattu-zitis, when he sent him to Egypt, to deliver the words: "Perhaps they do have a prince. They might be trying to deceive me and do not really want one of my sons to be King," the Egyptian Queen now replied in a letter as follows:

"Why do you say: They might be trying to deceive me? If I had a son, would I write to a foreign land in this manner, which is humiliating for me and my country? You do not trust me, and you say such a thing to me. He who was my husband died and I have no sons. Should I perhaps take one of my servants to be my husband? I have written to no other country. I have written only to you. The people say you have many sons. Give me one of your sons, and he will be my husband and King of Egypt."

[What follows is quite badly damaged. Suppiluliuma is offended by the insistence with which the Egyptian side is demanding that he give them a son. He also discusses with the Egyptian envoy his fear that the Egyptians might misuse one of his sons as a hostage, and is reassured.]

And so to please them, my father occupied himself with the question of a son. And then my father sent for the treaty document about how earlier the weather god had taken the man from Kurustama, the Hittite, and brought him into the land of Egypt and made them (the people of Kurustama) Egyptians; how they had become friends together for ever; how the tablet was read out before them. Then my father spoke the following to them: "Since days of yore, Hattusa and Egypt have been friends. And now this has happened between us. The land of Hatti and the land of Egypt will continue to be friends with one another for-ever."[21]

[21] See J. Assmann, *The Mind of Egypt*, 251–254 (see chapt. 1, n. 94).

This is indeed a form of history, and, in its richness of detail, color, and nuance, it outshines everything that has come down to us from Egypt and the Ancient Near East. The long and complex chain of events reported here is particularly unusual:

1. Suppiluliuma is in the land of Kargamis.
2. He opens up another front and sends troops into Amka, in Egyptian territory, under the command of two generals.
3. The Egyptians are afraid, particularly because their king (Akhnaton) has just died.
4. The Egyptian queen asks for a Hittite prince to succeed the dead Egyptian king.
5. Prolonged negotiations and declarations and an exchange of letters and envoys occur. Evidently (though there is a gap in the text here) the Egyptian envoys refer to an ancient treaty.
6. The treaty with the Egyptians is consulted.[22]
7. On the basis of this covenant, Suppiluliuma finally gives his consent.

Here, we are given insight into an event that is as unique as its documentation. Egyptian sources would never have recorded such an episode. An Egyptian queen, trying to arrange a political marriage with a foreign prince, so that a Hittite might mount the throne – this would truly be something monstrous, although it can be explained by the exceptional circumstances at the end of the Armana era.[23]

These, however, are the very factors that make this case so fascinating. What could the Hittite incentive be behind this interest in the past? The key lies in another text, also by Mursilis, that deals with exactly the same procedures but in the framework of a different literary genre or, to be more precise, in a different functional context. It is concerned with prayers to the Hittite storm god to get rid of a plague

---

[22] See Sürenhagen, *Paritätische Staatsverträge* (see chapt. 6, n. 15). In passing, it is worth mentioning briefly the way of looking at the past that was characteristic of the Hittites. Before Suppiluliuma gave his consent to the proposal of a political marriage, he consulted records of past relations between the two peoples, and it turned out that such a project had a sound basis. All Hittite contracts contained a more or less comprehensive historical introduction, detailing the shared prehistory of the partners and showing the past basis for a shared future.

[23] See Rolf Krauss, *Das Ende der Amarnazeit* (Hildesheim: Gerstenberg, 1979).

that has been ravaging the country for years and that is threatening to destroy the whole nation. The oracles have been consulted and they referred to the two ancient tablets mentioned earlier. One concerns sacrificial rites to the River Mala that have been neglected because of the plague. The other relates to the Kurustama covenant:

The Storm God of Hatti brought the people of Kurustama to Egypt and sealed a covenant about them with the Hittites, so that the latter were bound to him by oath. Although now both the Hittites and the Egyptians were under oath to the Storm God, the Hittites neglected to do their duties. They broke the oath of the gods. My father sent troops and chariots to attack the land of Amka, on Egyptian territory. But the Egyptians were afraid, and asked at once for one of his sons to take over the kingdom. But when my father gave them one of his sons, they killed him while they were taking him there. My father gave vent to his wrath, declared war on Egypt and attacked. He defeated the troops and war chariots of the land of Egypt. It was the will of the Storm God of Hatti, my Lord, to give victory to my father; he conquered and destroyed the troops and chariots of the land of Egypt. But when they brought the prisoners to Hatti, a plague broke out among them, and they died.

When they brought the prisoners to Hatti, these prisoners brought the plague to the land of Hatti. From that day onwards, the people in the land of Hatti died. When I had found the tablet about Egypt, I had questions put to the oracle: "These agreements which were made by the Hittite Storm God – namely, that the Egyptians as well as the Hittites were under oath to the Storm God, that the Damnassaras gods were present in the temple, and that the Hittites had immediately broken their word – is this perhaps the reason for the wrath of the Storm God of Hatti, my Lord? And this was confirmed."[24]

This text presents us with the same set of events, but it is extended by the following tragic episodes:

8. The king sends the prince, but he is killed on the way.
9. Suppiluliuma declares war on Egypt and is victorious.
10. The Egyptian prisoners bring plague to Hatti, and it rages for twenty years, claiming most of the population, including the king himself and his son and successor Arnuwandas.

---

[24] Albrecht Goetze, *Mursilis II. König der Hethiter. Die Annalen*, hethitischer Text und deutsche Übersetzung (Leipzig 1933, and Darmstadt: Wissenschaftliche Buchgesellschaft, 1967), 395.

A vital extension is made to the beginning of this chain of events. This reaches far back into the past, for one does not know when the covenant concerning the people of Kurustama was first drawn up between Hatti and Egypt. This agreement, though, forms the beginning of the tale, because an oath was sworn and the attack on Amka broke it.

Guilt and suffering act as incentives for this interest in the past. It is not the spectacular offer of marriage by the Egyptian queen, or any particular sense of history that sets this linear reconstruction of the past in motion: the trigger is the twenty-year plague, together with the conviction that deeds and consequences go together, and that catastrophe is the result of wrongdoing and guilt. The connection between deeds and consequences lies in the hands of the gods, who reward good and punish evil.[25]

The *Plague Prayers of Mursilis* are closely related to a procedure of sacral law with which we are familiar through, for example, the story of Oedipus. Disaster strikes the country – plague, drought, famine, and so forth – and it can only be explained in terms of punishment by an angry god. The king consults the oracle in order to find out the nature of the outrage that has occasioned the punishment, and to take the appropriate measures to atone for it. Expiation generally requires three steps: a major sacrifice, a public confession of guilt, and praise for the offended god, whose power has been so overwhelmingly proven by the acts of punishment and pardon. As G. Bornkamm pointed out in his article *Lobpreis, Bekenntnis und Opfer* (1964), this is why the Hebrew word *todah* encompasses exactly these three things: praise, confession, and sacrifice. This is the ritual of expiation laid down for such eventualities.[26]

---

[25] See Abraham Malamat, "Doctrines of Causality in Hittite and Biblical Historiography: A Parallel," *VT* 5 (1955), 1–12. I consider the concept of "causality" to be misleading in this context; see p. 232.

[26] Hattusil also refers to a performance of this ritual in his apology (Albrecht Goetze, *Hattusilis, Der Bericht über seine Thronbesteigung nebst den Parallettexten* [Darmstadt: Wissenschaftliche Buchgesellschaft, 1967], 22–23):

> Samuhas too, the city of God, he filled with impurity.
> But when I had returned from the land of Egypt,
> I went to the god to make a sacrifice
> And I performed the prescribed ritual to the god.

History becomes readable under the sign of guilt. It assumes significance, that is, it becomes semioticized and detrivialized. This in turn means that the ornamental ritualization of time, with its endless repetition of the same things, fades into the background, and it is the discontinuities, upheavals, reversals, developments, and chains of events that come to the fore. The chain does not manifest itself as some kind of abstract historical causality, but as the retributive will of an angry god who, with every event, delivers a new and even more terrible sign of his wrath. When and how did it all begin? How could it have led to such catastrophe? Which god has been offended? How can we mollify him? The reconstructive work of memory is not governed here by historical, but by legal and theological interests.

As guilt has to be uncovered and publicly confessed and atoned for, it becomes the incentive for memory and self-examination. This idea first saw the light of day in Mesopotamia, and then spread through the Ancient Near East and Egypt as far as Rome; significantly, it also sank particularly deep roots into Asia Minor, the land of the Hittites.[27] Against this background it is clear that suffering was basically seen as punishment, and that relief could only come through confession and reconciliation.

Semioticizing History under the Sign of Salvation

Guilt is only one incentive – albeit a very powerful one – for memory work, reconstruction of the past, self-examination, and the writing of history. It stems from the experience of suffering, which struggles against two premises: meaningless chance and cyclical recurrence. Suffering is both a sign and an exception. Its semioticization breaks

---

[27] "Biblical and Babylonian psalms, Egyptian and Sabaean confessional stelae [are] proofs of the public, written confession of sins that was once common throughout the East. [...] Augustine in his confessions brought such religious customs into literature" (P. Frisch, "Über die lydisch-phrygischen Sühneinschriften und die 'Confessiones' des Augustinus," *Epigraphica Anatolica* 2 (1983), 41–45, with additional literature). See also Georg Petzl, "Sünde, Strafe, Wiedergutmachung," *Epigraphica Anatolica* 12 (1988), 155–166. I am grateful to A. Chaniotis for these references. Franz Steinleitner, *Die Beicht im Zusammenhang mit der sakralen Rechtspflege in der Antike* (Leipzig: Theodor Weicher, 1913), put together a collection (with many gaps) of Lydian-Phrygian confessional inscriptions, which he saw as a precursor of the medieval practice of indulgence.

the circularity of time and simultaneously counters the contingency of history.

Events are proof of divine power. They are, however, not confined to retributive interventions – they may also be helpful. However, the latter type is also dependent on memory and confession, which in turn provide the incentive for a rich literature of self-examination. One example of this is *The Apology of Hattusilis III.* Just like Mursilis's *Plague Prayers,* this apology reconstructs past events as evidence of divine power, but not under the sign of wrath and punishment; this is an instance of mercy and blessing.

> These are the words of Tabarnas Hattusilis, the great King, the King of the land of Hatti, the son of Mursilis, the Great King, the King of the land of Hatti,
> the grandson of Suppiluliuma, the great King, the King of the land of Hatti,
> the descendant of Hattusilis, the King of Kussar.
>
> Of the rule of Ishtar I shall report
> and everyone shall hear of it.
> And in the future, among the gods of my sun,
> of the son, grandson and descendant of my sun
> shall be particular veneration of Ishtar.
> […]
> So long as I was a boy, I was an ass-like man.
> And Ishtar, my goddess, sent Muwatallis, my brother, to Mursilis, my father, as a consequence of a dream:
> 'For Hattusilis the years are yet short.
> He is not well. Give him to me;
> he shall be my priest.
> Then he will be well.'
> And my father took me, the little one, and gave me in service to the goddess.
> And I sacrificed to the goddess, performing the office of the priesthood.
> And then I experienced the reward at the hand of Ishtar, my goddess;
> And Ishtar, my goddess, took me by the hand and ruled over me.
> (Quoted after Goetze 1967, 7–9)

The story that follows relates in a lively and even exciting fashion how, after Mursilis's death, his brother Muwatallis becomes king and appoints Hattusilis as commander of the army. Hattusilis's success makes certain people envious, and they defame him to the king, who puts him on trial. The night before the trial, however, his goddess Ishtar appears to him in a dream and encourages him. He wins his case, and continues to command the army. During every campaign, Ishtar is by his side, helping him with spectacular victories and rescue operations. After the death of Muwatallis, Hattusilis puts his nephew Urkhi-Teshup on the throne as king, but the latter oppresses him for seven years out of jealousy. Finally, Hattusilis breaks away from him and summons him to be tried before a court of the gods.

Hattusilis's account is best described as an "aretalogy."[28] This is a miraculous tale told to glorify the rewarding or punishing powers of a deity. In Egypt this genre was known as *sdd b3w* (narrating the manifestations of power), and such texts can be found both in royal and in private inscriptions during the Ramesside Period, that is, at the same time as the reign of Mursilis II and Hattusilis III in Hatti.

From time immemorial, there were two distinct and mutually exclusive forms of monumental self-thematization in Egypt: accounts of royal deeds, and "autobiographical" tomb inscriptions. While private people never made individual feats the subject of monumental self-display, kings never gave a comprehensive account of their entire lives. However, this traditional dichotomy underwent a radical change during the decades around 1300 BCE – from which the Hittite texts derive. From that time on, inscribed stelae appeared on which private people did not give a general résumé of their lives, but on which they recounted single episodes that they viewed as exemplary of divine intervention. Such intervention made the episode significant and therefore worth recording, and it separated the highlighted event from the general process of living.

Two kinds of intervention were typical of these records: punishment and salvation. It may well be that these descriptions (stelae accounts) belong in the context of a similar institution of sacral law to that which we observed in the tale of Mursilis's *Plague Prayers*. Whoever has good reason to interpret an experience – a negative one such as illness or

---

[28] H. Tadmor classifies the text, in a more general perspective, as "royal apology;" see "Autobiographical Apology in the Royal Assyrian Literature," in H. Tadmor and M. Weinfeld (eds.), *History, Historiography and Interpretation. Studies in Biblical and Cuneiform Literatures* (Jerusalem: Magnes, and Leiden: E. J. Brill, 1986), 36–57.

infertility, or a miraculous cure – as divine intervention goes to the temple, makes a sacrifice, and erects a stela that stands either as a confession and a penance or as a thanksgiving to the respective deity. Hence the term "proclaiming the manifestation of power."

Such stelae are not to be found where there are royal inscriptions, and a text such as Mursilis's *Plague Prayers*, in which a king confesses the guilt of his father and takes expiation upon himself, would probably have been unthinkable in Egypt. Instead, the royal inscriptions translate the original form of the deed itself into a report on the divine aid that was experienced, whereas there are stelae containing prayers to the respective deity. These texts use the same vocabulary as private inscriptions, they express the same attitude toward the deity, and they illustrate that this is connected to a radical shift in the historical mentality and not to any sense of popular piety.[29] The record of Ramesses II's Battle of Qadesh,[30] and Ramesses III's hymn to Amun (*ÄHG* No. 196) are the most impressive examples of accounts of great deeds.

During the Battle of Qadesh, Ramesses II was ambushed by the Hittites. While some of his troops were still on the march, others fled, and therefore he found himself with just a few faithful followers trapped in a seemingly hopeless defensive battle against the surprise attack of the Hittites, until by sheer luck another elite brigade that was on a separate mission elsewhere happened to come along at just the right moment to rescue him. The course of this battle is described by means of a map-like representation with long texts reproducing all the essential details. As far as accuracy of detail is concerned, this record breaks every traditional mold. But Ramesses also adds an epic text that (using Egyptian sizes) extends over an entire scroll, describing his fortunate rescue as divine intervention. The text culminates in Ramesses' fervent prayer to Amun, to which Amun responds:

> I call to thee, my father Amun,
> While I am in the midst of the throng I do not know.
> All foreigners have united against me,
> While I am alone and no-one is beside me.
> I found that Amun had come when I called to him.
> He gave me his hand, and I rejoiced.

[29] For a fairly comprehensive collection of these texts, see J. Assmann, *Ägyptische Hymnen* Nos. 147–200 (see chapt. 5, n. 12).
[30] See J. Assmann, *The Mind of Egypt*, 245–271 (see chapt. 1, n. 94).

"I called to God – and I found that he had come" is the same formula used on private stelae:

> I called to my mistress,
> And I found that she had come in a sweet breath of air.[31]

"Coming" is the expression used for a miraculous rescue, or for any favorable intervention by a god. These parallels between private and royal inscriptions could be drawn in much greater depth, but what interests me here is simply the fact that no distinction is made between the biography of the individual, on whom the god has had a remarkable influence, and history at large, in which kings, battles, and the fate of nations are involved, and on which the god has exactly the same kind of influence. Both biographical and political history become areas of divine intervention.

THEOLOGIZING HISTORY UNDER THE SIGN OF A THEOLOGY OF THE WILL — FROM THE "CHARISMATIC EVENT" TO "CHARISMATIC HISTORY"

Signs and Miracles: Charismatic Events as the First Stage in the Theologization of History

When human fate and political history become areas of divine intervention, they change their structure. I describe this change in terms of the "event." Historical events stand in contrast to mythical events; they are distinguished by their uniqueness. The mythical event is a basic pattern that repeats itself in an endless cycle of rituals and festivals, whereas the historical event has a precise situation in time and place, and can never be repeated. With its cyclical repetition, the former structures or even "ornaments" time through its constant repetition (J. Assmann 1983), but the latter structures time by breaking into its natural circularity and splitting it into a before and after. The one makes time into a cycle and the other makes it linear. The mythical event therefore has to be celebrated, staged, and actualized; the historical, which is already actual, must be published, immortalized, remembered, and commemorated. Thus it is the historical and not the

---

[31] Assmann, *Ägyptische* Hymnen, Nos. 149 (see chapt. 5, n. 12).

mythical that provides an incentive for memory, historical awareness, and historiography.

The theologization of history begins with the historical event. The intervention of the divine in human affairs is not experienced as something continuous, as in the sphere of biocosmic Nature, but as something intermittent. B. Albrektson (1967) gave this principle of early theological history the programmatic subtitle *Historical Events as Divine Manifestations,* and he showed that the belief that the gods had a causative influence on the course of history and on individual human destiny was determinative not only for the Israelite but also for the whole Ancient Near Eastern concept of history. In the Anglo-Saxon world, this work was seen as opposing the thesis that the theologizing of history ("sacred history" or "history as revelation") was the sole province of the Jewish concept of God and history. But there are some important differences between divine intervention and sacred history. I distance myself from Albrektson[32] by outlining three very distinct concepts:

a) The "charismatic event," which is produced by divine intervention in the flow of human activity. Here, the stream of events is divided into the trivial nonsemiotic background of the commonplace and the semiotic foreground of the exceptional, whereby no distinction is made between historical (e.g., victories) and natural events (e.g., earthquakes).

b) The "charismatic history," which is produced by the covenant entered into by a people and a deity. Here the whole stream of events can be read as the history of this covenant; whatever ills befall the people will be connected to its faithfulness or unfaithfulness to the divine partner. It is not the plan that matters here,

---

[32] Albrektson, *History and the Gods* (see chapt. 6, n. 13) deals with the concept of "The History of Salvation" in chapter 5 ("The Divine Plan in History"), where he shows three things: (1) in the OT, there are relatively few mentions of Yahweh having a plan (*'sh* = plan, decision, purpose); (2) those few passages only refer to the purposeful nature of God's actions, but not of a single plan of "salvation"; and (3) in exactly the same sense of purposeful action, Mesopotamian sources *passim* speak of the plans of the gods. Here we have the concept that I have summarized under the heading of a "theology of the will," which was in fact characteristic of Mesopotamian religion. Albrektson therefore suggests confining the idea of a divine plan for salvation to the Apocalypse (Daniel).

but the reciprocal obligations of both sides. It is like a predated check, and whether it is honored or not will determine the course of history.

c) "Time and history," which are understood as a single manifestation – embracing the commonplace as well as the extraordinary – of the planned will of a deity. Only in this context can one speak of the (Christian) concept of the *History of Salvation*.

Variant "a" was typical of the Mesopotamian world, because of the age-old, extremely elaborate practice of divination. Thanks to the use of cuneiform script, this spread westward as far as Asia Minor, and then through the Etruscans as far as Rome.[33] Divination presupposes that events spring from the will of the gods, and by influencing the divine will, one can cause or prevent them. The opposite of a divination culture was, for example, that of Egypt, in which the will of the gods was linked to maintaining the world, and hence to the regular and the recurrent. The concept of happenings in the sense of individual events had a negative connotation and was associated with disorder, senselessness, and disaster. Instead of divination, the Egyptians had magic in the form of rituals, which as is made explicit in the *Instruction for Merikare* was given to them by the creator "in order to ward off the blows of events" (Papyrus Petersburg 1116A, lines 136–137, see J. Assmann 1989, 77 f.).[34] We may summarize the difference in what is undoubtedly an oversimplification: Egypt semioticized the rule, whereas Mesopotamia semioticized the exception.

In the New Kingdom, however, a theology of the will also imposed itself in Egypt and it led to a theologization of history.[35] Events were no longer thought of as the onset of chaos that had to be warded off through ritual, but as divine intervention (variant "a") and, at the

---

[33] *La divination en Mésopotamie*, Rencontre assyriologique, Jean Bottéro, "Symptômes, signes, écritures en Mésopotamie ancienne," in J. P. Vernant et al., *Divination et rationalité* (Paris: Éditions du Seuil, 1974), 70–197. See now also Stefan M. Maul, *Zukunftsbewältigung. Eine Untersuchung altorientalischen Denkens anhand der babylonisch-assyrischen Löserituale* (Namburi) Baghdader Forschungen, vol. 18 (Mainz: Philipp von Zabern, 1994).

[34] See J. Assmann, *The Mind of Egypt*, 190 f. (see chapt. 1, n. 94).

[35] I have described this process in J. Assmann, "State and Religion in the New Kingdom," in W. K. Simpson (ed.), *Religion and Philosophy in Ancient Egypt* (New Haven: Yale Egyptological Seminar, 1989), 55–88. See also J. Assmann, *Zeit und Ewigkeit im Alten Ägypten* (Heidelberg: Winter, 1975), 49–69.

highest theological level, as a manifestation of the divine creative will, which had produced not only time but also all that took place in it. "Thy Ka [will] is all that happens."[36]

The totality of all that happens as a manifestation of divine will (variant "c") is divided into good and bad events, according to whether they spring from the deity's grace (Egyptian *hzwt*) or from his wrath (*b3w*). But grace and wrath are, of course, not purely a matter of a god's arbitrary will, because if they were, there would be no guilt on the part of man. The concept of guilt is based on a type of law that man violates, thereby causing divine wrath. I look at this more closely in the last section.

Charismatic History as the Second Stage in the Theologization of History

A second stage in the presentation of history consists of a systematic analysis of the past from the standpoint of guilt; that is, when genuine historical records are compiled that judge past periods of government according to the good conduct of the king and the welfare of the people.

Once again, this principle was first introduced by the Hittites. The *Apology of Telepinus* was written ca. 1500 BCE. In this, a king passes a decree that incorporates a retrospective survey reaching far back into the past and encompassing over seven periods of government. Three good kings, Labarnas, Hattusilis I, and Mursilis I, whose periods of rule were marked by unity and success, were followed by four bad kings, whose reigns were characterized by intrigue, murder, and defeat. Telepinus justifies his usurpation of the throne as a turning point for the better and as a return to the blessed time of the founding kings. For this, he needs a double dose of the past: one from which he will turn away and the other that he will embrace. In the context of his justification, the connection between guilt and memory also plays a dual role: it relates to the guilt of the usurper who must defend his actions, and to the guilt of the former kings that is meant to vindicate

---

[36] Hymn in Theban Tomb No. 23, ed. J. Assmann, *Sonnenhymnen in thebanischen Gräbern* (Mainz: Philipp von Zabern, 1983), No. 17, 18–23. There are many other similar passages in J. Assmann, *Zeit und Ewigkeit*, 61–69 (see chapt. 6, n. 39).

his otherwise problematic usurpation.[37] Both cases involve guilt, although this is not based on theology. The question whether the bad kings had broken divine commandments is left as open, or as implicit, as the question whether the usurpation of the throne runs counter to the will of the gods. This early text reflects a stage that clearly precedes the theologization of history that became characteristic of the Late Bronze Age.

The oldest text in which we can see an analysis of the past in terms of theologically based guilt is the neo-Babylonian *Weidner Chronicle*. This also looks back far into the past at a succession of kings, examining their attitude toward the Esagila, the Marduk Temple of Babylon.[38] In various instances, the transfer of power from one dynasty to another is "based on a guilt which the rulers had taken upon themselves," and even the fall of the Empire of Ur is linked to the failings of King Shulgi (Wilcke 1988, 133). The concept of guilt brings meaning to the past and coherence to the sequence of kings and periods of government. It uncovers and indeed explains discontinuity, change, and upheaval. In this form, the past becomes meaningful, memorable, and a pointer to the future.

The Egyptian *Demotic Chronicle* should also be mentioned in this context. This is a text from a much later date (3rd century BCE) that uses the form of prophecies with commentaries to evaluate nine kings of the 28–30 Dynasties according to their piety and faithfulness to "the

---

[37] *The Apology of Hattusilis III*, written 300 years later, also belongs in this context, since Hattusilis III was also a usurper. He likewise justifies his actions through the guilt of his predecessor. However, he does not go very far back into the past, as he begins with his childhood, his illness, and his being chosen and then saved by Ishtar. The by now more intensive theologizing of history brought forth new patterns of meaning. Some scholars detect among the sources that the Book of Samuel worked into an account of the time of David a similar apology on behalf of David himself – an attractive idea that has a lot in its favor. See Harry A. Hoffner, "Propaganda and Political Justification in Hittite Historiography," in H. Goedicke and J. J. M. Roberts (eds.), *Unity and Diversity. Essays in the History, Literature, and Religion of the Ancient Near East* (Baltimore: Johns Hopkins University Press, 1975), 49–64 and, above all, Tadmor, "Autobiographical Apology" (see chapt. 6, n. 28).

[38] Albert K. Grayson, *Assyrian and Babylonian Chronicles. Texts from Cuneiform Sources* 5 (Locust Valley: J. J. Augustin, 1970), No. 19; J. v. Seters does not seem to have noticed the obvious parallels with Deuteronomy, and only refers briefly to this text on p. 85.

law," or to equate their failures with their "godlessness."[39] In China, it was customary for a new dynasty to write the history of the one that had preceded it in order to legitimize itself. This account had to show that although the preceding dynasty had received a mandate from Heaven and had initially fulfilled it, it then went increasingly off the rails, so to speak, so that a change became inevitable and the mandate passed to a new dynasty. Here too, the past was processed under the sign of guilt. The moral criterion of the mandate from Heaven endowed the events of the past with meaning, and it gave special prominence to the link between past and present.

Deuteronomy places obedience to the laws of the ruler at its very center. Here too we have a history of guilt, but it has not been written in order to justify a new dynasty that has returned to obedience, thereby regaining God's blessing. Here, the concern is to interpret and to cope with the catastrophic events of the present as the work of Yahweh (G. v. Rad 1958). Against the criterion of guilt, the sequence of these events builds up into a history that could only lead to disaster. This history, as recounted in the Book of Kings, has been generated by guilt, that has been established through the law. The latter, as codified by the Torah, is the will of God as revealed definitively for all time, thus making divination and fortunetelling superfluous.

Just as the twenty-year plague drove Mursilis II to search the sources and to dig deep into the past in order to draw up an account of his own and his father's deeds, Israel's catastrophes – the fall of the northern kingdom to the Assyrians in 722 BCE and of the southern kingdom to the Babylonians in 587 BCE, followed by exile – set memory work

---

[39] See Janet H. Johnson, "Is the Demotic Chronicle an anti-Greek Text?," in H.-J. Thissen (ed.), *Grammata demotika, Festschrift für Erich Lüddeckens* (Würzburg: Zauzich, 1984), 107–124. Meyer, "Ägyptische Dokumente" (see chapt. 5, n. 25), already drew attention to the parallel with Deuteronomy: he speaks of an *"Ethisierung der Religion"* that spread throughout the Ancient Near East during the middle of the first millennium. See Eberhard Otto, *Ägypten. Der Weg des Pharaonenreichs* (Stuttgart: Kohlhammer, 1955), 149: "The idea of the king being bound to ethical norms takes over from that of the king as the wielder of power, and the success or failure of his rule is taken as a sign of his accordance with God's will or his 'sinfulness.' While the classical Egyptian view regarded the success of the Pharaoh as a natural consequence of his divinity, Egyptians of the Late Period saw the failure of the dynasties as proof of their 'godlessness.'" See now J. Assmann, *The Mind of Egypt*, 377–388 (see chapt. 1, n. 94).

in motion. This led back to the Exodus from Egypt and from there
to the creation of the world, setting out all the major events and
bringing them together in terms of covenant and faithfulness, law
and obedience, guilt and responsibility. The very first man sinned by
disobeying a commandment, and this initial guilt set history in motion,
for Paradise was prehistory.

Charismatic history is the history of Yahweh and his people. The
covenant between them marked the true beginning, because from
then on it became a common story that could be remembered, narrated, and quoted. The story is repeated whenever the focus is on the
sealing or renewal of this bond: Josh. 24:2–13; Deut. 1:6–3, 17:18–29,
29:1–7; Neh. 9, and in many other passages that Baltzer has collated
and discussed in detail (1964, 29–70). Unlike the history of salvation,
this tale has a beginning and an end. It begins at the moment when
Yahweh himself becomes active as an historical character in the role
of one party to the agreement, and it ends when he ceases to influence the course of events directly. The Book of Esther is the only
canonical text to recount events *after* the end of charismatic history.
Otherwise the Hebrew Bible is defined as a codification of this history
that extends "from Moses to Artaxerxes."[40]

A periodic public reading of the text of the covenant helps to keep
it in memory. Even profane state contracts had to be read out regu-
larly to the signatory (Baltzer 1964, 91 f.; Cancik 1978), and this custom is continued in Deuteronomy, which commands that the Torah
be read out in public every seven years (Deut. 31:9–13). Every day
during the Feast of the Tabernacles, Ezrah read the Torah aloud to
the people from beginning to end (Neh. 8:18; Baltzer 1964, 91–93).
From this there developed the synagogue reading from the Torah
that must be read in its entirety in yearly cycles. Part of this liturgi-
cal memory is the recapitulation of the shared history: God's good
deeds and the failings of the people. The background to this story,
however, is no longer that of events (i.e., God's intervention), but
that of charismatic or sacred history. In one of the Qumran texts –
the "Manual of Discipline" – the liturgy of a religious group from the

---

[40] For example, Josephus, *Contra Apionem*, see p. 206 and 245. For this interpretation
of history, see especially Yosef H. Yerushalmi, *Zakhor. Jewish Memory and Jewish History*
(Seattle: University of Washington Press, 1982).

time of Jesus has been preserved, which presumably was not too different from both the Jewish and the Christian forms of worship. As Baltzer has shown, this liturgy corresponds to the renewal of a contract. The priests repeat the sacred history: "Then the priests recount the proofs of God's justice through His mighty deeds, and proclaim all His merciful faithfulness to Israel. And the Levites recount the guilty acts of the Israelites and all their reprehensible faults and their sins under the rule of Belial." Following on from this historical recapitulation, the covenant is sealed anew (Baltzer 1964, 171–173).

On the Genealogy of Guilt

The argument put forward in this chapter is that historical memory, as it originated in the Ancient East, is connected to guilt and an awareness of guilt arising from the breaking of oaths and contracts. Because an oath is especially sacred, history also takes on a kind of holiness that creates an obligation to remember.

What exactly is the sacred element in oaths and contracts? It is inherent in the oath that people had to swear by the gods. This created unconditional authority and an unbreakable bond. The gods supervised the fulfillment of the agreement; if they intervened when there was a violation, they did so within a context that they had been explicitly involved in by humans themselves. In other words, the gods were drawn into history at the behest of humans – which is, as it were, the reverse side of their intervention.

The theologizing of history, which in the second half of the second millennium spread throughout the Ancient Near East and the Mediterranean, was directly connected with the diplomatic practice of the time. All states, large and small, were at that time increasingly in contact with one another, and their links were largely regulated by contracts. It all began with the dyke that separated Umma and Lagash, and over the course of the next thousand years, a network arose that embraced the whole "ecumenical" world. All contracts required a sacred oath, and the gods were invoked as the powers to protect that oath (Weinfeld 1976; Tadmor 1982). The world of the gods functioned as the people's tribunal, ensuring that agreements were observed. The lofty art of diplomacy, which also had a theological side to it, was behind this process. The gods of one party to the agreement had to be "translatable" in terms of the other party's gods. In such a context, religious intolerance was unthinkable – one could not deny the existence of other gods.[41]

Given the degree to which the foreign policies of participating states were dependent on the diplomatic order of mutual understanding, the gods were inevitably and increasingly drawn into the unfolding of history. In this system, the ruler who held most conscientiously to the agreement was in the right, and the one who broke it, was in the wrong. Thus, breaking a contract became a kind of model of original sin.

Therefore, it becomes clear that history had to be theologized to a great extent once a people decided to invoke its god not only as the protector of a political contract but also as an active contract party, as if the god were the mighty king of Egypt or Assyria.[42] This development brought two completely new powers into play: god as the ruler and the people as the subject of history. Such a contract could never be provisional – it would obviously have to extend from the beginning until the end of time.[43] It was in the framework of this new theocratic constellation that the concept of sacred history came into being. *Iustitia connectiva* became the justice of God.[44]

The Mesopotamian view of history is as much a theodicy as the biblical view, but it stands completely under the sign of the event. Historical action by the gods is rare. However, in the biblical tradition, the event gradually loses its individual shape and merges into world history.[45] In Mesopotamian history there is still a rhythm of good and

[41] See J. Assmann, *Moses the Egyptian*, 44–54 (see chapt. 2, n. 63).

[42] G. E. Mendenhall, D. J. McCarthy, and K. Baltzer have shown that the Israelite theology of the covenant was based on the practice among Ancient Near Eastern states of making diplomatic agreements.

[43] Under Hittite state law, state agreements of parity were made to last forever: see Korošec, *Hethitische Staatsverträge*, 106 f. (see chapt. 5, n. 59).

[44] Jože Krašovec, *La justice (sdq) de dieu dans la bible hébraique et l'interprétation juive et chrétienne*, OBO 76 (Göttingen: Vandenhoeck & Ruprecht, 1988). The Hebrew expression for God's "holy deeds" meant literally "justices" or "proofs of justice": *s^{e}daqot*, plural of *s^{e}daqah*, "justice." The history of salvation is that of God's justice.

[45] The Book of Job is devoted to the problem of *iustitia connectiva* and its theologizing. In this great struggle, the "friends" take the traditional standpoint that all suffering results from guilt, and they advise Job to use his memory in order to find out what he has done wrong, so that he can be reconciled to God. But Job knows very well that in his case the connection between guilt and punishment has been broken, and so

evil, grace and wrath, whereas in the Bible profane history is seen ever more radically as an expression only of wrath, against which is set the one and only form of redemption, the Kingdom of God, as a kind of antihistory.

If one were to summarize these reflections, history is a function of *iustitia connectiva*. It is only possible to reconstruct the past on which memory and history depend through the establishment of binding obligations that bring order, meaning, and cohesion both to the temporal and the social dimensions of the world. That which is remembered is the binding obligation that must never be forgotten. Remembering the past is not the result of instinct, of some innate interest, but of a duty that is part of culture's impact on man. It is from the cultural construct of *iustitia connectiva* that the commemorative imperative arises: "Thou shalt remember. Thou shalt not forget." This is what is solidified into historical meaning in all cultures and in all individuals, each in their own way.

his suffering is meaningless, or at least it cannot be brought under the conventional heading of *iustitia connectiva*. But when God speaks to him at the end of the book, he acknowledges that God is right. In the world there is evil that does not come from God's will to punish, just as conversely God's will extends beyond the world and its events. This may also be seen as a step away from a history based on individual events.

7

Greece and Disciplined Thinking

The Alphabetical Writing System

Greece is generally regarded as the prototype of a literate culture. "The first society," write J. Goody and I. Watt, "that can truly be called literate did not evolve until the 6th and 5th centuries BCE in the city-states of Greece and Ionia."[1] Those who wish to study the social consequences of literacy must turn to Ancient Greece. According to I. J. Gelb, who put forward the theory that Phoenician script was a syllabary, the Greek alphabet was the first sign system to represent phonemes.[2] This development signified a huge simplification that led to an unprecedented democratization of writing in contrast to the syllabaries of the Semites and the ideographs of the Egyptians and Chinese, which were always confined to a small, professional elite; furthermore, it had an equally unprecedented effect on the human mind. The writing-induced "domestication of the mind" (J. Goody 1968) took a gigantic leap forward with alphabetization. It was not simply writing as such but the introduction of the alphabet that led to this

---

[1] Jack Goody and Ian Watt, "The Consequences of Literacy," in J. Goody (ed.), *Literacy in Traditional Societies* (Cambridge: Cambridge University Press, 1968), 27–68, 40.

[2] Ignace J. Gelb, *A Study of Writing* (Chicago: University of Chicago Press, 1952), 166. I would not subscribe to this theory, though.

new intellectual "discipline" that Eric Havelock convincingly argues represented the "birth of philosophy from the spirit of writing."[3]

What Havelock regards as being so special about the Greek alphabet is its abstractness. A writing system that splits spoken language into the component parts (consonants and vowels) that form its units of articulation is able, with its extreme flexibility, to transcribe any and every sequence of sounds. The atomization of language through an alphabet that can break down all semantic and phonetic units allows for a reorganization of elements that will emulate the style of spoken language better than any other system of notation. The Greek alphabet was the only one that was able to reproduce the spoken word in fluent and unabbreviated form, and thus for Havelock it was a true vehicle for Greek orality.

He illustrates this remarkable flexibility with an example,[4] comparing the account of the flood in the Epic of Gilgamesh with a similar account in Homer's *Iliad* (XII, 17–33). Both texts, as he makes clear right from the outset, "are of orally composed speech and therefore formulaic and repetitive to a degree which is uncharacteristic of literate discourse."[5] But even taking this common basis of written orality into consideration, Havelock ascribes significant differences to the different writing systems. He counts the number of words used, and calculates the ratio of those frequently used to the overall total:

Gilgamesh	Homer
23.3%	14%

Following this, he studies the repetitions of meanings (parallels), and finds a large number in Gilgamesh. The result: "The repetitive, not to say ritualistic character of the passage is obvious" (Havelock and Hershbell 1978, 7). The alphabetized, Greek description of the flood is, by comparison, "less tautological and less ritualistic than the

---

[3] Eric A. Havelock, *Preface to Plato* (Cambridge: Belknap Press, Harvard University Press, 1963), see also *Origins of Western Literacy* (Toronto: Ontario Institute for Studies in Education, 1976); *The Literate Revolution in Greece and its Cultural Consequences* (Princeton: Princeton University Press, 1982). On the writing of philosophy, see Thomas Szlezák, *Platon und die Schriftlichkeit der Philosophie* (Berlin: de Gruyter, 1985).

[4] Eric A. Havelock and Jackson P. Hershbell (eds.), *Communication Arts in the Ancient World* (New York: Hastings House, 1978), 3–21.

[5] Ibid., 8

cuneiform"(8). He concludes that the Greek system is superior to the Babylonian. No other writing system would have been able to capture the richness of oral poetry in this manner. For the first time in human history, argues Havelock, through Homer's text we have the "complete report of an undocumented culture"(10). "What might the Greek account of the Homeric flood have become if committed to a syllabary instead of an alphabet? Obviously we have no means of knowing; it is impossible for us to recreate the mental processes of a Mesopotamian scribe or a Mycenan one"(9). The special achievement of the Greeks lay not so much in the production of individual texts as in the invention of a system that was uniquely able to reproduce an oral account fluently and completely.

We can see from this example both the strengths and the weaknesses of Havelock's approach. The strengths include his concentration on the communicative quality of the texts, which he seeks to grasp empirically through quantifying methods. The weaknesses include the "absolutization" and the distortion involved in his view of the media.

As regards "absolutization," other formal rules and constrictions that technically influence the shaping of the text and therefore need to be taken into consideration are downgraded, overlooked, or excluded. The most obvious explanation – that the eastern texts (the "thought rhyme" of the *parallelismus membrorum*) rest on a different poetics – is explicitly rejected by Havelock. The question whether Homer's text was already more "literary" in its composition even prior to its being written down is not posed.[6] He also fails to ask whether perhaps the two texts belong to completely different genres. It is possible that the term "epic" conceals the fact that these texts were fashioned to perform

---

[6] The thesis that Homer's text was much more influenced by writing and constitutes "literature" in a completely different way from the Gilgamesh epic received strong support from Uvo Hölscher's research on the *Odyssey*; see Uvo Hölscher, *Die Odyssee. Epos zwischen Märchen und Literatur* (Munich: C. H. Beck, 1988). The following also believe that Homer's text was originally in written form: Joachim Latacz, *Homer* (Munich, Zürich: Arternis, 1985), and Alfred Heubeck, "Zum Erwachen der Schriftlichkeit im archaischen Griechentum," in *Kleine Schriften zur griechischen Sprache und Literatur*, Erlanger Forschungen (Erlangen: Universitätsbund Erlangen-Nürnberg, 1984), 57–74 (also Alfred Heubeck, *Schrift*. Archaeologia Homerica III.X [Göttingen: Vandenhoeck & Ruprecht, 1979]), and so one might state that, at least in Germany, the consensus tends toward this belief. For the opposite view cf. esp. the work of Gregory Nagy, *Homer's Text and Language*. Traditions (Champaign, IL: University of Illinois Press, 2004).

completely different functions in their societies.[7] Indeed, Havelock's comparison generally ignores all the political and social implications.[8] By concentrating almost exclusively on the medium, he foreshortens the perspective in a manner that also ignores the broader background of linguistic forms and traditions.

As regards "distortion," one can scarcely avoid the impression that, in his euphoria over the alphabetical script, and in his admiration for the unique achievements of the Greeks, Havelock underestimates the cultural achievements of neighboring societies (of course, this problem is not unique to him; it is common among western historians of literacy). His evaluation, for instance, of Egyptian hieroglyphs and their efficacy is based on several major misunderstandings. He believes in all seriousness that Egyptian society was barely able to use the hieroglyphic system "for written communication in any meaningful sense of the term."[9] He considers them to be "pictograms." It is certainly true that eastern scripts – especially Egyptian hieroglyphs

---

[7] Gerald K. Gresseth, "The Gilgamesh Epic and Homer," *Cuneiform Journal* 70, No. 4 (1975), 1-18, to whom Havelock refers, goes so far as to ascribe both texts to the same genre.

[8] The art form of the epic in general and of Homer in particular implies certain indispensable preconditions. We might subsume them under the heading of "heroic;" this always entails the memory of an "heroic age" that by definition, must be past. The epic is the form and the medium whereby it is made present. In fact S. N. Kramer speaks of "Mesopotamia's heroic age," which preserved memories of the Sumerian conquest of South Mesopotamia's alluvial land, in much the same manner as the Homeric epics commemorate Mycenaean culture, and the Vedic epics record Indo-European migration and the formative stages of the Vedic caste society (Samuel N. Kramer, *From the Tablets of Sumer* [Colorado: Falcon's Wing Press, 1956], 227 f.). Whether this thesis can be maintained for Mesopotamia (which seems unlikely) is not our concern here. What matters is that genres like the epic do not represent any metahistorical universals, but are tied to particular social and political factors.

[9] Eric A. Havelock, *The Muse Learns to Write: Reflections on Orality and Literacy from Antiquity to the Present* (New Haven: Yale University Press, 1986), 65. Havelock's ethnocentrism is indeed obtrusive. He takes it for granted that we are "the heirs of a 2,500-year-old experience of the written word," as if writing had been invented in 500 BCE (*The Greek Concept of Justice: From its Shadow in Homer to its Substance in Plato* [Cambridge: Harvard University Press, 1978], 4). In 500 BCE, the Egyptians and Babylonians were already able to look back over 2,500 years of experience with the written word. Other classical philologists also like to indulge in a similar underestimation of the efficiency of eastern scripts and an overestimation of the exoticism of their pictorial character. Øivind Andersen, "Mündlichkeit und Schriftlichkeit im frühen Griechentum," *Antike und Abendland* 33, (1987), 29-44, 33, for instance, thinks that only the Greeks were in a position to "write down everything that they heard and thought;" he distinguishes between "close to speech" and "rebus-like" communication.

and Mesopotamian cuneiform script (leaving aside later Semitic alphabets) – are harder to learn and use than the Greek alphabet.[10] But that does not make them any less efficient in the reproduction of the spoken language. The fact that there was no sound, no word, no sentence, and no thought in the respective language that the corresponding technique of writing was unable to express cannot be emphasized enough.[11] Havelock's reading of nonalphabetical scripts as difficult to use and thus extremely reductive in their quality of reproduction is based simply on ignorance.[12]

Similar objections to the thesis that only the Greek alphabetical script, with its abstract efficiency, could have promoted logic and abstract thinking may be raised from an orientalist's point of view.

[10] Havelock only recognizes the Greek writing system and those derived from it as alphabetical. He regards Semitic scripts, including Hebrew and Arabic, as "non-alphabetical" because (and here he sides with Gelb against Diringer) they did not comprise phonemes but only syllables, disregarding their vowel values.

[11] For instance, there is a precise distinction between "speech" and "narrative" in Egyptian narrative literature, mainly from the New Kingdom (15–11th century BCE). The interpolated direct speech is distinguished from the narrative text around it by lexis and syntax, and is clearly designed to give a realistic reproduction of spoken language, see Fritz Hintze, *Untersuchungen zu Stil und Sprache neuägyptischer Erzählungen* (Berlin: Akademie-Verlag, 1953). Late Egyptian commercial texts used a different idiom from that of literary texts and came very close to normal, everyday language. The literature of the Third Intermediary Period (e.g., *The Teachings of Amenemope*) was written purely in the vernacular, which is barely distinguishable from Coptic written in Greek letters.

[12] Havelock thought the "non-alphabetical" scripts were so difficult to read that they could only communicate familiar things to their readers. Therefore, even up to the present day, eastern literature could only communicate in clichés and formulae that reduced the complexity of experience to something easily recognizable. He saw the ability to write vowels as the unique achievement of the alphabet. No other script – and in this he was certainly right – could reproduce language in a manner that was independent of context. In Hebrew and Arabic, which only use consonants, the vowelization for those who have mastered the language emerges from the context. Words written in Greek can be read out of context and even without any knowledge of the language. This shows, however, that the efficiency of this script lies in very different areas, because in reproducing their own language, the Semitic, consonant-only scripts are in no way inferior to the Greek. It is only through their restriction to Semitic language structures that they are less suitable for reproducing foreign languages. The ability to reach beyond one's own language area was undoubtedly a driving force behind the development of writing, and it is anything but a coincidence that the pioneers of these scripts were seafaring traders such as the Greeks and the Phoenicians.

While writing phonemes as opposed to concrete sounds (like syllables) or sound sequences (words) offered an excellent medium for abstraction and rationalization, the Egyptian and Semitic principle of writing consonants – that is, dispensing with vowels – actually rested in itself on an efficient abstraction. However, we are not in a position to evaluate it properly because we are not familiar with the relevant linguistic structure. In Semitic languages, meaning depends on roots that generally have three consonants. These roots are lexemes that like phonemes are an abstraction. They only become concrete through prefixes, infixes, suffixes, and patterns of vocalization, which make them into verbs or nouns with their different forms of conjugation or declension. Writing penetrates the surface structure of formulated speech and targets the root structure of the lexeme, thereby distinguishing between carriers of meaning and forms of inflexion; this promotes awareness of semantic references, or a sort of thinking in "root meanings" that forms the basis of Semitic poetry, or what is called the *parallelismus membrorum.* The principle of writing only consonants is of Ancient Egyptian origin, and it was adopted by Ancient Canaanite, Phoenician, and Hebrew scripts. The methods of rabbinical and kabbalistic exegesis exploited the potential of a consonant script to extreme heights of speculative metaphysics of writing, of which its importance only becomes apparent through the perspective of J. Derrida's philosophical "grammatology." But Havelock only sees an obstacle to communication in the absence of vowels and not an actualized potential for abstraction in keeping with a particular linguistic structure.

Writing System and Scribal Culture (*Schriftkultur*)

Havelock's interpretations and evaluations are based on an identification of writing system (*Schriftsystem*) with scribal culture (*Schriftkultur*), but this is erroneous even though there are undoubtedly links between the two. The term "writing system" covers matters pertaining to the structures and functional modes of a particular script (e.g. whether it is ideographic or phonographic, syllabic or alphabetical, restricted to a single language or capable of reproducing the sounds/words/sentences of another language as well). "Scribal culture," on the other hand, covers the institutions and traditions of writing, how one approaches texts, and the position of writing and of written texts in society.[13] It is obvious that the consequences of writing will depend on the level of the social context, or "scribal culture."

One aspect of the latter is the social evaluation of scripts and of writing. The fact that they occupied a subordinate position in Greek society is well known. It is also revealing to consider philosophical evaluations of writing, not only Plato's famous verdict in *Phaidros* and in *The Seventh Letter* but also Aristotle's view: he thought that spoken language reproduced *tà en psychê* (that which is in the soul), while writing reproduced *tà en phonê* (that which is in the voice). Writing was external in two ways: its content side referred only to the phonetic and thus external side of speech. This theory resulted in three stages of detachment from the world: concepts referred to the world, language referred to the concepts, and writing referred to language – on the level not of conceptual but of phonetic articulation. The extreme opposite of all this was Egyptian hieroglyphics. With their realistic pictoriality, these referred directly to the world, and their function as signs related them to both the phonetic and the semantic level of language. Therefore they reproduced not only "what is in the voice" but also "what is in the psyche" and, furthermore, "what is in the world." Of course as a writing system they were more difficult to deal with than the Greek alphabet, but they accomplished something very different and were correspondingly held in higher esteem. The hieroglyphic script, with its sensual presence, went far beyond the reaches of the spoken word. Through it, language took on a more varied and referentially richer reality than it could through the voice. The alphabetical script, by comparison, was an abstract medium of expression for the voice, through which language took on its own presence and reality. Greek became a scribal culture only through the medium of language, whereas Egypt was also a pictorial culture and thus, a scribal

[13] See Georg Elwert, "Die gesellschaftliche Einbettung von Schriftgebrauch," in D. Becker et al. (eds.), *Theorie als Passion* (Frankfurt: Suhrkamp, 1987), 238–268. Distinctions such as "political system" v. "political culture" (society v. country), "legal system" v. "legal culture," etc. are on a comparable level. Under the concept of culture come questions concerning institutionalization, politics, law, etc.

culture in a much more comprehensive sense. The path to writing did not depend solely on language but also embraced a pictorial shaping and appropriation of the world. In this form, writing was valued as the loftiest and holiest means of expression that could be given to meaning.

Like Greece, however, Israel also turned away from pictures, launching itself into a specific word culture in which writing played a much more important cultural role. God wrote: he was the author and writer of the laws handed over on Mount Sinai, and he kept the accounts concerning the deeds of men.[14] As in Egypt, Israel developed writing as a key to the world. One might ask whether the actual expansion within society of the ability to write constituted the only or the decisive criterion for what we consider to be a scribal culture. And one might also ask whether the effects of literacy on a society's worldview might not be equally important, because even though only a small minority had mastered the art, they had succeeded in giving it a central position of enormous prestige in that society.

In our study of the connections between tradition and identity, and of organizational forms of cultural memory, it is extremely revealing that in Greece, as in Israel – but unlike Egypt – "great texts" formed the basis of cultural memory but, in contrast to Israel, all of these foundational texts reproduced oral speech: Homer's epics, the tragedies,[15] Plato's Dialogues.[16] Of course no one can deny that referring to these texts, not to mention creating them, would not have been possible without writing. But they do not flaunt their "writtenness;"[17] on the contrary, they emerge from and return to physical, live voices and interactions. Clearly writing is not taken here – as it was in Egypt and Israel – as an eternal, unchangeable, sacred counter to the

---

[14] But see also the "tablets of Zeus," which record the deeds of man, and Dike *deltographos* as Parhedros [assessor] of Zeus: Pfeiffer, *History of Classical Scholarship from the Beginnings*, 25ff. (see chapt. 2, n. 55)

[15] Charles P. Segal, "Tragédie, oralité, écriture," *Poétique* 13,1982, 131–54.

[16] Thomas A. Slezak, *Platon und die Schriftlichkeit der Philosophie*. Interpretationen zu den frühen und mittleren Dialogen. (Berlin: De Gruyter, 1985).

[17] In contrast to the writing of history, Gr. 'syn-graphé' (writing together, compilation), "ana-graphé" (record or documentation), and to the explicit justification of the written form in Thucydides as a "ktêma eìs aei."

transience of the spoken word. From this fact, we can extrapolate three characteristic features of the scribal culture of Greece:

1. It is open to orality in a different manner; it does not push it aside into a subculture, but takes up its forms and develops them to a new and enhanced level.[18]

2. Since writing in Greece did not constitute the key to sacred space, there are no sacred texts. As with the Celts, the Zoroastrian Persians, and especially the Vedic Indians, the Greeks entrusted their sacred texts to oral rather than written tradition (C. Colpe 1988; H. G. Kippenberg 1987).

3. As writing in Greece did not occupy any official place, no authorization was required for its use. That which Cicero once remarked with reference to the Romans was also applicable to the Greeks: "public memory entrusted to public writing" was an alien concept.[19]

The reason why Greek scribal culture contained so many oral or, more generally, archaic elements probably had nothing to do with the special nature of their writing system. It seems most likely that it lay in the unicity of social and political conditions in Greece. For reasons that we need not explore further here, the Greeks were free from the written laws of eastern societies.[20] Eastern scripts were developed as organs of political representation and economic organization, and they were inextricably linked to bureaucracy, which used them to

---

[18] It was anything but normal for a society to write down its oral tradition. As a rule, oral and written traditions existed side by side, until the written gradually dominated and the oral was downgraded to folklore or superstition. The oldest Greek literature seems in this respect to be unusual, in so far as it faithfully codified an oral tradition. But that was in keeping with Greek culture generally, as during its transposal into literature it never attempted to relegate its magic, shamanic, orgiastic, or other irrational roots into the shadows of some sort of remote subculture (like for instance the compromising element of heathenism that unexpectedly breaks through in the sacred plays of the Middle Ages). On the contrary, it was able to transfer the now fully formed meanings, aesthetic beauties, and anthropological truths into the rational forms of artistic and scholarly discourse. See A. and J. Assmann, "Das Doppelgesicht der Zeit im altägyptischen Denken," in A. Peisl and A. Mohler (eds.), *Die Zeit* (Munich, Wien: R. Oldenbourg, 1983), 267.

[19] Cicero, *De Leg.* 3, 20, 46: "publicis litteris consignatam memoriam publicam nullam habemus."

[20] Cf. now, however, Joachim Gehrke (ed.), *Rechtskodifizierung und soziale Normen im interkulturellen Vergleich*, Scriptoralia 66 (Tübingen: G. Narr, 1994).

facilitate the administration of large domains (for Mesopotamia, see M. Lambert 1960). Writing meant arranging, planning, dividing etc., and so, it was first and foremost an organizational, governmental instrument. The things that were written were discourses on power, relating to official identity, laws, permits, deeds, rituals, and sacrifices. Writing meant commitment, security, documentation, control, order, and classification. To borrow Foucault's expression, it was "dispositive of power." Whatever was written imposed a binding obligation.[21] Oral tradition as well as what we would call literature only had limited access to this form of writing. The worlds that divided the official scribes of Egypt or of Mesopotamia from the singer-poets of Greece were not simply those of writing technology, but of writing culture: the historical environment, the political climate, the audiences, and the experiences that existed in each respective society.[22]

The practice of writing was very different in Israel.[23] Compared to the scribal hierarchies of the neighboring kingdoms, Israel's priests and prophets had, to a certain extent, a freer hand. They at least had concerns outside of administration and organization. "Commitment" here applied to just one thing: the law, the "instructions" (*torah*), which they knew had been given to the people and must be kept and obeyed through all adversity. The connection between writing and obligation, reading and obeying was also valid here, but not in the context of the mundane apparatus of power. In Israel, writing was depoliticized, and it became the most important instrument for the exercise of God's power.

---

[21] See especially Jack Goody, *The Logic of Writing and the Organization of Society* (Cambridge: Cambridge University Press, 1986). The achievements (and limitations) of Babylonian and Egyptian scholarship are certainly unthinkable without writing, but they are due less to the "spirit of writing" than to the "spirit of bureaucracy" and its systematic listing and organizing of reality; see Jack Goody, *The Domestication of the Savage Mind* (Cambridge: Cambridge University Press, 1977). In Greece, these social, framing conditions of gaining, processing, and communicating knowledge did not exist. Instead the Greeks had institutions of forensic, agonistic communication. See also Fritz Jürss, *Geschichte des wissenschaftlichen Denkens im Altertum* (Berlin: Akademie-Verlag, 1982). On Egypt, see Schlott, *Schrift und Schreiber* (see chapt. 4, n. 6).

[22] I agree with Elwert, "Die gesellschaftliche Einbettung," 239 (see chapt. 7, n. 13): "It is not the use of writing in itself, but specific social institutions (situations relating to power, production and exchange) that use it and so create social change."

[23] See now Karl van der Toorn, *Scribal Culture and the Making of the Hebrew Bible* (Cambridge, MA: Harvard University Press, 2007).

The special nature of Greece's cultural development was the result not only of its writing system but also of something much more complex, and one has to ask where the instances of instruction were concentrated and how obligations were fixed and fulfilled. The answer lies in a sociopolitical use of writing that is best characterized in negative terms as a free space that was occupied neither by the commanding voice of a ruler nor by a god. This power vacuum favored orality's penetration of Greece's scribal culture.

Thus the influence of writing on Greek culture was completely different from that on Egyptian, Israelite, and also Chinese culture. A short essay by Rudolf Borchardt illustrates this clearly as follows:

The sacred basic language of the Greeks, what one might call their "Sanskrit," does not commit their descendants – unlike Indian or the classical languages of Ancient Israel, Ancient China or Ancient Iran – to religious charters. It is only in the eastern system that national eternity as a unit of law, doctrine (or teaching) and history has to be constantly caught up in the vessel of timeless language.

The national charter of the West is called poetry, on which depends the intellectual world of poetically produced individuality in literature and research. The danger never existed that Homer could become a bible for the pseudo-Greeks of the Hellenistic world The secret that made Hellas into a nation could never be reduced to so primitive a formula as a book or two, and the language of this secret could never be reduced to the tyrannical principle of a single primal time of a rigid primal language" (R. Borchardt 1973, 67).

If for a moment we can look away from a somewhat indigestible menu of one-sided evaluations, and focus solely on the evidence that Borchardt has in mind, we must acknowledge that these words have a certain justification. Rudolf Pfeiffer says something similar, though with greater brevity: "In the Greek world, a 'tyranny of the book' was never able to exert itself as it did in the eastern or medieval world." (R. Pfeiffer 1978, 52)

It may be helpful to set these comments against a diametrically opposite set of values that has the advantage of coming from a time much closer to that of the texts with which it deals. In his work *Contra Apionem*, written in Rome towards the end of the 1st century AD, the

Jewish historian Josephus Flavius compares Jewish and Greek historiography:

> With us it is not open to all to write history. That is why in the written text there are also no contradictions. Only the prophets had this privilege, for they acquired their knowledge of the most distant primal history thanks to divine inspiration, and they wrote down a clear account of the events of their time. Our books, to which credence is rightly given, are only 22 in number and contain a report on all times. 5 of these are the books of Moses, which contain the laws and traditional history from the origin of man to the death of the law-giver. History from Moses to Artaxerxes was written by the prophets in 13 books. The remaining 4 books contain hymns to God and precepts for the conduct of human life. From Artaxerxes to our own time there has been a tradition, but this does not enjoy the same esteem because the sequence of the prophets was broken. Only what they left behind do we honour as our writings. And although such a long period has elapsed, no-one has dared to add, take away or change even one syllable" (*Contra Apionem I* §§ 38–41).

The Greeks, on the other hand, had countless books, all of which were contradictory. Furthermore, tradition was only young:

> Admittedly, though, there are simply no Greek writings that are older than the poetry of Homer. But this is obviously later than the events of Troy, and it is said that not even he left behind any written version of his own poetry, but rather that it was later compiled from memory out of the songs (in circulation); and that is why it contains many contradictions (*diaphoniai*) (*CA* § 12).[24]

This critique of Greek scribal culture is directed against its structural orality. There were countless books full of contradictions, controversies, lies – a polemic dispute that invaded the realm of writing – and it was not about the truth but about the art of rhetoric and political influence. (We shall see later, however, that this multiplicity of contradictory voices, so obvious to an eastern observer, actually represented a specific achievement by the scribal culture.) Among the Jews, and in the East generally, the sphere of writing was sacred and therefore reserved for those who were authorized to deal in the sacred: the priests, who

---

[24] Quoted by Hubert Cancik, "Geschichtsschreibung und Priestertum. Zum Vergleich von orientalischer und hellenischer Historiographie bei Flavius Josephus, contra Apionem, Buch I," in E. L. Ehrlich, B. Klappert and U. Ast (eds.), "*Wie gut sind deine Zelte, Jaakow...,*" *Festschrift zum 60.Geburtstag von Reinhold Mayer* (Gerlingen: Bleicher, 1986), 41–62. My comments on Josephus are based largely on this essay.

"possess the oldest and most definitive tradition (*parádosis*) of memory (§ 8), firm, immovable, unchangeable, like the God whom it conveys."[25] In relation to the one and only truth, the books of the Jews are *symphonoi* [without contradiction]: they all say the same thing, and no one has the authority to make even the slightest change to the wording. This system, Josephus's critique appears to imply, is true written culture, and this is the great achievement that puts the East ahead of the Greeks.

It is all too obvious that Josephus's criticisms are as one-sided and malicious as the "neo-humanist" denunciation of the "eastern system" and "the tyranny of the book."[26] But it is equally evident that in this ideological dispute over true memory, a point has been made that brings a crucial distinction between the possible consequences of literacy to light. Writing, which in Israel led to the monolithic crystallization of tradition, led to fluidity, controversy, and hence to a variety of traditions in Greece. Both principles, the Jewish "harmony" (*symphonoi*) and the Greek "discord" (*diaphoniai*), are equidistant from the structure of oral tradition.

Furthermore, the contrast that Josephus draws between Greek and Jewish memory is in many respects reminiscent of Plato's comparison between Greek and Egyptian art. Here, too, we have a culture of constant, individual innovation under the sign of aesthetic effect set against a culture of hieratic, official stagnation under the sign of truth. Plato (*Laws* 656/657) confronts the Greeks with Egypt as a model of how to treat tradition in relation to which, as the vessel of a definitively known truth, "nothing may be added and nothing may be changed." In Greece, however, says Plato – praising the uniqueness of Egypt, just as Josephus praises the uniqueness of the Jews – "and everywhere else in the world," artists are free to invent whatever they like. The parallel is striking, and it does not derive from any sort of trend (Josephus would certainly not have had the Plato passage in mind, and probably did not even know it), but it arises out of a structurally different attitude toward tradition, that is, toward cultural memory, as found in the Greeks, the Jews, and the Egyptians.

---

[25] Ibid., 53, paraphrasing *CA* §§ 153, 167, 169, 189.
[26] See the careful corrections with which Cancik, "Geschichtsschreibung und Priestertum" (see chapt. 7, n. 14), adjusts the picture outlined by Josephus.

HOMER AND GREEK ETHNOGENESIS

The Heroic Age as Homeric Memory

One of Josephus's most potent arguments for the truth of Jewish tradition and for the unreliability of Greek is the claim that Jews died for their sacred literature, whereas no Greek died for Herodotus.[27] However, Josephus was wrong. Herodotus himself reports that the Athenians pronounced themselves ready to die for their "Greekdom." This declaration was carefully calculated and staged for its political effect. Toward the end of the Persian Wars, Alexandros of Macedonia came to Athens as a negotiator in order to persuade the Greeks to sign a treaty with the King of Persia. The Athenians dragged out the negotiations, "because they knew that the people of Sparta would hear of the arrival of the Persian envoy and of the proposed treaty and would hasten to send their own envoys." They had therefore deliberately waited in order to show the Spartans their true intentions. First, Alexandros was given a sharp refusal, and then the suspicious Spartans were taught a lesson: "And then there is Greekdom (*tò Hellenikón*), namely the same blood and language (*homaimón te kaì homóglosson*), common shrines and rituals, and the same customs (*étheá te homótropa*)."[28] This sense of belonging provides a guarantee that "so long as one Athenian is still alive, there will be no agreement with the Persians." In other words, they are prepared to die for "Greekdom."

This Panhellenic awareness, which the Athenians were so determined to proclaim in public, was anything but self-evident in a people who showed not the slightest hint of a political identity, and whose different political units were related to one another in solely nonpolitical ways. Their consciousness of Greekdom came about largely through the dissemination of one text: the *Iliad.* "On the basis of this epic narrative as a priceless national treasure, all the people of Greece, the 'Panhéllenes,' began to see themselves as one, despite all the

---

[27] *Contra Apionem* I §§ 42–45; Cancik, "Geschichtsschreibung und Priestertum," 59 (see chapt. 7, n. 24).

[28] Herodotus VIII, 144; see Moses Finley, "The Ancient Greeks and their Nation," in *The Use and Abuse of History* (London: Chatto and Windus, 1975), 120–133.

differences of tribes and classes, and regardless of changing political and social conditions."[29]

We therefore find ourselves confronted by the same phenomenon in Greece that we saw in Israel: both nations are formed by reverting to a foundational text. However, against the background of these parallels, what is really revealing is the contrast. In Israel, it is the memory of a dissident group, a movement of secession, that bases itself on the Torah under the sign of "distinction." The central memory figure is the history of a migration, a breakaway movement, and a liberation from what was alien. In Greece, we have a memory shared by many scattered groups based on the *Iliad* under the sign of "integration." The central memory figure is the history of a coalition, a Panhellenic closing of ranks against the common foe from the East.

This phenomenon is extraordinary for two reasons, and it needs to be explained by two different kinds of study. The first concerns the origin of the foundational text and the historical conditions that gave rise to it; the second is the history of the memory reversions. Both aspects of this process are significant because of the light that they shed on our discussion of forms and functions in relation to cultural memory. As far as the origin of the texts is concerned, we need to recognize that these were not myths or miraculous tales, but the "codification of memory." This raises the question: Why did the Greeks of the 8th century remember events that had taken place 500 years previously, in the form of an epic? The following may provide an explanation: the substantial cultural and social break between Mycenaean and ancient society made it possible to compose a "past" in the sense of an heroic age. An essential element of the past is precisely that it has gone and can never be continued. This past created the scenario for stories in which the aristocratic society of the 9th and 8th century BCE was able to experience and celebrate itself. It adopted these stories as its own past, and traced its genealogies back to the legendary figures of the Trojan War and all that was associated with it. The

---

[29] Pfeiffer, *History of Classical Scholarship from the Beginnings*, 5 (see chapt. 2, n. 55). Rudolf Borchardt is not quite right when he suggests that "the secret that made Hellas into a nation could never be reduced to so primitive a formula as a book or two." On the contrary, there could scarcely be a more apt way of describing the role of the *Iliad* in the ethnogenesis of Greece than "the secret that made Hellas into a nation."

Mycenaean past therefore took on the patina of age, with its heroic proportions, as a different epoch worlds away from the "mortals" of the present; at the same time, though, as a remembered, "lived-in" history it provided grounds for a genealogically based self-presentation and self-definition by the aristocracy. It was, in other words, a typical instance of continuity constructed across rupture.[30]

The question remains, however: why was this memory mobilized in particular in the 8th century? The rupture bridged by a fictitious continuity took place around 1200 BCE. Is it, then, possible that Homer's own century was also a time of crisis and upheaval? First of all, it must be noted that his epics mark the end of the heroic saga as a living, oral tradition. This suggests that they also belong to the end rather than the peak of the way of life and the world-view that they depict and that fits in with the appearance of such sagas. The heroic epic is the favorite genre of cultural memory in the framework of a particular form of society. This is what we might term "chivalry," that is aristocratic, warlike, and individualistic. Wherever in the world it occurs, chivalry entails a sense of superiority, a special kind of self-confidence that results, among other things, from land ownership (on a large enough scale for horse breeding) and from the "superhuman" speed of movement.[31]

The particular need for territory that goes together with this horse-breeding aristocracy led to the development of a certain lifestyle and personal profile that have been dubbed "loose (as opposed to "tight") society;"[32] this is not in the amoral sense, but in the sense of a desire

---

[30] See Hölscher, *Die Odyssee* (see chapt. 7, n. 6). The transition from the Late Bronze to the Iron Age (1100–900 BC) also caused a rupture and produced similar phenomena in other parts of the ancient world. In Mesopotamia, the neo-Assyrian Empire looked back to the time of Sargon of Akkade (2300 BC) as its cultural and political model, and during the 25th and 26th dynasties (8th-6th cts.), Egypt developed a kind of "renaissance," an artistic and literary revival of several classical periods, especially the Middle Kingdom (20th to 18th cts.). On Mesopotamia see now Gerdientje Jonker, *The Topography of Remembrance. The Dead, Tradition and Collective Memory in Mesopotamia* (Leiden: E. J. Brill, 1995); on Egypt, see de Manuelian, *Living in the Past*, (see chapt. 2, n. 13).

[31] See Hölscher, *Die Odyssee* (see chapt. 7, n. 6).

[32] Pertti Pelto, "The Difference between 'Tight' and 'Loose' Societies," *Transaction* (April 1968), 37–40; see John W. Berry, "Nomadic Style and Cognitive Style," in H. M. McGurk (ed.), *Ecological Factors in Human Development* (Amsterdam: North Holland, 1977), 228–245.

and need for freedom, initiative, independence, and honor. Perhaps Homer may stand at the end of the world he describes, and his poetry may be its monument. He establishes a tradition (oral), the social framework of which is decline and fall: an oral epic that flourished, not in the Mycenaean but in the early archaic age, when a special role was assigned to those legends based on the impressive ruins and other remains of the Mycenaean culture. It seems likely that Homer lived at a time of upheaval, in which Greek society was turning from "loose" to "tight." The beginning of the colonial movement is the most important indicator of this, and it may be interpreted as a sign of increased overpopulation in the motherland. The emerging city-state of the polis represented a typical case of a tight society, and in many respects this was the direct opposite of Homeric society. Homer's epics therefore should be seen in the context of an organizational form of cultural memory – as a reconstruction of the past that supported the self-image of a particular group. They constitute the end and also the pinnacle of this organizational form, because shortly before the final disappearance of their world, they bring together the whole of a tradition in a completely new kind of work, which can go on existing independently of the memory-bearing community, and thus can become the starting point of new memories.

This brings us to the second aspect pertaining to memory recursion, that is, to the memory of Homer, or tradition, and the dissemination of the text itself. Here we must keep in mind the fact that none of this took place in a culture of books and reading – the culture was one of recitation. The beginnings of an organized tradition and dissemination of Homer's work coincided with the end of the creative period of the Greek epic during the second half of the 6th century BCE.[33] This was no coincidence. In Israel too, the "end of prophecy" marked the beginning of canonization. The rhapsodists of the 6th century BCE were "professional reciters of established poetic works that were ascribed (to Homer)" (Pfeiffer). From the very beginning they combined tradition (looking after the text, *Textpflege*), interpretation

---

33 This and what follows is mainly based on Pfeiffer, *History of Classical Scholarship from the Beginnings*, (see chapt. 2, n. 55), and Uvo Hölscher, "Über die Kanonizität Homers," in A. and J. Assmann (eds.), *Kanon und Zensur* (see chapt. 1, n. 48). See now the controversy between Gregory Nagy and Martin West in Nagy, *Homer's Text and Language* (see chapt. 7, n. 6).

(looking after the meaning, *Sinnpflege*), and communication, functioning not only as entertainers but also as philologists and educators. Homer's epics are also "encyclopedias of conduct."[34] As Xenophanes, himself a rhapsodist, put it: "All have learned from Homer" (Diels, B 10).[35] The institution of Homer recitation contests began at the Panathenaean games, and spread to all Panhellenic festivals. In this first phase of organizing and institutionalizing cultural memory on a Panhellenic level, by way of a national internalization of Homer's work, reception assumed a festive, communal character. The epics circulated in the form of "ceremonial communication," and as they were inseparable from Panhellenic festivals, they formed the basis of a project of ethnogenesis that was beyond or at least independent of political identity. They became a "great tradition" that similar to in India kept a consciousness of belonging to a wider, "interlocational" community alive,[36] transcending all the petty squabbles, wars, border disputes, and differences that were equally as rife in Greece as in India. Together, the Panhellenic games and the Homer epic formed a collective unit whose integrative power was similar to that, in the later age of Athenian democracy, of the Great Dionysia and the tragedies in the formation of the collective identity of the Athenians.[37]

Remembering Homer: Classics and Classicism

The second phase of organizing Greek cultural memory began in Alexandria. It was preceded by a major rupture. The culture of rhapsodic recitation gave way to one of books and reading. But above all, the consciousness of time and history underwent a radical change. Tradition was now seen as works from a past that was ending and that could not have any continuation. For the culture change that took place in the 4th century BCE throughout the entire region of

---

34 Havelock, "The Alphabetisation of Homer," in Havelock and Hershbell (eds.), *Communication Arts*, 3–21 (see chapt. 7, n. 4).

35 On Homer as "praeceptor Graecia," see also Plato, *Prot.* 339 A and *Pol.* 606 E.

36 Robert Redfield, *Peasant Society and Culture. An Anthropological Approach to Civilisation* (Chicago: University of Chicago Press, 1956), especially 67 ff.; G. Obeyesekere, "The Great Tradition and the Little Tradition in the Perspective of Singhalese Buddhism," *Journal of Asian Studies* 22 (1963), 139–153.

37 See Christian Meier, "Zur Funktion der Feste in Athen im 5. Jh. v. Chr.," in Warning and Haug (eds.), *Das Fest*, 569–591 (see chapt. 1, n. 56).

the Mediterranean, the term "Hellenism" (or, Hellenization) is in fact misleading. It seems to imply a general adoption of the Greek way, with every culture changing accordingly, except for that of Greece itself. In reality, however, the unifying culture that spread was just as eastern as it was Greek, and it meant just as radical a change for the Greek city-states as it did for the rest of the Ancient World.[38] Elements of this change included such things as monarchy and bureaucracy, deification of rulers, legal codes, professional politicians, administration, science, military forces, the depoliticization of the individual, and much more. Most of these derived more from Persia than from Greece (see M. Smith 1971, 77 ff.). This raises the question whether perhaps Alexandrian classicism did not also contain elements of eastern scribal culture – the "eastern system" – resting on the sacredness of the text and the unchangeability of every letter.[39] It was not the texts themselves but the way they were dealt with that highlighted the influence of the East.

In relation to the classics, my own focus will not be on how they originated, but on how they were remembered. The transition from Greek to Hellenistic culture lies between the historical conditions of their origin and those of their remembrance. The fact that the language remained the same should not distract from the radicalness of this rupture. Basically, it was a new and different culture in Alexandria that retrospectively looked to Ancient Greece. "Newness" and "looking back" go together. The world of literature divides itself into "the old" (*hoi palaioi, antiqui*) and "the new" (*hoi neoteroi, moderni*), and

---

[38] In this context, it is highly significant that Josephus does not speak of "Hellenic", but of "common culture" (*koinòs bíos*) in dealing with the confrontation of orthodox and assimilated Jews during the Maccabaean Wars; see Erich Gruen, *Heritage and Hellenism. The Reinvention of Jewish Tradition* (Berkeley: University of California Press, 1998). Cf. also Glen W. Bowersock, *Hellenism in Late Antiquity* (Cambridge: Cambridge University Press, 1990).

[39] Such comments add additional weight to the information handed down by Cicero (*de or.* III 137) and others that the first written text of Homer's epics was produced and fixed in the reign of the tyrant Peisistratos of Athens, in connection with the "library" that, like Polycrates of Samos, he had built for himself. Rudolf Pfeiffer regards this tradition as a retrospective projection of Ptolemaic conditions onto Ancient Greece. However, one might also see an "orientalizing" tendency in these tyrants to emulate the book-collecting rulers of the East. See Morton Smith, *Palestinian Parties and Politics That Shaped the Old Testament* (New York: Columbia University Press, 1971), 139 ff.

the dialectic of innovation and antiquation determines what is old. It is not continuance but rupture that places the old on a pedestal of unmatchable perfection.[40] However, this break must not be total. In order for works to become classic, there has to be a rupture that renders tradition incapable of continuing, thus bringing the old to a standstill; on the other hand, however, an act of identification has to survive beyond the rupture so that the past is still recognizable as one's own, and the old can be recognized as the masters that they were. The past must be past, but it must not become alien.[41]

In certain respects, the Homer experience repeats itself. In Alexandria, we also have a codification of memory, of a relationship to the past beyond the break as a construct of cultural continuity. Thus both "the newborn art of poetry and the revival of old masterpieces stood under the protection of the daughters of memory" (Pfeiffer, 125), that is, the Muses, to whom the *Musaion* was dedicated – the institution that Ptolemy I of Egypt founded in Alexandria for the promotion of literature and the natural sciences. The Alexandrian way of dealing with tradition was through textual criticism, interpretation, and communication to an unprecedented degree of refinement and professionalism. The texts were collected, catalogued (*pinakes*), and compared; word lists were compiled; and definitions and explanations collated and developed into commentaries. The use of language by different authors and at different periods was studied as a basis for corrections and attributions. The sheer volume of work made it necessary to select the texts, and so the collection was evaluated and divided up into "treated" (*prattómenoi*) and classified (*enkrithéntes*) authors, while the rest were "excluded" (*ekkrithéntes*). The "canon of classics" was finally established after centuries of painstaking selection.[42]

---

[40] See Ernst A. Schmidt, "Historische Typologie der Orientierungsfunktionen von Kanon in der griechischen und römischen Literatur," in A. and J. Assmann (eds.), *Kanon und Zensur* (see chapt. 1, n. 48). On a similar phenomenon in Egypt during the Ramesside Period, see J. Assmann, "Die Entdeckung der Vergangenheit," 484 ff. (see chapt. 1, n. 79).

[41] See Mukarovsky: "a work that is alien to the people ceases to be a work of art;" see René Wellek, *Grenzziehungen. Beiträge zur Literaturkritik* (Stuttgart: Kohlhammer, 1972), 137.

[42] The Greeks do not speak here of "canon," with reference either to the lists of selected works – for which there does not appear to be a Greek word (Latin: *numerus* and *ordo*) – or to the total sum of classical authors and texts. However, the concept

Thus cultural meaning had been fixed in a manner whose resistance to time is in no way inferior to that of the Hebrew canon. The great tradition of foundational cultural texts was removed from the realm of ceremonial communication, whereas in Polis society it had in many areas remained an oral phenomenon, and it was transposed into the new institutional, educational framework of an international, Hellenistic society. Thus, a culture was born whose cohesion and continuity rested entirely on texts and their interpretation. Institutions of interpretation ensured cultural continuity, from *philologoi* to monks to humanists.

The two processes of selecting and fixing tradition – culminating in the 22- or 24-book canon of the Jewish scholars and the classical canon of the Alexandrian philologists – were not only almost concurrent, but they were also in contact with one another.[43] The Torah plays the same role as a crystallizing nucleus (a canon within a canon) in the Hebrew canon as Homer does in the Greek. And just as the Homer tradition functioned as a process of ethnogenesis in Greece, so too did the Torah in Israel. The fixing of the text was accompanied by a new consciousness of national and cultural belonging. Both processes had come to an end even before the Persian period, when the general change in Mediterranean culture began during which Greece became a book and reading culture, while in the Israel of the Second Temple written scholarship took on the guardianship of tradition and became the bearer of cultural memory. The scholar-scribes (*soferîm*) looked back to the prophets, just as the philologists looked back to the classics: both belonged to an era that had ended forever. In Israel it extended

---

of "classic" does have a linguistic source, even if it only goes back to the Roman reception of Alexandrian classics. "Classici," members of the *classis* or tax-paying upper classes, is a witty metaphor for the Greek term meaning "classified." For details, see Pfeiffer, *History of Classical Scholarship from the Beginnings* (see chapt. 2, n. 55) and Schmidt, "Historische Typologie der Orientierungsfunktionen" (see chapt. 7, n. 40).

43 This can hardly be the case with the virtually simultaneous development of the Buddhist and Confucianist canons, although they are not part of the present discussion. The sacred texts of Zoroastrianism, like the Vedic texts, were not allowed to be written down, and there were no written versions until the 3rd century AD. On the birth of the Buddhist canon and its effects on other canons in the eastern world, see Carsten Colpe, "Sakralisierung von Texten und Filiationen von Kanons," in A. and J. Assmann (eds.), *Kanon und Zensur*, 80–92, (see chapt. 1, n. 48).

from "Moses to Artaxerxes"[44] (Ezra and Nehemiah), and in Greece from Homer to Euripides.

In both cases, cultural meaning was fixed in a manner that was both time-resistant and universally accessible. The Greek classics provided the basis of cultural memory not only for the West but also in later times for classical philology in China and Africa. The Hebrew Bible underlies the scriptures of Christianity and of Islam, for the Koran is also unimaginable without the Old Testament.

III HYPOLEPSIS – SCRIBAL CULTURE AND THE EVOLUTION OF IDEAS IN GREECE

There is general agreement that the unique evolution of ideas[45] that, in the course of a few centuries, generated the foundational texts and intellectual traditions of western rationalism was largely triggered by scribal culture, and in particular by that of the Greeks. If we can identify religion and state as the respective achievements of Israelite and Egyptian scribal culture, then philosophy and science – i.e. the development of a discourse imposing logical rules on the search for truth – represent the special achievement of the Greeks.

There are two unique elements in Greek scribal culture. One, as already mentioned, is the fact that it did not turn away from the oral tradition but absorbed and developed it. In my view, the second is that it created a new form of intertextual relations. It was no longer a matter of speaker reacting to speaker, but of texts reacting to texts. Writing did not just convey information or instructions, or ensure interaction beyond the written sphere, for example in commercial or political contexts, but it also acted by way of references to other

---

44 According to Josephus Flavius and others, see Leiman, *The Canonization of Hebrew Scripture* (see chapt. 2, n. 58).

45 I have taken this concept over from N. Luhmann, to whom I am greatly indebted for much of this chapter. Luhmann frequently draws attention to the correlation between scribal culture and the evolution of ideas, and in this context was responsible for introducing the work of the American classical philologist E. A. Havelock in Germany. See Nikolas Luhmann, *Gesellschaftsstruktur und Semantik I* (Frankfurt: Suhrkamp, 1980), 17 ff., 45–71; *Soziale Systeme* (Frankfurt: Suhrkamp, 1984), 212–241; Engl. *Social Systems*, trans. J. Bednarz (Stanford: Stanford University Press, 1995), 147–175.

texts, that is within the written sphere, and in this sense it could even be self-referential or incorporate other texts written within the same framework of discourse. This gave rise to a new form of cultural continuity and coherence: reference to texts of the past, in the form of controlled variation that I like to call "hypolepsis." I must confess straight away that this term does not correspond to any conventional use of the word. The nearest equivalent would be Aristotle's *epidosis eis hauto* (adding to itself), which he uses to distinguish between man and the world of plants and animals, and to denote the unique ability of man "to be a part of the for-ever and the divine" (*de anima* II 4, 2). Johann Gustav Droysen in his *Historik* takes up this Aristotelian category in order to distinguish between "history and Nature." The continuity of Nature consists in repetition. "The grain of wheat laid in the earth will, through stem, floret and ear, grow to a repetition of the same grains. And so it is with animals and with all life on Earth, the whole sidereal world, whose essence for us is its regular rise and fall. The moment of time seems secondary to us, and the endless sequence of time divides itself in these forms into the same repeated circles or periods . . ." The continuity of culture, however, consists in progressive variation.

It is a continuity in which everything earlier extends and supplements itself through something later (*epidosis eis hauto*) – a continuity in which the whole sequence of known forms accumulates into progressive results, and every known form seems to contribute to the growing totality. In this ceaseless succession, in this self-enhancing continuity, the general view of time takes on a special content – that of an endless sequence of progressive becoming. The totality of these manifestations of becoming and progressing, as presented to us, is what we grasp as history.[46]

At the end of the first section of Chapter 2, I suggested replacing the simple distinction between Nature and history with a recursive form in which we followed the same criteria of repetition and progressive variation to draw a distinction within history itself. This is how we arrive at the narrower concept of history that I call "hypolepsis."

---

[46] Johann G. Droysen, *Historik. Vorlesungen zur Enzyklopädie und Methodologie der Geschichte*, ed. by R. Hübner (Darmstadt: Oldenbourg, 1972), 11 f.

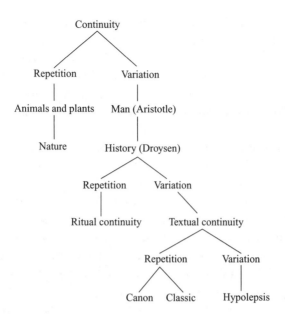

Forms of Hypoleptic Discourse Organization

The Greek term *hypólepsis* was used in two different contexts, both of which are relevant for our argument. One was the competition between rhapsodists, in which the word denoted the rule whereby the next contestant had to continue the Homer text from exactly where the previous one had left off.[47] The second context was rhetoric. Here *hypólepsis* meant linking up with what the previous speaker had said.[48] In both cases, the principle was not to begin from scratch but to build on a precedent, linking into a continuous process of communication. One might call this the "hypoleptic frame." In the competition between rhapsodists, this was the contest itself, whereas for rhetoric, it was the particular procedure, for example, a public meeting or a trial. In both cases, there was human interaction whose space-time borders were determined by the possibilities of such interaction. Our

[47] "ex hypolepseos ephexês": Plato, Hipparch, 228 B; in Diogenes Laert. I 57, the process is called "ex hypobolês;" see Pfeiffer, *History of Classical Scholarship from the Beginnings*, 8 (see chapt. 2, n. 55).

[48] Günther Bien, "Hypolepsis," in J. Ritter (ed.), *Historisches Wörterbuch der Philosophie* 4 (Basel: Schwabe, 1969), especially 64 and 66.

focus here is on how this hypoleptic frame could be extended beyond those borders into a sphere of communication that could dispense with interaction,[49] that is, an area in which "what the previous speaker had said" might have been said 2,000 years ago.

For such an area to come into existence, three things were necessary: writing, an institutional framework, and a concept of truth. Let us consider these three items in order.

There is not a great deal more to say about writing: it is obvious that if the previous speaker's words are to be present, even in the absence of the speaker, and made available for hypoleptic "reception" and continuation, they must be secured. This is only possible through writing. Even if in the oral tradition a preceding speech may also be handed down in a definitive form, so that centuries later someone can join in at a given point – "you have been told . . . but I say unto you . . . " – this is a form of retention that in the sphere of orality is itself exceptional, because memory is being used as a kind of writing. The point here is not the medium of writing, but the trans-situational retention of the spoken word in a text. In other words, although it is not written, it is still a text. One can only link up with texts, not with interactions.[50] Textuality occurs where language has separated itself from its practical embedding in situations (i.e., sociocultural interactions, or *Sitze im Leben*) and has taken on an independent form of its own. Normally, this fixed form is written. It would, however, be premature to assume that writing alone – even with the alphabetical script – already produces the phenomenon that we are proposing with the term *hypólepsis*.[51] Writing is simply a necessary tool; it does not in itself create sufficient conditions.

---

[49] I am adopting Luhmann's distinction between "interaction" and "interaction-free communication" here. See Luhmann, *Gesellschaftsstruktur*, (see chapt. 7, n. 45); *Social Systems* (see chapt. 7, n. 45).

[50] This concept of the text was developed by Konrad Ehlich, "Text und sprachliches Handeln. Die Entstehung von Texten aus dem Bedürfnis nach Überlieferung," in A. and J. Assmann (eds.), *Schrift und Gedächtnis*, 24–43 (see chapt. 1, n. 14).

[51] This appears to be the view of N. Luhmann, who sees the kind of factual discussion with preceding texts that we have called "hypolepsis" as a consequence of the alphabetical writing system, and for this he depends considerably on the work of E. A. Havelock: "As soon as alphabetized writing made it possible to carry communication beyond the temporally and spatially limited circle of those who are present at any particular time, one could no longer rely on the force of oral presentation; one needed to argue more strictly about the thing itself. 'Philosophy' seems to owe its beginnings to this. It is '*sophia*' as the skill required in such a tense situation to

This brings us to our second item: the institutional framework. We have noted that if it is to survive beyond that situation and make itself accessible for future reference, that which has been said, as the linguistic component of a complex process of interaction, has to be taken out of its situational context and given independent form as a text. However, once removed from its context, the meaning of the statement would be lost if the situation as such was not "extended." In other words, a new situational framework must be created to guide and organize both the act of passing on the statement and the hypoleptic act of linking up with it.[52] Once it has been uprooted, abstracted from its situation, and left helplessly exposed to all misunderstandings and rejections,[53] the original text must have a new framework to compensate for its loss of situational definition. "If the communication transcends the circle of those who were present at its inception, then understanding becomes more difficult and rejection easier; the interpretive assistance and pressure to accept provided by interaction are lacking" (N. Luhmann 1995, 160). This is the problem that literature and all forms of nonfiction face. In the case of literature, it is the text itself that gains autonomy by incorporating and making explicit its own situational framework. For instance, through Homer we learn all about the work of the bards and the performance of heroic epics, and through Alkaios we learn about the symposium as the performative frame of lyrical poetry. In other forms of writing, it is society that must provide the frame. These new conditions of what Luhmann calls "interaction-free communication" must not only ensure that the form of the text preserves what has been said and makes it comprehensible, but they must also set out the rules of "recursion," just as the original

---

enable communication that is serious, worthy of preservation, and universal (as far as the alphabet allows)" (Luhmann, *Social Systems*, 160 [see chapt. 7, n. 45]). As far as writing is concerned, he is content to simply point to eastern scribal cultures where this effect was not evident. This is why Havelock limits such effects to the alphabetical script. Once again, one might respond by pointing out that China – within the framework of a complex ideographical writing system – also developed a hypoleptically organized philosophical discourse that is in no way inferior to that of the Greeks.

52 On the concept of the "extended situation," see Ehlich, "Text und sprachliches Handeln," especially 32, (see chapt. 7, n. 50), and J. Assmann, "Die Macht der Bilder. Rahmenbedingungen ikonischen Handelns im alten Ägypten," in *Visible Religion VII* (1990), 1–20, 3–5.

53 See Plato's famous reservations about writing in *Phaidros* and the *Seventh Letter*.

frame – the contest of rhapsodists, and the legal or political speech – had done. All this requires the establishment of institutions in which such a dialogue with texts can take place.

Institutions of this nature included Plato's Academy and Aristotle's Peripatos. It is possible to argue, without any exaggeration, that without them, the hypoleptic frame of western philosophy could never have taken shape – a frame of "past speakers" that contained not only Plato and Aristotle themselves, but Descartes, Kant, Hegel, "etc., etc." Of course Plato and Aristotle can be incorporated as classics under the principle of classicism, and their texts are canonized under the principle of the canon, thus raising the question why the third principle of hypolepsis is necessary. Calling Plato and Aristotle "classics" emphasizes their unmatchable exemplarity. Their writings set the standard for what we mean by philosophy, just as Homer sets the standard for epic poetry. Calling these writings canonical highlights their absolute authority. This is precisely what happened during the Middle Ages. From this brief summary, it is clear that both forms of retrospective reference fail to cover the full range of philosophical interaction with these texts. A third form of reference is necessary that can distinguish between classic and canon, even if it also establishes connections.

The Hypoleptic Process as an Institutionalization of Authority and Criticism

The third item on our list was a concept of truth. We could just as aptly name it "information" or "concern." As N. Luhmann has emphasized, communication presupposes a distinction between the information itself and the way it is conveyed. In oral interaction, this distinction was generally imperceptible, and it was only through writing that it became necessary. "Writing and printing enforce an experience of the difference that constitutes communication: they are, in this precise sense, more communicative forms of communication, and they therefore require a more specific reaction by communication to communication than is possible orally."[54]

The principle of hypolepsis relates to these processes of checking truth and articulating doubt, which in turn are related to the

54 Luhmann, *Social Systems*, 162 f. (see chapt. 7, n. 45).

distinction between communication and information. These are polemic, agonistic principles. They regulate such things as competition between texts. Under the conditions of hypoleptic communication, scribal culture becomes a culture of conflict.[55]

This was the element of Greek scribal culture that Josephus Flavius had criticized. In contrast to the Jews, whose tradition rested on a single holy book, the Greeks had countless books that all contradicted one another. What Josephus could not see was that it was precisely the dissonant plurality (*Diaphonia*) of voices in Greek literature that constituted the unique achievement of this scribal culture. The unity of the biblical books, which he contrasted with Greek discord, depended on the principle of a certain and absolute truth. What makes a collection of texts into a canon is the decision that the statements fixed therein are to be seen as definitive, so that nothing must be added, altered, or taken away. Hypolepsis, on the other hand, proceeds from the belief that truth can never be more than an approximation, and the hypoleptic process is one of engaging in approximations. It draws its momentum from the awareness that knowledge is never complete, and there is always more to be had. You can only come closer to the truth – again, this is fundamental to hypolepsis – by freeing yourself from the delusion that you can keep starting afresh, by recognizing that you have been born into an ongoing process, by seeing which way things go, and by consciously, understandingly, but also critically learning what your predecessors have already said. Even scientific and philosophical revolutions cannot dispense with this hypoleptic location of the new. It is one of the framing conditions of science as an organized search for truth that the innovative relevance of a statement can only be seen against its hypoleptic background.

All such texts have a threefold relationship: (1) to earlier texts; (2) to the common subject matter or concern; (3) to criteria that check the claim to truth and monitor the distinction between communication and information. The scientific or philosophical text, unlike the literary, does not possess a purely intertextual coherence because in hypoleptically organized discourse, coherence is established through

---

55 N. Luhmann makes this feature of Greek scribal culture one of the central points of his general communications theory, and bases the constitutional improbability of (successful) communication on it.

criteria of truth shared in a three-way relationship between author, predecessor, and subject matter. This subject matter belongs completely to the frame of the "extended situation." After hundreds of years, it would be just as impossible to refer to the subject matter as to refer to what the predecessor had said, if special precautions were not taken to institutionalize permanence, so that the subject may remain present in the consciousness of later generations. This amounts to a trans-situational retention of relevance. It is not enough merely to write down what was said. It is not even enough to keep the relevant subject matter in view, if the significance is left out of the frame. Why is the subject matter important? Why should we be concerned with finding out the truth that underlies it? The semantic parallel to the "extended situation" is the constitution of a "thematic field."[56]

The form that a subject must take if its importance is to survive the concrete situation and bring later authors (which of course also means texts) back to it, is the "problem." Problems are the organizational element of hypoleptic discourse,[57] and for science they are the equivalent of mythomotor for society in general. They are a source of dynamic disturbance. Whereas the truth has become on the one hand problematic, it is on the other hand, at least in theory, soluble. Mythical discourse is therefore pacified in so far as it is not confronted by any visible contradiction, and all of its statements and images stand on an equal footing beside one another. Canonical discourse is also appeased because it simply does not allow any contradiction. But hypoleptic discourse is riddled with contradictions, and indeed its whole basis is a sharpened perception of contradictions, that is, of criticism that at the same time preserves the positions that it criticizes.

Anyone who is at home in the hypoleptic discipline of scientific or philosophical thought will usually tend to underestimate the tolerance we show toward the contradictions in our everyday lives. Daily life contains far more inconsistencies than our theoretical awareness could

---

[56] See Jürgen Markowitz, *Die soziale Situation* (Frankfurt: Suhrkamp, 1979), 115 f.; Luhmann, *Social Systems*, 148 ff. (see chapt. 7, n. 45).

[57] Luhmann, *Gesellschaftsstruktur und Semantik I*, 47 (see chapt. 7, n. 45), sees in "cognitive inconsistencies and problems, predominantly insoluble problems" an "additional mechanism" that accelerates variations. "The decisive guarantee of an evolution of ideas, as far as probability and tempo are concerned, lies in the fact that knowledge generally can only be systematized and held together with the aid of problems."

ever imagine. This applies in particular to past eras and so-called primitive cultures. Lévi-Strauss coined the term *pensée sauvage* (literally, "wild thought," "the savage mind") for this phenomenon. The process of *bricolage* is a manner of handling tradition that is diametrically opposed to hypoleptic discipline. *Bricolage* means tinkering around with recycled materials that are absorbed through their change of function. Hypolepsis, on the other hand, uses the materials found not in order to change their function but to give them new life within the framework of a shared functional context.

Does Thought Have History? Intellectual History as a Hypoleptic Process

The discipline of referral to existing texts is a precondition for the "evolution of ideas," but as we should emphasize again, this also depends on many other preconditions that are by no means covered by the invention of writing, not even that of alphabetical script. And of course this evolution was not an exclusively Greek achievement – Chinese philosophy flourished after Confucius, thanks to the same principle of hypolepsis. Referral to foundational texts, taking up what has been said by one's predecessors, subjecting them to criteria of relevance and truth or plausibility – these all allow for the kind of progress that Luhmann calls the "evolution of ideas" and that means that thought has a history. A history of ideas can only be written with reference to those cultural spheres in which it has unfolded.[58] That will soon become clear to anyone who tries to extend such a project to cultures that have not formed a hypoleptical structure. In Ancient Egypt, for instance, in just a few areas of tradition, there are the mere beginnings of a hypoleptical form of discourse: this can be seen in the sapiential discourse of the "instructions for life," which clearly – though rarely explicitly – refer to one another,[59] and also in the "theological

---

[58] On the historical dimension of thought and its historiography, see especially R. Rorty, B. Schneewind, and Q. Skinner (eds.), *Philosophy in Context. Essays on the Historiography of Philosophy* (Cambridge: Cambridge University Press, 1984).

[59] See H. Brunner, "Zitate aus Lebenslehren," in E. Hornung and O. Keel (eds.), *Studien zu altägyptischen Lebenslehren*, OBO 28 (Freiburg, Göttingen: Fribourg University Press, 1979), 105–171. In J. Assmann, *Ma'at*, chapter 2 (see chapt. 1, n. 11), I have attempted to reconstruct the (triangular) relationships that constitute a discourse.

discourse" of the hymnal texts of the New Kingdom.[60] In both instances, the historical and social framework for hypolepsis is apparent, but this form of discourse is confined to the school (instructions for living) and the temple (hymns); it is bound to the establishment and continuation of "thematic fields" – that is, to problems whose relevance is deemed to be central: for theological discourse on the problem of the oneness of God,[61] or for ethical discourse on the problem of social order or justice. If we look back over the entirety of Egypt's scribal culture, it is clear that these are tiny islands in the stream of tradition – exceptions that prove the rule. The rule itself was that the scribal culture remained generally embedded in institutions of ritual continuity, whose basic principle was repetition and not disciplined variation.[62]

The most important consequence of these observations is that they offer a satisfactory explanation for what K. Jaspers has made famous under the heading of "Axial Age," which in my view tends to obscure rather than illuminate. "The most extraordinary events," he argues,

are concentrated in this period. Confucius and Lao-tse were living in China and all of the schools of Chinese philosophy came into being, including those of Mo-ti, Chuang-tse, Lieh-tsu, and a host of others; India produced the Upanishads and Buddha and, similar to China, ran the whole gamut of philosophical possibilities down to skepticism, to materialism, sophism, and nihilism; Iran produced Zarathustra who taught a challenging view of the world as a struggle between good and evil; Palestine saw the prophets made their appearance, from Elijah, by way of Isaiah and Jeremiah to Deutero-Isaiah; Greece witnessed the appearance of Homer, of the philosophers – Parmenides, Heraclitus, and Plato – of the tragedians, Thucydides, and Archimedes. Everything implied

---

[60] See J. Assmann, *Re und Amun. Zur Krise des polytheistischen Weltbilds im Ägypten der 18.-20. Dynastie*, OBO 51 (Fribourg: Fribourg University Press, 1983); *Ägypten – Theologie und Frömmigkeit einer frühen Hochkultur* (Stuttgart: Kohlhammer, 1984), 192–285; Engl. *The Search for God in Ancient Egypt*, trans. David Lorton (Ithaca: Cornell University Press, 2001), chapter 9.

[61] See J. Assmann, "Arbeit am Polytheismus. Die Idee der Einheit Gottes und die Entfaltung des theologischen Diskurses in Ägypten," in Stietencron (ed.), *Theologen und Theologien* (see chapt. 5, n. 18), and now J. Assmann, *Moses the Egyptian* (see chapt. 2, n. 63).

[62] Jack Goody, *The Interface between the Written and the Oral* (Cambridge: Cambridge University Press, 1987), 37 ff., tackles the implications of writing in ancient eastern religions

by these names developed during these few centuries almost simultaneously in China, India, and the West, without any one of these regions knowing of the others.[63]

The puzzle of synchronicity swiftly dissolves into an optical illusion if Akhnaton and Muhammad are included in this collection (to which unquestionably they belong). Zoroaster's dates are now also considered to have been much earlier (before 1000 BCE). Thus the period in question expands from the 14th century BCE to the 7th century AD, losing all its significance. The time is obviously irrelevant to the phenomenon. One must simply assume that, given a degree of cultural sophistication, such breakthroughs kept occurring at various intervals. Only within the framework of a written, textual, and interpretive culture could their revolutionary consequences be transmitted and brought to bear. The case of Akhnaton is particularly revealing. His vision of one God was certainly the most radical of all monotheistic revolutions. It found expression in long texts that might well have become canonical if this religion had not remained a mere episode in Egypt's history. But the texts were then completely forgotten until, to the mounting astonishment of Egyptologists, they were rediscovered in the 19th century.

There was no epochal turning point but a cultural transformation that in some cases began earlier than in others, and underwent a certain acceleration during the first millennium BCE. What Jaspers sees as the birth of an intellectual world, taking place almost simultaneously in different places on the Earth that we still inhabit today, can be pinned down much more precisely. There was a transformation from ritual to textual coherence and continuity that happened quite naturally through the spread of literacy, which reached many different, very loosely connected cultures at around the same time – namely during the first millennium BCE. This period witnessed the birth not only of the foundational texts, but also of the cultural institutions that kept the normative and formative impetus of these texts alive

---

[63] Karl Jaspers, *The Origin and Goal of History*, trans. Michael Bullock (New Haven: Yale University Press, 1953), 2. See the critical analysis by A. Assmann, "Jaspers' Achsenzeit, oder Schwierigkeiten mit der Zentralperspektive in der Geschichte," in D. Harth (ed.), *Karl Jaspers. Denken zwischen Wissenschaft, Politik und Philosophie* (Stuttgart: Metzler, 1988), 187–205.

through all the changes in language, social systems, political orders, and other constructs of reality; thus, the framework of conditions was created that made a dialogue with predecessors from thousands of years ago possible. Karl Jaspers remained strangely blind to this institutional and technological framework of intellectual development, having completely ignored the role of writing in his reconstruction. Others like E. A. Havelock, J. Goody, and N. Luhmann, by contrast, tended to overestimate the importance of this role. The decisive factors are the level at which writing was embedded in society, how texts and written semantic formations were dealt with, and the art – with its many preconditions – of referral to foundational texts. It was not a matter of the use of writing, but of cultural mnemotechnics such as canonization and interpretation.

Nothing can demonstrate this more clearly than the fact that the characteristics of Axial Age or simply axial cultures can be lost. We are not dealing here with evolutionary achievements that can never be reversed – as Jaspers puts it (with a hint of Lady Macbeth): "It is done and cannot be undone."[64] It is possible for institutions of interpretation to disappear, for foundational texts to become incomprehensible or to lose their authority, for cultural mnemotechnics to vanish, and for cultures to revert to ritual coherence and continuity at any time.[65] What Jaspers describes is an organizational form of cultural memory that made unusual developments of ideas and also backgrounds for reference possible, whereby the foundational texts of the first millennium BCE are still able to speak to us.

Does thought have a history? The answer is yes, and this history unfolds within the hypoleptic framework of cultural memory. This means that the history of thought cannot be completely grasped if reconstructed solely in terms of evolution and progress. The concept of evolution, that is, of an accumulation by which the old is absorbed in the new, has to be complemented by the concept of memory, through

[64] Karl Jaspers, *Philosophie*, 3 vols. (Berlin, Heidelberg, New York: Springer, 1973), 832, quoted by A. Assmann, "Jaspers' Achsenzeit," 192 (see chapt. 7, n. 63).

[65] In the volume edited by Adam B. Seligmann (ed.), *Order and Transcendence. The Role of Utopias and the Dynamics of Civilizations* (Leiden: E. J. Brill, 1989), the authors speak of "de-axialisation" and "re-axialisation." An increasing number of critics are interpreting our own postmodern age as a "re-oralisation" and a "de-axialisation."

which the old remains present and valid, and progress is matched by recursion and even regression. The hypoleptic constitution of cultural memory implies not only reception and elaboration but also rejection and a return to once abandoned positions.

CULTURAL MEMORY

A Summary

I have now examined various theoretical approaches and historical examples in this quest to understand the changes that have taken place within the connective structure of societies by way of cultural memory. To sum up what I have found, it might be useful briefly to take a last look at these examples.

Late Period Egypt was a special case in the process of canonization, because it did not lead to a textual canon. The final form of this process was to be seen in the temples of the Greco-Roman period, which were much more than mere buildings. The temple gave solid form to a highly complex and strictly canonical groundplan, its walls were covered with writing, and it housed not only the rituals on which the Egyptians believed the life of society and the cosmos depended – as well as the connective structure of Ancient Egyptian culture, if my thesis is correct – but also a way of life whose strict adherence to the rules already showed all the features of what Max Weber called *methodische Lebensführung* [methodical lifestyle]. Plato had already read the temple as a canonical codification of Egypt's cultural grammar, which definitively laid down once and for all the rules of conduct and of art. The Egyptian view of the temple emphasizes two typical themes of the canon: revelation and closure. The groundplan and décor follow the instructions of a book that fell from Heaven, and nothing could be added to or subtracted from these.

If one takes a look at the historical conditions that framed this development, the striking element is that of foreign rule. The break with tradition on this political level led inevitably to a thorough reorganization of the cultural memory. According to the classic Egyptian view, the state was a salvational institution that kept the world going and guaranteed life after death to the individual by establishing Ma'at (order, truth, and justice) on earth. This idea of a beneficent continuation of life was now transferred exclusively to the temples. Although there was also a certain amount of literature available in order to retain the knowledge necessary for the rituals, the rituals themselves were still at the heart of Late Egyptian culture. What was brought to life in the temples bore the hallmark of contrapresent memory. This included the concept of a golden primal age in which the Ma'at still ruled over the Earth, thorns did not prick, and walls did not fall down. This age was now irrevocably past, but it could still be recalled by worshipping the dead gods who had lived in it, and by reviving Ma'at – who no longer lived on the Earth – through sacred rites.

By contrast, we can learn from Israel what a textual canon is, and how this exclusively linguistic narrowing down, codification, and canonization actually came about. There was a break in tradition on a political level here, initially in the comparatively mild form of vassaldom, then in the more extreme form of deportation. In the world of that time, deportation meant the end of collective identity. With the loss of home (*Heimat*), all the necessary frameworks of collective memory collapsed, the connective structure of culture fell apart, and the deported people dispersed in their new environment without a trace. This was the fate of the Israelite tribes of the northern kingdom, who were crushed by the Assyrians in 722 BCE. It appears that Jerusalem learned a lesson from this disaster. In 587 BC, when the deportees from Judah, the southern kingdom, went into exile, they may have done so accompanied by the Book of Deuteronomy (at least in its primal form), which laid the foundations for cultural mnemotechnics and contrapresent memory, dramatizing the dangers of forgetting through a change of circumstances, and teaching them to think beyond the borders of the land they were in. By warning the people of Jerusalem not to forget the Exodus from Egypt, this book provided hope for those in Babylon that they would return once more to Jerusalem. Contrapresent memory relativized their current place of abode by giving reality to another. We have steered clear of the debate between Old Testament scholars over the age of Deuteronomy and the historicity of Josiah's reforms, and have focused instead on the relationship between canon and exile, since each conditioned and reinforced the other. Without the canon, no matter what form it was in at the time, the exiles would not have survived without losing their identity, but had they not been in exile, the traditions they took with them would not have been retained in such a way that they became the Torah, which lay at the very heart of what later became the Hebrew canon. In Israel, history had to be remembered with all of one's heart and in all of one's actions in order to avoid a return to Egypt. But in Babylon it had to be remembered in order one day to be able to return to Israel.

This structure of reciprocal conditioning and reinforcing applies equally to the other paradigmatic factor of Israel's history, which is the formation of internal conflicts. Viewed from the internal perspective of the Bible, the canon precedes all these conflicts and brings them to the surface by confronting the people with a decision whether to adhere to its commandments (and promises) or give in to external pressure. Viewed from the external perspective of historical reconstruction, the situation is reversed: it is the endless sequence of internal secessions, oppositions, tensions, and schisms that demands an ever more precise explanation of cultural meaning, leading ultimately to a word-for-word freezing or fencing-in of tradition, and the three-story edifice of the canon.

To the two canonical motifs that we have already observed in Egypt – revelation and closure – we can now add a third: interpretation. Interpretation is an indispensable accompaniment to the cultural transformation that we have described as the transition from ritual to textual coherence. When the whole weight of cultural continuity is thrown onto foundational texts, everything depends on keeping those texts alive by bridging the ever widening gap between them and the changing reality of life. Initially, this happens within the text, through rewriting or continuation, or editorial adaptation to changing circumstances of comprehension. Then, when the text has been canonized – that is, irrevocably fixed in its wording and its volume – this bridge can only be built through a metatext: the commentary. We need to bear in mind that what to us is the familiar process of reading and comprehension represented a later stage in the history of reading. In Antiquity, the normal mode of reading was either memorizing, through which the reader internalized the text, or *hodegetic* reading, in which there was a dialogue with a teacher (*hodegetes*), who clarified the meaning. When Philip asks, "Understandest thou what thou readest?" the Ethiopian eunuch replies, "How can I, except some man should guide (*hodegesei*) me?" (Acts 8, 27 ff.) The consequence of this is that the guidance becomes as sacred as the text itself, and so there are genealogical chains of interpreters running, as it were, parallel to the text whose meaning they interpret. This is the basis of the rabbinical concept of the "oral Torah" and the Catholic concept of tradition.

The obligation to remember the text accompanies its canonization. Cultural mnemotechnics then became the basis of religion, and the ritual of sacrifice gave way to serving God's holy word. The imperative "Remember!" referred to two equally binding obligations: the laws set down by the covenant, which must be obeyed in all details and under all circumstances, and history, which delivered and justified these laws. It was through history that they acquired their true meaning. Only someone who remembered the Exodus from Egypt knew that the law meant freedom and was able to follow it. This was a completely new connection with the past. Of course, all communities lived under the spell of some kind of foundational story, which gave order and direction to their conduct. This was the principle we referred to as mythomotor. Such stories shed light on the present, and a shard also falls on the future to guide people's actions and expectations. But the story that had to be remembered in Israel was a myth of a completely new type. It had a fixed position in time, and it continued on into the present. These were events that not only formed the basis of present happenings – which is true of all myths – but that also told a story to which the present actually belonged. This marked it apart from the myths of the Middle Eastern, Egyptian, or Greek gods. How, then, did the new form of memory, past connection, and mythomotor come about?

This was the question that occasioned our digression into the world of cuneiform script. Our argument was that this concept of history and memory was derived from the sphere of the law, and together with the political and legal model of Israel's covenant with God, it developed into the form of historiography that we find in Deuteronomy and the deuteronomic tradition. History in this sense is a form of collective self-examination. It has the character of a confession. It recapitulates the failings of the people, in order that the difficulties of the present should not make them lose sight of the meanings of history. The point of disaster is punishment. The more catastrophic and impenetrable the present is, the more salvational is the memory of the history whose logic brings light to the darkness. This model, which attributes present misery to the intervention of an angry god, first occurs in Mesopotamian sources. Through the legal mode of the oath, gods are made the guardians of human affairs, that is human history. If a political oath is broken, like a treaty with another people, disaster may strike the whole country. This is the context that led to what we have called the "semioticization of history." When the gods are summoned as witnesses to and guardians of legal bonds and obligations, they become the instruments of justice. Man is then responsible to them. Therefore good or bad fortune can be interpreted within the framework of this relationship, which makes it into a sign of divine favor or punishment. History, then, is filled with meaning, but this is not the mythical, primal history whose basic patterns have shaped the world order; this is the history of everyday events taking place in linear time, in which everything depends on not forgetting the obligations entered into in the past. On the basis of this legalization of connective structures, meaning can be understood in terms of action and consequence.

Next we considered a group of Hittite texts from the 13th century BCE, in order to illustrate the forms of historical recapitulation that developed out of this semioticization of history. The main argument here was that remembrance of the past did not arise out of any universal sense of history (which would not have required any explanation), but was basically improbable and so needed to be explained according to whatever motives pertained under the circumstances. The past is only remembered to the degree in which it is needed, and can be filled with meaning and importance (i.e., semioticized). We singled out the concept of connective justice – the link between action and consequence – as a vital factor in such meaning.

The key term "justice" brings us directly to the theme of writing. Justice is the central element of the ancient eastern and Egyptian scribal culture, and it figures prominently in Egyptian and Mesopotamian literary "wisdom literature" as well as in Mesopotamian law books. Wisdom and law went together, and their point of convergence was in the tradition of writing. It would certainly not be wrong to link the concept of connective justice with the literate officials and sages of the houses of tablets (Babylon) and the houses of life (Egypt) as its carrier group. The same also applies, even more emphatically, to the Book of Deuteronomy. We discussed this book, paying particular attention to the themes of memory culture and political imagination: we saw it as the foundation of cultural mnemotechnics and contrapresent memory, and as the manifesto of a movement of national awakening after centuries of Assyrian oppression. We could also, with equal justification, have seen it as a landmark or turning point in the history of the media. Deuteronomy, as scholars have long since agreed, emerged from the circles of the wise scribes (*sôferîm hakhamîm*), who also had the task in Israel of passing down traditions, the ideology of connective justice, and insight into the connection between action and consequence that was synonymous with justice. Deuteronomy is in fact a book of law and wisdom, and as such it is the product of an advanced written culture.[66] Here, for the first time, customs and conventions, cult and ritual, oral tradition and implicit knowledge were set down definitively in the columns of a scroll. This linked the hope and aspiration to make Israel into a single "wise and understanding people" (Deut. 4, 6) with the idea of an education underpinned by the written word, which could fix the connective structure of society by giving it textual coherence and continuity. Through Deuteronomy, the scribes and the sages – precursors of the scholars of writing (*grammateîs*) in the New Testament – emerged as the representatives of Israel. These were the people whom Jeremiah had in mind when he said:

How do ye say, We are wise (*hakhamîm*), and the law of the Lord is with us? Lo, certainly in vain made he it; the pen of the scribes is in vain (Jer. 8, 8).[67]

Here, Jeremiah criticizes the naïve equation of text with meaning – the idea that one is in possession of wisdom and justice simply because one has put them in book form. This criticism does not really concern Deuteronomy, because internalizing, taking to heart and soul, is the true aim of the mnemotechnics prescribed here; he attacks instead the

---

[66] On the anchorage of Deuteronomy in the tradition of the copyists, see Weinfeld, *Deuteronomy*, 158 ff. (see chapt. 5, n. 5).

[67] Concerning this and the identification of the "Lord's Torah" with Deuteronomy, see Fishbane, *Biblical Interpretation*, 34 (with additional literature) (see chapt. 2, n. 11), see now also Karel van der Toorn, *Scribal Culture and the Making of the Hebrew Bible* (Cambridge, MA: Harvard University Press, 2007), 222, who interprets this oracle as a refusal to recognize any written text as the "Lord's Torah."

typical side effects of scribal scholarship, which in the context of a high-profile "literocracy" must have led to a great deal of tension. The same constellation of scribal scholarship, ethnic identity, historiographical memory work, and cultic reform is repeated again and again under "Ezra the Scribe" and in Greco-Roman times.

I have gone into a little more detail here about the relevance of written culture to this development, because I did not deal with it in the chapter on Israel, where my focus was on the connection between memory and identity. For the particular phenomenology of changes brought about by written culture, I used the example of Greece.

In Greece we find exactly the same constellation as in Israel and – *mutatis mutandis* – in Egypt: the formation of a national (Panhellenic) identity against the background of the Persian Wars, the birth of historiography as a result of changes in memory culture, political reform, and a comprehensive transposal of the connective structure into written form. Historiography in Greece did not have the moral and confessional character of collective self-examination that we observed in Mesopotamia or, especially, in Israel, and the subject of guilt did not play a central role in the formation of meaning. But guilt was far from being absent. Elements of connective justice, and hence of ancient eastern wisdom, are to be found throughout Herodotus. The ethnographic breadth of his vision, however, took him far beyond the eastern framework of "History as National Tradition" (van Seters 1989).

With the example of Greece, my aim was to show two specific developments of written culture that continue even today to define the connective structure of our own western cultural memory. I subsumed these under the headings of classics and hypolepsis. This brings us back to the concept of the extended situation with which we began. These two institutional frameworks help to construct a situation – an intertextual framework of references that we ourselves still occupy. Greece presents us with a unique instance of foundational texts that gradually formed a written culture. Undoubtedly the new medium of a vocalized alphabetical script played a substantial part in this, as it was easier to handle than other writing systems when it came to recording complex oral traditions. However, it is my view that Havelock greatly exaggerated its importance, just as he underestimated the recording capacity of eastern writing systems. Here, too, we should replace the monocausal model of explanation with a circular structure, or "reflexive loop." The script came together with a number of other factors in a process of reciprocal conditioning and reinforcing. These factors included on the one hand the pluralistic and multicentered composition of the political structure, and on the other, the agonistic, competitive basis of a loose society along with the tensions and ruptures that inevitably accompanied its transition into the tight society of the Polis. Homer's own codified memory of the Late Bronze Age Mycenaean way of life was already a bridge across a broken tradition, and, at the same time, it was foundational and contrapresent. To an even greater extent, this also applies to the memory that linked up with Homer's texts in the sense of a *traditum*. Holding onto Homer as a foundation even in the age of the Polis meant living in two times and two worlds at once. Thus Greece experienced a form of "living in quotations" (Thomas Mann), and gradually this developed into an interpretive culture like that of Israel.

As writing progressed, a project developed that gave itself the name philosophy, and this gave rise to a completely different form of intertextuality. What flourished here was the dynamic force inherent in writing itself – a force that was described strikingly by an Egyptian writer during the second half of the first millennium. Unlike the oral copyist, the writing author has to justify his work in the forum of existing texts, and give himself legitimacy by introducing something new and original of his own. Within Egyptian tradition, Khakheperre-sonb appears as an isolated precursor of this:

O that I had unknown sentences, strange sayings, New speech, that had never been heard before.

In Greece this problem led to critical intertextuality in the form of examining existing texts – an approach that established its own framework of cultural memory as scholarship or science. There was nothing similar in Egypt, Mesopotamia, or Israel; China and India, however, came up with a similar discipline. That is why I do not agree with Havelock and Goody, who regard this development as a consequence of the alphabetical writing culture. Clearly, it could not have happened without the use of writing, but that need not be alphabetical. The consequences of written culture were innumerable, and they followed different courses in different societies. However, in all cases the actual structure of the writing system – ideographic or phonographic, alphabetical or syllabic, with or without vowels – played a subordinate role. What was decisive was the interplay of various other factors (social, political, economic, and so on) that formed different configurations according to the individual cultures and periods. Within the framework of a theory of cultural memory, we have tried to bring together four concepts – tradition, the past, written culture, and identity – in order to stake out the parameters and the nature of those configurations.

References

Abadal i de Vinyals, Ramond d' (1958), "A propos du Legs Visigothique en Espagne," *Settimane di Studio del Centro Italiano di Studi sull' Alt, Medioevo 2*, 541–585.

Aland, K. (1970), "Das Problem des neutestamentlichen Kanons," in: E. Käsemann (ed.), *Das Neue Testament als Kanon* (Göttingen: Vandenhoeck & Ruprecht).

Albert, H. (1990), "Methodologischer Individualismus und historische Analyse," in: K. Acham, W. Schulze (eds.), *Teil und Ganzes (Theorie der Geschichte, Beiträge zur Historik 6)* (Munich: Deutscher Taschenbuchverlag), 219–239.

Albrektson, B. (1967), *History and the Gods. An Essay on the Idea of Historical Events as Divine Manifestations in the Ancient Near East and in Israel* (Lund: Gleerup).

Alliot, M. (1949), *Le culte d'Horus Edfou au temps des Ptolemées* (Beyrouth: Libraire du Liban, 1979).

Andersen, O. (1987), "Mündlichkeit und Schriftlichkeit im frühen Griechentum," *Antike und Abendland 33*, 29–44.

Anderson, B. (1983), *Imagined Communities: Reflections on the Origin and Spread of Nationalism* (London: Verso).

Anthes, P., Pahnke, D. (eds.) (1989), *Die Religion von Oberschichten* (Marburg: Diagonal).

Appadurai, A. (ed.) (1986), *The Social Life of Things. Commodities in Cultural Perspective* (Cambridge: Cambridge University Press).

Aristeas to Philocrates (Letter of Aristeas), ed. and trans. by Moses Hadas (New York: KTAV Publishing House, 1973).

Artzi, P. (1969), "The birth of the Middle East," in *Proceedings of the 5th World Congress of Jewish Studies*, Jerusalem, 120–124.

Armstrong J. (1983), *Nations before Nationalism* (Chapel Hill: North Carolina University Press).

Artzi, P. (1984), "Ideas and Practices of International Co-existence in the 3rd mill. BCE," *Bar Ilan Studies, History* 2, 25–39.

Assmann, A. (1986), "Opting In und Opting Out," in H. U. Gumbrecht, K. L. Pfeiffer (eds.), *Stil. Geschichten und Funktionen eines kulturwissenschaftlichen Diskurselements* (Frankfurt: Suhrkamp), 127–143.

Assmann, A. (1988) "Jaspers' Achsenzeit, oder Schwierigkeiten mit der Zentralperspektive in der Geschichte," in D. Harth (ed.), *Karl Jaspers. Denken zwischen Wissenschaft, Politik und Philosophie* (Stuttgart: Kohlhammer), 187–205.

Assmann, A. (1989), "Fiktion als Differenz," *Poetica* 21, 239–260.

Assmann, A. (1991), "Was ist Weisheit: Wegmarken in einem weiten Feld," in A. Assmann, D. Harth (eds.), *Weisheit. Archäologie der Literarischen Kommunikation III* (Munich: Fink), 15–44.

Assmann, A. (ed.) (1991), *Weisheit. Archäologie der Literarischen Kommunikation III* (Munich: Fink).

Assmann, A. (1991a), "Zur Metaphorik der Erinnerung," in A. Assmann, D. Harth (eds.), *Weisheit. Archäologie der Literarischen Kommunikation III* (Munich: Fink), 13–35.

Assmann, A. (1991b), "Kultur als Lebenswelt und Monument," in A. Assmann, D. Harth (eds.) *Weisheit. Archäologie der Literarischen Kommunikation III* (Munich: Fink), 11–25.

Assmann, A. (1999), *Erinnerungsräume. Formen und Wandlungen des kulturellen Gedächtnisses* (Munich: Beck).

Assmann, A. (2006), "Memory, Individual and Collective," in R. E. Goodin, C. Tilly (eds.), *The Oxford Handbook of Contextual Political Analysis* (Oxford: Oxford University Press), 2006, 210–224.

Assmann, A., Assmann, J. (eds.) (1987), *Kanon und Zensur* (Munich: Fink).

Assmann, A., Assmann, J. (1988), "Schrift, Tradition und Kultur," in W. Raible (ed.), *Zwischen Festtag und Alltag* (Tübingen: Narr), 25–50.

Assmann, A., Assmann, J. (1990), "Kultur und Konflikt. Aspekte einer Theorie des unkommunikativen Handelns," in J. Assmann, D. Harth (eds.), *Kultur und Konflikt* (Frankfurt: Suhrkamp), 11–48.

Assmann, A., Assmann, J. (1991), "Das Gestern im Heute. Medien des sozialen Gedächtnisses," *Studienbegleitbrief zur Studieneinheit 11 des Funkkollegs Medien und Kommunikation* (Weinheim).

Assmann, A., Harth, D. (eds.) (1991), *Mnemosyne* (Frankfurt: Suhrkamp).

Assmann, J. (1975), *Zeit und Ewigkeit im Alten Ägypten* (Heidelberg: Winter).

Assmann, J. (1977), "Die Verborgenheit des Mythos in Ägypten," in *Göttinger Miszellen* 25, 1-25.

Assmann, J. (1983), "Das Doppelgesicht der Zeit im altägyptischen Denken," in A. Peisl, A. Mohler (eds.), *Die Zeit* (Munich: Fink), 189–223.

Assmann, J. (1983a), *Re und Amun. Zur Krise des polytheistischen Weltbilds im Ägypten der 18.-20. Dynastie, OBO 51*; English version: *Egyptian Solar Religion in the New Kingdom*, trans. A. Alcock (London: Kegan Paul International, 1995).

Assmann, J. (1983b), "Tod und Initiation im altägyptischen Totenglauben," in H. P. Duerr (ed.), *Sehnsucht nach dem Ursprung. Zu Mircea Eliade* (Frankfurt: Syndikat), 336–359; English version: "Death and initiation in the funerary religion of ancient Egypt," in W. K. Simpson (ed.), *Religion and Philosophy in Ancient Egypt, YES 3,* 1989, 135–159.

Assmann, J. (1984), *Ägypten - Theologie und Frömmigkeit einer frühen Hochkultur* (Stuttgart: Kohlhammer); English version: *The Search of God in Ancient Egypt,* trans. D. Lorton (Ithaca: Cornell University Press, 1991).

Assmann, J. (1985), "Die Entdeckung der Vergangenheit. Innovation und Restauration in der ägyptischen Literaturgeschichte," in H. U. Gumbrecht, U. Link-Heer (eds.), *Epochenschwellen und Epochenstrukturen im Diskurs der Literatur- und Sprachhistorie,* (Frankfurt: Suhrkamp), 484–499.

Assmann, J. (1986), "Viel Stil am Nil? Ägypten und das Problem des Kulturstils," in H. U. Gumbrecht, K. L. Pfeiffer (eds.), *Stil. Geschichten und Funktionen eines kulturwissenschaftlichen Diskurselements* (Frankfurt: Suhrkamp), 522–524.

Assmann, J. (1986a), "Arbeit am Polytheismus. Die Idee der Einheit Gottes und die Entfaltung des theologischen Diskurses in Ägypten," in H. v. Stietencron, *Theologen und Theologien in verschiedenen Kulturkreise* (Düsseldorf: Patmos), 46–69.

Assmann, J. (1987), "Sepulkrale Selbstthematisierung im Alten Ägypten," in A. Hahn, V. Kapp (eds.), *Selbstthematisierung und Selbstzeugnis: Bekenntnis und Geständnis* (Frankfurt: Suhrkamp), 208–232.

Assmann, J. (1988), "Stein und Zeit. Das monumentale Gedächtnis des alten Ägypten," in Assmann, J., Hölscher, T. (eds.), *Kultur und Gedächtnis* (Frankfurt: Suhrkamp), 87–114.

Assmann, J. (1988a), "Kollektives Gedächtnis und kulturelle Identität," in J. Assmann, T. Hölscher (eds.), *Kultur und Gedächtnis* (Frankfurt: Suhrkamp), 9–19.

Assmann, J. (1989), "State and Religion in the New Kingdom," in W. K. Simpson (ed.), *Religion and Philosophy in Ancient Egypt* (New Haven: Yale Egyptological Seminar), 55–88.

Assmann, J. (1990), *Maat: Gerechtigkeit und Unsterblichkeit im alten Ägypten* (Munich: Fink).

Assmann, J. (1990a), "Der leidende Gerechte im alten Ägypten. Zum Konfliktpotential derägyptischen Religion," in C. Elsas, H. G. Kippenberg (eds.), *Loyalitätskonflikte in der Religionsgeschichte* (Würzburg: Königshausen and Neumann), 203–224.

Assmann, J. (1990b), "Die Macht der Bilder. Rahmenbedingungen ikonischen Handelns im alten Ägypten," *Vivible Religion VII,* 1–20.

Assmann, J. (1991), "Gebrauch und Gedächtnis. Die zwei Kulturen des pharaonischen Agypten," in D. Harth, A. Assmann (eds.), *Kultur als Lebenswelt und Monument* (Frankfurt: S. Fischer), 135–152.

Assmann, J. (1991a), "Der zweidimensionale Mensch. Das Fest als Medium des kulturellen Gedächtnisses," in J. Assmann, T. Sundermeier (eds.), *Das*

Fest und das Heilige. Religiöse Kontrapunkte des Alltags, Studien zum Verstehen fremder Religionen 1 (Gütersloh: Mohn), 13–30.

Assmann, J. (1991b), "Das altägyptische Prozessionsfest," in J. Assmann, T. Sundermeier (eds.), *Das Fest und das Heilige. Religiöse Kontrapunkte des Alltags, Studien zum Verstehenfremder Religionen 1* (Gütersloh: Mohn).

Assmann, J. (1997), *Moses the Egyptian. The Memory of Egypt in Western Monotheism* (Cambridge, MA: Harvard University Press).

Assmann, J. (2002), *The Mind of Egypt. History and Meaning in the Time of the Pharaohs*, trans. Andrew Jenkins (New York: Metropolitan Books; Cambridge: Harvard University Press).

Assmann, J. (2005), *Death and Salvation in Ancient Egypt*, trans. D. Lorton (Ithaca: Cornell University Press).

Assmann, J. (2010), *The Price of Monotheism* (Stanford: Stanford University Press).

Assmann, J., Hölscher, T. (eds.) (1988), *Kultur und Gedächtnis* (Frankfurt: Suhrkamp).

Baczko, B. (1984), *Les imaginaires sociaux, mémoires et espoirs collectifs* (Paris: Payot).

Balandier, G. (1988), *Le désordre. Éloge du mouvement* (Paris: Fayard).

Baltzer, K. (1964), *Das Bundesformular*, 2. ed. (Neukirchen: Neukirchner).

Barrow, R. (1976), *Greek and Roman Education* (London: Macmillan).

Bartlett, F. C. (1923), *Psychology and Primitive Culture* (Cambridge: Cambridge University Press).

Bartlett, F. C. (1932), *Remembering: a Study in Experimental Social Psychology* (Cambridge: Cambridge University Press).

Basset, J. C. et al. (ed.) (1988), *La mémoire des religions* (Geneva: Labor et Fides).

Bauer, W. (ed.) (1980), *China und die Fremden. 3000 Jahre Auseinandersetzung in Krieg und Frieden* (Munich: C. H. Beck).

Baumann, G. (ed.) (1986), *The Written Word* (Oxford: Oxford University Press).

Beauchard, J. (ed.) (1979), *Identités collectives et travail social* (Strasbourg, Toulouse).

Beck, F. A. G. (1964), *Greek Education 450–350 B.C.* (London: Methuen and Co.).

Berger, P. L., Luckmann, Th. (1966), *The Social Construction of Reality: A Treatise in the Sociology of Knowledge* (Garden City, NY: Anchor Books).

Bergson, H. (1896), *Matière et mémoire* (Paris: Alcan).

Berry, J. W. (1977), "Nomadic Style and Cognitive Style," in H. M. McGurk (ed.), *Ecological Factors in Human Development* (Amsterdam, New York, Oxford: North Holland), 228–245.

Bertrand, P. (1975), *L'oubli, révolution ou mort de l'histoire* (Paris: PUF).

Bethge, H. G. (1975), "Vom Ursprung der Welt: die fünfte Schrift aus Nag Hammadi CodexII" (Diss. Berlin <Ost>).

Bien, G. (1969), "Hypolepsis," in J. Ritter (ed.), *Historisches Wörterbuch der Philosophie 4* (Basel: Schwabe), 1252–1254.

Biesterfeldt, H. H. (1991), "Ibn Haldun: Erinnerung, historische Reflexion und die Idee der Solidarität," in A. Assmann, D. Harth (eds.), *Weisheit. Archäologie der Literarischen Kommunikation III* (Munich: Fink), 277–288.

Bleicken, J. (1985), *Die athenische Demokratie* (Paderborn: Schöningh).

Blenkinsopp, J. (1977), *Prophecy and Canon* (Notre Dame, IN: University of Notre Dame Press).

Bloch, M. (1925), "Mémoire collective, tradition et coutume," in *Revue de Synthèse Historique*, 73–83.

Blum, H. (1969), "Die antike Mnemotechnik" (Diss. 1964, Spudasmata 15).

Bolkestein, H. (1939), *Wohltätigkeit und Armenpflege im vorchristlichen Altertum* (Utrecht: A. Oosthoek).

Borchardt, R. (1973), "Die Tonscherbe," in *Prosa IV* (Stuttgart: Klett-Cotta).

Borgeaud, Ph. (1988), "Pour une approche anthropologique de la mémoire religieuse," in Basset, J. C. et al. (ed.), *La mémoire des religions* (Geneva: Labor et Fides), 7–20.

Boring, T. A. (1979), *Literacy in Ancient Sparta* (Leiden).

Bornkamm, G. (1964), "Lobpreis, Bekenntnis und Opfer," in *Apophoreta*, Berlin, 30, 46–63.

Bottéro, J. (1974), "Symptômes, signes, écritures en Mésopotamie ancienne," in Vernant, J. P. (ed.), *Divination et rationalité* (Paris: Éditions du Seuil), 70–197.

Bottéro, J. (1987), *Mésopotamie. L'écriture, la raison et les dieux* (Paris: Gallimard).

Bourdieu, Pierre (1979), *La distinction. Critique social du jugement* (Paris: Editions de Minuit);. Engl. version: *Distinction: a social critique of the judgement of taste*, trans. Richard Nice, (London: Routledge & Kegan Paul, 1986).

Boylan, P. (1922), *Thoth, the Hermes of Egypt* (London: Oxford University).

Brandon, Samuel G. F. (1967), *The Judgment of the Dead* (New York: Weidenfeld & Nicolson).

Bremmer, J. (1982), "Literacy and the Origins and Limitations of Greek Atheism," in J. den Boeft, A. H. M. Kessels (eds.), *Actus. Studies in Honour of H. L. W. Nelson* (Utrecht: Instituut voor Klassieke Talen), 43–55.

Brunner, H. (1970), "Zum Verständnis der archaisierenden Tendenzen der ägyptischen Spätzeit," in *Saeculum* 21, 150–161.

Brunner, H. (1983), "Seth und Apophis - Gegengötter im ägyptischen Pantheon?," *Saeculum* 34, 226–234.

Brunner, H. (1979), "Zitate aus Lebenslehren," in E. Hornung, O. Keel (eds.), *Studien zu altägyptischen Lebenslehren, OBO 28* (Freiburg, Göttingen: Fribourg University Press), 105–171.

Bubner, R. (1984), *Geschichtsprozesse und Handlungsnormen* (Frankfurt: Suhrkamp).

Burckhardt, J. (1984), *Die Kunst der Betrachtung. Aufsätze und Vorträge zur bildenden Kunst*, ed. Henning Ritter (Cologne: Dumont).

Burke, P. (1991), "Geschichte als soziales Gedächtnis," in A. Assmann, D. Harth (eds.), *Weisheit. Archäologie der Literarischen Kommunikation III* (Munich: Fink), 289–304.

Burkert, W. (1984), *Die orientalisierende Epoche in der griechischen Religion und Literatur* (Heidelberg: Winter).

Burns, A. (1981), "Athenian Literacy in the Fifth Century B.C.," *Journal of the History of Ideas* 42, 371–387.

Calvet, J.-L. (1984), *La tradition orale* (Paris: Presses universitaires de France).

Cancik, H. (1970), "Mythische und historische Wahrheit," *Stuttgarter Bibelstudien* 48.

Cancik, H. (1976), *Grundzüge der hethitischen und alttestamentlichen Geschichtsschreibung* (Wiesbaden: Harrassowitz).

Cancik, H. (1985/6), "Rome as a Sacred Landscape. Varro and the End of Republican Religion in Rome," in *Visible Religion*, 4/5, 250–265.

Cancik, H. (1986), "Geschichtsschreibung und Priestertum. Zum Vergleich von orientalischer und hellenischer Historiographie bei Flavius Josephus, contra Apionem, Buch I," in E. L. Ehrlich, B. Klappert, U. Ast (eds.), *Wie gut sind deine Zelte, Jaakow ... , Festschrift zum 60.Geburtstag von Reinhold Mayer* (Gerlingen: Bleicher), 41–62.

Cancik, H. (1990), "Grösse und Kolossalität als religiöse und ästhetische Kategorien. Versuch einer Begriffsbestimmung am Beispiel von Statius, Silve I 1: Ecus Maximus Domitiani Imperatoris," in *Visible Religion VII, Genres in Visual Representations* (Leiden: E. J. Brill), 51–68.

Cancik-Lindemeier, H., Cancik, H. (1987) "Zensur und Gedächtnis. Zu Tac. Ann. IV 32–38," in A. Assmann, J. Assmann (eds.), *Kanon und Zensur* (Munich: Fink). 169–189.

Cancik, H., Mohr, H. (1990), "Erinnerung/Gedächtnis," in *Handbuch religion swissenschaftlicher Grundbegriffe 2* (Stuttgart: Kohlhammer), 299–323.

Canfora, L., Liverani, M., Zaccagnini, C. (eds.) (1990), I Trattati nel Mondo Antico. Forma, Ideologia (Rome: Funzione).

Cassirer, E. (1923), *Philosophie der symbolischen Formen II. Das mythische Denken* (Darmstadt: Wissenschaftliche Buchgesellschft, 1958).

Castroriadis, C. (1975), "Temps identitaire et temps imaginaire: L'institution sociale du Temps," in C. Castroriadis, *L'institution imaginaire de la société* (Paris: Seuil).

Chatwin, Bruce. *The Songlines* (London), 1988.

Childs, B. S. (1962), *Memory and Tradition in Israel* (Naperville, IL: A.R. Allenson).

Cicero (2002), *On the Ideal Orator I*, trans. with introduction by James M. May and Jakob Wisse, (Oxford: Oxford University Press), 219.

Classen, P. (ed.) (1977), *Recht und Schrift im Mittelalter* (Sigmaringen: Thorbecke).

Claus, David B. (1981), Toward the Soul: An Inquiry into the Meaning of Soul before Plato (New Haven:Yale University Press).

Colpe, C. (1986), "Die Ausbildung des Heidenbegriffs von Israel zur Apologetik und das Zweideutigwerden des Christentums," in Faber, Schlesier (eds.), Restauration der Götter (Würzburg: Königshausen und Neumann), 61–87.

Colpe, C. (1987), "Sakralisierung von Texten und Filiationen von Kanons," in A. Assmann, J. Assmann (eds.), *Kanon und Zensur* (Munich: Fink). 80–92.

Colpe, C. (1988), "Heilige Schriften," in *Reallexikon für Antike und Christentum* *Lieferung* 112, 184–223.

Conrad, D. (1987), "Zum Normcharakter von 'Kanon' in rechtswissenschaftlicher Perspektive," in A. Assmann, J. Assmann (eds.), *Kanon und Zensur* (Munich: Fink), 46–61.

Crüsemann, F. (1987), "Das 'portative Vaterland'. Struktur und Genese des alttestamentlichen Kanons," in A. Assmann, J. Assmann (eds.), *Kanon und Zensur* (Munich: Fink), 63–79.

Davis, N. Z., Starn, R. (1989), "Memory and Counter-Memory," Special Issue, *Representations* 26.

Davis, W. M. (1982a), "Canonical representation in Egyptian Art," *Res 4: Anthropology and Aesthetics,* 20–46.

Davis, W. M. (1982b), "The Canonical Theory of Composition in Egyptian Art," *Göttinger Miszellen* 56, 9–26.

Davis, W. M. (1989), *The Canonical Tradition in Egyptian Art* (Cambridge: Cambridge University Press).

Deiber, A. (1904), "Clément d'Alexandrie et l'Égypte," *Mém. IFAO* 10 (Kairo).

Delling, G. (1987), *Die Bewältigung der Diasporasituation durch das hellenistische Judentum* (Göttingen: Vandenhoeck & Ruprecht).

Dentan, R. C. (ed.) (1955), The Idea of History in the Ancient Near East (New Haven: Yale University Press).

Derrida, J. (1967), *L'écriture et la différence* (Paris: Éditions du Seuil).

Derrida, J. (1974), *De la grammatologie* (Paris: Éditions de Minuit).

Détienne, M. (ed.) (1988), *Les savoirs de l'écriture. En Grèce ancienne* (Lille: Presses universitaires de Lille).

Diamond, St. (1971), "The rule of law versus the order of custom," in R. P. Wolf (ed.), *The Rule of Law* (New York: Simon and Schuster).

Diebner, B. J. (1991), "Gottes Welt, Moses Zelt und das Salomonische Heiligtum," in T. Römer (ed.), *Lectio Difficilior Probabilior? Mélanges offerts à Françoise Smyth-Florentin, Dielheimer Blätter zum Alten Testament und seiner Rezeption in der Alten Kirche,* Beiheft 12, Heidelberg, 127–154.

Diels, H., Kranz, W. *Die Fragmente der Vorsokratiker.* 2 vols. Hildesheim: Weidmann, 1951–1952, fragment B10.

Dihle, A. (1962), *Die Goldene Regel* (Göttingen: Vandenhoeck und Ruprecht).

Diringer, D. (1962), *Writing* (London, New York: Praege).

Diringer, D. (1968), *The Alphabet. A key to the history of mankind* (New York: Funk & Wagnalls).

Donald, Merlin (1991), *Origins of the Modern Mind. Three Stages in the Evolution of Culture and Cognition* (Cambridge, MA: Harvard University Press), 308–315.

Douglas, M. (1966), *Purity and Danger* (London: Routledge and Kegan Paul).

Douglas, M. (1970), *Natural Symbols: Explorations in Cosmology* (London: Barrie & Rockliff the Cresset Press).

Douglas, M. (1975), *Implicit Meanings. Essays in Anthropology* (London: Routledge and Kegan Paul).

Douglas, M. (1999), *Leviticus as Literature* (Oxford: Oxford University Press).

Douglas, M. (2001), *In the Wilderness: The Doctrine of Defilement in the Book of Numbers* (Oxford: Oxford University Press).

Droysen, J. G. (1972), *Vorlesungen zur Enzyklopädie und Methodologie der Geschichte*, R. Hübner (ed.) (Darmstadt: Wissenschaftliche Buchgesellschaft) (First print 1857).

Ehlich, K. (1983), "Text und sprachliches Handeln. Die Entstehung von Texten aus dem Bedürfnis nach Überlieferung," in A. Assmann, J. Assmann, C. Hardmeier, eds. Schrift und Gedächtnis. München: Funk, 24–43.

Eibl-Eibesfeldt, I. (1975), *Krieg und Frieden aus der Sicht der Verhaltensforschung* (Munich, Zürich: Piper).

Eibl-Eibesfeldt, I. (1976), *Liebe und Haß. Zur Naturgeschichte elementarer Verhaltensweisen* (Munich, Zürich: Piper).

Eickelmann, D. F. (1978), "The art of memory: Islamic education and its social reproduction," *Comparative Studies in Society and History* 20, 485–516.

Eisenstadt, S. N. (1987), *Kulturen der Achsenzeit*, 2 vols. (Frankfurt: Suhrkamp).

Eiwanger, J. (1983), "Die Entwicklung der vorgeschichtlichen Kultur in Ägypten," in J. Assmann, G. Burkard (eds.), *5000 Jahre Ägypten. Genese und Permanenz pharaonischer Kunst* (Nußloch b. Heidelberg: IS-Edition), 61–74.

Eliade, M. (1953), *Le mythe de l'éternel retour*, Paris 1950; English version: *The myth of the eternal return*, trans. Willard R. Trask (New York: Pantheon Books, 1965).

Elwert, G. (1987), "Die gesellschaftliche Einbettung von Schriftgebrauch," in D. Becker (eds.), Theorie als Passion (Frankfurt: Suhrkamp), 238–268.

Elwert, G. (1989), "Nationalismus und Ethnizität. Über die Bildung von Wir-Gruppen," in *Kölner Zeitschrift für Soziologie und Sozialpsychologie*, 440–464.

Engel, H. (1979), *Die Vorfahren Israels in Ägypten* (Frankfurt: Knecht).

Erdheim, M. (1984), *Die gesellschaftliche Produktion von Unbewusstheit* (Frankfurt: Suhrkamp).

Erdheim, M. (1988), *Die Psychoanalyse und Unbewusstheit in der Kultur* (Frankfurt: Suhrkamp).

Erikson, E. H. (1966), "Ontogeny of Ritualization in Man," *Philosoph. Trans. Royal Soc.*, 251 B, 337–349.

Fabry, H. J. (1988), "Gedenken und Gedächtnis im Alten Testament," in P. Gignoux (ed.), *La Commémoration* (Paris-Louvain), 141–154.

Fairman, H. W. (1958), "A Scene of the Offering of Truth in the Temple of Edfu," *Mitt. d. Dt. Arch. Inst. Kairo* 16, 86–92.

Falkenstein, A. (1965), "Fluch über Akkade," *Zeitschrift für Assyriologie* 57 (NF 23), 43ff.

Finley, M. (1975), "The ancient Greeks and their nation," in *The Use and Abuse of History*, London, 120–133.

Finley, M. I. (1986), *Das politische Leben in der antiken Welt* (Munich: C. H. Beck).

Finnegan, R. (1977), *Oral Poetry. Its Nature, Significance and Social Context* (Cambridge: Cambridge University Press).

Finnestad, R. B. (1985), *Image of the World and Symbol of the Creator. On the Cosmological and Iconological Values of the Temple of Edfu* (Wiesbaden: Harrassowitz).

Finscher, L. (1988), "Werk und Gattung in der Musik als Träger des kulturellen Gedächtnisses," in J. Assmann, T. Hölscher (eds.), *Kultur und Gedächtnis*, Frankfurt: Suhrkamp, 293–310.

Fischer, H. G. (1986), *L'écriture et l árt de l'Égypte ancienne* (Paris: Presses universitaires de France).

Fishbane, M. (1972), "Varia Deuteronomica," *Zeitschrift für die alttestamentliche Wissenschaft* 84, 349–352.

Fishbane, M. (1986), *Biblical Interpretation in Ancient Israel* (Oxford: Oxford University Press).

Fortes, M. (1945), *The Dynamics of Clanship among the Tallensi* (London: Publisher for the International African Institute by the Oxford University Press).

Fortes, M. (1978a), "Pietas in Ancestor Worship," in F. Kramer, C. Sigrist (eds.), *Gesellschaften ohne Staat, Gleichheit und Gegenseitigkeit*, 2 vols. (Frankfurt: Syndikat), 197–232.

Fortes, M. (1978b), "Verwandtschaft und das Axiom der Amity," in F. Kramer, C. Sigrist (ed.), *Gesellschaften ohne Staat II. Genealogie und Solidarität* (Frankfurt: Syndikat), 120–164.

Fowden, G. (1986), The Egyptian Hermes. A historical approach to the late pagan mind (Cambridge: Cambridge University Press).

Fränkel, H. (1960), "EPHEMEROS als Kennwort für die menschliche Natur," in *Wege und Formen frühgriechischen Denkens* (Munich: C. H. Beck), 23–39.

Frankfort, H. (1948), *Kingship and the Gods* (Chicago: Chicago University Press).

Frei, P., Koch, K. (1984), *Reichsidee und Reichsorganisation im Perserreich*, OBO 55 (Fribourg: Fribourg University Press).

Frisch, P. (1983) "Über die lydisch-phrygischen Sühneinschriften und die 'Confessiones' des Augustinus," *Epigraphica Anatolica* 2, 41–45.

Frisk, H. (1973), *Griech. Etymol. Wörterbuch* (Heidelberg: Winter).

Gadamer, H. G. (1960), *Wahrheit und Methode. Grundzüge einer philosophischen Hermeneutik* (Tübingen: Mohr-Siebeck).

Gardiner, A. H. (1909), *The Admonitions of an Egyptian Sage* (Leipzig: Hinrichs).

Gardiner, A. H. (1959), *The Royal Canon of Turin* (Oxford: Oxford University Press).

Geertz, C. (1983), "Common Sense as a Cultural System," in C. Geertz, *Local Knowledge* (New York: Basic Books), 73–93.

Gehlen, A. (1961), *Anthropologische Forschung* (Hamburg: Rowohlt).

Gelb, I. J. (1952), *A Study of Writing* (Chicago: University of Chicago Press).

Gellner, E. (1983), *Nations and Nationalism* (Oxford: Oxford University Press).

Gellrich, Jesse M. (1985), *The Idea of the Book in the Middle Ages: Language Theory, Mythology, and Fiction* (Ithaca: Cornell University Press).

Gerhardsson, B. (1961), *Memory and Manuscript: Oral Tradition and Written Transmission in Rabbinic Judaism and Early Christianity* (Lund: C. W. K. Gleerup).

Gese, H. (1958), "Geschichtliches Denken im Alten Orient und im Alten Testament," *Zeitschrift Theologie and Kirche* 55, 127–155.

Gignoux, P. (ed.) (1988), *La commémoration,* Colloque du centenaire de la section des sciences religieuses de l'EPHE (Louvain-Paris).

Goedicke, H. (ed.) (1985), *Perspectives on the Battle of Kadesh* (Baltimore: Halgo).

Goelman, H., Oberg, A., Smith, F. (eds.) (1984), *Awakening to Literacy* (Exeter: Heinemann Educational Books).

Goetze, A. (1929), "Die Pestgebete des Mursilis," *Kleinasiatische Forschungen* I, 61–251.

Goetze, A. (1933), *Mursilis II. König der Hethiter: Die Annalen, hethitischer Text und deutsche Übersetzung* (Darmstadt 1967, Leipzig: Hinrichs 1933).

Goetze, A. (1967), *Hattusilis. Der Bericht über seine Thronbesteigung. nebst den Paralleltexten* (Darmstadt: Wissenschaftliche Buchgesellschaft).

Goffman, E. (1974), *Frame Analysis: An Essay on the Organization of Experience* (Cambridge, MA: Harvard University Press).

Gombrich, A. (1970), *Aby Warburg: an Intellectual Biography* (London: The Warburg Institute).

Goody, J. (1977), *The Domestication of the Savage Mind* (Cambridge: Cambridge University Press).

Goody, J. (1986), *The Logic of Writing and the Organization of Society* (Cambridge: Cambridge University Press).

Goody, J. (1987), *The Interface between the Written and the Oral* (Cambridge: Cambridge University Press).

Goody, J., Watt, I., Gough, K. (eds.) (1968), *Literacy in Traditional Societies* (Cambridge, Cambridge University Press).

Graefe, E. (1990), "Die gute Reputation des Königs 'Snofru'," in *Studies in Egyptology, Festschrift Lichtheim* (Jerusalem: Magnes), 257–263.

Grayson, A. K. (1970), *Assyrian and Babylonian Chronicles. Texts from Cuneiform Sources* 5 (Locust Valley, NY: J. J. Augustin).

Grayson, A. K. (1980), "Histories and Historians in the Ancient Near East," *Orientalia* 49, 1980, 140–194.

Grieshammer, R. (1971), *Das Jenseitsgericht in den Sargtexten, Ägyptologische Abhandlung* 20 (Wiesbaden: Harrassowitz).

Grieshammer, R. (1974), "Zum 'Sitz im Leben' des negativen Sündenbekenntnisses," *ZDMG* Supplement II, 19ff.

Griffiths, J. G. (1960), *The Conflict of Horus and Seth* (Liverpool: Liverpool University Press).

Griffiths, J. G. (1979), "Egyptian Nationalism in the Edfu Temple Texts," in J. Ruffle, G. A. Gaballa, and K. A. Kitchen (eds.), *Glimpses of Ancient Egypt: Studies in Honour of H. W. Fairman* (Warminster, English version: Aris & Phillip), 174–179.

Gunnell, John G. (1968), *Political Philosophy of Time* (Middletown, CT: Wesleyan University Press).

Güterbock, H. G. (1934), "Die historische Tradition und ihre literarische Gestaltung bei Babyloniern und Hethitern I," *Zeitschrift fpr Assyriologie* 42.

Güterbock, H. G. (1956), "The deeds of Suppiluliuma as told by his son Mursili II," *Journal of Cuneiform Studies* 10, 41–50, 59–68, 75–85, 90–98, 107–130.

Güterbock, H. G. (1986), "Hittite historiography: a survey," in H. Tadmor, M. Weinfeld (eds.), *History, Historiography and Interpretation. Studies in Biblical and Cuneiform Literatures* (Jersualem: Magnes), 21–35.

Habermas, J. (1976), "Können komplexe Gesellschaften eine vernünftige Identität ausbilden?," in *Zur Rekonstruktion des Historischen Materialismus* (Frankfurt: Suhrkamp), 92–126.

Habsbawm, E., Ranger, T. (eds.) (1983), *The Invention of Tradition* (Cambridge: Cambridge University Press).

Hahn, A., Kapp, V. (eds.) (1987), *Selbstthematisierung und Selbstzeugnis. Bekenntnis und Geständnis* (Frankfurt: Suhrkamp).

Halbwachs, M. (1941), *La topographie legendaire des évangiles en Terre Sainte* (Paris: Presses universitaires de France).

Halbwachs, M. (1985a), *Les cadres sociaux de la mémoire* (Paris: Mouton, 1925).

Halbwachs, M. (1985b) *La mémoire collective* (Paris: Mouton, 1950); English version: *On Collective Memory* (Chicago: University of Chicago Press, 1992).

Hallo, W. W. (1986), "Sumerian Historiography," in Tadmor, H., Weinfeld, M. (eds.), *History, Historiography and Interpretation. Studies in Biblical and Cuneiform Literatures* (Jersualem: Magnes), 9–20.

Hartog, F. (1989), "Écriture, Généalogies, Archives, Histoire en Grèce ancienne," *Histoire et conscience historique (CCEPOA)* 5, 132.

Harvey, F. D. (1966), "Literacy in the Athenian Democracy," in *Révue des Études Grecques* 79, 585–635.

Havelock, E. A. (1963), *Preface to Plato* (Cambridge, MA: Harvard University Press).

Havelock, E. A. (1976), *Origins of Western Literacy* (Toronto: Ontario Institute for Studies in Education).

Havelock, E. A. (1978), *The Greek Concept of Justice from Its Shadow in Homer to Its Substance in Plato* (Cambridge, MA: Harvard University Press).

Havelock, E. A. (1978a), "The alphabetisation of Homer," in E. A. Havelock, Hershbell (eds.), *Communication Arts in the Ancient World* (New York: Hastings House), 3–21.

Havelock, E. A. (1980), "The oral composition of Greek drama," *Quaderni Urbinati di Cultura Classica* 35, 61–113.

Havelock, E. A. (1982), *The Literate Revolution in Greece and Its Cultural Consequences* (Princeton, NJ: Princeton University Press).

Havelock, E. A. (1984), "The orality of Socrates and the literacy of Plato," in E. Kelly (ed.), *New Essays on Socrates* (Lanham, MD: University Press of America), 67–93.

Havelock, E. A. (1986), *The Muse Learns to Write: Reflections on Orality and Literacy from Antiquity to the Present* (New Haven: Yale University Press).

Haverkamp, A., Lachmann R. (eds.) (1991), *Gedächtnis als Raum. Studien zur Mnemotechnik* (Frankfurt: Suhrkamp).

Heintz, R. (1969), "Maurice Halbwachs' Gedächtnisbegriff," *ZPhF* 23, 73–85.

Helck, W. (1964), "Die Ägypter und die Fremden," *Saeculum* 15, 103–114.

Helck, W. (1969), "Überlegungen zur Geschichte der 18. Dyn.," *Oriens Antiquus* 8, 281–327.

Helck, W. (1986), *Politische Gegensätze im alten Ägypten. Ein Versuch* (HÄB 23, Hildesheim: Gerstenberg).

Hengel, M. (1969), *Judentum und Hellenismus: Studien zu ihrer Begegnung unter besonderer Berücksichtigung Palästinas bis zur Mitte des 2. Jahrhundert vor Christus* (Tübingen: Mohr-Siebeck), 219–273.

Hengel, M. (1976), *Juden, Griechen und Barbaren. Aspekte der Hellenisierung des Judentums in vorchristlicher Zeit* (Stuttgart: KBW Verlag).

Hermann, A. (1938), *Die ägyptische Königsnovelle* (Glückstadt, New York: J. J. Augustin).

Heubeck, A. (1979), *Schrift (Archaeologia Homerica III.X)* (Göttingen: Vandenhoeck & Ruprecht).

Heubeck, A. (1984), "Zum Erwachen der Schriftlichkeit im archaischen Griechentum," in *Kleine Schriften zur griechischen Sprache und Literatur* (Erlangen), 57–74.

Hintze, F. (1953), *Untersuchungen zu Stil und Sprache neuägyptischer Erzählungen* (Berlin: Akademie-Verlag).

Hobsbawm, E., Ranger, T. (eds.) (1983), *The Invention of Tradition* (Cambridge: Cambridge University Press).

Hoffner, H. A. (1975), "Propaganda and Political Justification in Hittite Historiography," in H. Goedicke, J. J. M. Roberts (eds.), *Unity and Diversity. Essays in the History, Literature, and Religion of the Ancient Near East* (Baltimore: Johns Hopkins University Press), 49–64.

Hoffner, H. A. (1980), "Histories and Historians of the Near East: The Hittites," *Orientalia* 49, 1980, 283–332.

Hofstätter, P. R. (1973), *Einführung in die Sozialpsychologie* (Stuttgart: Kröner, 5. ed.).

Hölscher, T. (1988), "Tradition und Geschichte. Zwei Typen der Vergangenheit am Beispiel der griechischen Kunst," in J. Assmann, T. Hölscher (eds.), *Kultur und Gedächtnis* (Frankfurt: Suhrkamp), 115–149.

Hölscher, U. (1987), "Über die Kanonizität Homers," in A. Assmann, J. Assmann (eds.), *Kanon und Zensur* (Munich: Fink), 237–245.

Hölscher, U. (1988), *Die Odyssee. Epos zwischen Märchen und Literatur* (Munich: C. H. Beck).

Hölscher, U. (in print), "Kontinuität als epische Denkform. Zum Problem des 'dunklen Jahrhunderts'," in Museum Helveticum.

Hornung, E. (1966), *Geschichte als Fest. Zwei Vorträge zum Geschichtsbild der frühen Menschheit* (Darmstadt, Wissenschaftliche Buchgesellschaft).

Hornung, E. (1975), "Seth. Geschichte und Bedeutung eines ägyptischen Gottes," *Symbolon N.F.* 2, 49–63.

Hornung, E. (1982), Der ägyptische Mythos von der Himmelskuh. Eine Ätiologie des Unvollkommenen (Göttingen: Vandenhoeck & Ruprecht).

Hornung, E. (1982a), "Zum altägyptischen Geschichtsbewusstsein," in *Archäologie und Geschichtsbewusstsein. Kolloquien zur allgemeinen und vergleichenden Archäologie*, 3 (Munich), 13–30.

Union des Associations Internationales, *Identité et regions* (Bruxelles, 1981).

Illich, I., Sanders, B. (1988), *The alphabetization of the popular mind* (San Francisco: North Point).

Iversen, E. (1975), *Canon and Proportions in Egyptian Art* (London: Sidgwick and Jackson).

Jacobson-Widding, A. (ed.) (1983), *Identity: personal and socio-cultural* (Uppsala, Stockholm: Academiae Upsaliensis).

Jaspers, K. (1949), *Vom Ursprung und Ziel der Geschichte* (Munich: Piper).

Jaspers, K. (1973) *Philosophie*, 3 vols. (Berlin: Springer).

Jeffery, L. H. (1961), *The Local Scripts of Archaic Greece. A Study of the Origin of the Greek Alphabet and Its Development from the Eight to the Fifth Centuries B.C.* (Oxford: Oxford University Press).

Johnson, J. (1974), "The Demotic chronicle as a historical source," *Enchoria* 4, 1–18.

Johnston, A. (1983), "The extent and use of literacy. the archaeological evidence," in R. Hägg (ed.), *The Greek Renaissance of the Eight Century B.C. Tradition and Innovation*, (Stockholm), 63–68.

Jousse, M. (1925), *Le style oral rhythmique et mnémotechnique chez les Verbo-moteurs* (Paris).

Junge, F. (1984), "Zur Sprachwissenschaft der Ägypter," in *Studien zu Sprache und Religion Ägyptens (in honour of W. Westendorf)* (Wiesbaden: Harrassowitz), 257–272.

Jürss (Hg.), F. (1982), *Geschichte des wissenschaftlichen Denkens im Altertum, Veröffentlichungen des Zentralinstituts für Alte Geschichte und Archäologie der Akademie der Wissenschaften der DDR* (Berlin: Akademie-Verlag).

Kaiser, O. (ed.) (1983), "Texte aus der Umwelt des Alten Testaments," vol. I fasc.2, in R. Borger, M. Dietrich, E. Edel, O. Loretz, O. Rössler, E. v. Schular (eds.), *Staatsverträge* (Gütersloh: Gütersloher Verlagshaus).

Kakosy, L. (1981), "Ideas of the fallen state of the world in Egyptian religion: decline of the Golden Age," *Studia Aegyptiaca* VII, 81–92.

Karady, V. (1972), "Biographie de Maurice Halbwachs," in M. Halbwachs (ed.), *Classes sociales et morphologie* (Paris: Èditions de Minuit), 9–22.

Käsemann, E. (ed.) (1970), Das Neue Testament als Kanon (Göttingen: Vandenhoeck and Ruprecht).

Kaufmann, Y. (1988), *Christianity and Judaism. Two Covenants* (Jerusalem).

Kees, H. (1941), *Der Götterglaube im alten Ägypten* (Leipzig: Hinrichs).

Kelsen, H. (1941), *Vergeltung und Kausalität* (Hague, Chicago: W. P. van Stockum and University of Chicago Press).

Kemp, B. (1989), *Ancient Egypt. Anatomy of a Civilization* (London, New York: Routledge).

Kippenberg, H. G. (1986), "Die jüdischen Überlieferungen als patrioi nomoi," in R. Faber, R. Schlesier (eds.), Die Restauration der Götter. Antike Religion und Neo-Paganismus (Würzburg: Königshausen and Neumann), 45–60.

Kippenberg, H. G. (1987), "Codes and Codification," in M. Eliade (ed.), *The Encyclopaedia of Religion*, 3 vols. (New York: Macmillan), 352–358.

Kirk, G. S. (1977), *The Songs of Homer* (Cambridge: Cambridge University Press).

Knox, B. M. W. (1968), "Silent Reading in Antiquity," *GRBS* 9, 421–435.

Koch, K., et al. (1980), *Das Buch Daniel, EdF* (Darmstadt: Wissenschaftliche Buchgesellschaft).

Koch, K. (1986), "Auf der Suche nach der Geschichte," in *Biblica* 67, 109–117.

Koch, K. (1988), "Qädäm. Heilsgeschichte als mythische Urzeit im Alten (und Neuen) Testament," in J. Rohls, G. Wenz (eds.), *Vernunft des Glaubens (in honour of W. Pannenberg)* (Göttingen: Vandenhoeck and Ruprecht), 253–288.

Koller, H. (1963), *Dichtung und Musik im frühen Griechenland* (Bern: Francke).

Konte, L., *Unesco-Courier* 1985, 8, 7.

Korosec, V. (1931), *Hethitische Staatsverträge. Ein Beitrag zu ihrer juristischen Wertung. Leipziger rechtswissenschaftliche Studien 60* (Leipzig: T. Weicher).

Koselleck, R. (1979), "Kriegerdenkmale als Identitätsstiftungen der Überlebenden," in O. Marquard, K. Stierle (eds.), *Identität, Poetik und Hermeneutik VIII* (Munich: Fink). 255–276.

Kötting, B. (1965), *Der frühchristliche Reliquienkult und die Bestattung im Kirchengebäude*, (Cologne: Opladen).

Kramer, F. (1977), *Verkehrte Welten* (Frankfurt: Syndikat).

Krasovec, J. (1988), "La justice (sdq) de dieu dans la bible hébraique et l'interprétation juive et chrétienne," *OBO* 76.

Krauss, R. (1979), *Das Ende der Amarnazeit* (Hildesheim: Gerstenberg).

Krecher, J., Müller, H. P. (1975), "Vergangenheitsinteresse in Mesopotamien und Israel," *Saeculum* 26.

Kugler, F. (1848), *Handbuch der Kunstgeschichte*, 2nd ed. with additional material by Dr. Jacob Burckhardt (Stuttgart: Ebner Seubert).

Kurth, D. (1983), "Eine Welt aus Stein, Bild und Wort – Gedanken zur spätägyptischen Tempeldekoration," in J. Assmann, G. Burkard (eds.), *5000 Jahre Ägypten – Genese und Permanenz der pharaonischen Kunst* (Nußloch bei Heidelberg: IS-Edition), 89–101.

Kvanvig, H. S. (1988), "Roots of Apocalyptic. The Mesopotamian Background of the Enoch Figure and the Son of Man," *WMANT* 61 (Neukirchen: Neukirchner Verlag).

"L'identité, " *Actes de la recherche en sciences sociales, 35*, Paris 1980 (Contributions by G. Scholem, P. Bourdieu, R. Chartier et al.)

La mémoire des Français, éditions du CNRS.

Lacan, J. *Autres Écrits*, Paris: Seuil, 2001.

Lachmann, R. (1987), "Kanon und Gegenkanon in der russischen Kultur," in A. Assmann, J. Assmann (eds.), *Kanon und Zensur* (Munich: Fink), 124–137.

Lachmann, R. (1990). *Gedächtnis und Literatur* (Frankfurt: Suhrkamp); English. version: *Memory and Literature: Intertextuality in Russian Modernism* (Minneapolis: University of Minnesota Press, 1997).

Lambert, M. (1960), "La naissance de la bureaucratie," *Revue historique* 84, 1–26.

Lambert, W. G. (1957), "Ancestors, Authors and Canonicity," *Journal of Cuneiform Studies* 11, 1–14.

Lang, B. (ed.) (1981), *Der Einzige Gott* (Munich: C. H. Beck).

Lang, B. (1983), "The Yahweh-Alone Movement and the Making of Jewish Monotheism," in *Monotheism and the Prophetic Minority* (Sheffield, England: Almond Press), 13–59.

Lang, B. (1986), "Vom Propheten zum Schriftgelehrten. Charismatische Autorität im Frühjudentum," in H. v. Stietencron (ed.), *Theologen und Theologien in verschiedenen Kulturkreisen* (Düsseldorf: Patmos), 89–114.

Lanternari, V. (1960), *Movimenti religiosi di libertà e di salvezza dei popoli oppressi* (Milan: Feltrinelli); English version: *The Religions of the Oppressed: A Study of Modern Messianic Cults* (New York: Knopf, 1963).

Latacz, J. (1985), *Homer* (Munich, Zürich: Piper).

Lauterbach, J. (1913), "The Sadducees and the Pharisees," *Studies in Jewish Literature (in Honour of K. Kohler)* (Berlin).

Layton, R. (ed.) (1989), *Who Needs the Past? Indigenous Values and Archaeology* (London, Boston: Unwin Hyman).

Lebram, J. C. H. (1968), "König Antiochus im Buch Daniel," *Vetus Testamentum* 18, 737–773.

Ledderose, L. (1988), "Die Gedenkhalle für Mao Zedong. Ein Beispiel für Gedächtnisarchitektur," in J. Assmann, T. Hölscher (eds.), *Kultur und Gedächtnis* (Frankfurt: Suhrkamp), 311–339.

Leiman, S. Z. (1976), *The Canonization of Hebrew Scripture: The Talmudic and Midrashic Evidence* (Hamden, CT: Published for the Academy by Archon Books).

Leipoldt, J., Morenz, S. (1953), *Heilige Schriften. Betrachtungen zur Religionsgeschichte der antiken Mittelmeerwelt* (Leipzig: Harrassowitz).

Lévi-Strauss, C. (1966), *La pensée sauvage* (Paris: Plon, 1962); English version: *The Savage Mind* (Chicago: University of Chicago, 1966).

Lévi-Strauss, C. (1976), *Structural Anthropology*, vol. 2, trans. Monique Layton (Chicago: University of Chicago Press).

Lévi-Strauss, C. (1977), *Les structures élémentaires de la parenté* (Paris: B. Grasset, 1977/1983).

Lichtheim, M. (1973), *Ancient Egyptian Literature I* (Berkeley, Los Angeles, London: University of California Press, 1973).

Lloyd, A. B. (1982), "Nationalist Propaganda in Ptolemaic Egypt," *Historia. Zeitschrift für Alte Geschichte, Wiesbaden*, 31, 33–55.

Lloyd, A. B. (1982a), "The Inscription of Udjahorresnet, A Collaborator's Testament," *Journal of Egyptian Archaeology* 68, 166–180.

Lord, A. B. (1960), *Singer of Tales* (Cambridge, MA: Harvard University Press).

Lorenz, K. (1977), *Die Rückseite des Spiegels* (Munich: Piper); English version: *Behind the Mirror: A Search for a Natural History of Human Knowledge* (New York: Harcourt Brace Jovanovich).

Lotman, J., Uspenskij, B. (1977), "Die Rolle dualistischer Modelle in der Dynamik der russischen Kultur (bis zum Ende des 18. Jahrhunderts)," *Poetica* 9, 1ff.

Luckmann, T. (1979),"Persönliche Identität, sozialke Rolle und Rollendistanz," in: O. Marquard, K. Stierle, (eds.), *Identität (Poetik und Hermeneutik VIII)* (Munich: W. Fink), 293–313.

Luft, U. (1978), *Beiträge zur Historisierung der Götterwelt und zur Mythenschreibung* (Budapest: U. Luft).

Luhmann, N. (1971), "Sinn als Grundbegriff der Soziologie," in J. Habermas, N. Luhmann (eds.), *Theorie der Gesellschaft oder Sozialtechnologie* (Frankfurt: Suhrkamp), 25–100.

Luhmann, N. (1973), *Vertrauen. Ein Mechanismus der Reduktion sozialer Komplexität* (Stuttgart: Enke).

Luhmann, N. (1975), "Einführende Bemerkungen zu einer Theorie symbolisch generalisierter Kommunikationsmedien," in N. Luhmann (ed.), *Soziologische Aufklärung 2* (Cologne: Westdeutscher Verlag), 170–192.

Luhmann, N. (1975), "Selbst-Thematisierung des Gesellschaftssystems," in: *Aufsätze zur Theorie der Gesellschaft* (Opladen: Westdeutscher Verlag), 72–102.

Luhmann, N. (1979), "Identitätsgebrauch in selbstsubstitutiven Ordnungen, besonders Gesellschaften," in O. Marquardt, K. Stierle (eds.), *Identität* (Munich: Fink), 315–345.

Luhmann, N. (1980), *Gesellschaftsstruktur und Semantik I* (Frankfurt: Suhrkamp).

Luhmann, N. (1984), Soziale Systeme (Frankfurt: Suhrkamp); English version: *Social Systems*, trans. J. Bednarz (Stanford: Stanford University Press, 1995).

Luhmann, N. (1990), "Gleichzeitigkeit und Synchronisation," in *Soziologische Aufklärung 5* (Cologne: Westdeutscher Verlag), 95–130.

Lukacs, J. (1994), *Historical Consciousness or the Remembered Past* (New Brunswick, NJ: Transaction Publishers).

Luria, A. R. (1976), *Cognitive Development: Its Cultural and Social Foundations* (Cambridge, MA: Harvard University Press).

Maas, U. (1986), "'Die Schrift ist ein Zeichen für das, was in dem Geprochenen ist'. Zur Frühgeschichte der sprachwissenschaftlichen Schriftauffassung: das aristotelische und nacharistotelische (phonographische) Schriftverständnis'," in *Kodikas/Code* 9, 247–292.

Machinist, P. (1976), "Literature as Politics. The Tukulti-Ninurta Epic and the Bible," *Catholic Biblical Quarterly* 38, 455–482.

Machinist, P. (1985), "The Assyrians and their Babylonian Problem," *Jahrbuch des Wissenschaftskollegs zu Berlin* 84/85, 353–364.

Macmullen, R. (1964), "Nationalism in Roman Egypt," *Aegyptus* 44, 179–199.

Mahé, J. P. (1978), *Hermès en Haute-Égypte. Les textes hermétiques de Nag Hammadi et leurs parallèles grecs et latins* (Quebec: Presses de l'université Laval).

Malamat, A. (1955), "Doctrines of Causality in Hittite and Biblical Historiography: A Parallel," *VT* 5, 1–12.

Mann, Thomas (1974), "Freud und die Zukunft (1936)," *Gesammelte Werke*, vol. IX (Frankfurt: Fischer), 478–501.

Marcuse, H. (1964), *The One-Dimensional Man* (Boston: Beacon Press).

Markowitsch, J. (1979), *Die soziale Situation* (Frankfurt: Suhrkamp).

Marquard, O., Stierle, K. (eds.) (1979), *Identität, Poetik und Hermeneutik VIII* (Munich: Fink).

Marrou, H. I. (1977), *Geschichte der Erziehung im klassischen Altertum* (Munich: C. H. Beck).

Maschinist, P. (1976), "Literature as Politics. The Tukulti-Ninurta Epic and the Bible," *Catholic Biblical Quarterly* 38, 455–482.

Mauss, M. (1966), *Essai sur le don: forme et raison de l'échange dans les sociétés archaiques, Sociologie et anthropologie* (Paris, Alcan); English version: *The Gift: The Form and Reason for Exchange in Archaic Societies* (New York: W.W. Norton, 2000).

Mbunwe-Samba, P. (1989), "Oral Tradition and the African Past," in R. Layton (ed.), *Who Needs the Past? Indigenous Values and Archaeology* (London, Boston: Unwin Hyman), 105–118.

McCarthy, D. J. (1978), *Treaty and Covenant: A Study in Form in the Ancient Oriental Documents and in the Old Testament* (Rome: Biblical Institute).

Mead, G. H. (1934), *Mind, Self, Society. From the Standpoint of a Social Behaviorist* (Chicago: University of Chicago Press).

Meier, C. (1987), "Die Entstehung einer autonomen Intelligenz bei den Griechen," in S. N. Eisenstadt (ed.) *Kulturen der Achsenzeit*, 2 vols. (Frankfurt: Suhrkamp), I, 89–127.

Meier, C. (1989), "Zur Funktion der Feste in Athen im 5. Jh. v. Chr.," in R. Warning, W. Haug (eds.), *Das Fest, Poetik und Hermeneutik XIV* (Munich: Fink), 569–591.

Mendenhall, G. E. (1955) *Law and Covenant in Israel and in the Ancient Near East* (Pittsburgh: Biblical Colloquium).

Mentré, F. (1920), *Les générations sociales* (Paris, Bossard).

Merkelbach, R. (1968), "Ein ägyptischer Priestereid," *Zeitschrift für Philologie und Epigraphik* 2, 7–30.

Meyer, E. (1915), "Ägyptische Dokumente aus der Perserzeit," *Sitzungsberichte der Preussischen Akademie der Wissenschaft Berlin 1915. XVI.*

Meyer, E. (1928), "Gottesstaat, Militärherrschaft und Ständewesen in Ägypten," *Sitzungsberichte der Preussischen Akademie der Wissenschaften Berlin.*

Michaud, G. (ed.) (1978), *Identités collectives et relations interculturelles* (Bruxelles: Éditions Complexe).

Middleton, D., Edwards, D. (eds.) (1990), *Collective Remembering* (London: Sage).

Millar, F. (1978), "The background to Maccabaean Revolution," *JJS* 29, 1–21.

Millard, A. R. (1986), "The infancy of the alphabet," *World Archaeology* 17, 390–398.

Mol, H. (1976), *Identity and the Sacred. A Sketch for a New Social-Scientific Theory of Religion* (Oxford: Blackwell).

Mol, H. (ed.) (1978), *Identity and Religion. International, Cross-cultural Approaches* (London, Beverly Hills: Sage Publications).

Montet, P. (1950), "Le fruit défendu," *Kêmi* 11, 85–116.

Morenz, S. (1965), "Der Alte Orient. Von Bedeutung und Struktur seiner Geschichte," *Summa Historica. Propyläen Weltgeschichte Berlin* 11, 25–63.

Mühlmann, W. E. (1961), *Chiliasmus und Nativismus: Studien zur Psychologie, Soziologie und historischen Kasuistik der Umsturzbewegungen* (Berlin: D. Reimer).

Mühlmann, W. E. (1985), "Ethnogonie und Ethnogenese. Theoretisch-ethnologische und ideologiekritische Studie," *Studien zur Ethnogenese (Abhandlung der Rheinisch-Westfälischen Akademie der Wissenschaften)* 72.

Müller, K. E. (1987), *Das magische Universum der Identität. Elementarformen sozialen Verhaltens. Ein ethnologischer Grundriß* (Frankfurt, New York: Campus).

Munn-Rankin, J. (1956), "Diplomacy in Western Asia in the Early 2nd Mill BC," *Iraq* 18, 68-110.

Muszynski, M. (1974), "Le droit égyptien à travers la documentation grecque," *Le droit égyptien ancien.* Colloque organisé par l'Institut des Hautes Études de Belgie (Bruxelles), 163–180.

Nagel, T. (1988), *Die Festung des Glaubens. Triumph und Scheitern des islamischen Rationalismus im 11. Jahrhundert* (Munich: C. H. Beck).

Nagy, I. (1973), "Remarques sur le souci d'archaisme en Egypte à l'époque Saite," *Acta Antiqua Scient. Hungar* 21, 53–64.

Namer, G. (1987), *Mémoire et société* (Paris: Librairie des méridiens, Klincksieck).

Neisser, U. (1982), *Memory Observed* (San Francisco: W. H. Freeman).

Neisser, U., Winograd, E. (1988), *Remembering Reconsidered: Ecological and Traditional Approaches to the Study of Memory* (Cambridge, New York: Cambridge University Press).

New Literary History: *Aspects of Orality,* vol. 8/3 (1977); *Oral and Written Traditions in the Middle Ages,* vol. 16/1 (1984).

Nieddu, G. F. (1984), "La metafora della memoria comme scrittura e l'imagine dell'animo come deltos," *Quaderni di storia* 19, 213–219.

Niethammer, L. (ed.) (1985), *Lebenserfahrung und Kollektives Gedächtnis. Die Praxis der "Oral History"* (Frankfurt: Suhrkamp).

Nora, P. (ed.) (2009), *Les lieux de mémoire III: Les France* (Paris: Gallimard).

Nora, P. (ed.) (1984), *Les lieux de mémoire I: la république,* 3 vols (Paris: Gallimard).

Nora, P. (ed.) (1986), *Les lieux de mémoire II: La Nation* (Paris: Gallimard).

Nora, P. (1990), *Zwischen Geschichte und Gedächtnis* (Berlin: Wagenbach).

Notopoulos, J. A. (1938), "Mnemosyne in oral literature," *Translations of the American Philosophical Association* 69, 465–493.

Notopoulos, J. A. (1953), "The Introduction of the Alphabet into Oral Societies. Some Case Histories of Conflict between Oral and Written Literature," in I. T. Kakrides (ed.), *Profora eis Stilpona P. Kyriakiden (Hellenika. Periodikon syngramma hetaireia Makedonikon spoudon. Pararthema 4)* (Thessalonike), 516–524.

Obeyesekere, G. (1963), "The great tradition and the little tradition in the perspective of Singhalese Buddhism," *Journal of Asian Studies* 22, 139–153.

Ockinga, B. G. (1983), "The burden of Khackheperrecsonbu," *JEA* 69, 88–95.

Oexle, O. G. (1976), "Memoria und Memorialüberlieferung im frühen Mittelalter," *Frühmittelalterliche Studien* 10, 79ff.

Oexle, O. G. (1983), "Die Gegenwart der Toten," in H. Braet, W. Verbeke (eds.), *Death in the Middle Ages* (Leuven: Leuven University Press), 48ff.

Oexle, O. G. (1985), "Die Gegenwart der Lebenden und der Toten. Gedanken über Memoria," in K. Schmidt (ed.), *Kulturen der Achsenzeit*, 2 vols. (Frankfurt: Suhrkamp), 74–107.

Offner, G. (1950), "A propos de la sauvegarde des tablettes en Assyro-Babylonie," *RA* 44, 135–143.

Ong, W. J. (1967), *The Presence of the Word* (New Haven: Yale University Press).

Ong, W. J. (1977), "African talking drums and oral noetics," in *New Literary History* 8.3, 409–429.

Ong, W. J. (1982), *Orality and Literacy. The Technologizing of the Word* (London, New York: Methuen).

Ong, W. J. (1986), "Writing Is a technology that restructures thought," in G. Baumann (ed.), *The Written Word* (Oxford: Clarendon Press, New York: Oxford University Press), 25–50.

Oppel, H. (1937), KANON. Zur Bedeutungsgeschichte des Wortes und seinen lateinischen Entsprechungen (regula – norma), *Philologus*, Suppl. XXX H.4, Leipzig.

Oppenheim, L. (1964), *Ancient Mesopotamia. Portrait of a Dead Civilization* (Chicago University Press).

Otto, E. (1938), "Die Lehre von den beiden Ländern Ägyptens in der ägyptischen Religionsgeschichte," *Studia Aegyptiaca I = Analecta Orientalia* 17, 10–35.

Otto, E. (1966), "Geschichtsbild und Geschichtsschreibung im alten Ägypten," *Die Welt des Orients* 3.

Otto, E. (1969), "Das 'Goldene Zeitalter' in einem ägyptischen Text," *Religions en Égypte hellénistique et romaine (BCESS)* (Paris), 92–108.

Otto, W. (1908), *Priester und Tempel im hellenistischen Ägypten II* (Leipzig, Berlin: B. G. Teubner).

Overbeck, F. (1919), *Christentum und Kultur* (Basel: Schwabe).

Parry, M. (1971), "The making of Homeric verse," in A. Parry (ed.), *The Collected Papers of M. Parry* (Oxford: Clarendon Press).

Pelto, P. (1968), "The difference between 'tight' and 'loose' societies," *Transaction*, April, 37–40.

Petzl, G. (1988), "Sünde, Strafe, Wiedergutmachung," *Epigraphica anatolica* 12, 155–166.

Pfeiffer, R. (1968), *History of Classical Scholarship from the Beginnings to the End of the Hellenistic Age* (Oxford: Clarendon Press).

Pfeiffer, R. (1976), *History of Classical Scholarship. From 1300 to 1850* (Oxford: Clarendon Press).

Pfohl, G. (ed.) (1968), *Das Alphabet. Entstehung und Entwicklung der griechischen Schrift* (Darmstadt: Wissenschaftliche Buchgesellschaft).

Piekara, F. H., Ciesinger, K. G., Muthig, K. P. (1987), "Notizenanfertigen und Behalten," *Zeitschrift für Pädagogische Psychologie* 1/4, 267–280.

Posener, G. (1956), *Littérature et politique dans l'Égypte de la XIIe dynastie* (Paris: H. Champion).

Pury, A. de, Römer, T. (1989), "Memoire et catechisme dans l'Ancien Testament," *Histoire et conscience historique (CCEPOA)* 5, 81–92.

Quaegebeur, J. (1980/81), "Sur la 'loi sacrée' dans l'Égypte gréco-romaine," *Ancient Society* 11/12, 227–240.

Quecke, H. (1977), "Ich habe nichts hinzugefügt und nichts weggenommen. Zur Wahrheitsbeteuerung koptischer Martyrien," in J. Assmann, E. Feucht (eds.), *Fragen an die altägyptische Literatur. Gedenkschrift E. Otto* (Wiesbaden: Reichert), 399–416.

Rad, G. von (1947), *Deuteronomium-Studien* (Göttingen, Vandenhoeck & Ruprecht).

Rad, G. von (1958), "Die deuteronomistische Geschichtstheologie in den Königsbüchern," in G.v. Rad (ed.), *Gesammelte Studien zum Alten Testament* (Munich: C. Kaiser), 189–204.

Rad, G. von (1961), "Der Anfang der Geschichtsschreibung im alten Israel," *Gesammelte Studien zum AT* (Munich: C. Kaiser).

Redfield, R. (1955), *The Little Community* (Chicago: University of Chicago Press). [[date 1956 on query ref. list]]

Redfield, R. (1956), *Peasant Society and Culture. An Anthropological Approach to Civilisation* (Chicago: University of Chicago Press).

Redford, D. B. (1986), *Pharaonic King-Lists, Annals and Day Books* (Mississauga: Benben).

Reshef, U. (1988), "Une commémoration impossible: l'holocauste en Israel," *Gignoux*, 351–367.

Reventlow, H. G. (1961), *Das Heiligkeitsgesetz, formgeschichtlich untersucht* (Neukirchen: Neukirchener Verlag).

Reymond, E. A. E. (1969), *The Mythical Origin of the Egyptian Temple* (Manchester, New York: Manchester University Press).

Ritschl, D. (1967), *Memory and Hope. An Inquiry Concerning the Presence of Christ* (New York: Macmillan).

Ritschl, D. (1985), "Die Erfahrung der Wahrheit. Die Steuerung von Denken und Handeln durch implizite Axiome," *Heidelberger Jahrbücher* 29, 35–49.

Ritter, A. M. (1987), "Die Entstehung des neutestamentlichen Kanons," in A. Assmann and J. Assmann (eds.) *Kanon und Zensur* (Munich: Fink), 93–99.

Ritter, J. (1969), *Metaphysik und Politik. Studien zu Aristoteles und Hegel* (Frankfurt: Suhrkamp).

Robertson, R., Holzner, B. (eds.) (1980), *Identity and Authority. Exploration in the Theory of Society* (Oxford: Oxford University Press).

Röllig, W. (1985), Über die Anfänge unseres Alphabets," *Das Altertum* 3, 83–91.

Rorty, R., Schneewind, J. B., Skinner, Q. (eds.) (1984), *Philosophy in Context. Essays on the Historiography of Philosophy* (Cambridge, New York: Cambridge University Press).

Rossi, L. E. (1978), "I poemi omerici come testimonianza di poesia orale," G. P. Carratelli (ed.), *Origini e sviluppo della città* (Milan: Bompiani), 73–147.

Rüstow, A. (1952), *Ortsbestimmung der Gegenwart. Eine universalgeschichtliche Kulturkritik*, vol. 2 (Zurich: Rentsch), 12.

Sahlins, M. (1972), *Stone Age Economics* (Chicago, Aldine-Atherton).

Said, E. W. (1978), *Orientalism* (London: Routledge & Kegan Paul).

Sanders, E. P. (1981), "Aspects of Judaism in the Graeco-Roman Period," vol. 2, in *Jewish and Christian Self-Definition*, 3 vols (Philadelphia: Philadelphia: Fortress Press), 1980ff.

Schachermeyr, F. (1984), *Die griechische Rückerinnerung* (Wien: Verlag der Österreichischen Akademie der Wissenschaften).

Schlott, A. (1989), *Schrift und Schreiber im Alten Ägypten* (Munich: C. H. Beck).

Schmale, F. J. (1985), *Funktionen und Formen mittelalterlicher Geschichtsschreibung* (Darmstadt: Wissenschaftliche Buchgesellschaft).

Schmid, H. H., "Gerechtigkeit als Thema biblischer Theologie" (unpublished script).

Schmid, H. H. (1968), *Gerechtigkeit als Weltordnung* (Tübingen: Mohr-Siebeck).

Schmidt, E. A. (1987), "Historische Typologie der Orientierungsfunktionen von Kanon in der griechischen und römischen Literatur," in A. Assmann, J. Assmann, (eds.) *Kanon und Zensur* (Munich: Fink) 246–258.

Schmidt, K. (ed.) (1985), *Gedächtnis, das Gemeinschaft stiftet* (Munich: Schnell & Steiner).

Schmidt, K., Wollasch, J. (eds.) (1984), *Memoria. Der geschichtliche Zeugniswert des liturgischen Gedenkens im Mittelalter. Münstersche Mittelalter-Schriften 48* (Munich: Fink).

Schott, R. (1968), "Das Geschichtsbewußtsein schriftloser Völker," *Archiv für Begriffsgeschichte* 12, 166–205.

Schottroff, W. (1964), *'Gedenken' im Alten Orient und im Alten Testament. Die Wurzel zakar im semitischen Sprachkreis* (Neukirchen: Neukirchener Verlag).

Schottroff, W. (1969), *Der altisraelitische Fluchspruch* (Neukirchen: Neukirchener Verlag).

Schuster, M. (1988), "Zur Konstruktion von Geschichte in Kulturen ohne Schrift," in J. v. Ungern-Sternberg, H. Reinau (eds.), *Vergangenheit in mündlicher Überlieferung* (Stuttgart: B.G. Teubner), 57–71.

Segal, C. (1982), "Tragédie, oralité, écriture," *Poétique* 13, 131–154.

Segal, C. (1984), "Greek tragedy: Writing, truth, and the representation of self," H. Evjen (ed.), *Mnemai. Studies K. Hulley* (Chico, CA: Scholars Press).

Seligman, A. B. (ed.) (1989), *Order and Transcendence. The Role of Utopias and the Dynamics of Civilizations* (Leiden, New York: E. J. Brill).

Seters, J. van (1983), *In Search of History* (New Haven: Yale University Press).

Seters, J. van (1989), "Tradition and history: History as national tradition," *Histoire et conscience historique (CCEPOA)* 5, 63–74.

Sevenster, J. N. (1975), *The Roots of Pagan Anti-Semitism in the Ancient World* (Leiden: E. J. Brill).

Shils, E. (1981), *Tradition* (Chicago: University of Chicago Press).

Shotter, J. (1990), "The social construction of remembering and forgetting," in D. Middleton, D. Edwards (eds.), *Collective Remembering* (London: Sage). 120–138. [[book name ok?]]

Smend, R. (1968), *Elemente alttestamentlichen Geschichtsdenkens* (Zürich: EVZ-Verlag).

Smith, A. D. (1986), *The Ethnic Origins of Nations* (Oxford, New York: B. Blackwell).

Smith, M. (1971), *Palestinian Parties and Politics That Shaped the Old Testament* (New York: Columbia University Press).

Smyth-Florentin, F. (1989), "Modeles de recits d' origine et structures du pouvoir," *Histoire et conscience historique (CCEPOA)* 5, 41–48.

"Social memory," *Sonderheft Communication* 11(2).

Spicer, E. H. (1971), "Persistent cultural systems. A comparative study of identity systems that can adapt to contrasting environments," *Science* 174 (4011), 795–800.

Spieckermann, H. (1982), *Juda unter Assur in der Sargonidenzeit* (Göttingen: Vandenhoeck & Ruprecht).

Spiegel, J. (1935), *Die Idee des Totengerichts in der ägyptischen Religion, LÄS* 2.

Spiegelberg, W. (1914), *Die sogenannte Demotische Chronik* (Leipzig: J. C. Hinrichs).

Stadelmann, H. (1980), *Ben Sira als Schriftgelehrter* (Tübingen: Mohr-Siebeck).

Staudacher, W. (1968), *Die Trennung von Himmel und Erde. Ein vorgriechischer Schöpfungsmythos bei Hesiod und den Orphikern* (Darmstadt: Wissenschaftliche Buchgesellschaft).

Steinleitner, F. (1913), *Die Beicht im Zusammenhang mit der sakralen Rechtspflege in der Antike* (Leipzig: Kommissionsverlag der Dieterich'schen Verlagsbuchhandlung, Theodor Weicher).

Steinmetzer, F. X. (1922), *Die babylonischen Kudurru. Grenzsteine als Urkundenform* (Paderborn: Schöningh).

Stone, M. (ed.) (1984), *Jewish Writings of the Second Temple Period* (Assen, Netherlands, Philadelphia: Van Gorcum, Fortress Press).

Stone, M. E. (1987), "Eschatologie, Remythologisierung und kosmische Aporie," in S. N. Eisenstadt (ed.), *Kulturen der Achsenzeit*, 2 vols (Frankfurt: Suhrkamp), 19–37.

Street, B. (1987), "Orality and literacy as ideological constructions: Some problems in cross-cultural studies," *Culture and History* 2, 7–30.

Svenbro, J. (1987), "The 'voice' of letters in Ancient Greece: On silent reading and the representation of speech," *Culture and History* 2, 31–47.

Szlezák, T. A. (1985), *Platon und die Schriftlichkeit der Philosophie* (Berlin, New York: W. de Gruyter).

Tadmor, H. (1982), "Treaty and oath in the Ancient Near East: An historian's approach," in G. M. Tucker, D. A. Knight (eds.), *Humanizing America's Iconic Book* (Chico, CA: Scholars Press), 127–152.

Tadmor, H., Weinfeld, M. (eds.) (1986), *History, Historiography and Interpretation. Studies in Biblical and Cuneiform Literatures* (Jerusalem, Leiden: Magnes, E. J. Brill).

te Velde, H. (1977), "The theme of the separation of heaven and earth in Egyptian mythology," *Stud. Aeg.* 3, 161–170.

Tenbruck, F. H. (1986), *Geschichte und Gesellschaft* (Berlin: Duncker & Humblot).

Tenbruck, F. H. (1989), "Gesellschaftsgeschichte oder Weltgeschichte?," *Kölner Zeitschrift für Soziologie und Sozialpsychologie* 41, 417–439.

Theißen, G. (1977), *Soziologie der Jesusbewegung. Eion Beitrag zur Entstehungsgeschichte des Urchristentums*, 3. ed. 1981 (Tübingen: Mohr-Siebeck).

Theißen, G. (1988), "Tradition und Entscheidung. Der Beitrag des biblischen Glaubens zum kulturellen Gedächtnis," in J. Assmann, T. Hölscher (eds.), *Kultur und Gedächtnis* (Frankfurt: Suhrkamp), 170–196.

Thienemann, F. (1979), *Jüdisches Fest und jüdischer Brauch*, reprint, orig. 1937 (Königstein/Ts).

Thomas, K. (1983), The perception of the past in early modern England (London: University of London).

Tunnik, W. C. van (1949), "De la règle mäte prostheinai mäte aphelein dans l'histoire du canon," *Vigiliae christianae* 3, 1–36.

Ungern-Sternberg, J. v., Reinau, H. (eds.) (1988), *Vergangenheit in mündlicher Überlieferung* (Stuttgart: Teubner).

Vansina, J. (1985), *Oral Tradition as History* (Madison: University of Wisconsin Press).

Veblen, T. (1899), *A Theory of the Leisure Class* (New York, London: Macmillan Co.).

Veenhof, K. R. (ed.) (1986), *Cuneiform Archives and Libraries* (Leiden, Netherlands: Historisch-Archaeologisch Instituut te Istanbul).

Velde, H. te (1967), *Seth, God of Confusion*, trans. G. E. van Baaren-Pape (Leiden: E. J. Brill).

Vidal-Naquet, P. (1981), *Les juifs, la mémoire et le present* (Paris: F. Maspero).

Vidal-Naquet, P. (1989), "Flavius Josephe et les prophetes," *Histoire et conscience historique (CCEPOA)* 5, 11–32.

Voegelin, E. (1966), *Anamnesis. Zur Theorie der Geschichte und Politik* (Munich: Piper).

Voegelin, E. (1974), "The Ecumenic Age," vol. IV, in *Order and History*, 4 vols. (Louisiana: Baton Rouge).

Vollrath, H. (1979), "Gesetzgebung und Schriftlichkeit: Das Beispiel der angelsächsischen Gesetze," *Historisches Jahrbuch* 99, 28–54.

Wachtel, N. (1986), "Memory and history: Introduction," *History and Anthropology* 2.2, 207–224.

Walzer, M. (1988), *Exodus and Revolution* (New York: Basic Books).

Watanabe, K. (1987), *Die adê-Vereidigung anlässlich der Thronfolgeregelung Asarhaddons, Baghdader Mitteilungen*, vol. 3 (Berlin: Gebr. Mann).

Way, T. (1984), *Die Textüberlieferung Ramses' II. zur Qadeš-Schlacht* (Hildesheim: Gerstenberg).

Weber, H. J. (1986), *Kanon und Methode. Zum Prozess zivilisatorischer Begründung* (Würzburg: Könighausen and Neumann).

Weber, M. (1978), *Wirtschaft und Gesellschaft* (Tübingen: Mohr-Siebeck).

Wehler, H. U. (1989), "Geschichtswissenschaft heutzutage: Aufklärung oder 'Sinnstiftung'," in *Zwischenbetrachtungen*. *Im Prozeß der Aufklärung* (Frankfurt: Suhrkamp), 775–793.

Weidner, E. (1954–1956), "Hof- und Haremserlasse assyrischer Könige," in *AfO* 17, 257–293.

Weinfeld, M. (1972), *Deuteronomy and the Deuteronomic School* (Oxford: Clarendon Press).

Weinfeld, M. (1976), "The loyalty oath in the ancient Near East," *Ugaritische Forschungen* 8, 379–414.

Weinfeld, M. (1990), "The common heritage of the covenantal traditions in the ancient world," in L. Canfora, M. Liverani, C. Zaccagnini (eds.), *I Trattati nel Mondo Antico. Forma, Ideologia* (Rome: Funzione), 175–191.

Weippert, M. (1990), "Synkretismus und Monotheismus. Religionsinterne Konfliktbewältigung im alten Israel," in J. Assmann, D. Harth (eds.), *Kultur und Konflikt* (Frankfurt: Suhrkamp), 143–173.

Wilcke, C. (1988), "Die Sumerische Königsliste und erzählte Vergangenheit," in J. v. Ungern-Sternberg, H. Reinau (eds.), *Vergangenheit in mündlicher Überlieferung* (Stuttgart: Teubner), 113–140.

Wildung, D. (1977), *Imhotep und Amenhotep. Gottwerdung im Alten Ägypten* (Munich: Deutscher Kunstverlag).

Will, E., Orrieux, C. (1986), *Ioudaïsmos - Hellenismos, essai sur le judaïsme judéen à l'époque hellénistique* (Nancy: Nantes: Press University).

Winter, E. (1989), "Hieroglyphen," *RAC Lieferung* 113, Stuttgart, 83–103.

Woodbury, L. (1983), "The literate revolution: A review article," *Classical Views / Echos du monde Classique* 27, 329–352.

Worsley, P. (1968), *The Trumpet Shall Sound. A Study of 'Cargo'-Cults in Melanesia* (New York: Schocken Books).

Yates, F. (1968), *The Art of Memory* (Chicago: Chicago University Press).

Yerushalmi, Y. C. (1982), *Zakhor. Jewish Memory and Jewish History* (Seattle: University of Washington Press).

Young, J. E. (1986), "Memory and monument," in G. H. Hartman (ed.), *Bitburg in Moral and Political Perspective* (Bloomington: Indiana University Press), 103–113.

Yoyotte, J. (1961), "Le jugement des morts dans l'Égypte ancienne," *Sources Orientales* 4, Paris.

Zirker, H. (1986), "Religion," in G. Bitter, G. Miller (eds.), *Handbuch religionspädagogischer Grundbegriffe* 2 (Munich: Kösel), 635–643.

Zumthor, P. (1983), *Introduction à la poésie orale* (Paris: Seuil).

Name Index

d'Abadal I de Vinyals, R., 63 n. 90
Abimilki of Tyrus, 177 n. 9
Abush, T., 123 n. 14
Adorno, T. W., 68
Aeschylus, 109
Ahasveros, 66
Akhenaten, 85, 177 n. 8, 178, 184 n. 20,
    217, 265
Aland, K., 94 n. 50
Albert, H., 112, n. 2
Albrektson, B., 211, 212 n. 13, 225
Albright, W. F., 177 n. 9
Alexandre, J., 47
Alexandros of Macedonia, 247
Alkaios, 259
Alliot, M., 168 n. 36, 169 n. 40
Alt, A., 177 n. 8
Amasis, 186
Amenemhet I, 19, 65
Amenemope, 238 n. 11
Amun, 178, 182, 223, 264 n. 60
Andersen, Ø., 237 n. 9
Anderson, B., 47, 115, 121 n. 9, 140
Anthes, P., 137 n. 37
Antiochus IV Epiphanes, 64, 188
Apollo, 43, 57
Appadurai, A., 25 n. 30
Archimedes, 265
Archytas of Tarent, 105
Aristeas, 88, 177 n. 7
Aristophanes, 92 n. 46
Aristotle, 86, 119, 128, 155, 240, 256ff.

Armstrong, J., 171 n. 47
Arnold, D., 19 n. 9
Arnuwandas, 218
Artaxerxes, 206, 230, 245, 255
Asarhaddon, 138 n. 41
Asclepius, 176 n. 3
Ashurbanipal, 138 n. 41
Assmann, A., 4, 7, 11, 16 n. 2, 40 n. 51,
    43 n. 58, 56, 80, 87 n. 29, 131 n. 26,
    210 n. 9, 265 n. 63
Assmann, A. and J., 7 n. 5, 20 n. 14,
    36 n. 47, 39 n. 50, 58, 69 n. 103,
    90 n. 38, 94 n. 50, 97 n. 54, 132 n. 28,
    200 n. 62, 242 n. 18
Assmann, A./Harth D., 16 n. 2, 29 n. 35,
    40 n. 53
Assur, 182
Athanasius, 87 n. 29
Aton, 178, 184 n. 20
Augustine, 44 n. 69, 220 n. 27
Averroes, 155

Baal, 182, 195
Baczko, B., 115
Balandier, G., 118, 124
Baltzer, K., 199 n. 59, 200 n. 61, 230f.
Bar-Kochbah, 179, 189
Barlett, F. C., 22 n. 23
Bauer, W., 131 n. 24
Beauchard, J., 111 n. 1
Belial, 231
Berger, P./Luckmann, T., 2 n. 2, 33

Index

abomination, 159, 169, 203
abstraction, 30, 239
Academy (Plato's), 260
administration, 80, 129, 167, 243, 252
aemulatio, 92
age, 34f., 58, 77, 174, 247, 249ff. (*See also* dark age, golden age, heroic age, middle ages, mythical age etc.)
age, axial, 10, 81, 174, 264, 266
akribeia, 91 n. 40, 93, 105
Alexandrian, 251ff.
alienation, 83, 135f.
alphabet, 234–240, 274
alphabetization, 234
amity, 211
amixia, 189f.
Amka, 215–219
Amun(-Re), 178, 182, 223
anachronous structures, 10
ancestor, 20, 35, 43f., 46, 81f., 102
ancient world, 4, 131, 143, 154, 172, 174
annals, 51, 56ff., 149, 164, 214f.
antagonism, 11, 134f., 183
antagonistic power, 69
anthropological universal, 50, 64, 94
anthropology/anthropological, 50, 60, 116, 125, 154
anti-Semitism, 189 n. 36
anti-traditionalism, 109
apocalypse, 27
apocalypticism, 55, 188

apocryphal, 78, 80, 103, 107
apology, 221f.
apostasy, 182, 191
apostolic status, 101
archetype, 33, 158
archive, 36, 54, 76 n. 10, 77, 80
architecture, 93, 109, 127, 150, 152, 158f., 164
aretalogy, 222
ars memoriae, 15f., 18, 193
art, 15, 39, 41ff., 100, 102, 104f., 150ff., 174, 237 n. 8, 246, 253, 267
artefact, 30, 32
artist, 39, 91 n. 41, 99, 193, 246
art of memory/memory art, 15ff., 44, 192ff., 203f.
art of rhetoric, 245
Asia Minor, 226
assimilation, 131f., 156, 175, 189, 204
Assur, 182
Assyria, 106, 173, 189, 232
Assyrians, 131, 140, 145, 178, 185, 190, 229, 268, 272
Athen(ians), 247, 251
Athenian democracy, 251
authority, 19, 49, 80, 83ff., 99ff., 186, 200, 212, 231, 260, 266
autobiographical memory, 19
autobiographical tomb inscription, 222
autochthony, 180
autonomous reason, 109
autonomy, 100, 259